THE BIRTH AND EVOLUTION OF ISLAMIC POLITICAL THEORY

THE BIRTH AND EVOLUTION OF ISLAMIC POLITICAL THEORY

Political Rationalism from Ibn Al-Muqaffa to Ibn Khaldun

Gokhan Bacik

EDINBURGH
University Press

Edinburgh University Press is one of the leading university presses in the UK. We publish academic books and journals in our selected subject areas across the humanities and social sciences, combining cutting-edge scholarship with high editorial and production values to produce academic works of lasting importance. For more information visit our website: edinburghuniversitypress.com

© Gokhan Bacik, 2025

Edinburgh University Press Ltd
13 Infirmary Street
Edinburgh EH1 1LT

Typeset in 11/15 Adobe Garamond by
IDSUK (DataConnection) Ltd, and
printed and bound in Great Britain

A CIP record for this book is available from the British Library

ISBN 978 1 3995 2201 4 (hardback)
ISBN 978 1 3995 2203 8 (webready PDF)
ISBN 978 1 3995 2204 5 (epub)

The right of Gokhan Bacik to be identified as author of this work has been asserted in accordance with the Copyright, Designs and Patents Act 1988 and the Copyright and Related Rights Regulations 2003 (SI No. 2498).

CONTENTS

List of Figures and Maps	vi
Acknowledgements	vii
Introduction: What is Islamic Political Theory?	1
1 Ibn al-Muqaffa: The Birth of Islamic Political Theory	24
2 Al-Mawardi: Islamic Political Theory in the Provincial Order	75
3 Nizam al-Mulk: Islamic Political Theory in the Age of States	123
4 Ibn Tufayl: Political Rationalism in an Elitist Order	171
5 Ibn Khaldun: A Proto-modern Islamic Political Theory	220
Conclusion: Political Rationalism from Past to Present	258
Bibliography	264
Index	311

FIGURES AND MAPS

Figure 1.1	Ibn al-Muqaffa and the Abbasid revolution	26
Figure 1.2	Explaining politics according to three paradigms of political thought	56
Figure 1.3	Ibn al-Muqaffa and the evolution of state in Islamic history	57
Figure 2.1	The rulers in the Abbasid–Buwayhid cohabitation	90
Figure 2.2	Al-Mawardi in Islamic political history	95
Figure 3.1	Nizam al-Mulk and political actors	126
Figure 3.2	Nizam al-Mulk and the historical setting	133
Figure 4.1	Ibn Tufayl in political history	193
Map 1.1	The Abbasid Empire in $c.800$	38
Map 2.1	The Islamic world in $c.950$	79
Map 3.1	The Islamic world in $c.950$	131
Map 4.1	The Almohads	177
Map 5.1	Ibn Khaldun's historical context: the post-Almohad Maghrib	223

ACKNOWLEDGEMENTS

The research for this book began after I left Turkey for political reasons. My academic survival has been possible thanks to so many people whom I have met in the past seven years. I am therefore first greatly indebted to Scholar Rescue Fund (IIE-SRF), which supported me during the difficult times of my transition. I am also equally indebted to the Palacky University in the Czech Republic, an institution of higher education that should be globally appreciated for its historical role in supporting scholars at risk from different countries. It is in this vein, I owe much to my Czech colleagues Jaroslav Miller, Jiří Lach, Tomáš Lebeda, and the Czech diplomat Jakub Dürr (d. 2023), who offered their unwavering support to have me settled in Olomouc. I would also like to thank the then Minister of Education Robert Plaga for his support in the subsequent process. I also acknowledge the help of Sophie Johnson, Abu Leyla Khaled Ashour, Rachel Bridgewater, Isa Afacan, Serkan Seker, Bülent İbicioğlu, Ahmet Kuru, Yavuz Baydar and Ergun Babahan. Last but not least, I owe a special debt of gratitude to my family, Semra, Bensu and Leyla.

INTRODUCTION
WHAT IS ISLAMIC POLITICAL THEORY?

In June 632, tribal representatives gathered in Saqifah, in the bower of the Banu Saʿida clan, soon after Muhammad's death, with the urgent task of electing a new leader. Muhammad's death ended the period when God's Apostle commanded politics by divine inspiration. Tribes quickly embarked on a fierce political competition to have their favoured candidates elected by the appropriate means of persuasion and power. Al-Tabari (d. 923) reports Abu Sufyan – the former leader of the Meccan oligarchs defeated by Muhammad – saying in Saqifah that 'I see a cloud of smoke that nothing but blood will clear.'[1] The prediction was soon confirmed by a series of political crises, including civil wars, where thousands of Muslims killed one another.

Muslims' recourse to war or bargain was not unexpected, because the vacuum left by the Prophet was occupied by politics. As a matter of fact, tense disputes in Saqifah that led to scuffles proved that Muslims were not aware of an agreed set of religious principles that might have been invoked to arbitrate their disputes.[2] There being no divinely prescribed model, even events such as the invention of the caliphate, and the election of Abu Bakr as the first caliph, were determined by reflex actions such as resort to the Early

---

[1] Al-Tabari 1997, 199.
[2] Öztürk 2018, 31.

Muslims' interpretation of Islam, tribal customs and tribal balance of power.[3] For example, the critical factor in the Aws tribe's support of the election of Abu Bakr was the rival Khazraj tribe's dropping out of the race.[4] The Saqifah meeting, as Muhammad Abed al-Jabri noted, 'was a purely political discussion, decided by the political-social balance of power'.[5]

Al-Ash'ari, the founder of the Sunni theological school named after him, lauds Abu Bakr's election (in *Al-Ibanah*) as a fundamental item of faith by referencing Qur'an and the traditions as proof.[6] This method is critical, for it explains politics in terms of religious norms, even in the absence of a prophet to mediate between the people and the divine. The Shi'i explanation posits also that Ali should have been the caliph after Muhammad's death. So, Abu Bakr's election was wrong: Muhammad had already picked Ali as his successor, as Qur'an texts and the traditions confirm.[7]

In contrast, Ibn Khaldun explains Abu Bakr's election as an outcome of the tribal balance of power in the early Muslim community, in particular, the influence of the Quraysh. According to him, had political power been entrusted to any tribe other than the Quraysh, it would not have been possible to keep the community united, for the rival tribes would have broken the whole thing up. This attests to the fact that references to religious arguments during the election of first caliph constructed narratives to justify power and interest.[8]

Various perspectives are noted in the trajectory of Islamic political thought, as the above cases display. However, the strain of political thought in the Islamic tradition that explains politics outside the religious perspective is ignored. Calling that ignored trajectory 'Islamic political theory', the purpose of this book is to demonstrate and explain this as a separate branch of Islamic political thought derived from the works of Ibn al-Muqaffa (d. 759), al-Mawardi (d. 1058), Nizam al-Mulk (d. 1092), Ibn Tufayl (d. 1185) and Ibn Khaldun (d. 1406).

[3] For Azmeh (2016, 186), the caliphate was not a blueprint for government mandated by God.
[4] Crone 2005, 18.
[5] Al-Jabri 2009, 8.
[6] Al-Ash'ari 1940, 133–6.
[7] Tabataba'i 1975, 36–7.
[8] Ibn Khaldun 1958a, 400.

Categorising Islamic Political Thought

The literature on Islamic political thought is methodologically organised to overlap the typical characteristic of the arbitrary use of religious, philosophical and political perspectives as if the differences among them have no effect. As an indication, words like 'ideology', 'theory', 'philosophy', 'paradigm', and the less common 'political regard', are used in a discretionary manner.[9]

Reading the literature, one enters a nebulous field where religious, philosophical and political perspectives intersect almost freely, without systematic categorisation. Even when the literature detects differences among the various strains of Islamic political thought, it still retains an overlapping approach without heeding the need for a systematic analysis of the possible outcomes of those differences. This is chiefly because of the perception that medieval Islamic political thought was essentially a religious-philosophical construct that does not allow a clear separation of religious, philosophical and political strains.

To overcome various confusions created by the overlapping approach, I first define Islamic political thought as *the collection of all sorts of views on politics expressed from a religious, philosophical, political, and any other perspective*. 'Political thought' is defined here as an umbrella term, or, as Hayrettin Yücesoy wrote, 'a euphemism only for the sake of convenience, and as a shorthand description to signify diverse strains of political thought in medieval Islamic history'.[10]

For example, Ibn Khaldun, al-Farabi and al-Ash'ari are natural subjects of Islamic political thought, even though they represent different strains. But, as underlined earlier, such an all-inclusive definition causes an overlapping approach, the cost of which is arbitrary reference to religious, philosophical and political perspectives. As a solution, I study Islamic political thought as three distinct categorical groups: the religious view of politics, Islamic political philosophy and Islamic political theory.

Religious view of politics

On the religious view of it, 'politics' is justified and explained according to religious rules. This is what Patricia Crone calls 'the idea that all polities

---
[9] Yavari 2019, 52–73.
[10] Yücesoy 2006, 623.

rested on religious law brought by a prophet'.[11] The religious view effectively displaces political theory with the law by not leaving significant space for dynamics other than religious rules to explain and justify politics. Political analysis is thus transformed into a specific reasoning where politics is explained and justified according to religious principles. As noted earlier, al-Ash'ari's position on the caliphate is an example of the religious view: the religious view of politics is the view of jurists and religious scholars.

The religious view regards its rules as granted, universal and ahistorical, thus not determined by social, political and economic dynamics such as group solidarity, political power, security concerns and personal interest. The origin of this understanding is that the authority of the Prophet has a spiritual basis.[12] In this category, knowledge is absolute; it is not a product of worldly dynamics. It is relevant and adequate in any spatial and temporal context, for it transcends history.[13] Thus, political knowledge is connected to the religious interpretation of the cosmic system. This is summarised by Crone thus:

> All the power in the universe and all the physical and moral laws by which it is regulated reflect the same ultimate reality, God. God rules in the most literal sense of the word, appointing rulers, governors, judges, and deputies and ordering armies to be sent against insubordinate subjects.[14]

From the religious view, rules and institutions are therefore taken for granted because 'the function and general form of the state have been laid down once and for all, irrespective of historical circumstances or other social factors'.[15] The ideal nature of those rules and institutions is not subject to change caused by historical dynamics. Simply, politics is seen as ontologically religious. Reflecting this, the religious view promotes a methodology that reads politics through rules. In so doing, as Erwin I. J. Rosenthal notes, religious law (or theology) is vindicated in the face of divergent practices in political reality.[16]

---

[11] Crone 2015, 240.
[12] Razek 2012, 107.
[13] Al-Attas 1993, 30.
[14] Crone 2005, 6.
[15] Gibb 1955a, 3.
[16] Rosenthal 1962, 113.

The historical proof for such a rationale is the change in Arab society by the divine rules brought by Muhammad.

The religious view of politics rests on the concept of an ideal society where religious norms are perfectly applied. As Rosenthal says, the sharia-state is the ideal state of Islam, as the Republic was for Plato, and for the other ideal states of the various philosophers. This is not a utopia: the ideal society was already realised by Prophet Muhammad. Therefore, the gap between the ideal society and an existing society is only a sign of imperfectness. So, we always have a confrontation of Islamic norms and historical and political reality.[17] But that confrontation does not make the religious view relinquish its view of the granted norms as the prime elements in the explanation and justification of politics. Confrontation is only proof of the imperfectness of a society in its attainment of the religious norms, as the historical and the political reality never has the capacity to legislate norms. Thus, politics is no more than the sum of efforts to bring a society to a level where religious norms are perfectly applied. In other words, the political field, a passive entity, is a receptacle for Islamic rules.[18] In short, politics is a branch of religion.

Islamic political philosophy

Islamic political philosophy is similarly normative. The difference is in the references: while the religious view recognises the revelation as the sole resource, Islamic political philosophy espouses also the philosophical norms, that is, the *nomos*. *Nomos* is absolute, universal, timeless and ahistorical. It did not come into being in this world. Philosophical norms exist perfectly on a higher plane of reality. Ours is a world where things exist in an imperfect way. So, a society is an imperfect state where political leadership and its constituency lack knowledge of the universals.[19] Logically, the philosophical norms like 'wisdom' and 'truth' that exist perfectly only in the ideal realm are expected, in Islamic political philosophy, to guide politics.[20]

---

[17] Ibid., 118 and 31.
[18] Ibid., 24.
[19] Marmura 1979, 312.
[20] Wansbrough 1978, 131. Berlin (1964, 10) names ideal models as 'stylized models of society'. They are only 'useful abstraction'.

Reflecting Greek philosophy,[21] Islamic political philosophy has human happiness and perfection as its central concerns.[22] So its central theme is the creation of a virtuous political order 'whose guiding principle is the realization of human excellence'.[23] Thus, politics is not an autonomous field in Islamic political philosophy; it is a branch of philosophy. Reflecting this philosophical core, Islamic political philosophy rests on a metaphysical view of the cosmos, exactly like the religious view of politics. Muhsin Mahdi illustrates how these views arise from a metaphysical idea of the cosmos

> Both begin with a god as the ultimate cause of legislation, and consider correct beliefs about divine beings and the world of nature as essential for the constitution of a good political regime . . . In both, these beliefs should reflect an adequate image of the cosmos . . .[24]

This conceptualisation is easily observed in al-Farabi (d. 950), the leading representative of Islamic political philosophy. His *The Virtuous City* begins with the cosmic principles that connect the human universe to the spiritual universe.[25] We need to know those principles, since they determine politics.[26] But this makes of political philosophy also a quest for universal knowledge, the knowledge of the whole.[27] At this point, politics is both metaphysical and cosmological.[28] So, social, political and economic dynamics are secondary in al-Farabi. Reflecting this, *The Virtuous City* has long sections on God, cosmology, the soul, the intellect, and virtue and happiness, whereas the section on 'the communal setting in which virtue might be achieved' is short.[29]

The lack of interest in the practical aspects of politics is unsurprising, since neither the mind nor the soul is a derivative of the body.[30] The absolute

---

[21] Leaman 1987, 147; Walzer 1963, 44. Also see Rosenthal 1962, 111–12.
[22] Najjar 1961, 57; McDermott 2008, 12.
[23] Mahdi 1987, 209.
[24] Ibid., 207–8.
[25] Al-Farabi 1995, 25–106.
[26] Lapidus 2002, 152; Butterworth 1987, 235.
[27] Strauss 1957, 343–5.
[28] Parens 2016, 15. For Marmura (1979, 312), al-Farabi's views are 'metaphysical-political'.
[29] Crone 2005, 169.
[30] Mahdi 1987, 207.

knowledge of society, on which social, political or other dynamics have no effect, exists independently. Even so, 'absolute knowledge' is the reference point of politics.

Al-Farabi's ruler is an ideal ruler, a philosopher/prophet-king, equipped with universal knowledge.[31] His prime mission is to connect people with the divine beings and knowledge. Response to daily problems is not part of his prime mission.[32] Political philosophers have no responsibility to set forth any political programme.[33] That is, political philosophy is not a historical discipline.[34] It is normative. Its axioms cannot be tested empirically: they are not subject to observation.[35]

Islamic political theory

Various developments, such as the Abbasid revolution in 750, when a power-struggle emerged to determine politics in the Muslim world, and the disintegration of political unity that gave way to a power competition in the Muslim world in the tenth century, challenged the normative perception of politics among Muslims. Meanwhile, the birth and evolution of statehood in Muslim societies gradually imposed its power-oriented solutions against the normative formulations of politics.[36] All such developments and trends transformed Muslim politics into a field of continuous power struggles.[37]

Islamic political theory was a response to these developments' having transformed politics into a field of contest that challenged the previous norms-centred political perceptions. This response, however, formed gradually over time, evolving according to sequential historical conjectures. Thus, Islamic political theory is studied in this book across a wide time span, from the eighth to the beginning of the fifteenth century, through its five prominent exponents: Ibn al-Muqaffa, al-Mawardi, Nizam al-Mulk, Ibn Tufayl and Ibn Khaldun.

---

[31] Fakhry 2002, 104; Strauss 1990, 14; Campanini 2004, 46.
[32] Mahdi 1987, 212–13.
[33] Bosworth 2000, 137.
[34] Strauss 1957, 56.
[35] McDermott 2008, 17.
[36] Humphreys 2006, 110; Donner 1986, 289–90.
[37] Siddiqi 1942, 89.

Interpreting historical developments as imposers of new dynamics in politics that are strong enough to push religious or philosophical norms aside, Islamic political theory proposed instead to *explain and justify politics by invoking autonomous variables completely or partially independent of religious and philosophical norms*.[38]

An autonomous variable (such as political power, interest, group solidarity, and survival motive) is a social, political or economic dynamic that has a role in continuing or changing a given state of affairs. Autonomous variables are the prime dynamics, both in maintaining solidarity and equilibrium, and in causing changes in the arrangement and functioning of units in a society.[39] In other words, an autonomous variable determines sequence and change in a society.[40]

The distinctive nature of an autonomous variable is in that it imposes its own rationale, which often has the capacity to bend a normative rationale, be it religious or philosophical. This makes autonomous variables inherently 'secular' in the sense that they are non-religious phenomena, that is, indifferent to religion, or not motivated by a religious norm. As importantly, autonomous variables characterise politics as dynamic phenomena actualised by the power and network relations of a given context. The methodological

---

[38] Islamic political theory is still 'Islamic' even when it explains politics by invoking autonomous variables independent of religious norms. As Ahmed (2016, 5–6 and 544) wrote, Islam can be studied as a matter of Divine Command or a matter of human fact in history. Therefore, 'what is Islamic' at doctrinal and experimental levels can be construed variously. The alternate ways of studying Islam conclude that 'all acts and statements of meaning-making for the Self by Muslims and non-Muslims that are carried out in terms of Islam – that is, in terms of any of Pre-Text, Text or Con-Text – should properly be understood as Islamic'. On this account, the five names I study in the manuscript are still Islamic, for they engage with Islam as Con-text/context even when they explain politics completely independent of religious norms. There are examples in recent scholarship that adhere to this approach. Ghobadzadeh's (2014) 'religious secularity' should be reminded here. Similarly, Kuru (2020, 91–104) argued that the essentialist idea that Islam inherently rejects religion–state separation is misleading. Kuru's approach endorses defining 'Islamic' in terms of context. The perspective proposed by Dressler and Mandair (2011, 3–36) is another example according to which 'religion and secularity are regarded as co-emergent and co-dependent'.

[39] Bogue 1952, 565.

[40] Vance 1944, 123–31.

outcome of this characterisation is the need to focus on autonomous variables to explain politics *before* or *along with* institutions and norms.

Islamic political theory, rather like modern political theory,[41] is interested in the behaviours of actors, not in their abstract thoughts about politics and society. In this regard, Islamic political theory deals also with a restricted set of primary variables and their interrelations. Reading politics as it does through autonomous variables in a given historical context, Islamic political theory is essentially not normative. Nor does it rely on a religious or on the philosophical interpretation of the cosmic order. This results in Islamic political theory having no claim to theoretical excellence. While political philosophy is interested in the big issues like 'wisdom' and 'harmony with nature',[42] Islamic political theory is about practical issues such as security, legitimacy, taxation, food prices, civil unrest and change in leadership.[43] It is satisfied with responding to the existing problems.[44] So, there is no notion of the ideal society in Islamic political theory. Therefore, the existing society is the normal state of politics that cannot be seen as imperfect or ignorant.

Having defined Islamic political theory broadly, I can now proceed to supply its details:

Empirical and Historical

Islamic political theory is historical inasmuch as it responds to the problems and circumstances of given historical settings. And it is empirical, for the source of its arguments that explain and justify political behaviour and thought is the historical setting alone; no philosophy is called upon to characterise it. Thus, Islamic political theory is not zero-context; it is time-bound and historical.

Derived from the historical context, knowledge in Islamic political theory does not transcend the observable things. That is, autonomous variables,

---

[41] Parsons 1963, 233.
[42] Procope 1988, 23.
[43] Shorten 2016, 1.
[44] On this aspect of modern political theory, see MacIntyre 1983, 23. Shorten's (2016, 1) approach is similar: political theory is 'an activity rather than a body of knowledge'. It is what people 'do' rather than what they 'know about'.

not universal timeless ideas, are referenced by it. This determines another key feature of Islamic political theory: the historical context is its objective framework. Hence, it is testable in terms of its congruity with autonomous variables in the historical setting. This is never possible in the religious view of politics, nor in Islamic political philosophy, for their axioms transcend the observable world, leaving no objective framework to test them.[45]

The empirical and historical nature of Islamic political theory creates significant methodological outcomes. Firstly, that study engages in the analysis of the causal and constitutive interactions of autonomous variables and political phenomena in the given real-life context. So the subjects under analysis are the ideas, behaviours and institutions of that context. Religious and philosophical principles are no longer the monopolistic elements that bear upon politics. In this regard, Islamic political theory is a break from the Platonic tradition, according to which we cannot prove empirically, nor even explain, the concept 'absolute knowledge'.[46]

Secondly, the works of Islamic political theory should not be interpreted with literal and formal approaches. Literal and formal approaches are the usual methods of the religious view of politics, and of Islamic political philosophy, for they follow the granted norms and institutions. However, literal and formal approaches to understanding the works of Islamic political theory would provide only a snapshot view of political life, for they are not zero-context. Thus, the study of Islamic political theory is only possible when the impact of autonomous variables that construct the political phenomena are taken into consideration. Otherwise, what we get is always only the decontextualised picture of the political phenomena.

Briefly, in Islamic political theory, history is not only informative about, but also constitutive of, the political phenomena.[47] In other words, history is

---

[45] This is the argument observed by scholars like Berlin. Accordingly, political philosophy became irrelevant from a scientific viewpoint for it is normative and not fact-based. Berlin 1964, 5. Also see Strauss and Cropsey 1987, 1–6.

[46] Reichenbach 1968, 30–1.

[47] From a New Historicist approach, 'history as information' is never satisfactory as there is no 'clear-cut boundary between a work of art on the one hand and its historical background on the other'. Schmitz 2007, 164.

not a passive timeline. Instead, it is the record of the autonomous variables (such as the network effects or power relations) that impose their preconditions upon politics and society.[48] By this account, religious and philosophical norms are no longer studied independently of the causal power of temporal connections.

However, the mainstream literature concerned with Islamic political thought is dominated by the formal approach that underestimates the autonomous variables. The consequence is treating the works of Islamic political theory as if they are zero-context, as is the religious view of politics and Islamic political philosophy. But this leads to the vehement consequence of failing to notice that Islamic political theory exists as an independent strain of Islamic political thought. These problems in the literature on Islamic political thought arise in significant part because that field is dominated by scholars of religion and philosophy. Their disciples' tools are significantly different from those of the political scientists. Not surprisingly, therefore, the methodology and terminology of contemporary political science is almost absent from the literature, and this makes it lean heavily into the religious-philosophical study of Islamic political thought. In this regard, what Colin Hay underlines while discussing the consequences of a formal approach in political studies is also valid for the study of Islamic political thought:

i. confining political analysis to a method where temporal traces are removed;
ii. obtaining a timeless snapshot of how societies and political systems function, with political choices often analyzed in isolation from their historical context;
iii. institutions and social structures are treated as given entities rather than as ongoing processes;
iv. treating time as noteworthy only when discussing the rare moments of sudden change.[49]

As a result, works that should be recognised as examples of Islamic political theory are wrongly interpreted from a religious or philosophical perspective,

---

[48] Pierson 2004, 20–1 and 37–9.
[49] As adapted in Bryson 2007, 10.

and their discussions are left scattered among texts of the religious view of politics, and of Islamic political philosophy. This amounts to being the theologising or philosophising of politics, and subsequently, of Islamic political theory.

Reflectivism

Being empirical and historical, Islamic political theory is necessarily reflective, meaning that the works of Islamic political theory should be read from a historicist perspective.[50] Written as responses to various problems, *not* as general theoretical formulations, it is necessary to read a work of Islamic political theory according to what it meant in its time. To do this is 'to understand the thinkers of the past exactly as they understood themselves'.[51] Ideas do not originate in a historical vacuum. Rather, 'they are produced in certain historical and social conditions', so knowledge of these conditions is required in the interpretation of those ideas.[52]

However, major books of Islamic political theory are medieval texts divorced from their physical and social surroundings.[53] Detached from their historical context, on a Ricoeurian perspective, they no longer transmit the contextual components of their content.[54] Therefore, a literal reading of those works would inevitably lead to the frameless interpretations of presentism, or to misleading generalisations.[55] The solution is to consider 'the social logic of the text' when interpreting the works of Islamic political theory.[56] The question 'what does it mean?' is replaced by 'where does it mean?' or 'to whom does it mean?'[57] When that is done, our view of political life in those texts shifts from 'snapshots to moving pictures', meaning that we can imagine the meaning of the text in its historical context as a living phenomenon, rather than as snapshot photos.[58]

---

[50] 'Positivism necessarily transforms itself into historicism.' Strauss 1957, 354.
[51] Strauss 1959, 67.
[52] Schmitz 2007, 160.
[53] On reading medieval texts, see Caie 2008, 10.
[54] Ricoeur 1976, 25–7.
[55] See Searle 1979, 117.
[56] Spiegel 1990, 59. Also see Ricoeur 1976, 9; Caie and Renevey 2008, 2.
[57] Machan 1991, 4–6.
[58] Pierson 2004, 1–2. This is what Abu-Zayd (2004, 13) names as the 'humanistic hermeneutics', which is to imagine a text as a living phenomenon in its historical context.

Reflectivism, however, should not be confused with empiricism; while empiricism sees ideas as the product of historical variables, reflectivism sees them as expressed according to the historical mindset. Accordingly, texts have a culturally specific nature, and they are the products of particular periods and discursive formations.[59] For example, on an empiricist account, slavery in the Middle Ages is a result of various economic, social and political causes. On the reflective account, medieval opinions on slavery are reflections of the standard discourse, according to which slavery was 'normal'.

As a consequence of the overlapping approach, the literature usually interprets works of Islamic political theory by ignoring their reflective nature. This results in the theologising or philosophising of those works, as if they had been written as general works of religion or philosophy.

Power Oriented

Political rationalism, as expected, brings us to power, which is the most influential autonomous variable in politics.[60] However, two grand trajectories of Islamic political thought, that is, the religious view of politics and Islamic political philosophy, approach power sceptically. This is so because both are committed to a moralistic understanding of society where power yields perfectly to the norms. They imagine power as static and controllable by religion. So the question of power is usually side-stepped by Islamic scholars who adhere to those moralistic views.[61] For example, in al-Farabi, a representative of Islamic political philosophy, the ideal state will be free of all kinds of violence, for it is the concomitant feature of the ignorant, errant and imperfect political regimes.[62] For al-Shafi'i, a representative of the religious view of politics, power is similarly static: he defines war as a religious ritual that should be practised by Muslims independently of any reason that forces them to practice it. Imagining power as a dependent variable of religion, he explains jihad as 'obligatory for all believers, exempting no one, just as prayer, pilgrimage and [payment of] alms are performed'.[63] This is simply a theologising of power.

---

[59] Spiegel 1990, 70–1.
[60] Harris 1957, 2.
[61] Lambton 1956, 125.
[62] Maroth 2018, 164.
[63] Al-Shafi'i 1997, 84.

In contrast, Islamic political theory defines norms in terms of political power. When power is not distributed in harmony with a norm in a system, that norm not only loses its monopoly on determining political action, but it also becomes subject to power. As stated earlier, the incongruity of norms and power in a system is therefore the historical origin of Islamic political theory. Thus, though the birth of politics and Islamic political thought occurred in the early periods of Islam, the birth of Islamic political theory is a later phenomenon.[64]

Subjected to the influential consequences of various structural changes, Islamic society has never managed to re-unite itself to again become the society it was in the earlier period of Islamic history. Inevitably, autonomous variables became major elements to shape Islamic politics. Surveyed thus, the case of Muslim politics is comparable to what we read in Machiavelli as the inevitable situation in life when *necessita* overcomes *virtu*, for *necessita* justifies the use of any and all means.[65] Hobbes calls this 'the right of doing any act'.[66] Similarly, Islamic politics gave birth to the same dichotomy of power versus norms, which was effectively a split from the religious view of politics and Islamic political philosophy. The key dynamic that made this split possible was indeed the rise of power.

Power cannot be controlled unless there is an equal or a superior other power.[67] Power can therefore autonomously determine the causal effects in politics.[68] This helps us see how power has an inherently 'secular' nature, for its autonomy enables escape from religion's command.[69] We are now on a different echelon, the one where power creates and enforces social and political values[70] for it shapes also the reasons that move people to think and act as they do.[71] That is to accept into the mainstream of societal life a second authority other than religion that generates its own *rationale* in politics.

---

[64] 'Islamic political thought starts with Islam.' Al-Azmeh 2007, 207.
[65] Machiavelli 1998, 70.
[66] Hobbes 1998, 114. Also see Duke 2014, 618.
[67] Gibb 1962, 38.
[68] Murphy 2011, 88.
[69] Parsons 1963, 232; Rudolph 1986, 78.
[70] Bachrach and Baratz 1962, 948.
[71] Gilabert 2018, 79; Forst 2015, 124.

Once politics is imagined as a reflection of autonomous variables, particularly power, a completely different understanding of politics emerges. Political institutions, decisions, and even ideas, are no longer seen as granted. Nor is the law independent of power relations in a society. Advanced legal systems may prevail in a society, but they never annul political analysis based on power relations. For example, we never imagine that today's modern law, which regulates life in more detail than any previous law, eliminates the need for political analysis. Departments of political science cooperate with the schools of law.

However, the mainstream literature on Islamic political thought, which is dominated by the formal methodology of the religious view of politics, has the tendency to read politics from the law. Medieval Islamic politics is mostly explained as a religious construct, as if (Islamic) law perfectly encompasses politics, leaving no space for the autonomous variables of (mainly) political power. This feeds the misleading view of 'politics as law'.

One historical fact that boosts the religious view is that religion was a major organiser of human affairs in medieval Muslim societies, interwoven with everything else, not constituting a separate sphere of its own, as in medieval European society.[72] Since Islam was the law in medieval Muslim society, disobeying a law was never 'simply to infringe a rule of the social order: it is an act of religious disobedience, a sin, and as such, involves a religious penalty'.[73] This confused the semantics of religion and politics, for there was no social science, nor any other proper medium in medieval Muslim society, to explain politics.[74] The inevitable consequence is the interpretation of politics in a way that mostly fits the discourse of the religious view of politics, where detecting 'secular' autonomous variables like power is not easy.

However, a power-oriented analysis provides a different picture of medieval Muslim politics. This is not necessarily to deny that Islamic law was the legal framework. So, while religion is regarded as the formal framework, politics is

---

[72] Southern 1990, 16; Taylor 2007, 2.
[73] Lambton 1991a, 1.
[74] Al-Alwani 2005, 229.

read from the lens of autonomous variables. Mohammed Abed al-Jabri's account of political events in the early period of Islam is a good example:

> disagreements, and the resulting clashes and wars, were only incidental political conflicts provoked by kinship and interests. Religion was not a point of contention, nor was it ever an element in these conflicts. All the contenders, competitors and combatants were Companions, and all of them understood their religion, practiced it and abided by it in their personal conduct. In other words, religion was not an authoritative referent in this contention, as the disagreement was political in the general sense of the word. It was neither in the name of religion nor against religion.[75]

Similarly, reminding us that Islamic politics has always been contested since the election of the first caliph, Abu Bakr, Ali Abdel Raziq notes that 'coercion has always been the basis of the caliphate', for it was provided by instruments of power, such as the armed forces. Inspired by Ibn Khaldun, Raziq reminds us that royal authority means the power to rule by force; kingship is nothing but coercion. For Raziq, this is a natural consequence of the autonomy of power. Power simply dictates its rationale, challenging any superior, even 'the most scientific kind of intellectual inquiry'.[76] What lies at the heart of those argumentations is that 'politics as law' might not be possible in all societies. Accordingly, no matter how the law is organised in a society, politics is an ongoing process continuously determined by power-politics.[77] In this approach, more attention is paid to the political realities of the times than to the religious principles.[78]

Political Rationalism

The autonomy of the political – that is, the existence of autonomous variables to explain and justify politics[79] – dictates another attribute of Islamic political

---

[75] Al-Jabri 2009, 11.
[76] Razek 2012, 44–51.
[77] This is power politics in modern scholarship as observed in Morgenthau (1948, 13) who wrote that even if it appears to us as the Crusaders wanted the free holy places or Woodrow Wilson wanted to make the world safe for democracy, they are all for striving for power.
[78] Zaman 2002, 94.
[79] Marchart 2007, 36.

theory: rationalism, the position that human reason is capable of articulating reasoned solutions and observation beyond the capacity of religious texts.[80] However, rationalism should be treated differently in Islamic political theory.

Rationality is usually analysed in the binary of 'rationalism versus traditionalism' in Islamic thought, where it is mostly a function of how theological and philosophical propositions are interpreted, and it has no strong empirical dimension. Accordingly, there are rationalist schools, such as the Muʿtazila, or rationalist scholars like Ibn Sina and Ibn Rushd, and the traditional schools (mainly Ashʿari), and scholars like al-Ghazali.[81] However, the application of such a theological-philosophical notion of rationality to Islamic political theory, of which the prime nature is empirical, is problematic and confusing.[82] But again, the mainstream literature – as an inevitable result of the overlapping approach – has wrongly justified the use of theological-philosophical rationalism in the study of Islamic political thought. This creates three problems: firstly, it leads to wrong interpretations on various issues such as actors' intentions and motives. Secondly, it causes the frequent mistake of incorporating Islamic political theory into the religious view of politics, or the Islamic political philosophy. Thirdly, it promotes a formal approach where politics is analysed mainly through rules or institutions that ignore the impact of autonomous variables. Instead, an alternative rationalism with a political character determines reasoning in politics.

This political rationalism gets its distinctive attribute from the empirical nature of politics, which is essentially 'the conduct of affairs', and 'a matter of solving problems'.[83] The mind now responds to various impacts of the autonomous variables, such as power and interest. Political rationality is thus never a pure abstract reasoning like it is in theological-philosophical rationality. In Michael Oakeshott's terms, political reasoning is determined by the appropriate *technique* of the practice, rather than by the technical or abstract principles of the ideal frameworks. This is to accept that autonomous variables may deliver a reasoning different from what a theological-philosophical reasoning would normally dictate. It is simply to reject susceptibility to theological or

---

[80] Bacik 2021, 9.
[81] Makdisi 1973, 155–68; Gibb 1982, 3–3; Goldziher 1994, 40.
[82] For philosophical and political rationalism, see Miller 2001, 809.
[83] Oakeshott 1962, 100.

philosophical formulations. In this regard, political rationalism has its roots in the recognition of the impossibility of a perfect match between ideal norms and political realities. Even imagining that politics is ruled by granted and fixed norms is 'a piece of mysticism and nonsense' for political theory. Politics, from a political rationalist perspective, is naturally a succession of crises.[84]

Political rationality is a major departure of Islamic political theory from the religious view of politics, and from Islamic political philosophy. All names that I study in this book as representatives of Islamic political theory are deeply involved in the political affairs of their time, and are particularly attentive to political roles. They did not write their books as scholars isolated from political experience; instead, their works were written as responses to the political problems of their historical contexts. Their engagement with political affairs is the indispensable enabler of their displays of the practical dynamics of rationality in politics.

Ibn al-Muqaffa's career began as a bureaucrat in the late Umayyad period. After the Abbasid revolution, he resumed his job in the ranks of the new regime. As a high-level bureaucrat, he dealt with the complex problems of the transition from the Umayyads to the Abbasids. Al-Mawardi was a member of the Abbasid bureaucracy. He was sent as a diplomat to provincial states' rulers, like Seljuq Sultan Tugrul, to fix the power-sharing problems between them and the Abbasid caliphate. Nizam al-Mulk was the grand vizier of the Saljuqs (or Seljuqs) for twenty-nine years. Ibn Tufayl was a man of politics: as a court advisor, he was at the centre of the Almohad elites. He held an advisory position to two Almohad caliphs. He wrote *Hayy ibn Yaqzan* when he was in government service. Ibn Khaldun was involved in high politics in different capacities. He was sent as ambassador by Muhammad V of Granada on a mission to Pedro the Cruel, the king of Castile. He also acted as a negotiator on behalf of his patrons among the Arab and Berber tribes of North Africa.

The Cases and the Book's Content

There is no standard for defining the scope of works on Islamic political thought. This is mostly a result of the 'overlapping approach'. Books with that approach either include as many names as possible, or they pick up

---

[84] Ibid., 4–5 and 10–11.

names they consider the most influential. However, those methods usually result in a collection of the works from the various strains of Islamic political thought. For example, following the method of including as many names as possible, Patricia Crone's *Medieval Islamic Political Thought* studies pretty much any actor since Muhammad: the Muʿtazila, the Zaydis, the Qarmati, the Ibadis, the Kharijites, the Sunnis, the Umayyads, the Iranian Ghulat.[85] But, this method provokes several questions: to begin with, is it realistic to study, for example, the Ibadis within the context of Islamic political thought? If yes, then, why are other groups excluded? Why, for instance, did Crone not analyse the leaders of the Zanj rebellion, the slaves' uprising against the Abbasids in the late ninth century?[86]

The main problem with the method of concentrating on the most influential names is that the writer has no objective criteria for choosing the names to study. To illustrate this problem through several examples: Anthony Black's *The History of Islamic Political Thought* emphasises several names, such as al-Tusi and al-Jahiz.[87] But no such attention to al-Jahiz is observed in Crone. Badr al-Din al-Jamaʿa, who is highlighted in Ann K. S. Lambton's *State and Government in Medieval Islam*, merits no reference from Crone.[88] While Erwin Rosenthal's *Political Thought in Medieval Islam* treats al-Mawardi as a key name, Crone does not. Haroon Sherwani's *Studies in the History of Early Muslim Political Thought* begins his account of Islamic political thought with Ibn Abiʾr Rabi, who lived at the time of the Abbasid caliph Muʿtasim.[89] But, Rabi is not even considered seriously by other books. The selection criteria might also be affected by regional preferences: for example, Sherwani includes Mahmud Gawan (d. 1481), whose impact was felt more among Indian Muslims.[90] But Gawan is not even recorded by scholars who live in Europe and North America, nor by those in the Western Muslim world.

---

[85] Crone 2005, 219.
[86] There is only one short footnote on the Zanj rebellion in Crone (2005, 351).
[87] Black 2011, 28.
[88] Lambton 1991a, 138.
[89] Sherwani 1942, 69.
[90] Originally an Iranian merchant, Gawan later became the chief state executive of the Deccan-Bahmani sultanate. Eaton 2005, 59–77.

As the above examples illustrate, the 'as many names as possible' method and the 'most influential names' method, both operate arbitrarily. In fact, this was once confirmed by Lambton when she wrote that her selection of authors was guided 'partly by personal choice, partly by the work of others in the field before me'.[91] Expecting that it will remove problems caused by this sort of selection procedure, I pick up names by a three-fold method. Firstly, I include in this book only cases of Islamic political theory. Any name that represents the religious view of politics, or Islamic political philosophy, is excluded. For example, neither al-Farabi nor Ibn Sina is studied, for they represent Islamic political philosophy. Similarly, neither al-Ghazali nor al-Juwayni is included, for they represent the religious view of politics. In fact, this book is the first to study the representatives of Islamic political theory exclusively.

Secondly, the cases are selected from the three major regions of the medieval Muslim society: Ibn Tufayl and Ibn Khaldun represent the Muslim West; Nizam al-Mulk represents the Muslim East, particularly the Turkish-Persian cultural zone; and Ibn al-Muqaffa and al-Mawardi (for this selection purpose) represent the Muslim East, particularly the Arab-Persian cultural zone.

Thirdly, it being empirical and historical, the very nature of Islamic political theory requires the study of its historical evolution. Correspondingly, this book has the ambitious goal of narrating the birth and evolution of Islamic political theory in the general course of Islamic history, from the eighth to the early fifteenth century. The cases were selected from the relevant historical periods because they are either the only or the most influential representatives of Islamic political theory. On this scheme, Ibn al-Muqaffa, the subject of Chapter 1, symbolises the birth of Islamic political theory during the revolutionary transition from the Umayyads to the Abbasids in the eighth century. His thought was formed in the age of Abbasid consolidation. The Chapter 2 case is al-Mawardi, who lived in the age of the Abbasid decline, when the caliphate transferred its temporal powers to local states as a survival strategy. Al-Mawardi's political thought illustrates the evolution of Islamic political theory in that critical setting of the decline of the caliphate. Nizam al-Mulk, the Chapter 3 case, lived when independent states emerged as the main actors of Islamic politics. In his time, the caliphate was no longer an influential institution. Nizam al-Mulk

[91] Lambton 1991a, xviii.

developed the first state-centred perspective. Therefore, his political thought is critical for an understanding of the evolution of Islamic political theory in the age of independent states. Ibn Tufayl, whose political thought represents the evolution of Islamic political theory in the Muslim Maghrib during the revolutionary transition from Almoravids to Almohads, is the Chapter 4 case. In Chapter 5, Ibn Khaldun is studied to examine the post-Almohad period in the Muslim West. By studying these cases, this book examines the birth and the development of Islamic political theory, from the early Abbasid period to the late Middle Ages, as a historical continuity.

Method, Argumentation, Limits and Purpose

How I define (above) Islamic political theory determines the methodology of this book: my intention is to illustrate how the political thought of the selected cases was determined by the autonomous dynamics of the time. To achieve this, I dovetail political history and intellectual history by contextualising each case study in its historical setting. Thus, each chapter provides detailed background information about the historical setting of the case being studied.

Each chapter has also a section where I analyse the political ideas of the case to hand by using the textual analysis methodology (including critical discourse analysis) to show that the writings of each case were his response to various developments in his historical setting. My purpose is to show how those texts reflect the social, political and economic dynamics of the period.

Pragmatically, the above-described methodology defines the limits of this work: this book does not intend to analyse any historical question (like 'were *mawali* the primary agents of the Abbasid revolution?'), nor any intellectual question (like 'was Ibn Tufayl closed to Muʿtazila?'). Its sole purpose is to illustrate that, and how, the political thinking of each of the five cases that this book studies was determined by autonomous dynamics that are partially or completely independent of religion and political philosophy.

A purpose of this book, as stated before, is to demonstrate that Islamic political theory is a separate branch of Islamic political thought: it is a line of thought that is markedly different from those of its religious and philosophical counterparts. The works of each of the five political-theory names is studied to demonstrate this. But this does not mean that the book has only this methodological purpose. There is also a pragmatic purpose: I am proposing 'Islamic political theory' because it provides an alternate and efficient perspective on the gamut of political discourses present in the times of each of its exponents. The ideas that populate Islamic political theory are formed by the social, economic and political dynamics of the historical setting of each of its exponents. Their great legacy is that they enable the study of political ideas while they are interplaying with the historical dynamics of their times. This makes them more authentic recorders of their times than are the dry retrospective textual analyses in which the historical dimension is lost.

How Does this Book Help the Reader Understand the Muslim World of Today?

In this book I examine a period in which what we know as 'Islam as a political paradigm' is finalised. Contemporary Muslims' reference to Islam in daily and political life is essentially an engagement with ideas that formed in this period. The content of this book can therefore be imagined as an outline of the historical foundation of Islamic political thought that still affects Muslims. Accordingly, this book provides five important tips for understanding contemporary Muslims.

Firstly, this book will provide insights into the contemporary democratisation debate among Muslims. A major subject of this book is how legitimacy was defined in medieval Muslim societies. This will provide important historical clues about how the concept 'people' was understood and contextualised in political thought by Muslims in the past. I believe this is crucial in an effort to understand contemporary Muslim societies, for they are societies that have faced problems with developing institutions that require popular sovereignty at the centre, evidenced by institutionalised structures such as parliament, free elections and the rule of law.

Secondly, this book, of which a major subject is the evolution of statehood in medieval Muslim society, will provide insights into the state–society relations of Muslims, in particular, about why they have a state-centred political and economic system, but also a weak civil-and-peripheral balancing power. The historical origins of state centrism are subject matter of this book.

Thirdly, the book will provide insights to the secularism debate among Muslims. It provides many debates on how medieval Muslims imagined the 'non-religious' view of politics. Thus, this book will promote an understanding of the resistance to secularism among some Muslims, and enable the reader to decide whether this resistance is the consequence of a historical legacy or a contemporary invention.

Fourthly, the book will provide critical insights unto Islamism. The following pages will provide important hints concerning various questions like: 'Did the early Islamic political theorists such as Ibn al-Muqaffa and al-Mawardi understand the concept "state" ontologically, religiously, or as a non-canonical historical construct?' Also, the findings of this book will help the reader construct informed answers to questions like: 'Is Islamism correct when it says that Islam is also state?' 'Is Islamism a continuation of the classical Islamic political thought?'

Finally, history, after law and theology, is another pillar of the contemporary Muslim world. It plays a key role in the achievement of a religious, cultural and social unity among Muslims.[92] This book might prove helpful in gaining an understanding of contemporary Muslims' engagement with history, particularly for the reader who asks questions like: 'Why are contemporary Muslims proud of the Almohad civilization despite that it declared that other Muslims are apostates?' 'What does it mean to Sunnis that the early Abbasids generated legitimacy through an Alid discourse?' 'How is it that Nizam al-Mulk, the patron of Sunnism, wrote a chapter on the etiquette of wine drinking?' This book's discourses will inspire the reader's formulations of answers to such questions. Answers in this area are of critical importance, for they explain how contemporary Muslims interpret Islamic history.

---

[92] Gibb 1955b, 5.

1

IBN AL-MUQAFFA: THE BIRTH OF ISLAMIC POLITICAL THEORY

An inquiry into Islamic political theory brings us to Ibn al-Muqaffa, for his *Risala fi al-Sahaba* (A Memorandum on the [Caliph's] Entourage) is the first work in this field.

Risala fi al-Sahaba (hereafter *Risala*) was written between 754 and 757.[1] Ibn al-Muqaffa's political thought formed during the transition from the Umayyads to the Abbasids through a revolution in 750, and the subsequent period of regime consolidation. This is a convenient period to observe the role of power in politics, as the justification of the replacement of the Umayyad order was sheer power.[2] The Abbasid revolution gave way to complex changes in the configuration of political elites and institutions, as well as the social basis of political authority.[3] *Risala* was written as a response to the various problems of that historical setting. Ibn al-Muqaffa, following a non-religious perspective, explained political issues as the product of autonomous dynamics like power, tribal relations and political geography. To analyse this in detail, we need to take a closer look at his times, a period when the Abbasids were in a regime-building phase after a revolution.

---

[1] Hamori 2013, 232; Latham 1990, 64.
[2] El-Hibri 2004, 6–8.
[3] Agha 2003, xv–xxxiii.

Ibn al-Muqaffa: A Scribe

Ibn al-Muqaffa, originally Ruzbeh, was born in Gor (southern Iran) to a Zoroastrian family in *c.*720. As the Arab conquest of Iran (651) had occurred not long ago, Iran was still in a complicated transition from Zoroastrianism to Islam. He received from his family a knowledge of Pahlavi (Middle Persian) and of the Zoroastrian faith. He was first taught by his father, Dadawayh, who was a tax collector during the rule of al-Hajjaj, the Umayyads' Iraqi governor.[4] Dadawayh, who died a Zoroastrian, was a *dihqan*. *Dihqan* were a lower class of the former Sasanid nobility that had retained important roles due to their knowledge about crop yields, the tax base, ethnic composition and the laws.[5]

Ibn al-Muqaffa was educated in Basra, where he read Aristotle's works.[6] He socialised with members of the high literati, which helped him excel in Arabic.[7] With different groups like Christian ascetics, Manichaeans and neo-Mazdakites, along with Muslims, Basra had a pluralistic and Persified culture combined with the rational scepticism affected by scribes who hold universalist opinions.[8] Basra, founded as a garrison city in 638 under Caliph Umar,[9] was different from Kufa, another city founded by Muslims, for the latter was the hub of the Alid groups. It was a period when new political ideas were in formation in such cities, creating contending geopolitical dynamics.[10]

Ibn al-Muqaffa began his public career as a scribe during the Umayyads. He worked in Fars (southwest Iran) after 743. He undertook the important tasks of mediating in Fars between the warring officials in 744, when the Umayyad rule disintegrated. He met his future Abbasid bosses, like Isa bin Ali, there.[11] When

---

[4] Ibn Isfandiyar 1905, 5. As his father's fingers were shrivelled in a politically motivated investigation by the Umayyads, he was called 'the son of the shriveled', i.e. Ibn al-Muqaffa. Van Ess 2017, 26.
[5] Zarrinkub 2007, 43–4.
[6] Yousefi 2017, 4; Sourdel 1954, 308
[7] Latham 1990, 48.
[8] Arjomand 1994, 20.
[9] Al-Ya'qubi 2018b, 69; al-Tabari 1992, 161–3.
[10] Masudi (1989, 61) reports the accounts of Basran people cursing Kufa.
[11] Arjomand 1994, 16–17.

	Political Actors		Political Events
Ibn al-Muqaffa (720–759)	The last Umayyad Caliph Marwan II (744–750)	Abbasid Imam Muhammad b. Ali (d. 743)	The clandestine organisation and propaganda in Khurasan (718–747)
		Abbasid Imam Ibrahim b. Muhammad (743–749)	The Revolution (747–750)
	The 1st Abbasid Caliph Al-Saffah (749–754)		Regime consolidation
	The 2nd Abbasid Caliph Al-Mansur (754–775)		

Figure 1.1 Ibn al-Muqaffa and the Abbasid revolution.

the region was taken over by the Abbasid groups around 745, he was transferred to the service of Dawud bin Umar, the last Umayyad governor of Iraq.[12] When the Umayyads attempted to re-claim the lost provinces, Ibn al-Muqaffa was sent back to the region. He worked for the fiscal *diwan* in Kirman (central Iran). Ibn al-Muqaffa, however, left the region before the collapse of the Umayyads. He returned to Basra, where local contacts helped him switch sides in the revolution.[13] After the revolution, he first became secretary to Sulayman bin Ali. He later worked for Isa bin Ali, the uncle of the first and the second Abbasid caliphs.[14]

Ibn Khallikan (d. 1282) presents Ibn al-Muqaffa first as a scribe (*katib*).[15] As a scribe, he was exposed to politics while working for the highest political dignitaries in the turbulent times preceding and following the Abbasid revolution.[16] Naturally, he developed his ideas on politics as a bureaucrat, not as a scholar or jurist.

[12] Van Ess 2017, 26.
[13] Yousefi 2009, 97.
[14] Qina 2000, 14.
[15] Ibn Khallikan 1843a, 431.
[16] Kristo-Nagy 2019, 163.

The scribes, an esteemed group in Persian political culture, were first introduced to Islamic society during Caliph Umar's reign. This later became a systematic policy when Ziyad, the Umayyad governor of Iraq, organised a local *diwan* with the help of a Persian scribe.[17] Their impact peaked in the early Abbasid period, as many viziers and other officers were Persian.[18]

Scribes represented a distinctive knowledge, as they analysed social, political and economic issues through practical engagement. Various accounts of scribes in *Al-Fihrist* of al-Nadim (d. 990) illustrate that they were well connected in political life.[19] But, holding official responsibility, they had to provide accurate analysis. *Qabusnama*, written by Kai Kaus, an eleventh-century Ziyarid (a dynasty in Northern Iran) ruler, warned that proficiency in clear writing is possible with detailed knowledge of the relevant subjects. Reminding that their works guide government policies, he warned that forgery would result in punishment.[20]

The works of scribes detected how various issues, such as the assessment of taxes, are related to political issues like legitimacy.[21] Their role was not merely to provide statistics, but also to discern how numbers are relevant in a given social context. This was a new field of knowledge where social and political issues are explained in a causal way through empirical data. The last Umayyad caliph, Marwan II's secretary Abd al-Hamid (d. 750) warned that a scribe should know religious sciences, the Arabic language, the political events of Arabs and non-Arabs (from the narratives of both sides) and accounting. According to him, bare facts are not satisfactory; a scribe should discover the causal links of events, because one thing contains the clues to another, and this enables the scribe to be guided in future works by previous experiences.[22]

Because the scribal text presents the causal understanding of social and political issues, it is the literary foundation of Islamic political theory.[23]

---

[17] Arjomand 1994, 11–12.
[18] Yarshater 1998, 6.
[19] Al-Nadim 2019, 357–425.
[20] Kai Kaus 1951, 200–10.
[21] Yousefi 2009, 79.
[22] Ibn Khaldun 1958b, 20–34; al-Qadi 2019, 219–20. Ibn Khallikan (1843b, 174) noted that the footsteps of Abd al-Hamid were followed by all scribes.
[23] See Tor 2015, 1.

Breaking with the previous poetic and other informal works, the scribal text developed a compositional syntactic style.[24] A scribe was not a scholar, nor was he a philosopher or a jurist. His perspective was determined by practical factors such as culture, geography and political power. Many scribes wrote books on politics, culture and geography. These works contributed to the development of the Arabic prose and vocabulary that became the foundation of the scientific texts of the Muslim world.[25] Effectively, it was they who formed the political intelligentsia of the early Islamic society.[26]

The scribes brought the Persian administrative traditions into Islamic culture with their translations of Pahlavi works. These translations introduced a humanistic and secular dimension because the scribes contextualised their subjects into the larger frameworks, including Persian history, thereby reaching beyond the Arabic/Islamic context.[27] Equally importantly, they incorporated power into their analyses, as they were true observers of how power affects politics.[28]

Ibn al-Muqaffa's is a pioneering name both in the bringing of Persian cultural elements into Islam, and in the formation of the early Arabic prose. He is regarded as the creator of Arabic prose.[29] His translation of *Kalila and Dimna* from Pahlavi is the first work of Arabic prose.[30] He translated other books, including *Khudaynama*, *The Testament of Ardashir*, *The Letter of Tansar* and *Kitab Mazdak*.[31] Breaking with the earlier poetic style, he introduced a literary style suitable for administrative writing.[32] J. D. Latham compares Ibn al-Muqaffa to Jacques Amyot (d. 1593), who contributed to the birth of a French prose style by his translation of Plutarch in the Renaissance years.[33] In this regard, *Risala* symbolises the transition to abstract and sophisticated worldly thinking.[34]

---

[24] Hanaway 2012, 99–100.
[25] Nasr 2007a, 397.
[26] Kristo-Nagy 2009, 286.
[27] Wacks 2003, 181. Al-Jabri (2011, 76) criticised Ibn al-Muqaffa for not quoting the Qur'an satisfactorily while referencing the Persian humanistic heritage.
[28] Kristo-Nagy 2019, 180.
[29] Ibid., 166.
[30] Wacks 2003, 179; Yarshater 1998, 57; Nasr 2007b, 420.
[31] Venetis 2006, 48 and 129; Bosworth 1983, 487.
[32] Serjeant 1983, 114–46; El-Hibri 2021, 62.
[33] Latham 1990, 53.
[34] Tor 2018, 7.

Ibn al-Muqaffa's works also exposed examples of humanistic and secularist tenets. He imagines politics as ruled by general laws shared by all nations.[35] *Kalila and Dimna* talks on 'good principles common to all creeds'.[36] This is repeated in *Al-Adab al-Sagir*: there is no branch of knowledge that was not narrated by a previous person or book.[37] The books left by the ancients (*kitab al-baqiyya*) prove this, as they were written well before us, with a lasting validity.[38] Being general and non-religious, this knowledge is transferable from culture to culture.[39]

Though Ibn al-Muqaffa embraced Islam, he was faulted for being a *zindiq*[40] (secretly keeping Zoroastrianism) because of his engagement with Persian culture.[41] His sarcastic comments on the Arab culture and glorification of Persian culture made him a 'usual suspect'.[42] Ibn Khallikan quotes Caliph al-Mansur as saying that 'I have never found a book on Zendikism that does not owe its origin to Ibn al-Muqaffa'.[43] A book by Zaidi imam al-Qasim bin Ibrahim (d. 868), which was written against Manichaeism, had the title *The Book of Refutation Against the Damned Zandiq Ibn al-Muqaffa*. Though the book's goal is to refute the Manichean dualistic doctrine,[44] it has harsh passages on Ibn al-Muqaffa, like 'the devil is on Ibn al-Muqaffa's tongue'.[45]

Unsurprisingly, when Ibn al-Muqaffa was killed in *c.*758, the perpetrators raised his allegedly heretic views to justify the murder. In fact, the event that incented Ibn al-Muqaffa's killing was a power struggle in the Abbasid court.

---

[35] Kristo-Nagy 2009, 289.
[36] Inostranzev 1918, 123. Goiten (2010, 151) attributes the introduction to Ibn al-Muqaffa.
[37] Ibn al-Muqaffa 1989c, 284.
[38] Ibn al-Muqaffa 1989b, 245.
[39] Ibn al-Muqaffa 1989c, 284.
[40] *Zindiq*, a general term for heresy, originally meant followers of Zand (Mani), the founder of Manichaeism.
[41] Al-Jabri (2011, 76) criticises Ibn al-Muqaffa for founding a culture inside Muslim society by referencing Persian culture. This is a case that illustrates how the same debates are still with us today.
[42] Van Ess 2017, 26. For example, he wrote *Muʿaradat al-Quran* that challenges the inimitability of Qurʾan.
[43] Ibn Khallikan 1843a, 431–2.
[44] Esmailpour 2007, 174.
[45] Ibrahim 1927, 28.

When Abd Allah bin Ali made a bid for power against Caliph al-Mansur, the tension was solved by an agreement of safe-conduct (*aman*) between them. However, the *aman* – which was written by Ibn al-Muqaffa – had strict binding commitments that were resented by the caliph. Al-Mansur ordered Ibn al-Muqaffa's killing.[46]

I shall revisit this killing later. But first, I shall present the political background to which Ibn al-Muqaffa was exposed. Understanding this background is crucial, as Ibn al-Muqaffa, who was a bureaucrat, developed his political thought by responding to various problems and events that he observed, and was sometimes involved in.

The Birth of the Abbasids

The political movement associated with the Abbasid family emerged in Kufa in 716, eight years before Ibn al-Muqaffa's birth. Founded in 638 by Muslim general Saʿd bin Abi Waqqas, Kufa was planned as a garrison city destined to become an Arab hub in the Sasanian heartland.[47] Despite that it was far from the Arab heartland, the inhabitants always imagined themselves as central actors.[48] This peaked when Ali made Kufa his powerbase against Muʿawiya. Kufa's Alid identity continued beyond this. At the time of Caliph Abd al-Malik, the city became a hub of pro-Alid activism where large and small anti-Umayyad revolts became routine.[49] The hallmark of pro-Alid groups was to claim leadership through kinship.

The Abbasid political movement arose within Kufa's pro-Alid environment. Shiʿa groups normally claimed leadership through Ali's sons from Muhammad's daughter Fatima. However, Muhammad bin al-Hanafiyya (d. 700/1), Ali's son from another wife, Hanifa, claimed leadership through his kinship. Because Muhammad bin al-Hanafiyya was not a grandson of Prophet Muhammad, his genealogical association with the Prophet was an indirect one through Ali's father, Abu Talib, the Prophet's uncle. This was a new political genealogy

---

[46] Ibn Khallikan 1843a, 433; al-Nadim 2019, 259.
[47] Al-Baladhuri 1916, 434 and 448; al-Tabari 1992, 10.
[48] Lassner 1965, 135.
[49] Hitti 1937, 207; Lassner 1980, 139.

where 'uncle' is a hereditary connection. Muhammad bin al-Hanafiyya's followers became known as Kaysaniyya.[50]

A dramatic development to change the fate of the Kaysaniyya was the Mukhtar revolt (685–7) in the Second Muslim Civil War. Mukhtar led a rebellion to revenge the murder of Husayn, Ali's son, by the Umayyads. Mukhtar (d. 687) controlled the region from eastern Anatolia to central Iran, including Azerbaijan. Meanwhile, the Umayyads were able to retain control only in Syria, as Hejaz, Khurasan and surrounding regions were under the control of Abdullah ibn al-Zubayr (who created a state in Madina). And western Arabia and southwest Iran were controlled by Kharijites.

The Muslims were no longer a united community. They were split into groups, and differences among them generated political tensions. Among them were non-Arab Muslims (*mawali*) who supported Mukhtar because he recognised their right to booty and army stipends. This cooperation brought the *mawali*, who would later become the basis of the Abbasids, to the centre of politics.[51] Mukhtar later recognised Muhammad bin al-Hanafiyya as the divinely ordained leader, which not only empowered the Kaysaniyya but also created the connection between the movement and the *mawali*.

In 701, Muhammad bin al-Hanafiyya died, and a majority of his supporters followed his son, Abu Hashim. In 716, Abu Hashim died, causing a split among his followers. But when a large group of them followed Muhammad bin Ali bin Abdullah al-Abbas (henceforth the Abbasid Imam Muhammad), the leadership passed to the house of Abbas.[52] As Imam Muhammad had no genealogical connection with Abu Hashim, the transfer was justified as a spiritual one. Paradoxically, though they were not Alid or Shi'a, the very origin of the Abbasid claim for authority was framed on a Shi'ite vocabulary.[53]

The Abbasids later developed the Kaysaniyya's genealogy through 'uncle' by redefining it through an Abbasid, Ibn Abbas, the Prophet's uncle.[54] The Abbasid defence of genealogy through 'uncle' is illustrated in a letter by

---

[50] Daniel 1979, 28; Daftary 2007, 59.
[51] Browne 1951, 229.
[52] Al-Shahrastani 1984, 127–9; Ibn Khaldun 1958a, 406–9.
[53] Van Ess 2006, 138.
[54] Al-Shahrastani 1984, 129; al-Ya'qubi 2018d, 626, 636–9 and 644. The person that secured the genealogical legitimacy became the state's name in the case of the Abbasids and the Fatimids.

the first Abbasid caliph al-Mansur to Muhammad bin Abdullah, an Alid who revolted in Madina in 762/3:

> My, how you pride yourself on kinship through women ... But God did not make women equal [in such matters] to uncles and fathers or [even] to paternal relations and guardians. God gave the uncle status equal to a father, giving him [legal] precedence in His book over the less significant mother ...[55]

That letter, a fascinating text that displays the interplay of politics and legitimacy, proves that, like the Shi'a, the Abbasids claimed that their right to the caliphate is made obligatory by divine mandate, not by the agreement of men.[56] Ironically, the Kharijites, who supported an egalitarian view of leadership, were declared as heretics.[57] As the Umayyads were already purged, Islamic politics operated on a native theory of divine mandate from the early eighth century.

By taking over the Kaysaniyya network, the Abbasid movement (*da'wa*) began.[58] It was a clandestine organisation. Even the leader was unknown to the public.[59] Al-Humaymah, a village on the south side of the Dead Sea, a good location for its closeness to the caravan routes used by pilgrims, became the headquarters.[60] Imam Muhammad met trusted individuals during the pilgrimage season as a precautionary strategy. He directed the *da'wa* through an executive council of twelve representatives, the *naqibs*.[61]

Social and Economic Grievances

The Abbasid propaganda combined religious and political motifs to delegitimise the Umayyads by addressing social and economic grievances.[62] They promised

---

[55] Al-Tabari 1995, 169–71.
[56] Mottahedeh 2007, 58.
[57] Not coincidentally, in 740, the revolting Berbers embraced Kharijism, of which the motto was 'any just Muslim, even a Berber slave, has the right of *imamate*'. Savage 1992, 351.
[58] O'Leary 1923, 98–9.
[59] Blankinship 1988, 590; Marin-Guzman 1994, 244.
[60] Future Abbasid caliphs al-Saffah and al-Mansur were born in al-Humaymah. Ibn Khallikan 1843b, 220.
[61] Daniel 1979, 32.
[62] Zaman 1990, 30.

a true Islamic government where people would be treated justly, which was a treatment that the Umayyad 'usurpers' did not deliver.[63] The primary target was Khurasanis, including the *mawali*, who were angered by problems associated with the Umayyads, like corruption, tribalism and economic injustice.[64]

The Abbasids manipulated the tensions among the tribes. Those tensions were caused by the Umayyad tactic of playing the tribes (mainly the southern and the northern tribes) against one another.[65] Meanwhile, the Abbasid claim for leadership, which was framed in a Shi'a narrative, enabled the Messianic motifs, which were strong in Khurasan.[66] The Umayyads tried to restore their legitimacy in Khurasan through the reforms of Nasr bin Sayyar, their last governor. However, the reforms failed, as the Umayyads had no strong local support.[67] The Umayyads were already in turmoil since the assassination of Caliph Walid II in 744. This prevented their instigation of effective agendas.

Among the grievances associated with the Umayyads, the problems related to taxation were critical. The early contracts agreed by the Arabs and the *dihqans* had fixed the taxation issue in Khurasan.[68] When conversions to Islam gradually diminished the tax base (Muslims do not pay poll tax), the *dihqans* kept taxing converted Muslims (*mawali*), thereby creating inequality between old and new Muslims.[69] To avoid a drop in their revenues, the Arab rulers tolerated such inegalitarian practices.[70]

Predictably, such problems gradually transformed the *mawali* into a constituency of the Abbasids.[71] All twenty founding fathers of the Abbasid movement in Kufa were *mawali*.[72] The problems linked to taxation helped

---

[63] Mottahedeh 2007, 58.
[64] Shaban 1970, xv; Judd 2010, 89.
[65] Wellhausen 1927, 70; Kennedy 1981b, 28.
[66] They propagated the idea that Ali deposited divine knowledge in a scroll which passed through his sons to the Abbasids. Agha 2003, 4.
[67] Hawting 2000; Sharon 1990, 35–6.
[68] Islahi 2014, 49; Zarrinkub 2007, 47.
[69] Zaman 1987, 121; Marin-Guzman 1994, 234.
[70] Hoyland 2015, 198–9.
[71] I do not mean the thesis of Wellhausen (1927, 397 and 492), that described the Abbasid revolution as a Persian reaction to Arabism.
[72] Agha 2003, 6.

the Abbasids form a large constituency by bringing together the dissatisfied people of various backgrounds.[73] They could draw support also from the Arab population, including the Arab *muqatila* (warriors) in Khurasan.[74]

The Rise of the East

Around 717, the Abbasids, having realised their limits in pro-Alid Kufa, expanded their *da'wa* to Khurasan, which later became the epicentre of their activism.[75] This caused the *da'wa* to sprout on the geopolitical tension between Khurasan and Syria.

Khurasan had everything the Abbasids needed.[76] It was not only a region of disgruntled peoples, but a region of millenarian beliefs that facilitated people's attachment to the Abbasid propaganda.[77] Its distance from Damascus obstructed a strong Umayyad control.[78] The militaristic culture with experienced warriors, a result of Khurasan's frontier status in holy war, was another advantage.[79]

The *da'wa* in Khurasan gained momentum during the second Abbasid Imam Ibrahim, particularly when he appointed Abu Muslim as the new local leader.[80] Abu Muslim, who was popular among the local people, was directly instructed by the imam.[81] Various Khurasani millennial groups were among his supporters.[82] Abu Muslim quickly became the most influential actor in the most decisive stage of the Abbasid revolution.[83]

In 747, Abu Muslim proclaimed the revolution, which was followed by a phase of armed conflict with the Umayyad forces led by Nasr bin Sayyar.

---

[73] Berkey 2003, 106.
[74] Lapidus 1975, 366.
[75] Zarrinkub 2007, 50; Agha 1999, 212.
[76] El-Hibri 2021, 36.
[77] Marsham 2009, 183.
[78] Kennedy 1981a, 43.
[79] Kennedy 2016, 109. Al-Ya'qubi (2018b, 70) described Khurasan as surrounded on all sides by battle-hungry warriors.
[80] Wellhausen 1927, 517. According to al-Tabari (1985b, 66 and 120), Abu Muslim was introduced to the Abbasid imam during the meetings of pilgrimage in 741–2. He was imagined as a good candidate to attract the support of the *mawali*. Kennedy 1981a, 43; Omar 1967, 99.
[81] Al-Tabari 1985b, 71–3.
[82] Daniel 1979, 105.
[83] Sharon 1990, 66.

He conquered Marv in the same year.[84] Soon, the Umayyad rule in Khurasan disintegrated. In 748, the Abbasids, led by Qahtabah bin Shahib, captured Kufa.[85] Caliph Marwan II retaliated by killing Imam Ibrahim in 749, at a time of decisive battles, to determine the Abbasids' fate.[86] This, however, did not make a botch of the revolution, as the Abbasids successfully managed the transition of power by electing Abu'l Abbas. Finally, the Abbasid army, led by Abdullah bin Ali, the new imam's uncle, defeated the Umayyads in the Battle of Zab on 26 February 750. Marwan II, for a while an escapee, was killed.[87]

The Revolution

The Abbasid army, led by Abdullah bin Ali, entered Damascus in 750.[88] Next came a ruthless purge, with mass executions not only in Damascus but also in places like Mosul.[89] The violence exceeded the cultural limits.[90] Imam Abu'l Abbas became Caliph al-Saffah, the blood-shedder. The Abbasids attempted to literally exterminate the Umayyads by killing every male descendant.[91] The rage is illustrated by al-Ya'qubi as follows:

> [Abdullah bin Ali] gave orders to dig up the tombs of the Umayyads, and he had the bodies removed and burned; he spared none of them . . . he had Caliph Hisham bin Abd al-Malik exhumed. He found him in a cave atop his throne – he had been painted with a liquid to preserve him. He had the body brought out, and he struck its face with a club. He had the body suspended between two stakes and flogged one hundred and twenty times, until the body parts were strewn about. He then had it collected and burned.[92]

---

[84] Al-Tabari 1985b, 63–8 and 93.
[85] Shaban 1971, 185.
[86] Al-Ya'qubi 2018d, 1065.
[87] Al-Tabari 1985b, 162–6 and 170.
[88] Ibn Khayyat 2015, 305.
[89] Al-Tabari 1985b, 196; al-Ya'qubi 2018d, 1079.
[90] Robinson 2010, 227 and 236–44.
[91] Hitti 1937, 285–6; Strange 1900, 4.
[92] Al-Ya'qubi 2018d, 1084–5. Marwan II's head was cut off and sent to Abdullah bin Ali. Seeing a cat tear out the tongue, he said: 'If time had shown us no wonder other than Marwan's tongue in a cat's mouth, it would have been enough for us.' Al-Suyuti 2015, 84.

The violence traumatised Syria, where the impact of the Abbasid revolution was intense.[93] The city was the stage of a dramatic surrender, as the Abbasids attacked almost all foundations of the Umayyad regime. Public buildings were sacked.[94]

Meanwhile, the Abbasid family, whose affairs were managed by Abu Muslim's local men, were in Kufa during the critical days of the revolution.[95] The Abbasid era officially began with Caliph Abu'l Abbas' sermon in the Grand Mosque, where he proclaimed that 'the sun has risen from its rising place, the arrow has returned to the archers, the bow to its maker, and right has returned to its source among the people of the Prophet's house'.[96]

Ibn al-Muqaffa's Political Thought

Ibn al-Muqaffa made a smooth transition to the Abbasid regime. After working for Sulayman bin Ali, he became the secretary of Isa bin Ali, the uncle of the first and second Abbasid caliphs.

In 754, Caliph al-Saffah died and was succeeded by his son, Abu Ja'far, as Caliph al-Mansur. It was a challenging transition, as Abdullah bin Ali revolted against al-Saffah, and that was followed by the murder of Abu Muslim. *Risala* probably emerged in the meantime, as it refers obliquely to these events.[97] This happened between 754 and 757, the aftermath of the revolution, when the Abbasids were building a new regime.[98] *Risala* was written as a response to the political and social developments of the period. Below, I shall analyse Ibn al-Muqaffa's political thought to demonstrate how it connects to his historical context.

The Geopolitics of the Abbasid Regime

Born on a Khurasani base, the Abbasid regime needed to consider the geopolitical balance among the loyalist Khurasan, Syria, the former epicentre of the

---

[93] Cobb 2001, 5 and 3.
[94] Elisséeff 2007, 111.
[95] Kennedy 1981a, 45; al-Ya'qubi 2018d, 1070.
[96] Al-Ya'qubi 2018d, 1077. When the inauguration was performed, Marwan II had not yet been killed. Mottahedeh 2007, 59.
[97] Lassner 1980, 106.
[98] Kristo-Nagy 2009, 293.

Umayyads, and Iraq, the hub of pro-Alid groups. The Abbasids already knew of regional differences. Back in 717, Imam Muhammad had authorised the expansion to Khurasan by reminding people that Kufans would never support anyone except the Alids, and the Syrians were devoted pro-Umayyads.[99] In the inaugural sermon in Kufa, Dawud bin Ali, who spoke after al-Saffah, cursed the Umayyads by calling al-Marwan 'Satan's ally'. He glorified Khurasanis as helpers given by God.[100]

A section of *Risala* deals with the geopolitics of the Abbasid regime-building. Ibn al-Muqaffa provides the earliest example of incorporating regional differences into Islamic political thought. 'Muslims' is replaced in Ibn al-Muqaffa's text with 'Khurasanis, Syrians and Iraqis'. As each region had a different political interpretation of Islam in Ibn al-Muqaffa's political thinking, it was no longer religion but the Abbasid regime that united those regions.

Syria: 'ancient regime'

The Abbasid revolution was the fall of Syria. Imagining Syria as the embodiment of the ancient regime, the Abbasids felt obliged to insulate themselves against risks that might originate in Syria.[101] The ultimate consequence of this strategy was to transfer the epicentre of politics to the eastern regions.[102]

For Ibn al-Muqaffa, too, the Syria days were the past. He wrote that the Syrians would be treated as they had treated others: they had deprived people; they would now be deprived. Syria had received taxes from other regions; Syrians would now send their taxes to other regions. They had excluded others from government; they would now face exclusion. According to Ibn al-Muqaffa, the caliph should not expect friendship from Syrians, as they are the harshest people in enmity and deception.[103]

Ibn al-Muqaffa's recommendations reflected the Abbasid attitude to Syrians. They were seen as an Umayyad region because of a complex history that connected Syria to the Umayyads. The Umayyads' relations with

---

[99] Daniel 1979, 30.
[100] Al-Yaʿqubi 2018d, 1077; al-Tabari 1985b, 155–6.
[101] Omar 1967, 330.
[102] Judd 2010, 89.
[103] Ibn al-Muqaffa 1989a, 318.

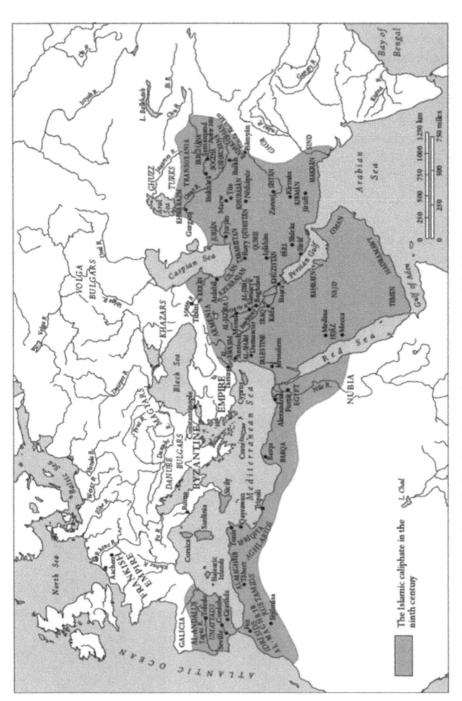

Map 1.1 The Abbasid Empire in *c.*800 (*The New Cambridge History of Islam Vol. I*, 2011).

Syria (when Muʿawiya's father, Abu Sufyan, had economic relations with the region) preceded Islam.[104] Those relations continued with Islam.

In 634, Muʿawiya and his brother Yazid had fought in the armies that conquered Syria.[105] After the deaths of Yazid and Abu Ubayda, the first governor of the region,[106] and Khalid bin Walid's dismissal by Caliph Umar, Muʿawiya became the governor of Damascus in 640.[107] He ruled Syria for twenty years, during which time he developed a strong relationship with the region. He also managed the settling of the Arabs, which enabled him to shape the province.[108] He built up a system of tribal alliances in which he appeared to be the main tribal leader. This helped him generate popular legitimacy after he transferred authority from Madina to Damascus.[109]

He then constructed the Umayyad state as a Syria-Arab empire where Syrians had privileges.[110] While the Syrian troops became the pillar of the Umayyad regime,[111] the Syrian people were his power base.[112] To symbolise that Damascus was the new centre, Muʿawiya ordered that the pulpit of the prophet in Madina be transported to Syria in 670/671.[113] The rise of Syria created political and economic resentments in Madina. The split triggered military battles where Syrians killed many companions in 683.[114]

Though the systematic inclusion of Khurasan into the Islamic state was achieved under the Umayyad governor Qutayba ibn Muslim,[115] the Umayyads

[104] Shaban 1971, 43.
[105] Al-Tabari 1992, 193; al-Baladhuri 1916, 166.
[106] Al-Waqidi 2005, 407.
[107] Al-Tabari 1989c, 98–100. According to Kennedy (2016, 49), Umar favoured the Umayyads above the Makhzum family (to which Khalid bin Walid belonged) who had been promoted by Abu Bakr. Muʿawiya was in close contact with Umar during the conquest of Syria. al-Tabari 1992, 185. Al-Suyuti (2015, 2) narrates that Umar called the Muawiyya 'the Khusraw of the Arabs'.
[108] Al-Baladhuri 1916, 278.
[109] Whitcomb 2009, 247–8.
[110] Gaube 2012, 349.
[111] Gibb 1962, 49. Also see al-Tabari 1996, 2, 8 and 29.
[112] Al-Yaʿqubi 2018b, 69.
[113] Al-Tabari 1987b, 101.
[114] Al-Tabari 1990, 221–2; Ibn Khayyat 2015, 101 and 104.
[115] Al-Tabari 1987b, 21, 72, 92 and 199; al-Baladhuri 1924, 186.

could not make another loyal region of Khurasan. On his deathbed, Nasr bin Sayyar warned: 'Stay in Syria!'[116] Syria was the Umayyad homeland.

Returning to Ibn al-Muqaffa's advice, he did not want the caliph to approach the Syrians with enmity. His was the realist stance. He therefore suggested that only trustworthy Syrians be given public roles. Ibn al-Muqaffa's suggestions leaned towards a strategy that was more integrational, as Syria was no longer the central province. That strategy included other suggestions, such as spending the tax collected in Syria on them, creating a new *diwan* for Syrian soldiers, and assigning each Syrian soldier with the task of caring for the poor and the orphans.[117]

This cautious policy also commended itself because of the ongoing pro-Umayyad revolts in Syria.[118] For example, the revolt led by Abu al-Ward, which broke out just after the revolution, was affiliated with the Umayyads.[119] This was followed by a series of Sufyani revolts, associated with Abu Muhammad al-Sufyani, who was the Umayyad prince pretender.[120] Such revolts kept the Abbasids on alert with regards Syria. Besides, the use of Khurasani troops to quell the rebels prolonged the revolutionary mentality, particularly the grudge between Syria and Khurasan.

The worst happened after the death of Caliph al-Saffah in 754, when his uncle, Abdullah bin Ali (hereafter Abdullah), revolted and claimed the throne.[121] Abdullah had distinguished himself in the fight against Marwan II, and in the subsequent campaigns in Jazira and Syria.[122] The Abbasid army entered Damascus under his command. What complicated the revolt was its connection to Syria. Al-Ja'far (who would become the Caliph al-Mansur) saw the revolt as an instance of Syrian revanchism.

Abdullah was the first Abbasid governor of Syria. Caliph al-Saffah assigned to him a campaign against Byzantium, and an army that included Syrians. The news of al-Saffah's death came right after that, and Abdullah invited

---

[116] Ibn Khayyat 2015, 295.
[117] Ibn al-Muqaffa 1989a, 318.
[118] Kennedy 2016, 112.
[119] Al-Tabari 1985b, 176.
[120] Al-Ya'qubi 2018d, 1018.
[121] Al-Tabari 1995, 14.
[122] Shaban 1976, 6.

people to support his claim to the caliphate. Next, unsure of their loyalty,[123] he purged the Khurasani troops. This left his army composed mostly of Syrians (remnants of the army of Marwan II) with whom he had developed close relations as governor.[124]

Actually, Abdullah had long been a supporter of reintegrating the Marwanid forces into the Abbasid army.[125] Various Syrian leaders immediately welcomed his claim for the caliphate.[126] When al-Mansur sent Abu Muslim to quell the revolt, the crisis turned out to be a reincarnation of the Khurasani–Syrian rivalry.[127] The Khurasani troops defeated Abdullah in 754, after three months of insurgence.[128]

Though it was not the only post-revolutionary revolt, the Abdullah affair panicked the Abbasids, as it revealed that the Syrian dynamics were dangerously active. Al-Mansur used the crisis to put an end to any lingering political opposition in Syria, and to reorganise the military in line with his interests.[129]

The revolt also triggered the events that resulted in the murder of Ibn al-Muqaffa. The defeated Abdullah fled to Basra to seek safe haven from his brother, Sulayman bin Ali. Sulayman asked for safe conduct from his cousin, Caliph al-Mansur.[130] Ibn al-Muqaffa, who was working for Isa bin Ali, was assigned the task of writing the safe-conduct document. He wrote a text that gaves strong guarantees to Abdullah, such as unrestricted movement that allowed him to travel anywhere. This text included clauses to bind the caliph, such as: his failure to honour his promises will see his wives regarded as divorced, and his army under no obligation to obey him.[131] Al-Ya'qubi narrates that, al-Mansur, having

---

[123] Al-Tabari 1995, 5–6 and 12.
[124] Mottahedeh 2007, 64.
[125] Bligh-Abramski 2012, 393.
[126] Omar 1967, 327.
[127] Al-Tabari 1995, 10.
[128] Al-Ya'qubi 2018d, 1099.
[129] Lassner 1980, 12.
[130] Al-Tabari 1995, 17–18.
[131] Marsham and Robinson 2007, 249–57. According to Arjomand (1994, 26), *Risala* might have been written after the death of al-Saffah, when Ibn al-Muqaffa's boss Isa bin Ali was master of the situation at Anbar, the seat of the caliphate, and his brother Abdullah had revolted. *Risala* may have been presented to al-Mansur, along with the safe-conduct document, during the negotiations following Abdullah's defeat. Similarly, Goiten (2010, 154) speculates that *Risala* might be linked to Ibn al-Muqaffa's murder.

read the safe-conduct document, asked 'Who wrote this?' The answer he received determined Ibn al-Muqaffa's fate.[132]

Iraq: a strategy for change

As the hub of the Alid groups, Iraq was never a pro-Umayyad region. Muʿawiya offered Iraq to Ali, while keeping Syria for himself.[133] Iraq had developed an anti-Umayyad stance well before Khurasan.

Though the Abbasids were pleased by Iraq's indifference to the Umayyads, its pro-Alid attitude was still a problem. Some Shiʿa groups, in view of their kinship theory of leadership, were unfriendly to the Abbasids.[134] As explained above, the Abbasids had benefitted from that Shiʿa narrative before the revolution. But they distanced themselves from the Alid groups after the revolution, seeing their narrative marginalised and ineffective for attaining popular legitimacy.[135] Meanwhile, Shiʿa revolts broke out in Iraq after the revolution.[136] The Shiʿa opposition continued right up until the third Abbasid caliph al-Mahdi (r. 775–85).[137] As a more distressing development, reminiscent of the Abdullah affair, Abu Salama – a key actor of the revolution in Khurasani and the Iraqi phases, and a minister (*wazir*) of the Abbasid family[138] – negotiated secretly with Alid groups, offering them the caliphate during the critical days of the revolution before the coronation of the first Abbasid caliph.[139]

Ibn al-Muqaffa witnessed all these developments, including the Abu Salama affair. His views on Iraq are reflected in his observations about it. Echoing the balanced Abbasid view, Ibn al-Muqaffa saw Iraqis as a virtuous people. He was of the view that the caliph may safely appoint them to

---

[132] Al-Yaʿqubi 2018d, 1101–12.
[133] Al-Tabari 1996, 209.
[134] Bennison 2009, 29.
[135] Al-Yaʿqubi 2018a, 45; Zaman 1997b, 49.
[136] Al-Tabari 1994, 142–5.
[137] Elad 2010, 67.
[138] Al-Tabari 1985b, 184.
[139] Ibid., 151; al-Yaʿqubi 2018d, 1079. Various names within the Abbasid *daʿwa* tried to persuade Shiʿa Imam Jaʿfar bin Muhammad to seek the caliphate. According to al-Shahrastani (1984, 132), Abu Muslim was among them.

his staff.[140] His view of the Iraqis is never like his view of the Syrians. Ibn al-Muqaffa saw the problems in Iraq as the results of Umayyad maladministration. It was his candid opinion that attributing such problems to the Iraqis was to ignore their virtues.

Ibn al-Muqaffa therefore criticises the Abbasid regime for its failure to terminate the misguided administration policy on Iraq by ceasing to appoint unqualified administrators who see the region in negative terms. This failure, Ibn al-Muqaffa deems is responsible for creating a fissure with the local notables.[141] The officials he complained about were probably former revolutionary activists who had no administrative experience. He wanted them replaced by qualified administrators capable of nurturing better relations with the Iraqi notables.[142] Urging the need for better administrators, Ibn al-Muqaffa highlighted the need to end the state of revolution with a transition to bureaucratic order.[143] The Abbasids' various policies in Iraq ran parallel with Ibn al-Muqaffa's suggestions. They integrated Umayyad judges and bureaucrats. For example, Yahya bin Said al-Ansari (d. 760), the Umayyads' judge in Madina, was appointed to Iraq.[144]

Given the problems in Syria, Ibn al-Muqaffa saw Iraq as essential to the Abbasid regime. The regime could not survive merely by dependance on Khurasan, which is far from the Muslim heartland. This made Iraq the best alternate region for regime consolidation. Ibn al-Muqaffa also defined Iraqis as 'helpers of Khurasanis'. They were the most supportive people to the Abbasids after the Khurasanis. He reminded people that Basrans and Kufans live together with Khurasanis.[145] Probably, Ibn al-Muqaffa imagined Iraq as an ideal place to mix Khurasanis with other people.[146] In fact, Khurasanis

---

[140] Ibn al-Muqaffa 1989a, 315. While promoting Iraqis, Ibn al-Muqaffa points out that some of them have high qualities in *fiqh*, reason and ethics. As noted by Schacht (1967, 276), this might be a reference to the nascent *ahl ra'y* school in Iraq.
[141] Ibn al-Muqaffa 1989a, 315–16.
[142] Demirci 2005, 143.
[143] Kristo-Nagy 2019, 169.
[144] Bligh-Abramski 2012, 395 and 399.
[145] Ibn al-Muqaffa 1989a, 315 and 321.
[146] Goiten 2010, 159–60.

had already begun to settle in Iraqi cities like Kufa.[147] Later, that became an official policy.[148]

The Abbasids soon created Baghdad, and moved their political centre to Iraq in 762. The decision reflected the major goals of Abbasid regime-building: detachment from Syria, and the creation of a new political centre in the eastern part of the empire.[149] They could not have moved the centre to Khurasan because Iraq provided by far the largest share of the revenues of the caliphate;[150] and Khurasan was too far from the central regions of the empire.[151] Baghdad was far from Syria and close to Khurasan.[152] It was well located in terms of the routes to Khurasan.[153] Its distance from Kufa, a city of potential Shiʿa opposition, was another advantage.[154]

Meanwhile, the new capital enabled the Abbasids to create a loyalist class by providing opportunities for them, such as land ownership.[155] This turned out to be the process that gradually marginalised the Syrian aristocracy.[156] Syria, the former centre of the Umayyad era, was reduced to a western flank province.[157]

Aware of the geopolitical differences among their regions, the Abbasids looked for a balance that would fit their regime-building. This search reflected itself in the names of Baghdad's four gates: Khurasan, Kufa, Basra, Syria. But the Khurasan gate was 'the Dynasty Gate',[158] symbolising preeminence.[159]

---

[147] Djaït 2007, 293.
[148] Wellhausen 1927, 558.
[149] Zychowicz-Coghill 2022, 130; Judd 2010, 89.
[150] Kennedy 1981a, 87.
[151] Lassner 1980, 143.
[152] Strange 1900, 4.
[153] Duri 2007, 31. The channels of the Euphrates and Tigris connected Baghdad to the Persian Gulf, Raqqah, Anbar, and the pilgrimage routes to Hejaz. Masudi 1989, 29; Lassner 1965, 139.
[154] Wellhausen 1927, 558.
[155] Kennedy 1981a, 86.
[156] Lassner 1965, 140–1.
[157] Bennison 2009, 26.
[158] Masudi 1989, 29.
[159] Al-Yaʿqubi 2018b, 72; Duri 2007, 32.

Khurasan: army and politics

A major political legacy of the revolution was dependency on Khurasani troops.[160] However, the Abbasids still had no systematic control over them. The frontier status of Khurasan, and its consequent militaristic culture, prevented the demarcation of political, fiscal and military fields.[161] Still organised as a revolutionary army, command of the troops was in the hands of leaders/commanders who were mostly drawn from families of Arab origin that had settled in Khurasan.[162] Some of them were reluctant to transfer their powers to the Abbasids. Having no concept of state loyalty, these military elites could easily change their positions. For example, Bassam, a commander in Khurasan, left the Abbasids in 751.[163] Despite such risks, the Abbasids could not easily replace these commanders, as they were from prominent local families.[164]

In the meantime, Abu Muslim, leader of the revolution in Khurasan and the commander of Khurasani troops, was killed by Caliph al-Mansur in 755.[165] Abu Muslim's was probably the highest profile among the individuals serving the Abbasids.[166] He saved the new regime by quelling revolts, including that of Abdullah and Abu Salama.[167] By killing Abu Muslim, having already eliminated Abdullah and Abu Salama, the Abbasids had purged three prominent names of the revolution.

Al-Mansur (before his caliphate as al-Ja'far) had always sought Abu Muslim's purge.[168] Caliph al-Saffah objected to this, considering Abu Muslim's service. But al-Saffah permitted his son to investigate Abu Muslim in Khurasan.[169] The son was treated badly by Abu Muslim.[170] During his visit, Abu Muslim

---

[160] Kennedy 1981b, 26.
[161] Luce 2009, 1–14.
[162] Kennedy 1981a, 78.
[163] Al-Tabari 1985b, 199.
[164] Kennedy 1981a, 79.
[165] Al-Tabari 1995, 42; al-Ya'qubi 2018d, 1101; al-Qazwini 1913, 58.
[166] Lassner 1984, 165.
[167] Al-Tabari 1985b, 205; 1995, 4. Al-Ya'qubi (2018d, 1098) narrates al-Mansur telling Abu Muslim that 'no one but I and you can deal with Abdullah bin Ali'.
[168] Kristo-Nagy 2019, 163.
[169] Al-Tabari 1985b, 210; al-Qazwini 1913, 57.
[170] Al-Ya'qubi 2018d, 1077–8.

executed Suleyman bin Kathir, a senior representative of the Abbasid. This was a deliberate act to remind the Abbasids of their limits in Khurasan.[171] The Abbasids interpreted these developments as confirming their fears that Abu Muslim was not under their control.

One reason behind Abu Muslim's self-confidence was the premature death of Qahtabah ibn Shabib after a battle against the Umayyads in 749/50. This effectively left Abu Muslim the commander with uncontested prestige.[172] Qahtabah was a major figure of the revolution as the general commander of the Abbasid troops, first in eastern regions like Ray, then in Basra and Kufa.[173] As an original *naqib*,[174] Qahtabah was a trusted man for the Abbasids, particularly in their dialogue with the troops.[175] In contrast, the troops led by Abu Muslim had no direct contact with the Abbasid family.[176]

Qahtabah's death transformed Abbasid politics into a competition between Abu Ja'far and Abu Muslim, where the latter was the shareholder preventing a strong caliphate.[177] When Abu Muslim defeated Abdullah, al-Mansur sent a representative to watch over the division of the booty, a reminder that the Abbasids were the ultimate authority.[178] Abu Muslim did indeed acknowledge the Abbasid authority, but he behaved as an independent leader, sometimes even intervening in general politics.[179] When the caliph asked Abu Muslim to take charge of Egypt and Syria, with the intention of keeping him far from Khurasan, his response was proof of a power competition: 'Khurasan is mine.'[180] Khurasanis saw him as their political leader, which was a consequence of his

---

[171] Al-Tabari 1985b, 185. As original *naqib*, Sulayman was among those who met Imam Muhammad in Mecca in 741/2. Al-Tabari 1995, 38.

[172] Ibn Khayyat 2015, 300; al-Tabari 1985b, 137.

[173] Al-Tabari 1985b, 126; al-Ya'qubi 2018b, 138–9.

[174] Al-Tabari 1985b, 26.

[175] Blankinship 1988, 591; Kennedy 1981a, 44.

[176] Kennedy 2016, 110.

[177] Agha 2003, 106. When Caliph al-Saffah died, Abu Muslim wrote a letter of condolence to Abu Ja'far. But he did not congratulate Abu Ja'far on becoming caliph. Al-Tabari 1995, 20.

[178] Al-Tabari 1995, 23; Gardizi 2011, 30.

[179] Kennedy 1981a, 52–4.

[180] Al-Tabari 1995, 24.

policies, like running a military *diwan*,[181] and minting coins that proclaimed him as *amir*.[182]

Ibn al-Muqaffa finished *Risala* close to the time of Abu Muslim's death.[183] Working at the Abbasid court, he had witnessed the developments and debates that led to Abu Muslim's murder. This helped him discern the Abbasid army strategy of transforming revolutionary troops into a formal army, indoctrinating them in loyalty, and moving the army back to its usual position by ending its influence in non-military fields, particularly the economy.

Ibn al-Muqaffa first concentrated on transforming the Khurasani troops into a formal army. After technical issues, such as the importance of employing commanders with better credentials, he delved into the complicated subject of loyalty. According to him, Khurasani troops had no match in Islam in terms of militaristic skills, but they were not optimally aware of the standards of the formal army in which there was a strong culture of loyalty. They therefore should be trained in the awareness of the power of their hands, opinions and speeches.[184] They needed to learn not only civil virtues, but also the code of behaviour in the political order that required troops' respect for life, property and the civilian population.[185]

Ibn al-Muqaffa imagined loyalty as the shared idea among troops that connects them to the political authority. However, that did not exist in the Khurasani army, as there were people among the troops with the extreme views of the various regions.[186] Having an army without a shared idea of loyalty was risky. Ibn al-Muqaffa explains this risk through the metaphor of riding a lion.[187] The message is sharp: relying on troops who do not share your views is a danger, as they may attack you. It is a weakness that appears as strength. To bolster his argument, Ibn al-Muqaffa warned that there are instructors

---

[181] Abu Muslim registered troops to *diwan* according to their place of origin, which was an egalitarian method unlike the Umayyad tribal registration. Sharon 1990, 270.
[182] Guest 1932, 555; Miles 2007, 369.
[183] Van Ess 2017, 27.
[184] Ibn al-Muqaffa 1989a, 311–14.
[185] Goiten 2010, 155.
[186] Ibn al-Muqaffa 1989a, 311.
[187] Ibid., 311

among commanders who seek to imbue their troops with a sense of obedience thus: if the caliph orders the mountains walk, they will walk; if he orders a reverse *qibla* in prayer, they will obey.[188] Ibn al-Muqaffa problematises two interconnected problems here. Firstly, there are extremists in the army who influence the troops, and this injures military hierarchy.[189] Secondly, even if such extremist views sustain a loyalty that might now please the caliph, it is precarious loyalty that can easily be abused and manipulated.

Several developments after the revolution (before and after *Risala* was completed) verified Ibn al-Muqaffa's warnings. Sinbadh, a local aristocrat who had been promoted to the rank of general by Abu Muslim, revolted two months after the latter's murder, using a neo-Mazdakite propaganda, and captured Nishapur and Ray. Manipulating various views, such as 'Abu Muslim did not die but assumed a divinity', Sinbad gathered many troops. As a dramatic follow-up, Jahwar, a Persian commander who was appointed by al-Mansur to quell Sinbad, also revolted.[190] Many other revolts followed, in which millennial beliefs, like that of Khurramiyya, played a role.[191] There was, for example, the revolt of Ishaq bin Turk, who also motivated people with neo-Mazdakite beliefs.[192] In 758/9, the Rawandiyah revolted, making a case that perfectly fitted Ibn al-Muqaffa's lion metaphor, as they had previously recognised Caliph al-Mansur's divinity.[193]

Beyond the problems created by military revolts, Ibn al-Muqaffa drew attention to the fact that most of the troops imagined the caliph as an imam in Shi'i terms, rather than as a political leader.[194] Those religious – mostly Shi'ite – views had helped the Abbasids in the past. But the birth of the Abbasid state required all religious groups to be united around itself.

---

[188] Ibid., 311. 'Moving mountain' appears in *Denkard VI*. Emetan and Shaked 1979, 23.

[189] Ibn al-Muqaffa might have seen Abu Muslim in this group; extremist groups had relations with Abu Muslim. Al-Shahrastani 1984, 131; al-Tabari 1995, 45.

[190] Nizam al-Mulk 2002, 206; al-Ya'qubi 2018b, 139; al-Shahrastani 1984, 150.

[191] Al-Tabari 1995, 44–7.

[192] Arjomand 2022, 208. Another was the revolt of Ustadsis. Al-Tabari 1995, 49–50; Anthony 2012, 641–55.

[193] Al-Tabari 1995, 62–3.

[194] Zaman 1997b, 40.

Those ideas became anachronistic within the Abbasid political order. Ibn al-Muqaffa suggested constructing a political loyalty that went beyond the tribal and religious forms of loyalty. To this end, he problematised the fact that army members come from various *qawm*s, that is, nations and tribes.[195] This was also an allusion to the Umayyads, whose divisions within the army along tribal lines weakened them in Khurasan. Yet the Umayyads had tribal ties with the Syrians, and those did not exist between the Khurasani troops and the Abbasids.[196]

To achieve his commended political loyalty that was beyond tribal lines, Ibn al-Muqaffa suggested that the caliph prepare a directive to explain to soldiers what is permitted, and what is prohibited, in a clear, comprehensive and eloquent way. This would also be instruction on the Qur'an and the Sunna. But this instruction must proceed along the lines of the example set by the caliph, so that soldiers did not fall prey to the heretics. People should memorise it.[197] This is not to suggest a general religious education. Ibn al-Muqaffa wanted to cultivate an understanding according to the examples set by the caliph.[198] Though religion is referenced, Ibn al-Muqaffa's model is political. The goal is to indoctrinate troops according to the Abbasid interpretation of politics, religion and other issues, expecting that this can generate a political concept of loyalty.[199] By emphasising that the directive be eloquent, Ibn al-Muqaffa desired a model based on persuasion, unlike the previous forms of loyalty that had operated through extremist beliefs or revolutionary devotion.[200]

Ibn al-Muqaffa imagined the state as the ultimate authority around which the troops would be united. Religion was not rejected, but given a status in terms of politics. This was normal, as political divisions among Muslims, particularly among the Abbasids, and the purge of the Umayyads in the revolution, virtually ended religion's role as an autonomous uniting framework.

---

[195] Ibn al-Muqaffa 1989a, 311.
[196] Lambton 1991a, 51.
[197] Ibn al-Muqaffa 1989a, 311. According to Shaked (1995, 244) and Van Ess (2017, 57–8), the proposal might have been inspired by Sasanian precedents.
[198] Lambton 1991a, 52.
[199] Ibn al-Muqaffa 1989a, 311.
[200] Black 2011, 22.

In this regard, Ibn al-Muqaffa's proposal was a foray into legal-theoretical territory in the cause of military loyalty.[201] But, according to Ibn al-Muqaffa, military issues were exclusively within the jurisdiction of the political leader, and not subject to religious rules.[202]

With this argument, Ibn al-Muqaffa provided a key principle of Islamic political theory: political and religious realms do not overlap perfectly. Based on this, Ibn al-Muqaffa defined 'the military' as exclusively a political field where the state is the monopolistic authority. Religion was not rejected, but it was subject to the standard set by political power. Only in so doing could Ibn al-Muqaffa ask the caliph not to tolerate the religious instructors in the army who interpreted religion differently.[203] This was not a debate among jurists; it was the Abbasid Army, where the state imposes the rules, including how religion should be interpreted.

However, Ibn al-Muqaffa's concept of loyalty was not risk-free. He was correct in criticising the old concepts of loyalty, as they relied on extremist views. He even mocked them for requiring allegiance to the ruler even if he rebels against God. The better way was not to obey the ruler if he ordered rebellion against God; obedience to the ruler was only valid so long as the ruler ordered righteous things. But this rational tenet worried Ibn al-Muqaffa, as it might be taken as a license to disobey the ruler.[204] Furthermore, the Abbasid army had a revolutionary habit of protesting an unjust rule. 'No obedience to the ruler who disobeys God' was a slogan of the troops during the revolution.

To overcome this caveat, Ibn al-Muqaffa developed an argument to deprive soldiers of any weight to judge the caliph's orders.[205] Accordingly, he separated 'anarchy' and 'order'. Once an order is given, it immediately creates its own autonomy, which requires issues concerning the ruling of people and military affairs to be exclusively left to politics, excluding religion. The categorisation implies that rebelling was legitimate only in anarchy. However, by the creation of the Abbasids, the anarchy ended, and the rule was established.

---

[201] Lowry 2008, 29.
[202] Ibn al-Muqaffa 1989a, 312.
[203] Ibid., 311–15.
[204] Ibn al-Muqaffa 1989a, 312.
[205] Lowry 2008, 30.

Soldiers should no longer intervene in affairs that were exclusively left to the political authority. Practically, Ibn al-Muqaffa revokes troops' ability to evaluate the caliph on religious criteria. This could happen only when it came to strictly religious matters, such as if the ruler forbade pilgrimage and fasting.[206]

Army, Economy and Society

Ibn al-Muqaffa suggested a regular payment for troops, as this would free soldiers from economic concerns. Even the smallest complaint about salaries should be heard with due concern, lest it affect the whole army. The issue was of such critical importance that Ibn al-Muqaffa asked the caliph to develop alternative methods of payment in kind (food and animal feed) to protect soldiers' incomes from being devalued by rising prices.[207] Ibn al-Muqaffa's regular salary advice was aimed at preventing soldiers from seeking alternate forms of revenue, as this would lead to independent behaviour.[208]

Another critical issue was the demarcation of the military and economic fields, which had vanished during the revolution. Ibn al-Muqaffa's views in this area reflect the causal relationships that drove the economy, society and the army in medieval Muslim society. Accordingly, agriculture taxes formed a major part of public revenue, most of which was used to finance the army. This generated a sensitive equilibrium between the army and the people. The balance was disturbed when the rulers demand more taxes to finance the army. Ibn al-Muqaffa thus warned that the financing of troops in times when the economy is experiencing inflation should not be allowed to damage land-owners/farmers.[209]

A worse policy was soldiers' involvement in taxation. Rulers, facing financial deficit, gave roles to troops in tax collection in exchange for their services. This created problems of arbitrary taxation, which irritated society, and caused a fall in agricultural production. Ibn al-Muqaffa was categorically opposed to troops' being given a role in taxation. He said that corrupts the army, for it weakens professional and militaristic honour, and creates complications

---

[206] Ibn al-Muqaffa 1989a, 312.
[207] Ibid., 314–15.
[208] Lassner 1980, 108–9.
[209] Ibn al-Muqaffa 1989a, 314–15.

between state and people. He called for the abolition of all ongoing methods of tax collection that involved soldiers.[210] Ibn al-Muqaffa's strict position against the involvement of troops in taxation might have been linked to a concern that the Abbasids might employ soldiers in taxation in regions like Khurasan, where they lacked an efficient administration.[211]

As already noted, the lack of a fair taxation regime in Khurasan facilitated the formation of a large anti-Umayyad opposition. Though the Umayyads reformed the taxation regime during the rule of Nasr ibn Sayyar, their efforts fell well short of success.[212] Ibn al-Muqaffa's comments on taxation were indeed influenced by that negative memory. He knew that Khurasan was still fragile for lack of a fair taxation regime. Confirming his fears, troops in Khurasan were already involved in social turmoil after the revolution.[213]

Discovering the State

Ibn al-Muqaffa observed that the courts in Basra and Kufa brought down the same verdicts on a crime type, but meted out unequal punishments in instances of it. Judges' verdicts, even in the core categories of crime – financial matters, adultery and murder – were often contradictory. The judges in Kufa reached contradictory decisions even when one crime was indistinguishable from another. This situation triggered resentment and protests.

To resolve this problem, Ibn al-Muqaffa proposed that the caliph establish a central body to supervise court decisions with the purpose of achieving their standardisation. He wanted the experts to keep a book (*kitaban jami'an*), under the caliph's patronage, that made final judicial decisions available for review. He imagined this book as a permanent record that would evolve with later caliphs' contributions.[214] This proposal might have been

---

[210] Ibid., 313.

[211] Goiten 2010, 158–9.

[212] Gardizi 2011, 26.

[213] Kennedy 1981b, 30.

[214] Ibn al-Muqaffa 1989a, 316–17. Ibn al-Muqaffa's proposal is discussed with a narrative that Caliph al-Mansur intended to promulgate the *Muwatta* of Malik bin Anas (d. 795) as the uniform basis of legal decisions. Malik rejected the offer. Zaman (1997a, 7) summarised the moral of the narrative as 'no one has the authority to draw up a code which might be given the sanction of law'. But *Muwatta* reflected the codification trend, as it has an approach based on a Madina doctrine. For various examples, see Malik bin Enes 1982, 54, 195 and 273.

inspired by Persian precedents.[215] Sasanian kings kept compilations of laws.[216] *Khwaday-namag*, probably compiled by Khusraw I, is an example;[217] it was translated into Arabic by Ibn al-Muqaffa himself.[218] However, there are other views: while Black likens the proposed book to late Roman praxis,[219] Goiten rejects both Persian and Roman influence.[220] All in all, therefore, it is better to call the proposed book the result of Ibn al-Muqaffa's observations of the community and its needs.[221]

Ibn al-Muqaffa criticised judges' contradictory verdicts from a political perspective. He was a scribe, not a jurist or a scholar of law. As his concern was a unified administration,[222] he saw contradictory decisions as dangerous, for they imperilled the government's good relations with the people. This inspired him to introduce the idea of legislation into Islamic thought by proposing the assignment of a political body that exercised not only the executive but also the legislative power.[223]

He was fully committed to the idea that the concept 'the political authority' (the state) entails the necessity of its autonomy. This is so because the state is the ultimate framework that unites the people, the land and the law. Not even religion has that level of autonomy. The political authority – the moment it is identified as 'the state', and therefore as the caretaker of society and the land – accepts responsibility for its own autonomy, hence for its absolute administrative unity.[224]

Let me illustrate this with an example: while Abu Yusuf requires the taxing of pearl and amber, Abu Hanifa is against it.[225] At a scholarly level, this

---

[215] Berkey 2003, 126.
[216] Perikhanian 1983, 630.
[217] Corcoran 2011, 101.
[218] Yarshater 1983, 993–4.
[219] Black 2011, 23.
[220] Goiten 2010, 163.
[221] Shaked 1995, 242.
[222] Lambton 1991a, 49.
[223] March 2019, 20; Schacht 1955, 61.
[224] Another example that displays how Ibn al-Muqaffa (1989a, 322) saw the state as the ultimate authority is his proposal to appoint people (whose livelihood would be guaranteed) to guide them on moral issues.
[225] Kallek 1997a, 5.

difference is the same as the difference that arises among jurists. Now, imagine judges in a country practising the views of Abu Yusuf and Abu Hanifa simultaneously. That would create financial problems, like losses of revenue, as well as the political problem of social unrest, because such differences in practice are prone to making particular people and the society resentful. If we imagine judges enforcing the different laws (Ibn al-Muqaffa criticised) that are the opinions of jurists in the critical matters of punishment and property, the results would be painful. This brings us to a question: shall the political authority allow the coexistence of contradictory judicial decisions, knowing that this engenders serious problems?

Islamic laws are imagined as having a divine origin, but scholars and jurists are entitled to interpret them. It is they who have the power to finalise the interpretation of Islamic law.[226] This idealistic model, however, became problematic once Muslim societies developed the structure called 'the state', the political authority that is monopolistic in all its domains. The state, which claims monopolistic authority in all its domains, introduced a power-dimension into the relations between the political authority and law by distinguishing 'legal opinion' and 'legislation' (state law). As Fred M. Donner underlined, judicial activism within the state imposes on state law the acceptance of an abstract concept of law: an overarching 'justice' that purports to regulate the affairs of all.[227] This transforms state law, which was previously handled by independent or semi-independent individuals, into an administrative issue of political power.[228] The role of these independent or semi-independent individuals in legal affairs and law enforcement is therefore gradually weakened.[229] The power elite, who see themselves as monopolistic actors in the construction of the overriding law, decline to delegate the authority of enforcing laws to second parties. Also, as

---

[226] Zubaida 2003, 43; Mouline 2014, 2.
[227] Donner 1986, 283–5.
[228] Zubaida 2003, 42 and 17; Robinson 2000, 166.
[229] Donner 1986, 290–1. In modern terminology, the legal-political aspect is where the semantics of politics and law overlap. Wintgens 2002, 1–9. As clarified by Kelsen (2006, 181–2), the state exists alongside its juristic concept, and takes priority over it. This conceptualisation later evolved in Europe through names like Rousseau, for whom 'it is not through the laws that the state subsists, it is through the legislative power'. Kriegel 1995, 62–3.

Ibn al-Muqaffa mentions, the power elites do not want independent and semi-independent actors' different decisions to put political order at risk.

Ibn al-Muqaffa proposed that the political elites be the ultimate authority in enforcing a uniformity of laws.[230] The proposal was forced by two inconsistent phenomena: while Muslims had the tradition of jurists and scholars commenting on the law, they developed the state in the period between Caliph Umar and the Umayyad caliph Abd al-Malik. Ibn al-Muqaffa was the first to detect this inconsistency of norm holders and power holders. Asserting that no power holder would tolerate scholars' or jurists' decisions about the final law of the land, Ibn al-Muqaffa proposed incorporating power-relations into the equilibrium. Ibn al-Muqaffa's thought was thus the earliest exploration of how to locate state autonomy in the Muslim community, particularly in regard to the law of the land.[231]

Ibn al-Muqaffa detected that legal pluralism, of which scholars are proud, is not compatible with the state. In so doing, he effectively distinguished the two faces of the law: judicial and legislative-political. On the judicial level, a state should provide for a fair trial. Though the judges are appointed by the political authority, a border is required that keeps the political elite separate from the judges. Judges should monopolise the court.[232] However, when it comes to the legislative-political aspect, it is about deciding which laws should be applied in uniformity in a given place. This is the higher level that is above scholars' opinions and jurists' decisions. At this level, no actor can monopolise the making of the law other than the political elite. As religion is no longer an autonomous dynamic there, this naturally changes the status of judges: they are now a state organ.[233] They can enjoy professional autonomy, but this never allows them to bypass the political elite.

Ibn al-Muqaffa's proposal illustrates that the evolution in Islam of Islamic political theory and the evolution of statehood are interconnected. To put this in a theoretical framework (Fig. 1.2): the state requires a new type of rationality of which the actors and parameters differ from the religious view of politics

---

[230] Yousefi 2009, 114.
[231] Lowry 2008, 26.
[232] Masud 2002, 141; Zaman 1997b, 105.
[233] Zaman 1997a, 5–6.

	State of politics	Parameters	Agents
Islamic political theory	The actual state	Autonomous variables	Power elites
Religious view of politics	The ideal state	Given rules	Jurists, scholars
Political philosophy	The ideal state	Given norms	Philosophers

Figure 1.2 Explaining politics according to three paradigms of political thought.

and political philosophy. This naturally weakens or destroys the autonomy of religious and philosophical rules, as they are now exposed to political power.

Ibn al-Muqaffa proposed a system which adapts to the practical reality that the political authority is the highest dynamic regarding the legal-political dimensions of the law. Imposing general laws has therefore a political nature; it is never purely a legal matter. He differentiated the state law and the jurist opinion: scholars and jurists have the right to propose opinions or doctrines; but those opinions become the law only if endorsed by the political authority.

The subject that Ibn al-Muqaffa highlighted is a gap in Islamic thought that has not been closed persuasively. The idea that Islam yields this task to scholars and jurists is a richness in thought that is meaningful at the intellectual level. This sort of thinking is mostly the legacy of early Muslim thinkers who disregard the question of power. Those thinkers did not treat power as autonomous; instead, they imagined it as a function of moral rules. This nurtured the naive assumption, which is divorced from actual practice, that political stability can be assured by normative orthodoxy.[234] The birth of the state destroyed that naive thinking. Yet the gap inevitably paved the way to the dominance of the political elite over jurists and scholars.[235] Ibn al-Muqaffa reminds us of the reality that, so long as religion is the law, the political elite would dominate its agents, that is, the jurists and scholars.

The birth and evolution of the state in Islamic society

As Ibn al-Muqaffa was born shortly after the reign of Abd al-Malik, his proposal was not independent of the fact that he lived in the late Umayyad period, where an Islamic-society concept of state had already emerged (see Fig. 1.3).[236]

---

[234] Lambton 1956, 125–7.
[235] Rosenthal 1962, 68.
[236] Robinson 2000, 166; Crone 2005, iix.

	Periods	Events	Political Model
	610–632	Muhammad receiving revelation	Prophet-ruler
	632–661	From Muhammad's death to Mu'awiya's caliphate	Classical caliphate
Ibn al-Muqaffa (720–759)	661–743	From Mu'awiya's caliphate to the death of Caliph Hisham	Early Islamic state
	743–750	Abbasid Revolution	Power struggle
	750–	Consolidation of the Abbasid regime	Abbasid state

Figure 1.3 Ibn al-Muqaffa and the evolution of state in Islamic history.

Ibn al-Muqaffa's thought reflects the condition of state-and-religion at the crossroads, where their relationship had to be defined.[237]

To illustrate this briefly: according to the mainstream narrative, the state emerged in Islamic society in the period that spans the reign of Caliph Umar to that of Abd al-Malik bin Marwan. Previously, Islamic society was a community without institutions where people managed their affairs in personalistic ways.[238] This narrative was originally invented by al-Mawardi, and later developed by Ibn Khaldun. Nuances notwithstanding, this narrative survives in the works of contemporary scholars.

The turning point was the creation of *diwan*, a department with specialised tasks, such as taxation. Ibn Khaldun wrote that *diwan* appeared when statehood emerged during the reign of Caliph Umar.[239] Umar created *diwan* to overcome complex problems of administration, including booty, military governance and taxation after the conquest of Sawad (the arable lands of southern Iraq). What was left from the previous Islamic experience was not sufficient to deal with such complexities.[240] When Arabs came to rule the new realms, they still did not have the institutions of a sedentary culture.[241] Muslims thus, paradoxically,

---

[237] Goiten 2010, 164. Ibn al-Muqaffa (1989a, 315) used the term '*dawla*' (state) for the Abbasids.
[238] Wellhausen 1927, 3; Sharon 2012a, 17.
[239] Ibn Khaldun 1958b, 21.
[240] Al-Ya'qubi 2018d, 776 and 783; Ibn Khaldun 1958b, 21; al-Baladhuri 1924, 251.
[241] Ibn Khaldun 1958b, 268.

adapted Persian institutions when they dominated Persia, because they did not have equivalents of them.[242]

Whether inspired by Persians or Romans, *diwan* was necessarily a non-canonical institution.[243] Ibn Khaldun wrote that *diwan* had to be explained to Umar, as he did not know its meaning.[244] Pragmatically, such borrowings from Persians, as D. G. Tor summarises it, filled a gaping hole in Islamic political life with the already available Persian institution, just like the Muslims filled the gap in their medical knowledge with Galen.[245]

Diwan reveals the foundation of the Islamic state, as it was a shift from the personalistic way of governance to an institutional setting.[246] Managing revenues through *diwan*, Umar did not observe the former practice of distributing the conquered lands to warriors. He found the former practice inapplicable, since a large population lived in the conquered lands.[247] This, however, meant taking booty from the conquerors and passing it to the state. Some conquerors reacted to Umar, as they did not comprehend the rationale behind keeping lands for the public.[248] Similarly, Umar's new practice of *aʿta* (pension), the distributing of booty according to political criteria that replaced the previous methods, was criticised.[249] All these changes meant a shift from the former personalistic and egalitarian methods to new ones that operated on political criteria.[250] Gradually, the expansion of the caliph's

---

[242] Bell 2012, 218; Danner 2007, 575; Bosworth 1973, 53.

[243] Al-Yaʿqubi 2018d, 783; Ibn Khaldun 1958b, 20. According to al-Tabari (1995, 115–16), the idea of *diwan* came from al-Walid bin Hisham who saw it in Syria.

[244] Ibn Khaldun 1958b, 21. The discussions of other Muslims on *diwan* reveal that it was new to them. Al-Tabari 1994, 115–16; al-Baladhuri, 1924, 241.

[245] Tor 2011a, 116.

[246] Duri 2011, 87; Husaini 1976, 63 and 40.

[247] Al-Tabari 1992, 155; al-Yaʿqubi 2018d, 782; al-Baladhuri 1916, 423, 430–1.

[248] Wellhausen 1927, 44; Duri 2011, 89.

[249] Al-Tabari 1994, 115; al-Yaʿqubi 2018d, 783–4. Umar's practices, like instituting a calendar, and dating documents and stamping them with clay were other reflections of this shift. Al-Tabari 1994, 114.

[250] Ibn Khaldun 1958b, 97.

duties required other rules and institutions.[251] The administrative complexity created by those institutions subsequently inserted a boundary between rulers and people. This symbolised the corporate nature of the state. For example, Umar appointed judges, no longer interested in exercising this office himself directly.[252]

The embryonic state that began with Umar's *diwan* evolved, giving way to an Islamic state in the time of Muʿawiya (r. 685–705). It later acquired a sophisticated nature under Abd al-Malik (r. 661–80).[253] The literature displays this evolution with references to its various developments.

The most visible of these developments was the appearance of Muʿawiya's name and images in public places to symbolise the central government.[254] For instance, he was depicted seated on a throne as he signed official documents.[255] Public display was made of Islam-part-of-state policies under Abd al-Malik bin Marwan.[256] Public signs, such as milestones, were used to define him as the sovereign;[257] his image on his now-standardised coinage[258] underlined that status.[259] He imposed Arabic on the bureaucracy.[260] Also, the Umayyads planned

---

[251] Ibn Khaldun 1958a, 454. Symbolising the rise of *the political*, Umar reincorporated those who fought against the Muslim community in the Ridda wars, who had been excluded by Abu Bakr based on religious concerns. Political reasons were behind Umar's decision, such as the lack of manpower as well as to unite Arabs against the Persians. Al-Tabari 1992, 18; 1993, 75 and 151. Also see al-Yaʿqubi 2018d, 752–5; Kennedy 2016, 57.

[252] Ibn Khaldun 1958a, 452–3. Illustrating this point, Ibn al-Muqaffa (1989a, 320) notes that the caliph's acts are no longer personal, they are public.

[253] Ibn Khaldun 1958b, 22; Foss 2010, 76 and 84; Donner 1986, 285. Hoyland (2006, 398) starts the state with Abd al-Malik.

[254] Hoyland 2015, 98.

[255] Ibn Khaldun 1958b, 53 and 63–4.

[256] Hoyland 2015, 195.

[257] Sharon 2012b, 293; Danner 2007, 575. The erection of milestones, as well as buildings such as the Dome of Rock, were imageries that asserted the Umayyads' claims to be autonomous rulers. Donner 2012b, 7.

[258] Ibn Khaldun 1958b, 59.

[259] Al-Tabari 1989b, 90–2; al-Suyuti 2015, 32; al-Yaʿqubi 2018d, 986.

[260] Ibn Khaldun 1958b, 22.

the urban space on a state-based perspective by introducing new boundaries between government offices and the people. The people were asked to observe the protocols of respectful behaviour in those spaces.[261] Official units of weights and measures were issued to display that the state had the exclusive legitimate authority to impose the relevant law in this field.[262] A slew of sophisticated central and provincial administrations came into play,[263] perhaps the most glamorous of them being an army that was maintained to be at the service of the government.[264] The Court of Redress of Grievances (*mazalim*) was founded,[265] and security forces were created in cities. A system was put in place to control the collection of revenues when they were being extracted in the provinces. That system also oversaw the spending of those revenues.[266]

All the above-listed institutions meant the birth of a state that claims a monopolistic autonomy on imposing an overarching law.[267] Each item in the list is a political instrument that connects people to the state by power and legitimacy.[268] As the state became the political uniter of the people, it easily imposed unity around itself, and adjudicated all sorts of differences, including legal issues. This transformation was the historical background in which Islamic political theory emerged. In short, the state made Islamic political theory possible (and inevitable) by creating the autonomous political authority to impose its own rules.

---

[261] Foss 2010, 79–80; Elisséeff 2007, 110. Al-Ya'qubi (2018d, 911–12; 2018a, 37) summarises this transformation: 'Muwiyya was the first in Islam to institute bodyguards, chamberlains, police forces, and gate-keepers; to drape curtains … to sit on a throne with people below him; to institute the office of the seal; to erect tall buildings.'

[262] Donner 1986, 290.

[263] Hawting 2000, 35–6. Others, like the Umayyad governor Ziyad who created regular chanceries, also played roles in this context. Al-Baladhuri 1924, 259–66.

[264] Hawting 2000, 62.

[265] Shahin 2015, 79.

[266] Foss 2010, 77 and 92.

[267] Razek 2012, 30; Walmsley 2010, 26.

[268] Donner 2012a, xiv. For example, coins carried the message to inhabitants about the continuing rule of a caliphate, and illustrated the ability of the state to unify economic measures. Ilisch 2010, 125 and 142.

A case: taxation and state

To return to Ibn al-Muqaffa, his search for a uniform taxation law through the agency of the political authority provides additional insights into his state-oriented thought.

The Abbasids inherited from the Umayyads an agriculture-based economy without a uniform taxation regime.[269] Ibn al-Muqaffa describes it in detail: There are different taxation rules across the country. Those rules are not standard even in the same place. People no longer know the rules. The resultant chaos is most detrimental to landowners (farmers) who need clear taxation rules. Without proportional taxation rules, the system victimises villagers when the price of their products falls. The chaos inhibits the work of the supervising tax officers. They either chase villagers to find whatever they can tax, or they tax those who use the land, which is only a punishment of hardworking villagers.[270] The message of Ibn al-Muqaffa's complaints about taxation is essentially the same as his complaints about the courts' ruling inconsistently: until someone secures uniformity in the law, contradictory rules will only damage public order.

As another solution through political authority, Ibn al-Muqaffa suggested to the caliph that he fix the taxation rules.[271] But how is that possible from the perspective of Islamic law? Ibn al-Muqaffa finds a justification by categorising the collecting of taxes and the spending of them as a case of 'taking from Muslims and distributing to Muslims' according to the exclusive discretion of the political authority.[272] This proposal fits with his previous proposal of codifying laws, as both tend to impose strict oversight on arbitrary enforcements of the law.[273] Ibn al-Muqaffa had simply proposed a uniformity in the interest of the state.[274]

Ibn al-Muqaffa justified the rationale of looking for a political solution to problems concerning taxation by arguing that jurists' methods are not

---

[269] Shaban 1976, 16.
[270] Ibn al-Muqaffa 1989a, 321–2.
[271] Ibid., 321–2 Also see Rosenthal 1962, 73.
[272] Ibn al-Muqaffa 1989a, 312.
[273] Yousefi 2009, 116.
[274] Ibn al-Muqaffa 1989a, 317.

conducive to the aim of standardising law.²⁷⁵ Not only do the jurists lack the political power to impose a law, but their methods are flawed, for they have no objective framework that can deliver standard rulings. Jurists justify their contradictory rulings by relying on the Sunna. The Sunna is, however, a personal view usually based on contradictory historical precedents. Judges cannot even present a systematic Sunna.²⁷⁶ Such defects notwithstanding, the Sunna is still treated by jurists as if it were a standard framework. Equally problematical is that jurists rely on analogy (*qiyas*), which is not a proper method of standardisation, as it is prone to subjective decisions.²⁷⁷ The different resources or narratives are referenced by analogy. This only perplexes those who use it. Similarly, people cannot dispense with it, because they believe that abandoning analogy is wrong.²⁷⁸ For Ibn al-Muqaffa, jurists' methods rely on subjective argumentation that lacks an objective basis.

Ibn al-Muqaffa's views display how the concept of law is different in Islamic political theory from that of the jurists. In the case of taxation, he observed that the discipline of law is more complicated than the juristic narratives lead us to believe.²⁷⁹ The juristic narrative, which has an idealistic concept of law, creates problems of stagnancy.²⁸⁰ Jurists imagine the laws as external to society. Thus, their logical methods like analogy are only an analytic inductive method that references ideal rules. These methods do not help when practical problems are addressed. Simply, analogy does not take the empirically observed situation as the main reference point. In contrast, the method of Ibn al-Muqaffa, for whom there is no ideal rule that transcends society, is empirical, as he sees

---

[275] Lowry 2008, 28.
[276] Ibn al-Muqaffa 1989a, 316–17.
[277] Hamori 2013, 232; Schacht 1967, 275.
[278] Ibn al-Muqaffa 1989a, 317. Ibn al-Muqaffa's rigorous critique of analogy is unsurprising, as he is the translator of Aristotle's works on analogy like *Categories* and *The Isagoge* of Porphyry. Ighbariah 2020, 57–97.
[279] Ibid., 95. Also see Zaman 1997b, 104.
[280] Duri 2011, 87.
[281] Yousefi 2019, 104–5.

law through the practical experiences of people.[281] That practical awareness is better at providing an objective framework in politics that addresses people's problems than are the subjective and idealistic assumptions of jurists. Ibn al-Muqaffa's proposal on taxation was therefore not an example of fiscal jurisprudence.[282] Behind his proposal was a political reasoning.

Theorising Political Rationalism in Ibn al-Muqaffa

Ibn al-Muqaffa's point of departure is the actual state of politics, not idealistic conceptions of it. According to him, it is not possible to satisfy all people.[283] Since a perfect society is not attainable, the best strategy is to find solutions within the limits of the actual state of politics.[284] Reflecting the empirical dimension of his thought, he does not justify himself by quoting idealistic religious norms; he references the relevant dynamics of society and politics. Ibn al-Muqaffa's politics is therefore never an idealistic vision; it is a field of continuous fluctuations.

Autonomous variables like the political and the economic are decisive in Ibn al-Muqaffa's thought. That is, the king survives as king only while he retains his 'property', meaning all his economic assets and capacities. Political authority (*mulk*) cannot survive without economic power.[285] Thus, 'poverty' is the worst of disasters, for it can destroy everything in life, even morality and knowledge.[286]

In *Al-Adab Al-Sagir*, we get further details on how norms are affected by power. Accordingly, those who have no power have nothing. Power is the pillar of the state.[287] Even opinions are determined by the dynamic interactions of the economy and power.[288] For example, legitimacy is a function of

---

[281] Yousefi 2019, 104–5.
[282] Goiten 2010, 153.
[283] Ibn al-Muqaffa 1989b, 248.
[284] Ibn al-Muqaffa 1989c, 297.
[285] Ibn al-Muqaffa 1989b, 247. [*Ar.* mal]
[286] Ibn al-Muqaffa 1989c, 304.
[287] Kristo-Nagy 2009, 294.
[288] Ibn al-Muqaffa 1989c, 304.

power: 'Power comes from legitimacy, and legitimacy comes from power.'[289] He formulates 'legitimacy' in terms of power, not in the terms of the religious criteria provided in jurists' and scholars' books. Legitimacy is negotiated, not an ideal phenomenon to be determined by religious rules. The king should be in continuous quest of attaining legitimacy with popular ideas and works designed to 'make his rule [look] beautiful to the people'.[290] The apex of political rationalism in Ibn al-Muqaffa is observed in *Al-Adab al-Kabir*, when he writes: 'morality is impossible with power (or the king)'.[291] He differs from the religious view of politics, and from Islamic political philosophy, both of which see power as the servant of a supreme norm. For him, power is autonomous to a point that it creates its own normative justification.

Ibn al-Muqaffa underlines reason in several passages of his works. *Al-Adab al-Sagir* begins with an emphasis on reason.[292] However, it is substantially the empirical nature of Ibn al-Muqaffa's thought that defines him. This is mostly visible in his clear rational inquiry of religion. Religion is not a matter of argumentation and persuasion for Ibn al-Muqaffa. He makes a firm distinction between faith and opinion/knowledge.[293] One surrenders (*teslim*) to religion. Opinion, unlike the surrender to religion, gains strength with argumentation in the process of rational inquiry. Opinions can be proved, or at least defended, by argumentation, whereas religion cannot be defended or proved by rational arguments.[294] Religion survives through cultural mechanisms, or simply as habit. In the 'Borzuya Introduction' of *Kalila and Dimna*, it is explained that people believe in religions not because they have verified it themselves, but because religion has captured their imagination in the process of their socialisation. That is why conversations with people to find the best religion are so unsatisfactory.[295]

---

[289] Ibn al-Muqaffa 1989b, 253.
[290] Ibid., 253.
[291] Ibn al-Muqaffa 1989b, 253. [*Ar.* fe'in al-akhlaq mustahille ma'a al-mulk (*or*) al-melik]
[292] Ibn al-Muqaffa 1989c, 284 and 291.
[293] Rosenthal 1962, 70.
[294] Ibn al-Muqaffa 1989c, 294.
[295] Ibn al-Muqaffa 1819, 71–2.

This passage distinguishes socialisation and intellectual engagement, and defines faith as a product of the former. So, religion does not belong to the rational realm. Though he still thinks religion 'the most esteemed talent/gift', he reminds us even so that it is something that people get by birth.[296] Thus reverence for religion is one realm of being. The rational realm is another. Rational inquiry into religions brings no satisfactory proof.[297] In this way, Ibn al-Muqaffa re-defined religion's status without rejecting it. It now belongs to the field of culture governed by socialisation, not rational inquiry.[298]

Locating religion outside of rational inquiry has the important implication of the demarcating line between politics and religion. Religion and politics do not overlap perfectly in Ibn al-Muqaffa's thinking. Politics is therefore left to human opinion (*ra'y*). As a consequence, there is a field where the king can decide unilaterally on matters that are not clearly ruled by religion.[299] The king's authority is vested, for example, in his political power in various fields like war, security and taxation.[300] The logic here is simple: given that religion and rational inquiry reference different modes of thoughts, the obvious deduction is that religion cannot embrace the whole of life, particularly in fields like politics, where rational inquiry reigns. Those fields belong to free opinion.[301]

On this account, Ibn al-Muqaffa's model has two levels of separation. On the first level, he categorises Islamic law into two sections, according to whether they are open to human interpretation or not. On the second level, he defines a field where religion is silent, as that field is completely left to human opinion. This is not a field where religious rules are open to interpretation; it is a field where there are no religious rules. To justify this, Ibn al-Muqaffa says

---

[296] Ibn al-Muqaffa 1989c, 294. [*Ar.* afdhal al-mawahib]
[297] Ibn al-Muqaffa 1819, 71.
[298] Ibn al-Muqaffa (1989c, 299) rebuts the value of 'memorizing or protecting without reasoning'.
[299] Ibn al-Muqaffa 1989a, 312–13. Ibn al-Muqaffa's giving the central role to the holders of power is described by Black (2011, 24) as a Hobbesian twist.
[300] Yousefi 2017, 19.
[301] Goiten 2010, 157.

that had God sent rules by religion for every detail of life, 'without sacrificing even one letter of it', that would have been an unbearable burden for people. It would perplex humans by making reason useless for lack of a function, because reason would do only things that are defined by revelation.[302]

This has another important consequence that Ibn al-Muqaffa delivers: religion and opinion cannot explain each other. Debating on religion, which is an attempt at rational inquiry into religion, is meaningless, as religion is not a field of rational inquiry. Debate there is only a mistaken attempt to turn religion into an opinion. For him, treating opinion as religion is wrong.[303] An attempt to understand politics, which is a field left to opinion, from a religious point of view is tantamount to treating politics as religion. Ibn al-Muqaffa clearly separates opinion from religion, and he locates politics in the realm of the former.

However, this is not to argue that Ibn al-Muqaffa rejects the social function of religion. He disapproves disbelief by reminding that 'believing in magic is better than believing in nothing'.[304] Reason needs religion, for Ibn al-Muqaffa.[305] This is more about religion's socio-political functions.[306] It is more like a political instrument, but a necessary one.[307] Shaul Shaked explains this using of religion as a notion relating to the psychology of the individual, rather than as an institutional concept.[308] This instrumental approach to religion also affected also his reasoning: even when he quotes religious texts, they work as helpful customs or ancient wisdoms.[309] Religion itself is not *per se* a proof or argument, it is a sociological phenomenon in Ibn al-Muqaffa's works.[310]

---

[302] Ibn al-Muqaffa 1989a, 313. According to Black (2011, 24), Ibn al-Muqaffa's view on the relationship between religion and reason is like that which subsequently developed in the West.

[303] Ibn al-Muqaffa 1989c, 294.

[304] Ibid., 297. Similar statements appear in *Denkard VI*. Emetan and Shaked 1979, 15.

[305] Ibn al-Muqaffa 1989c, 302.

[306] El-Hibri 2021, 64.

[307] Kristo-Nagy 2009, 290; 2019, 173.

[308] Shaked 1995, 246.

[309] Arjomand 1994, 33.

[310] Ibn al-Muqaffa 1989c, 295. Kai Kaus (1951, 201) warned scribes to embellish their letters with quotations from the Qur'an. This is observed in Ibn al-Muqaffa's translation of *The Letter of Tansar*. Tansar 1968, 39.

Revisiting the Iranian Influence

The Persian impact on Islamic societies was consequential for two reasons. Firstly, many institutions that effected the evolution of Islamic political theory had Persian origins. For example, the Redress of Grievances was created by Abd al-Malik on the model of the Sasanian court of appeals.[311] Secondly, major ideas that formed the historical foundation of Islamic political theory were inspired by Persian culture. If philosophical rationalism in Islam is a fruit of the interaction with Greek philosophy, Islamic political rationalism is a fruit of the interaction with Persian administrative culture.[312] In *Uyun al-Akhbar*, Ibn Qutayba (d. 889) narrates Prince Walid once asking his father, Caliph Abd al-Malik, 'What is politics?' In his response, the caliph's reference was 'as [written] in the books of Persians'.[313]

Given its formative impact on Islamic political theory, revisiting the Persian influence is a necessity for this book. The main problem in this regard is that the Iranian impact is presented by a mainstream thesis as a reason behind the decline of Islamic civilisation. This is, however, constructed mostly on frameless and reductionist views of Persian culture.[314] I am interested in this problem in this book because that mainstream thesis prevents the correct understanding of the origins of Islamic political theory. As the scope of Persian influence goes beyond the limits of this chapter, I shall be satisfied with selected subjects.

To begin with, Persianisation among Muslims is not a late phenomenon. It began as early as Caliph Umar's reign. His taxation regime was an adaptation of the Sasanian model as designed by Anushirwan.[315] The Persian impact is observed even on major taxes like *jizya* and *kharaj*.[316] The origins

---

[311] al-Mawardi 1881, 74; Nizam al-Mulk 2002, 14.
[312] According to Yarshater (1998, 4–5), early Islamic society was composed of Arabic faith, Greek philosophy, and the Sasanian administrative tradition and political theory.
[313] Ibn Qutayba 1900, 27.
[314] I myself made this mistake. Bacik 2019, 28–30.
[315] Al-Tabari 1999, 260–260; al-Tabari 1992, 155; Morony 1984, 100; Davaran 2010, 51; Islahi 2014, 49; Goodman 1983, 476; Cahen 1997, 1030. On Anushirwan's tax reform, see al-Yaʿqubi 2018c, 461–2; Brosius 2006, 185.
[316] Pourshariati 2008, 502; Kallek 1997b, 72; Hitti 1937, 171. Muslims introduced *kharaj* to various regions such as Egypt later, as 'the assimilation of *kharaj* into Islamic law involved a long process of nearly two centuries'. Yousefi 2019, 106–7.

of *kharaj* trace back to the Parthians of the third century BC. *Jizya* was the Persian *gozet*.[317] Umar's adaptations made the Persian impact a 'canonical' foundation, as they were incorporated into Islamic law as part of *muwafaqat of Umar*.[318] Later jurists drew their reasoning procedures from the relevant procedures of Umar's decisions.[319] The canonisation of Anushirwan's rules through Umar generated different responses: some brought to bear the narratives of land tax seemingly grounded in Qur'an and the traditions.[320] For others, the Sasanid legacy was sanctioned, as observed in pseudo-Ghazali: *Nasihat al-Muluk* narrates Muhammad saying that 'I was born in the time of the Just King', and explains him as Anushirwan.[321]

Secondly, some scholars presented Persian society as despisers of merchants and commercial activity.[322] This is an essentialist and misleading claim. But for the usual stagnancies in times of economic crisis, as was the case in the later Sasanid period, the Persians engaged in energetic trade activities. They were well connected to international trade, with connections to China and Rome.[323] With their economic network in the Near East, the Persians even engaged in trade wars with the Romans.[324] Trade was the second pillar of the Sasanian economy, after agriculture.[325] The Persians had a law to protect property rights, including hereditary rights and the having/buying of land.[326] Ibn Khaldun wrote that the Persians had specific laws that prohibited the King's personal involvement in trade, or his buying a farm, as this would be harmful to the market.[327] Finally, Zoroastrianism was not an anti-trade

[317] Lukonin 1983, 744; Becker 2012, 191–2; Papaconstantinou 2010, 58.
[318] Hakim 2017, 207.
[319] In an account on Sawad, al-Baladhuri (1924, 237) shows how jurists like Abu Yusuf took Umar's decisions as canonical rules.
[320] Yousefi 2019, 95.
[321] Al-Ghazali 1964, 55.
[322] Marlow 1997, 8.
[323] Wiesehöfer 2001, 146–8; Canepa 2009, 24–6.
[324] Daryaee 2009, 149. In 298, Rome attempted to curb the Sasanians to gain direct access to Chinese silk.
[325] Brosius 2006, 182. Brunner's (1983, 747–77) detailed account of Persians' economic life does not provide any proof for an antagonistic approach towards merchants.
[326] Perikhanian 1983, 655–8 and 669.
[327] Ibn Khaldun 1958b, 95.

religion.[328] Merchants played roles in the expansion of Zoroastrianism.[329] It should be remembered also that the fiscal rules that Muslims used during their prosperous times were inspired by the Iranians.

Thirdly, a dry concept of centralisation is attributed to the Persian culture. This leads to the exaggerated explanation of every Islamic practice of centralisation as the result of Persian influence. Persian history includes Achaemenids (sixth century BC), the Parthians (third century BC–third century AD) and the Sasanians (third century–seventh century AD). It is therefore frameless and essentialist to identify a practice as typically Persian unless its context is defined. Persians had no 'centralisation for centralisation's sake' motto. The centralisation policies they pursued at times were the result of their adaption to the problems they faced. Otherwise, Iranian history shows instances of antagonism between feudalism/decentralisation and centralisation.[330]

The reforms of Khusraw I Anushirwan (r. 531–79), which affected the later Sasanian society, are informative in this regard. The period is significant also for being inspirational for Muslims. Anushirwan wanted to reform the fiscal system, mainly the taxation regime, to ensure a stable source of income for the treasury.[331] However, such reforms have been subtracted from their context, and interpreted in the reductionist manner to claim that Persian culture promoted an administrative centralisation that overlooks economic realities.

Against that interpretation, Anushirwan's reforms increased the impact of centrifugal dynamics like the *dihqan* system.[332] Representing the solidarity of the village community,[333] *dihqan* was expected to secure stability in landholdings and taxation. It represented local power.[334] This was a strategy to enhance taxation and agricultural production through a social class that was not detached from local realities. *Dihqan* thus represented the complex social relationship of the centre and the local.[335] It also symbolised the policy

---

[328] Davaran 2010, 142.
[329] Boyce 1979, 76.
[330] Zakeri 1995, 22–3.
[331] Pourshariati 2008, 85; Brosius 2006, 156.
[332] Paul 2013, 2 and 104; Canepa 2009, 224; Tafazzoli 2000, 41.
[333] Cahen 2007, 311.
[334] Paul 2015, 105.
[335] Lambton 1991b, 253; Wiesehöfer 2001, 174.

of counterbalancing big aristocracy by protecting local economic activities.[336] It is thus not possible to reduce Anushirwan's reforms to a dry centralisation that is detached from economic concerns. As a matter of fact, various centralisation policies of Islamic rulers that put economic rationality at risk, such as the involvement of troops in taxation, were firstly and vehemently criticised by Ibn al-Muqaffa[337] and Ibn al-Miskawayh,[338] the conveyors of Persian culture.[339]

Fourthly, Persian society, as described in *Letter of Tansar*,[340] was imagined as founded on a four-tier social system that rebutted sociological dynamics across society. Mohsen Zakeri, according to whom it is open to question whether such an idealised caste-like society had ever existed, argues that the model is not supported by the major resources of Persian culture. After analysing resources such as *Arda Wiraz-namak* and the inscription of King Shapur I (d. 271) at Hajji-abad, Zakeri found that they display a more complex social system. For Zakeri, the four-tier system as presented by *Letter of Tansar* is a theoretical imagining rather than a model in actual operation.[341]

Letter of Tansar, originally written by a priest in the third century during the reign of Ardashir I (r. 224–41), was reincarnated in the sixth century after Anushirwan's reforms as Sassanid propaganda that aimed at achieving a new social equilibrium in response to the Mazdakite revolt.[342] Anushirwan's most important goal was to cope with the social and political unrest.[343] The work recollected various maxims, which traced back to the time of Ardashir I, to

---

[336] Campopiano 2018, 477; Zakeri 1995, 30; Daryaee 2009, 147–8. Khosrow I ordered his troops to avoid the cultivated fields, and to cause no harm to any of the landholders (*dahaqin*). Al-Tabari 1999, 296.

[337] Ibn al-Muqaffa 1989a, 313.

[338] Ibn Miskawaihi 1921, 100–1.

[339] There is also the issue of inconsistency: Ibn al-Muqaffa, who promoted a centralist government, and al-Mawardi, the theorist of delegating authority, are both described as promoting Persian administrative culture.

[340] Tansar 1968, 38.

[341] Zakeri 1995, 17–22.

[342] Frye 1983, 153; Campopiano 2009, 3.

[343] Al-Tabari 1999, 147.

support Anushirwan's goal of a stable society.[344] Anushirwan's rigid family rules that prohibited marriage across the strata were a reaction to the Mazdakite revolt that had attacked the Zoroastrian family law.[345] Thus, *Letter of Tansar* represents a religious view[346] ('a literary fiction'[347]) that idealises Anushirwan's policies.[348] It is a legitimating text rather than a realistic description of society. More problematically, it is a text of overlapping contexts and meanings. Behind the work are two different historical contexts: the times of Anushirwan and of Ardashir I.

Similarly, Anahit Perikhanian found no mention in sources of the Achaemenian and Parthian periods of the ancient division of society into such classes. No evidence is observed that such a division existed in the first half of the Sassanian period. That such a division existed in the subsequent period is verified only by Pahlawi sources, from the works of Byzantine writers, and Arab writers bred in the Persian tradition. Overall, as Perikhanian underlined, a four-estate model, which was introduced as a bureaucratic agenda, never ended the social dynamics among the different groups. None of these estates should be imagined as stagnant, since the development of urban life, the crafts and trade, and the appearance of a bureaucracy generated dynamics and changes affecting all classes.[349]

Fifthly, the four-tier structure is interpreted as essentially anti-trade and anti-intellectual. I have already commented on the former. When it comes to the latter, Anushirwan revived art and sciences. Greek medicine was promoted at his intellectual-friendly court.[350] He invited Western philosophers after the closure of their school in Athens in 529.[351] Translations from Greek

---

[344] Pourshariati 2008, 86.
[345] Lukonin 1983, 690; Canepa 2009, 103.
[346] Boyce 1968, 6–7.
[347] Canepa 2009, 40.
[348] Zakeri 1995, 22. The Persian response to the Mazdak revolt was later inherited by Muslims. This is visible in the account of the Mazdak revolt in Nizam al-Mulk (2002, 191–206). The revolt was interpreted as a case to display how a heretic movement disrupts society.
[349] Perikhanian 1983, 632–3.
[350] Brosius 2006, 156–7 and 171.
[351] Huyse 2008, 148; Browne 1951, 167.

and Sanskrit were made during his time. A medical school following Greek ideas was established at Gundeshapur which lasted into Islamic times.[352] According to S. Hussain Nasr, the hospital system of the Islamic period was built largely upon the traditions of the Gundeshapur hospital.[353] As a matter of fact, Islamic sciences had many contributors with Persian backgrounds, like Ibn Sina, al-Farabi, al-Kindi, al-Razi and al-Biruni.[354] This should settle the issue of continuity within the Iranian tradition. The Samanids, one of the most advanced Islamic societies in science and trade ever, was the symbol of Persian cultural revival.

Sixthly, a highly simplistic concept of church–state collaboration is attributed to Persian culture. This also needs to be seen from a more critical perspective, because, as Pervaneh Pourshariati put it, it is more a propagandistic endeavour of the clergy and of the monarchy, articulated late in the Sasanian period, than the reality of the religious landscape. There are precedents in Iranian history that challenge this narrative.[355] According to Richard N. Frye, the king's law was the supreme law in ancient Iran, and 'Iranians have avoided the old Mesopotamian practice of one primary ruler of both church and state'. It was later, with the Arab invasion of Iran, that the caliph became head both of the state and religion.[356]

Shaked writes similarly that there are precedents in the Sasanian period that go against the assumption that Zoroastrianism was the state religion. Yet resources support this thesis in religious literature, mainly in Pahlavi, from the post-Sasanian period.[357] For example, many works quote the *Letter of Tansar* on this subject.[358] However, in this context, the letter refers to church

---

[352] Frye 1983, 161.
[353] Nasr 2007a, 414.
[354] Ibn Khaldun 1958c, 311–14; Nasr 2007b, 419–41; Saliba 1998, 126–46.
[355] Pourshariati 2008, 324–38.
[356] Frye 2005, 28. For Frye, the supremacy of the 'secular' state was the rule in Iranian tradition until Khomeini established a theocracy in which secular authority was completely subordinate to religious rule.
[357] Shaked 2008, 104–5. Also see Adhami 2003, 225.
[358] Tansar (1968, 33–4): 'for church/religion and state were born of the one womb, joined together and never to be sundered'.

and state collaboration in the context of the period when Ardashir I united a coalition to overthrow the Parthians.[359] Tansar, a cleric (*mowbed*), was promoting a single Zoroastrian church under the direct authority of the Persian ruler. His expectation was that a devout and orthodox dynasty would be a truer upholder of the faith. This narrative was in harmony with Ardashir's policy of uniting Persia by religious propaganda.[360] Mary Boyce calls Tansar 'a religious propagandist'.[361] Similarly, in *Denkard* (written in the tenth century), another oft-quoted text on this subject, there is evidence that its authors presumed that their work would be read by Muslims.[362] Many arguments of the literature rely on the later Pahlavi texts, so those arguments lack a solid foundation of historical evidence.

Above, I highlighted the need for a more critical engagement with the Persian political culture. There was no Persian administrative culture that can be called an essentialist construct that delivers standard outcomes independently of context. Making this point is not to categorically repudiate the value of the critical literature that problematises the Iranian influence on Islamic societies. The purpose is to demonstrate that the various perceptions of Persian political culture are constructed on frameless and essentialist arguments.[363]

Conclusion: Setting the Standards of Islamic Political Theory

Ibn al-Muqaffa incorporated the birth-of-the-state concept into political thought, with the result that he analyses the birth of Islamic political theory. His political thought made the autonomous dynamics, such as political power and geopolitical dynamics, the focal points of analysis. He also submitted

---

[359] Frye 1983, 118.
[360] Boyce 1979, 102. Tansar was a Zoroastrian priest and counsellor of Ardashir. Latham 1990, 56.
[361] Boyce 1979, 102.
[362] Rezania 2017, 343 and 358–9.
[363] Other subjects, like imagining Persians as having a uniform concept of sacral kinship, should also be remembered. The works of various scholars, like Choksy (1988, 49), Lukonin (1983, 693), Huff (2008, 25) and Daryaee (2008, 60) provide evidence that shows how sacral kingship was a contested phenomenon in Iranian history.

a parallel epistemological framework where faith and opinion are separated from each other. Ibn al-Muqaffa defined opinion as argument-dependent, and sidelined belief as an irrational concept acquired by socialisation alone, and immune to change by argument. He then suggested that opinion is the fortress of the political field. It was a huge epistemic license to construe politics as independent of religion. Ibn al-Muqaffa explained politics as a cross-cultural phenomenon that is beyond the boundaries of Islam.

By inventing 'the state problem' in Islamic political thought, Ibn al-Muqaffa detected the dilemma of the political and religious elites in Islamic societies. He correctly predicted that the political elite would dominate the political realm by not sharing their powers with the religious elite. Later developments in Islamic societies confirmed his prediction.

On this account, Ibn al-Muqaffa set the standards of Islamic political theory. Several elements of his political thought, such as his argument that politics is subject to general rules shared by all nations, later became the foundation of Islamic political theory. As the following chapters will illustrate in detail, later political rationalists like al-Mawardi, Nizam al-Mulk and Ibn Khaldun used and developed his arguments.

2

AL-MAWARDI: ISLAMIC POLITICAL THEORY IN THE PROVINCIAL ORDER

Chapter 1 studied Ibn al-Muqaffa, who lived in the age of the consolidation of Abbasid power. This chapter will examine al-Mawardi (974–1058), who lived during the Abbasid decline.

Al-Mawardi lived during the provincial order when the Abbasids, deprived of military and economic power, survived by delegating their powers to local states. The model created a league of autonomous states around the spiritual leadership of the Abbasid caliphate. To make the situation worse, the Zaydi-Shiʿa Buwayhid state (a local state) had ruled Baghdad, the seat of the caliphate, for over a century, in cohabitation with the Abbasids. The caliph had become little more than a powerless religious figurehead. Meanwhile, the Ismaili-Shiʿas, having established the Fatimid state, emerged as an external rival to the Abbasids. The Shiʿa states were on the rise. The Sunni world was in crisis.

Al-Mawardi developed his political thought by responding to this historic setting as an Abbasid official. Among major issues, his responses were to the Buwayhid-Abbasid cohabitation in Baghdad, and to the Abbasids' survival strategy by religious means, as there were no temporal powers to speak of, and the external Fatimid threat occupied his thoughts. The main quandary of al-Mawardi's political thought was the Abbasid weakness in a divided Islamic world where, ironically, power was the most effective authority. Ibn al-Muqaffa had proposed solutions knowing that there was a strong Abbasid power to realise them. In contrast, al-Mawardi submitted his opinions to a context where political power was distributed among local states.

The Birth of the Provincial Order

Al-Mawardi's political thought had at its centre a weak Abbasid caliph. A pragmatic thinker, he developed solutions that could best serve a caliph who had almost no temporal powers. A detailed analysis of the dynamics and events that had brought the Abbasids to this point is required to understand the rationale of al-Mawardi's argumentation on political issues. In what follows, I shall first explain the historical developments that created the provincial order. That provincial order, which affected the Muslim society for almost two centuries, is so critical in Islamic history because it was the main form of political structure from the mid-ninth century to the mid-eleventh century, and that affected daily life, politics, as well as intellectual life. As the provincial order determined a special way of organising power, legitimacy and politics across the Muslim world, it is critical to examine and explain that historical context before any political thinker's output can be analysed sensibly.

After a corrosive civil war (809–33), the Abbasids entered a period of crisis during which problems concerning the military continually worsened the situation. They had already adopted the policy of replacing the Khurasani troops with Turkish and other mercenaries.[1] This trend accelerated after Caliph Mu'tasim (r. 833–42) who had transformed the slave soldiers into the army's core.[2] These soldiers later gained autonomy, turning the reign of Caliph Mu'tazz (r. 866–9) into a period of riots.[3] This was no longer a military issue, as the military had become influential within the bureaucracy.[4]

The mercenaries were not isolated warriors. They brought their nomadic networks with them, and inevitably broke the traditional Abbasid order of land tenure, and of the bureaucracy. The militarisation of the system was distressing for urban groups, particularly for the merchants. Social and political

---

[1] Bosworth 1965/6, 144.
[2] Lassner 1980, 16; Kennedy 2016, 136.
[3] Al-Tabari 1985a, 35 and 140.
[4] Hitti 1937, 467.

cohesion had weakened.[5] Seeking a solution, the Abbasids turned to radical policies, such as al-Muʾtasim's making Samarra (125 kilometres north of Baghdad) the new capital in 835/6, in the expectation that isolating the army would ease problems.[6] Contrary to expectations, the caliphs were isolated, and fell into the grip of the Turkish troops.[7]

Even worse, the soldiers developed new ways of making an impact on politics: in 886, they blocked the supply chain. That caused sharp inflation, and protests in Baghdad.[8] This happened at a time when the military forces of Baghdad and Samarra were fighting each other. The soldiers in Samarra even declared an alternate caliph.[9] The Abbasids faced similar military troubles in the reign of al-Mutawakkil (r. 847–61).[10] Turkish soldiers organised protests in Samarra, paralysing the Abbasid rule. Al-Mutawakkil even planned to find another new capital. He dissolved the army in Samarra; but this led to his murder by soldiers in 861.[11] Efforts to end the military tutelage stalled as the Abbasids fell into another period of chaos. The Samarran experience and later developments seriously weakened the Abbasids' administrative ability to control the provinces.[12]

As the upheavals paralysed the economy, critical infrastructural investments, especially in irrigation, were neglected. This triggered various complications in the Tigris region, like depopulation.[13] The taxation system simultaneously broke down, which meant a sharp decline in Iraqi revenues that were indispensable to the maintenance of a functioning government.[14] That factionalised the bureaucracy. Naturally, the Abbasids' capacity to impose a central government diminished seriously. The chaos in the government

---

[5] Lapidus 2002, 114. Al-Tabari (1985a, 35) describes the caliph complaining that Turks make their children soldiers.

[6] Al-Yaʿqubi 2018b, 87 and 93; al-Tabari 1985a, 34.

[7] Gibb 1969, 83.

[8] Al-Tabari 1987a, 151.

[9] Al-Tabari 1985a, 41. Also see Gordon 2001, 71 and 79.

[10] Al-Tabari 1987a, 10.

[11] Masudi 1989, 260; Cobb 1999, 241.

[12] Bennison 2009, 39.

[13] Lapidus 2002, 110; Waines 1977, 195.

[14] Campopiano 2012, 1; Duri 2011, 141.

generated social grievances and discontent. This was a complex crisis that eroded the political bonds between the Abbasids and the various social groups across the country.

Though there were relatively stable periods during the reigns of al-Mu'tadid, al-Mu'tazid and al-Muqtafi – from 879 to 908 – structural problems returned during the reign of al-Muqtadir (r. 908–28). The army suffered further collapse, as did the bureaucracy.[15] Al-Muqtadir was the last caliph to exercise authority over the heartlands of the caliphate.[16] Eventually, the Abbasids were unable to prevent the Buwayhids' taking control of Iran during the reign of al-Qahir (r. 932–40). Only Iraq and Khuzestan remained under their direct rule. But the deterioration continued: as of 935, the only region under their control was Baghdad.

When the crisis brought the Abbasids to the point of being unable to mobilise the standard means of central government, such as the recruiting of troops and the extracting of revenues, they developed the strategy of giving political concessions to emerging groups across the empire, anticipating that this would impede a complete disintegration. Predictably, this policy made the Abbasids dependent on local actors both financially and militarily.[17] By the reign of al-Radi (934–40), irregular resources, including gifts and tributes from local states, made up the majority of the Abbasid budget.[18] In fact, local dynasties, such as the Samanids and the Tahirids, had emerged by assuming important roles. For example, the Tahirids, who had replaced the Turks in the policing and securing of Baghdad, became Caliph al-Ma'mun's major ally in the civil war (809–33). The Tahirids' contribution from Khurasan became a major part of the Abbasid tax revenues.[19]

The transformation of local dynasties into provincial sovereigns was finalised when the caliph relinquished his temporal powers to them. This was the opposite of the traditional model in which the provinces were ruled by centrally appointed governors with absolute power.[20] That centralist model

---

[15] Berkel *et al.* 2013, 1. Also see Masudi 1989, 329.
[16] Kennedy 2013, 13.
[17] Shaban 1976, 124 and 115; Bonner 2011, 348.
[18] Waines 1977, 283.
[19] Masudi 1989, 147; Bosworth 2007a, 95.
[20] Kennedy 1981b, 26.

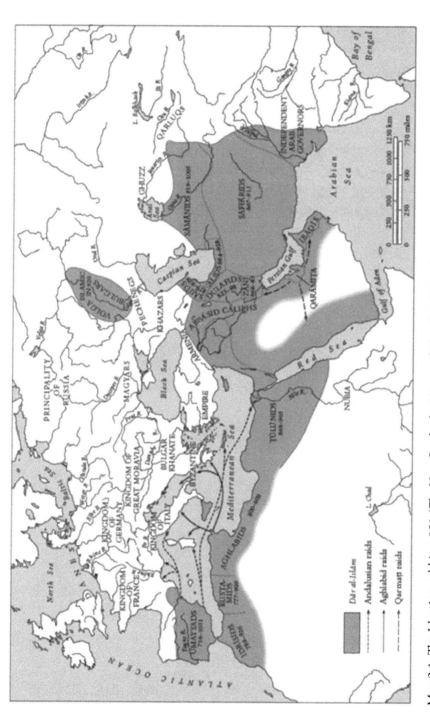

Map 2.1 The Islamic world in c.950 (*The New Cambridge History of Islam Vol. I*, 2011).

was, however, left behind in the past: once the local powers felt confident, they easily challenged the caliph. For example, the caliphal governor of Fars was expelled in 902.[21]

The Tahirids became the first autonomous dynasty – that is, provincial state – in the east, controlling Khurasan and a part of Persia.[22] The caliph later gave them an investiture to symbolise formal recognition.[23] They were followed by others, like the Samanids, the Saffarids, the Ghaznawids, the Saljuqis, the Qarakhanids and the Buwayhids.[24] The system worked on a simple contract: the caliph gave formal investiture to a provincial state's ruler, and that made him the legitimate and independent ruler in his region. This was done in exchange for the recognition of the caliph as the leader of the Muslim community, and accordingly, leaving religious affairs to the caliph's discretion.[25]

The caliphal recognition was formalised with titles and investitures.[26] This was the 'constitutional' etiquette that declared a provincial ruler's sovereignty to the public. The provincial order thus expanded the titles and symbols of political authority, every detail of which was significant.[27] This contract required provincial rulers to perform the symbolic acts of including the caliph's name in khutba and on the coinage.[28] But it was never a contract among equals: provincial states imposed themselves on the caliph by the sheer dint of their power.

The Abbasids grudgingly recognised the provincial states.[29] Ibn Isfandiyar (d. c.1217) says of the Saffarids that they had transformed themselves into a

---

[21] Bosworth 1968a, 552.
[22] Al-Bayhaqi 2004, 175; Bosworth 1969, 105. Given their long loyalty to the Abbasids, the split of the Tahirids symbolised the ideological collapse of the Abbasids.
[23] Al-Tabari 1985a, 23; Gardizi 2011, 45.
[24] Ibn Khaldun 1958b, 128.
[25] Morgan 2016, 1; Sherwani 1942, 138. Provincial rulers offered gifts and standard payments for those titles. Bosworth 1962b, 211.
[26] Kennedy 2011, 364.
[27] Ibn Khaldun 1958a, 469. The caliph decided how many drums (*nawbah*) the Buwayhid ruler could beat at his palace. Donohue 2003, 28.
[28] *The Numismatic History of Rayy* of Miles (1938) illustrates the coinage of the Ghaznawids (190–2), Buwayhids (177–9) and Samanids (136–43) having the caliph's name.
[29] Bosworth 2007a, 107.

state, thanks to the weakness of the Abbasids.[30] The Abbasids had to recognise such impositions because, as Ibn Khaldun (d. 1406) wrote, they simply had no power to rule their lands.[31] Politics in the provincial order was determined simply by power. Illustrating this, Gardizi (d. 1061) describes Ya'qub, the Saffarid ruler, brandishing his sword and saying: 'This is my document of appointment!' when asked about his caliphal investiture.[32]

The provincial order was comparable to European medievalism, which was a 'system of overlapping authority and multiple loyalty'.[33] Likewise, the provincial order had a weak centre that allowed local states to develop their own political agendas. There was no centralised authority, and no clearly demarcated set of territorial units. Instead, there was a tangle of overlapping jurisdictions, plural allegiances and asymmetrical suzerainties.[34] Logically, politics in the provincial order was mainly determined by the power relations among actors.

Balance of Power in the Provincial Order

Having summarised the birth of the provincial order, I shall next explain how the provincial order operated. This subject is highly significant in an analysis of al-Mawardi's political thought. This is so because he contextualised his arguments within the functioning provincial order, and not as universally applicable principles.

In that provincial order, any local authority that secured the control of a territory could appeal for caliphal legitimacy.[35] Yesterday's rebels could become today's legitimate rulers. The Abbasids had to distribute investitures according to the balance of power within the system, lest the prestige of caliphal recognition depreciate.[36] They supervised the correct use of titles. The caliph, for example, once asked the Buwayhid ruler, Abu Kalijar, to not

---

[30] Ibn Isfandiyar 1905, 181.
[31] Ibn Khaldun 1958a, 129.
[32] Gardizi 2011, 47–58.
[33] Bull 1977, 254.
[34] Holzgrefe 1989, 11.
[35] Mottahedeh 1980, 18.
[36] Bosworth 1962b, 225.

use the title *malik al-umam* (king of Muslims), but to use *malik al-dawla* (king of state).[37] Naturally, the Abbasid policy was to keep the highest title for the caliph.[38] The proper use of titles also mattered to the people: in 1037, the caliph permitting Jalal al-Dawla to use the title *malik al-muluk* (king of kings) created popular objection.[39]

A provincial state was the vassal of the Abbasids. But a provincial state was allowed its own vassal (sub-provincial) state. For example, in the eleventh century, Makramid Oman was the sub-provincial state of the Buwayhids, which was a provincial state of the Abbasids.[40] The Makramid coins carried the names of the rulers: the Makramids', the Buwayhids' and the Abbasids'.[41] The Ghaznawids' was once the sub-provincial state of the Samanids.[42] Formed in this way, the provincial system was a power hierarchy. Changes in power relations caused changes in the hierarchy among states. This generated two standard policies: a sub-provincial state sought independence from its suzerain; a provincial state either cooperated with friendly states, or sought to weaken its rival. For example, the Saffarids, once a sub-provincial state of the Tahirids and Samanids, later fought against them, and even destroyed the Tahirids.[43] They then established a transient empire stretching from Kabul to Isfahan. This was the first great breach of Abbasid integrity.[44] The Ghaznawids emerged as a vassal state to the Samanids, but they later destroyed them.[45]

As examples of the balance of power: in 874, when Ismail, the brother of the Samanid ruler Nuh, rebelled, the Tahirids supported him.[46] Balancing might take the form of competition over control of the sub-provincial states. When the Ghaznawids became stronger in the eleventh century, they claimed Oman,[47] and the Makramid sub-provincial rule there shifted its

---

[37] M. Y. Khan 2001, 1.
[38] Amedroz 1905, 393–9.
[39] Ibn al-Athir 1998b, 227–8; Ibn al-Jawzi 1992b, 26.
[40] Rudhrawari and Muhassin 1921, 103; Al-Salimi 2005, 247–53.
[41] Biwar and Stern 1958, 151–2.
[42] Al-Bayhaqi 2004, 175.
[43] Shaban 1976, 99; Morgan 2016, 2.
[44] Bosworth 2007a, 107.
[45] Al-Qazwini 1913, 78–9; Gardizi 2011, 82.
[46] Al-Bayhaqi 2004, 177.
[47] Bosworth 1962a, 74.

loyalty from the Buwayhids to the Ghaznawids.[48] Likewise, there was fierce competition between the Samanids and the Ghaznawids to transform various sub-provincial states into their vassals. For example, the Ghaznawid Sultan Mahmud brought several Samanid sub-provincial states in Guzgan (northern Afghanistan) under his suzerainty.[49] Logically, each provincial state had a strategy to control its sub-provincial state. In the late tenth century, for instance, the Buwayhids used military power to discipline their vassal Hasanwahyids, a local Kurdish dynasty near the Zagros mountains.[50]

The Abbasids survived by adapting to the balance of power among the provincial states. Their being the monopolistic authority in the distribution of formal legitimacy was their main policy instrument.[51] To illustrate this through various cases: when the Saffarids expanded in 874, the caliph asked the Tahirids to stop them.[52] But when Yaqub b. Layth (861–79), the Saffarid ruler, seized the territories of the Tahirids in Khurasan, the Abbasids recognised him as the ruler of Khurasan.[53] However, the caliph was not happy, given the Tahirids' service to the Abbasids: he assembled the pilgrims of Khurasan, denounced Ya'qub, and renounced his annexation as unlawful.[54] But, having no power, the caliph asked the Samanid ruler, Ismail bin Ahmad, to stop the Saffarid expansion.[55] The Samanids became the effective defenders of the Abbasids against the Saffarids. When the Samanids dominated the region, the Abbasids conferred some parts of the Saffarids' lands upon them in 875.[56]

Later, however, the Saffarid ruler Amr (r. 879–901) gained control of Khurasan; he asked the caliph to recognise him as the legitimate ruler, and thereby replace the Samanids there. Though the caliph seemed to have accepted the request, he secretly urged the Samanids to resist the Saffarids.[57]

[48] Nazım 1931, 79.
[49] Bosworth 2007b, 171–2.
[50] Paul 2018a, 68.
[51] Barthold 1968, 226.
[52] Al-Qazwini 1913, 72.
[53] Ibn Isfandiyar 1905, 181.
[54] Bosworth 2007a, 116.
[55] Nizam al-Mulk 2002, 18.
[56] Al-Qazwini 1913, 73.
[57] Treadwell 2005, 152; Frye 2007, 137.

That sort of pragmatic balancing was observed even at lower levels: in Kirman (southeastern Iran), Caliph Mu'tazz once granted investitures simultaneously to two Saffarid rulers, intending to stir up a war between them.[58]

The anarchic nature of the provincial order, inasmuch as it had no central power to unilaterally impose a norm, caused everything in the system to be highly volatile. For example, when the Byzantine threat approached, Caliph al-Muwaffaq gave concessions to the Tahirids in 889, to secure their support. But when the caliph rescinded the concessions a year later, the Tahirids omitted his name from khutba.[59]

Naturally, confident provincial states were less interested in caliphal investitures. The Saffarids, when they felt themselves strong, were not particularly interested in caliphal investitures. However, they became willing supporters of caliphal legitimacy, realising that it would help them consolidate their power in Khurasan.[60] Similarly, the Samanids at times dispensed with caliphal legitimacy. This made the Samanid-Abbasid relations thorny, though the normal expectation was their amicable attitudes, for both were champions of Sunnism.[61]

But pragmatism reigned: the Samanids did not recognise Caliph al-Qadir for two years, arguing that he was a Buwayhid and Ghaznawid puppet whose allegiance was with the deposed Caliph al-Tai.[62] This was a highly disturbing attitude for the Abbasids. Even so, they constantly put difficulties in the way of sending regular taxes to the caliph.[63] When they felt confident, the provincial states did not even refrain from more disturbing policies: the Tahirids forced the caliph to abdicate in 865,[64] and the Saffarids attempted to replace the caliph in 876.[65]

---

[58] Barthold 1968, 217.
[59] Bosworth 2007a, 119–20.
[60] Bosworth 1968a, 535.
[61] Frye 2007, 153; Tor 2009, 287.
[62] Siddiqi 1942, 82; Bosworth 1962a, 60. The Samanid ruler Nuh (r. 976–97) similarly refused to recognise Caliph al-Muti for nine years and struck coins in the deposed Caliph al-Mustakfi's name. Treadwell 1991, 216–17.
[63] Frye 2007, 140.
[64] Gardizi 2011, 48.
[65] Al-Qazwini 1913, 72.

The Need for Caliphal Legitimacy

However, the power-centred mechanism of the provincial order never meant that there was no longer a need for a caliph. The provincial states were in constant search for legitimacy. Legitimacy in the medieval Muslim society was the successful persuasion of people that a certain dynasty (or state), and not another, should rule. But since there was no popular legitimacy to rely on, the states used any available means to confer legitimacy. Typically, the legitimacy builders were patronage, marriage, oath, lineage, tribal loyalty, and professional cooperations of clerks or soldiers.[66]

As lineage was the most effective one to appeal to people, many provincial states used the Persian lineage discourses. The Tahirids claimed to be descendants of Rustam-i Dastan, a mythological Persian figure.[67] The Samanids claimed the genealogy of Bahram Chubin, the rebellious commander who ruled the Sasanian Empire between 590 and 591, before Khusrau II re-established control.[68] The Ziyarids claimed Persian royal ancestry, alleging that they were descended from Arghush Farhadan, king of Gilan in the time of the legendary Kai-Khusrau.[69] Others, like the Ghaznawids and the Saffarids, also claimed legitimacy through Persian elements. However, none of these proved to be a viable substitute for caliphal legitimacy.

Several things can account for this, not least of them being the domestic rifts within the provincial states. For example, the Ghaznawids' was a Turkish provincial state with a Persian bureaucracy. It was therefore never easy for the Ghaznawids to encompass such divisions sufficiently to develop a semblance of a shared legitimacy The provincial states, born as military organisations, had that history as an inhibitor of popular legitimacy.[70]

Meanwhile, the fragmentation of the Islamic world, which saw rulers and dynasties changed incessantly, made it difficult for people to feel strong allegiance to local rulers.[71] The caliph's mandate in religious affairs, in the proceedings of the law, and in the oversight of the decisions of judges, especially in

---

[66] Mottahedeh 1980, 42.
[67] Bosworth 1973, 51–62; Meisami 2007, 15.
[68] Al-Qazwini 1913, 7; Tor 2011a, 116; Peacock 2007, 115.
[69] Madelung 2007, 212.
[70] Haug 2019, 170.
[71] Goiten 2010, 40.

the sensitive common cases like marriage and inheritance, made the caliphal legitimacy look indispensable.[72] Thanks to such dynamics, caliphal legitimacy remained the primary constitutional legitimacy for local rulers.[73] Large or small, the local actors were unable to dispense with it. In 1012, a local Kurdish leader, who had the title Nasir al-Dawla from Caliph al-Qadir, was declared the legitimate ruler of a small territory in southeast Anatolia.[74]

There was also a special reason for caliphal legitimacy: it linked to the fact that many of the provincial states were in Khurasan, a main frontier (*thughur*) of holy war.[75] Local dynamics in Khurasan were predominantly shaped by the dynamics of holy war (jihad). That made caliphal recognition a significant element in the attainment of social and political legitimacy.[76] Provincial rulers demanded caliphal legitimacy strategically to present themselves as aligned with the jihad mission.[77] In this context, provincial rulers also needed caliphal legitimacy to cooperate with the local religious actors (be that a scholar, an imam, a preacher, a local ascetic, a theologian or a judge) in Khurasan.[78] These local actors had recourses like piety and religious knowledge to rally the local people.[79] This was crucial in the building of local legitimacy.[80]

Military politics also came into it: the Abbasid decline caused the 'privatisation' of holy war by volunteers (*mutatawwila*), formerly a primary state task.[81] As a result, local people and rulers accepted that the mission fell upon them, they being nearest to the non-Muslims.[82] This transformed Khurasan

---

[72] Gibb 1969, 84.
[73] Mottahedeh 2007, 18.
[74] Tholib 2002, 141.
[75] Ibn Miskawaihi 1921, 213; Hawting 2000, 39; Brauer 1995, 9–13.
[76] Tor 2015, 3.
[77] Treadwell 1991, 97 and 286.
[78] Bosworth 1962b, 232; 1968a, 535.
[79] Starr 2013, 245; Mouline 2014, 19–20; Marlow 2016, 182.
[80] For example, Ibn Abu Hafs, a local ascetic, led the holy war against the Turks around Bukhara, which made him a critical actor for Samanid rulers. Religious actors like him contributed to the consolidation of Samanid rule. Treadwell 1991, 85 and 98; Paul 1994, 8.
[81] Tor 2005, 555–73.
[82] Lambton 1991a, 212.

into a hub of volunteer fighters who became the backbone of the local armies.[83] But it was never easy to manage volunteers, as they were usually not registered in the military *diwan*.[84] That made caliphal legitimacy necessary, both in the recruiting and controlling of volunteers.

There was also a financial dimension: provincial rulers needed caliphal legitimacy as military finance was linked to jihad.[85] To illustrate, the Samanids, who controlled a large area of the frontier region, needed caliphal endorsement not only to attract more fighters,[86] but also for social legitimacy, as they relied on the jihad ideology.[87] That applied to the Ghaznawids, as Mahmud used the caliphal endorsement to justify his expeditions into India.[88] When he gained caliphal investiture in 999, he aimed to lead an expedition to India every year.[89] He organised sixteen major expeditions to India between 1000 and 1025.[90] In these 'plunder raids',[91] the Ghaznawids collected a vast amount of Indian gold.[92] The Saffarids, too, needed caliphal legitimacy, for their military system depended on holy war. This included the strategy of exploiting silver mines in Panjshir.[93] Both states regularly sent gifts from their plunders to the caliph.[94]

The Abbasid–Buwayhid Cohabitation

In 945, the Shiʿa provincial state of the Buwayhids changed the course of Islamic history by capturing Baghdad, and staying there until 1055 to control

---

[83] Tor 2009, 287.
[84] Mottahedeh 1980, 83. Al-Mawardi (2012, 271) defined military politics in his time as the hardest task of the rulers.
[85] Bosworth 1965/6, 166.
[86] Haug 2019, 183. Jihad also provided the Samanid with a huge share in the slave market. Haug 2011, 181.
[87] Treadwell 2005, 165.
[88] Crone 2004, 221; Haug 2011, 639.
[89] Nazım 1931, 86.
[90] Merçil 1989, 16–26. Also see Bosworth 2007b, 169.
[91] Bosworth 2007b, 179.
[92] Nizam al-Mulk 2002, 49.
[93] Tor 2002, 293–5.
[94] Hanne 2007, 68; Güner 2002, 21.

Iraq, and much of Persia and Oman.[95] This brought about the cohabitation of the Buwayhids and the Abbasids. The cohabitation operated within the standard rules of the provincial order. However, it was a special case because the Buwayhids and the Abbasids overlapped spatially. This 110-year overlap, during which time al-Mawardi's political thought emerged, resulted in radical changes in how political subjects like power and legitimacy were formulated.

The Buwayhids, former vassals of the Ziyarids, emerged in Daylam, a mountainous region of northern Iran on the southwest coast of the Caspian Sea.[96] As Islam arrived late to this region, it was never fully integrated into the caliphate. There was instead an expansion here of heterodox beliefs.[97] As the region became a safe haven also for the Alid groups, Zaydism became a part of the local groups' resistance to the Abbasids, and to the local provincial state of the Tahirids.[98]

The Buwayhids were a militaristic ethnic group. *Hudud al-'Alam*, a tenth-century Persian geography book, described the inhabitants of Daylam as a warlike people.[99] Their political organisation was militaristic.[100] Though militarism created strong bonds of loyalty, it prevented central rule. This left the Buwayhids rather like a confederation in which their royals ruled regions like Fars and Iraq.[101]

The Buwayhids were Zaydi, a branch of the Shi'a that owed allegiance to Zayd bin Ali (d. 740). They contended that the leader should be a descendant of the Prophet through Ali, not only because he was the designated successor, but also because he is the most excellent.[102] This generated the doctrine that leadership should belong to whichever member of the Alid family proved willing and capable of undertaking that position.[103] In fact, this doctrine was

---

[95] Ibn Khallikan 1843a, 156; Ibn Isfandiyar 1905, 223.
[96] Al-Shahrastani 1992, 156.
[97] Bonner 2011, 346; Bosworth 2007a, 100.
[98] Madelung 2007, 206; Mottahedeh 1980, 37.
[99] Minorsky 1982, 133.
[100] Piacentini 2005, 196; Busse 2007, 251. Levy (1929, 155) likened it to a military camp.
[101] Bowen 1929, 226–8.
[102] Al-Shahrastani 1992, 154; al-Baghdadi 1920, 44.
[103] Kennedy 1981a, 38.

the justification behind Zayd's unsuccessful revolt against the Umayyads in 740.[104] The Zaydi doctrine generated a variation in theology by opening the leadership role to any willing and capable person with prophetic descendance through Ali. The caliphate of Abu Bakr and Umar was no longer a theological sin, but an error of judgement: Ali was the better candidate.[105] This set them apart from other Shi'as (the Twelvers), and deemed them the Shi'a sect closest to Sunnism.[106]

The cohabitation began in 945, when the caliph recognised the Buwayhid ruler, Ahmad, with the title *Mu'izz al-Dawla*. Mu'izz became *amir al-umara*, the highest political authority.[107] In exchange, the Buwayhids recognised the caliph as the supreme religious authority, and included his name in khutba and on their coins.[108] Having lost his temporal powers, the caliph had become a mere religious leader. This was a huge anomaly because a Shi'a state that does not acknowledge the Abbasid caliphate theologically had come to dominate the centre of the Sunni world.[109]

Mu'izz al-Dawla first considered abolishing the caliphate by replacing it with an Alid.[110] But the Buwayhids later realised that the caliphate is powerful leverage in the hands of whoever controls it, and getting rid of it would create more problems than solutions.[111] As a matter of fact, the Buwayhids benefitted from the caliphate more than their Sunni rivals. It was effective,

---

[104] Al-Tabari 1989a 27, 17 and 41. Abbasids were in the earlier phase of revolution during Zayd's revolt. Imam Muhammad bin Ali asked his followers to stay out of the revolt. Daniel 1979, 38.

[105] Al-Shahrastani 1984, 136. This is the case particularly in the Sulaimaniya branch of Zaydiyya, which is important for al-Mawardi's references to Zaydiyya who were mostly from this branch.

[106] Haider 2021, 203; Zysow 2013, 605. According to Daftary (1998a, 59) the Zaydis 'retained the politically militant but religiously moderate stance of the early Shi'a of Kufa'.

[107] Al-Qazwini 1913, 87.

[108] Miles 2007, 375.

[109] Morgan 2016, 5–6.

[110] Kabir 1964, 186.

[111] Busse 2007, 271. The Buwayhids were also preoccupied with regime consolidation. Ibn Miskawaihi (1921, 100) noted that Mu'izz al-Dawla was busy quelling the mutiny of the Dailami soldiers.

Buwayhids		Abbasids
Mu'izz al-Dawla (945–967)		Al-Mustakfi (944–945)
'Izz al-Dawla (967–977)		
'Adud al-Dawla (977–983)		Al-Muti (945–973)
Samsam al-Dawla (983–987)		Al-Ta'i (973–991)
Sharaf al-Dawla (987–989)	Al-Mawardi	
Baha al-Dawla (989–1012)	(974–1058)	Al-Qadir (991–1031)
Sultan al-Dawla (1012–1021)		
Musharraf al-Dawla (1021–1025)		
Jalal al-Dawla (1027–1044)		
Abu Kalijar (1044–1048)		Al-Qaim (1031–1075)
Al Malik al-Rahim (1048–1055)		

Figure 2.1 The rulers in the Abbasid–Buwayhid cohabitation.

for example, against the Samanids, who had a strategy of counterbalancing the Shi'a powers in Iran.[112] Abolishing the caliphate would indeed put the Buwayhids in a complex crisis with the Sunni states, as well as with the Sunni people in their territories.[113]

The caliphate was a huge tool of legitimacy for the Buwayhids, the outsiders in a Sunni world.[114] It gave them an advantage in their control of their Sunni subjects, particularly those in Baghdad, where the Sunni-Shi'a tension was endemic.[115] That applied also to the Turkish soldiers, most of them Sunnis, whom the Buwayhids had recruited. They remembered particularly the frequent tensions between them and the Dailami soldiers, who were ruled by independent generals.[116] The caliph sometimes mediated those tensions.[117] Unlike their situation with the Dailamis, whose loyalty was a function of their identity as people of Iranian origin, sustaining the loyalty of Turkish soldiers who were only professionals was difficult and costly.[118]

---

[112] Tholib 2002, 52; Frye 2007, 151. In 956, the Buwayhids were forced to sign a humiliating treaty by the Samanids. Jiwa 1992, 68.
[113] Crone 2004, 220.
[114] Kennedy 2016, 187.
[115] Mottahedeh 1980, 38.
[116] Ibn Miskawaihi 1921, 365; Rudhrawari and Muhassin 1921, 37.
[117] Ibn al-Jawzi 1992b, 170.
[118] Bonner 2011, 346; Bosworth 1965/6, 144–57.

Last but not least, the Buwayhids were the target of Fatimid ideological and political threats, despite them both being Shiʿa.[119] The Fatimid policy of diverting trade from the Persian Gulf to the Red Sea was a potential threat to the Iraqi economy, and it was a direct threat to the Buwayhids. On the ideological level, the Ismaili missionaries' activities in Syria were equally disturbing.[120] For example, the Uqaylids, normally a Buwayhid sub-provincial state, proclaimed allegiance to the Fatimids in 1010.[121] The caliph's support was valuable in diverting those threats.[122] Political interests made the Sunni caliphate and the Shiʿa Buwayhids unite against the Shiʿa superpower, the Fatimids.

The External Ideological Threat

Al-Mawardi was a Sunni Muslim who worked for the Abbasid caliph. Naturally, the Fatimid threat, which affected Abbasid politics, was among the parameters he considered while formulating his views. A brief analysis of how the Fatimid threat was relevant to the Abbasids is therefore required to convey a better sense of the historical setting to which al-Mawardi responded.

In 909, the Ismaili Shiʿites established the Fatimid state in Egypt. This enabled Ismailism, which had long been a religious movement, to assume the title 'caliphate' in the reach of its government's authority and in its legal codes.[123] The Fatimids came rapidly from Morocco in North Africa to encompass Sicily, Egypt, Palestine, parts of Syria and the Hejaz. As one of their most annoying policies for the Abbasids, the Fatimids set the policy of establishing a firm grip on Syria during the reign of the Fatimid caliph al-Aziz (r. 975–96).[124] Their troops entered Damascus in 969. Syria was subject to Fatimid campaigns until this was stopped by Turks in 1060. The next Fatimid caliph, al-Hakim (r. 996–1021), also pursued an aggressive policy of sending Ismaili missionaries into Abbasid territories. By the time the Abbasid al-Qadir became caliph in

---

[119] Starr 2013, 242.
[120] Jiwa 1992, 65–7; Howes 2011, 879.
[121] Kennedy 2016, 207.
[122] Bosworth 1962a, 67; Ibish 1966, 43–4.
[123] Mottahedeh 1980, 24; Walker 1993, 161–82.
[124] Daftary 2007, 173.

992, some local rulers in Iraq had already included the Fatimid caliph's name in khutba and on the coinage.

The Ismailis claimed a universal caliphate based exclusively on the lineage of Muhammad through his daughter Fatima. This was a challenge to the Abbasid uncle-based genealogy. The Ismaili caliph was the pole (*qutb*) of faith, *ipso facto* the sovereign of the world.[125] As he was divinely appointed, any contender, including the Abbasid caliph, was a usurper.[126] This doctrine, once in a real-life context, made the Fatimids pursue anti-Abbasid politics.[127] Furthermore, the Fatimid state was not only a state but also a doctrine.[128]

Along with their state (*dawla*), the Ismailis had the *da'wa*, a network of missionaries (*dai*) preaching their doctrine. They worked to 'proselytise' the Sunnis, and to overthrow Sunni regimes and replace them with Ismaili rule.[129] This paved the way for the religio-political rivalry between the Abbasids and the Fatimids.[130] Ismaili missionaries were active everywhere from Yemen to Pakistan, but more alarmingly, in Khurasan and Syria.[131] They even influenced the local elites, notably the Samanids, including their ruler Nasr (r. 914–43).[132] This was, however, a competition of unequal rivals: the Sunni world was in crisis, whereas the tenth century was the Shi'a Golden Age.[133]

Ismaili ideology was propagated by poets, theologians and philosophers, and represented a Shi'a pinnacle of the sciences and the arts. The highly influential 'The Epistle of the Brethren of Purity', a tenth-century encyclopedia, revealed a serious Ismaili discipline of thought.[134] Azhar College was

---

[125] Brett 1996, 431 and 438–9.
[126] Daftary 1998b, 63.
[127] Halm 2001, 1–2.
[128] Brett 1996, 431.
[129] Lev 2009, 72. *Iftitah al-Dawla* of al-Qadi al-Nu'man (2006, 68 and 75), an exponent of Fatimid jurisprudence, illustrates this anti-Abbasid stance.
[130] Meanwhile, Qarmatians, breakaways from Ismailism, were strong in eastern Arabia and Oman. In 930, they carried the Blackstone in Ka'ba to their capital Ahsa and kept it for twenty years, which was a serious problem for the Abbasids. De Blois 1986, 13–21; Daftary 2013, 446.
[131] Muir 1891, 573.
[132] Nizam al-Mulk 2002, 212.
[133] Tignor 2011, 147; Jiwa 1992, 57.
[134] B. Lewis 1969, 102–3; Stern 1964, 417.

founded as a Fatimid institution. Meanwhile, the Abbasids, who had to respond to this intellectual and political challenge, had no power to liberate Baghdad, the seat of the Sunni caliphate, from the Shiʿa Buwayhid state.

Having summarised the general political setting, I shall proceed to present a brief account of Al-Mawardi's life, then analyse his political views to show how they were proposed and justified in the context of the political and social developments of his place and period.

Al-Mawardi: His Life

Abu al-Hasan al-Mawardi was born in Basra in 974. Among his teachers was Abu Hamid al-Isfarayini (d. 1016), who taught him hadith, law and other disciplines, like dialectic.[135] Ibn Khallikan identifies Shafi law as the foundation of al-Mawardi's perspectives.[136] Al-Mawardi was also instructed by other scholars, such as al-Jabali, al-Minqari, and al-Bafi, an eminent scholar of grammar, literature and poetry.[137] Another attention-grabbing scholar among his teachers, al-Saymari (d. 1044), known for his Muʿtazila inclinations, taught him legal theory.[138] Reflecting this broad intellectual background, al-Mawardi authored books in different fields, like politics, grammar and Qurʾanic exegesis,[139] and engaged with different schools of thought.[140]

Al-Mawardi worked as a judge in Ustuwa, Nishapur and Baghdad. In 1037, he was given the honorific title of *aqda al-qudat*, the highest title for a judge.[141] He was also an active participant in political life as a statesman and diplomat, and enjoyed close relations with both Abbasid and Buwayhid rulers. He worked as counsellor to the Caliphs al-Qadir and al-Qaim, and played important roles in critical events where Abbasid interests were at stake.[142] When al-Qaim became caliph in 1031, he sent al-Mawardi to Abu

---

[135] M. Y. Khan 2001, 1.
[136] Ibn Khallikan 1843b, 225.
[137] Sherwani 1942, 161–8.
[138] Kallek 2003, 180.
[139] Tumanian 2020, 573; Ibn Khallikan 1843b, 225.
[140] Mikhail 1985, 10; Fakhry 1994, 158.
[141] Brockelman 1991, 869; Judd 2014, 95.
[142] Hanne 2004, 53–4.

Kalijar, the Buwayhid ruler, to receive his oath of allegiance, and ask him to read the caliph's name in Friday sermons.[143] In 1036, al-Qaim sent al-Mawardi as ambassador to make a deal between the Buwayhid rulers, Jalal al-Dawla and his nephew Abu Kalijar, on the partition of the regions among them.[144] Later, Al-Mawardi was again sent to Abu Kalijar to ask him not to use the title *malik al-umam* (king of Muslims) but *malik al-dawla* (king of state).[145] Five years later, al-Mawardi was sent to the Saljuqi ruler Tugrul to ask him not to use his own name, but the caliph's name, in khutba.

Al-Mawardi supervised Saljuq's emergence as a provincial state in line with the caliphal procedures. In 1041, the caliph sent al-Mawardi to Jalal al-Dawla to persuade him not to intercept the caliph's revenues. In 1043, he was sent to make peace between the Saljuq ruler Tughrul, and the Buwayhid rulers Jalal al-Dawla and Abu Kalijar.[146] Al-Mawardi also participated in key events in Baghdad. When people reacted to the caliph's permission to Jalal al-Dawla to use the title *malik al-muluk* (king of states) and *shahanshah* (king of kings), al-Mawardi was part of the diplomatic mission gathered by the caliph to solve the problem.[147]

Exposed to politics at all levels, al-Mawardi's political career provided him with ample terrain on which he was able to observe the significance of political power, and how that power overrides the legal norms. Al-Mawardi left active politics around 1046. He died in Baghdad in 1058.

Al-Mawardi and Islamic Political Theory

I study al-Mawardi as a representative of Islamic political theory by analysing his works, primarily *al-Ahkam al-Sultaniyya* (henceforth *Ahkam*).[148] Al-Mawardi's political thought is never an abstract speculation of normative idealism (as observed in the discourses of jurists and philosophers). His attention was always focused on the empirical dynamics that determine the

---

[143] Ibn al-Jawzi 1992b, 225; Ibn al-Athir 1998b, 199.
[144] Güner 2003, 230.
[145] Al-Baghdadi 1981, 39.
[146] Ibn al-Athir 2002, 56–7.
[147] Ibn al-Jawzi 1992b, 26; Ibn al-Athir 1998b, 227–8.
[148] *Ahkam* was written either for al-Qadir or al-Qaim.

	Periods	Events	The Political Model
	810–900	Decline of the Abbasids	Rise of first provincial states
	900 onwards	Dissolution of the Abbasid state	Consolidation of provincial system
	909	Fatimid state in Egypt	Political and ideological rivalry between the Abbasids and the Fatimids
Al-Mawardi (974–1058)	945	Buwayhid rule in Baghdad	Buwayhid–Abbasid cohabitation
	991	Sunni revivalism and the Abbasid restoration	

Figure 2.2 Al-Mawardi in Islamic political history.

loci, like political power, of the active decision-makers.[149] This resulted in his attempting to solve the mismatch between political reality and the law. To that end, he recommended the abandoning of the legalistic idealism of jurists,[150] and the political idealism of the philosophers.[151] He proposed political solutions that were partially, and at times completely, independent of religion.

Al-Mawardi's political thought is a response to the cohabitation of the Abbasids and the Buwayhids, the Fatimid threat, and the political relations in the provincial system. His responses to the historical context that contained him provided the empirical foundation of his thought (Fig. 2.2). Basically, he recognised that power is the main dynamic in the design of politics, and that the political and the religious powers are irretrievably separated.[152] While responding to his historical context, al-Mawardi developed three groups of views:

i. he justified the traditional arguments in terms of the motifs of traditional reasoning;

---

[149] M. Y. Khan 2001, 3 and 33; Marcinkowski 2001, 282.
[150] Black 2008, 25.
[151] Kallek 2003, 182; Gibb 1962, 153; Lambton 1991a, xiv and 1; Hurwitz 2013, 135; Kerr 1966, 6–12. Also see Fakhry 1994, 160.
[152] Campanini 2011, 229.

ii. however, he justified traditional arguments in terms of the new reasoning that references the autonomous, not the religious, dynamics;
iii. his justifications of the new arguments referenced the autonomous, not the religious, dynamics.

Al-Mawardi's arguments of the second and third kinds are examples of Islamic political theory. His thought was empirical and historical: he saw the political as a phenomenon as it exists outside the text determined by the autonomous dynamics.[153] In *Tashil al-Nazar*, al-Mawardi framed this as 'every time and period has its realities'.[154]

The Sunni approach is usually seen as accommodating the existing situations with theory.[155] For al-Mawardi, this can only be partially valid. He went beyond that accommodating routine to advance the field with a reasoning justified by autonomous dynamics. This was mainly because he formulated his political views not as an isolated jurist or scholar, but as a statesman and diplomat who was deeply involved in political affairs.

In this regard, al-Mawardi's political thought is different from that formulated in al-Baghdadi's (980–1037) *Usul al-Din* and al-Baqillani's (950–1013) *Tamhid*, two works that reflect the religious view of politics. Al-Baghdadi and al-Baqillani were contemporaries of al-Mawardi who were known for their contributions to the advancement of Ashʿarism, the mainstream Sunni tradition.[156] Thus, as Tayeb El-Hibri put it, while the works of al-Baqillani and al-Baghdadi are 'religious treatises', *Ahkam* 'reads more like a political manifesto'.[157] The differences that characterise al-Mawardi's thought, given its historical and empirical nature, are the subject of the discussion that follows.

Political rationalism in al-Mawardi: some preliminary notes

Al-Mawardi wrote on political issues in a climate where there were Sunni and Shiʿa states with different leadership doctrines, including the Fatimid theory

---

[153] Hamid 2001, 14; Mikhail 1985, 19; Black 2011, 89.
[154] Al-Mawardi 2012, 126.
[155] Gibb 1962, 148, 155 and 162; Rosenthal 1962, 30.
[156] Rudhrawari and Muhassin 1921, 23 and 25–7.
[157] El-Hibri 2021, 198. Though al-Baqillani was also exposed to power relations (Adud al-Dawla sent him as an ambassador to the Byzantine empire), his work 'does not necessarily fully represent the theory and practice of the government of the community'. Lambton 1991a, 73.

of divine leadership. As an Abbasid official, he could not propose a theory that would put the caliph at risk. His arguments had to work against both the Shi'a and the Sunni states. As importantly, his theory had to point out that the caliph survives through his religious powers, he being without temporal power. This forced al-Mawardi to interpret religious arguments strictly in line with Abbasid interests. Thus, al-Mawardi's political rationalism sometimes comes over as religious argumentation. As the backbone of al-Mawardi's method, rational and religious arguments are developed or interpreted to best serve the Abbasids.

A case that reflects Abbasid politics in al-Mawardi's thinking is his explanation of the need for a leader. He makes that explanation in terms of both reason and religion. He proves the necessity of leadership by reason, because human beings can grasp the need for an order rationally. But reason cannot know the details of the revelation that informs the leadership.[158] So at this point, al-Mawardi separates 'political leadership' (which operates on the general rules shared by all people) and 'the caliphate' (which operates on Islamic rules shared by Muslims).[159] This reasoning reflects al-Mawardi's pragmatic quest for a framework that uses both rational and religious arguments to develop a theory that will best serve the Abbasids.

In other words, al-Mawardi imagined the caliph as the person who holds both political and religious powers. Logically, the political dimension enables the proposing of new rules because that operates on rational grounds. In practice, this is political reasoning. This reasoning is most clear at the opening of *Ahkam* where he defines leadership with reference to the public interest (*masalih al-umma*), the most important subject that pertains to administrative rules.[160] 'Public interest' here does not only imply significance, but also the reasoning beyond the religious text.

Unsurprisingly, like Ibn al-Muqaffa, al-Mawardi also took an instrumentalist view of religion. Religion is required, for it maintains people's support and loyalty.[161] It matters in the participation in public order.[162] Religion functions as

---

[158] Al-Mawardi 1881, 4.
[159] Their separation at institutional level would culminate with Ibn Khaldun.
[160] Al-Mawardi 1881, 3–4.
[161] Al-Mawardi 2012, 247–8, 250–2 and 351.
[162] Moosa 2018, 40.

a psychological force, or identity, that leads to social cohesion.[163] For example, al-Mawardi is critical of previous kings who ruled merely by relying on their armies.[164] However, that instrumentalist perspective does not see religion as sufficient to keep people from wrongdoing. There is a need also for an authority that coerces people.[165] That authority is the state, because it operates through political power.[166] In *Tashil al-Nazar*, al-Mawardi framed this as 'the state comes into being with power, and ends with weakness'.[167]

However, al-Mawardi did not define religion as the ontological arm of the state. Though he appreciates the role of religion, he attributes the stability of the state to its grounding in politics (*siyasah*) and institutions.[168] In so doing, al-Mawardi moved politics into a completely practical field. Neither politics (*siyasah*) nor institutions can be analysed as idealistic notions detached from the human (and historical) context in which they are embedded. As a matter of fact, as another important feature of his political thought, politics is ruled by its own rules (*qanun al-siyasiyya*).[169] Those are general rules not limited to religion because they have been proved valid by earlier peoples.[170] As we remember from Ibn al-Muqaffa, this is the separating of political and religious rules by a defining of the former as the universal set shared by all people.

Another significant subject is al-Mawardi's concept of political authority. How did al-Mawardi imagine political authority? Actually, I have already presented al-Mawardi's stance on this point in Chapter 1. The mainstream narrative on the birth of the state in Islamic societies as outlined there is basically dependent on his inferences. We can now revisit that narrative, this time by examining al-Mawardi's original account.

We find how al-Mawardi's conceptualised political authority in his views on *mazalim* tribunes. In general, *mazalim* tribunes deal with officials who

---

[163] Hamid 2001, 5.
[164] Al-Mawardi 2012, 248.
[165] Fakhry 1994, 163; Mikhail 1985, 10.
[166] Kallek 2004, 247.
[167] Al-Mawardi 2012, 253 and 255.
[168] Ibid., 251.
[169] Ibid., 338.
[170] Ibid., 126.

misbehave by taking advantage of their governmental power.[171] Al-Mawardi is regarded as the first to develop an extensive theoretical consideration of *mazalim* tribunes.[172] Though this might at first seem to be a limited subject, we soon discover that as al-Mawardi frames his arguments here, he provides us with significant clues about how he imagined politics, institutions, and their relationship in Islamic history.

To begin with, according to al-Mawardi, *mazalim* tribunes emerged later. This is because there was no need for special tribunes in the early period of Islam, for the problems of those time were solved in personalistic ways. He saw that period as a community based on personal or communal relations rather than on advanced institutions. It was an age of strong faith; people achieved their purposes without needing institutions. Their problems were not complex. Put differently, al-Mawardi saw the early period of Islam as a community, not as a state.

However, according to al-Mawardi, social and political life gradually advanced into complex structures, so the nature of problems also changed. Thus, the former personalistic methods were no longer satisfactory. Al-Mawardi counted the wrongdoings of officers as an example of the new complex problems. We infer here that al-Mawardi did not see the early personalistic methods as appropriate means of dealing with the problems caused by officers. That need, for him, gave way to the *mazalim* tribune, in which judges are more flexible and have more authority.[173] But, the Muslims did not invent these tribunes; they were inspired by the Persians.

Al-Mawardi notes that these tribunes were founded during the reign of the Umayyad caliph Abd al-Malik. He explains also that the origin of the *mazalim* court was in the practice of Persian kings. Logically, this narrative saw those institutions as non-canonical, in the sense that they were not dictated by religious norms at the outset. So, if they were not canonical, what is the origin of their power? Al-Mawardi has the answer when he reminds us that the Persian kings regarded those tribunes as *qawaid al-mulk* (the pillars

---

[171] Hurwitz 2013, 141.
[172] Berkel 2014, 232.
[173] Al-Mawardi 1881, 74–9.

of sovereignty/political power).¹⁷⁴ That is why the political rulers involved themselves in the *mazalim* tribunes.¹⁷⁵ Al-Mawardi himself narrated that Abd al-Malik (and the following caliphs) dealt directly with those tribunes.¹⁷⁶

To conclude this part: al-Mawardi's account of *mazalim* gives us three major points helpful for gaining an understanding of how he imagined politics and political authority. He explains Islamic society as having made the transition from individualistic to institutional governance. This transition accommodated new institutions that were non-canonical (not religious); they derive their legitimacy from political power.¹⁷⁷ This marked the invention of 'the public', which was the step that took politics beyond the former personalistic methods: problems were now to be resolved by new institutions justified by political power.¹⁷⁸ With this, al-Mawardi explains Islamic history in the terms of the general rules of human history, meaning thereby that there are general rules that explain the political phenomena, no matter whether or not they are occurrences among Muslims.

A spiritual caliphate

The gist of al-Mawardi's approach is his definition of the caliphate as a spiritual leadership. This was the general principle that affected his approach to any subject under investigation. His method can even give rise to the following question: what would be the best solution in Case X for the Abbasid caliph who survives through religious means because he has no temporal power?

This is seen when al-Mawardi defined the caliph as the bearer of the first duty to guard the faith and combat innovations that intrude into it. The caliph's second duty is to enforce the law on disputing parties, and thereby

---

[174] Ibid., 74. Al-Mawardi's (ibid., 189) account of the birth of bureaucratic units (*diwan*) is framed on the same logic. Accordingly, Caliph Umar, facing the problem of excessive revenues, created the first *diwan* imitating the Persian model.

[175] Hurwitz 2013, 143; Berkel 2014, 237.

[176] Al-Mawardi 1881, 74 and 80.

[177] While interpreting the verse (8:46) which is usually translated as 'do not dispute with one another . . . your *power* would disappear', al-Mawardi interprets the word *wind* (*rih*) not as *power* but state/*dawla*. Al-Mawardi 1881, 36.

[178] Mikhail (1985, 11) describes *Ahkam* as the first Muslim book on public law. Liebesny (1975, 228) describes al-Mawardi as a scholar of constitutional theory.

end their disagreements by letting justice prevail.[179] This definition was tailored to serve the interest of the Abbasids: while the first theorises the Abbasid caliph's survival pursuant to his being the bearer of the duty to exert influence, through religious powers, on his Sunni subjects,[180] the second part theorises the caliph as the bearer of the duty to safeguard the provincial order. In this way, Al-Mawardi effectively redefined the caliphate in line with the political dynamics of the provincial order, of which the Abbasid–Buwayhid cohabitation is an integral part.

Above, I summarised the Abbasid–Buwayhid cohabitation with the goal of presenting it in the list of the major events of the period. Thus, I shall now revisit cohabitation, but with the different goal of examining the distribution of temporal and religious powers between the Abbasids and the Buwayhids. In so doing, I shall explain more clearly why al-Mawardi defined 'guarding the faith' and 'combatting innovations' as the top duties of the caliph, or simply, why he framed 'the spiritual caliph'. This subject is important also in the analysis of al-Mawardi's stance on numerous other technical issues that will be reviewed in the later sections of this chapter.

Division of temporal and religious powers was the rule in the provincial order.[181] This rule was not confined to Baghdad. We however observe this more clearly in the Buwayhids' and Abbasids' physically overlapping condition. Otherwise, the caliph had no temporal impact in other provincial states, be it the Saffarids' or the Ghaznawids'.

Accordingly, the caliph recognised the Buwayhid rulers as the legitimate rulers.[182] The Abbasids had no role in the election of the Buwayhid ruler: for example, the Buwayhids finalised all the details of the transition after the death of Adud al-Dawla, and later, they requested the formal recognition of Caliph al-Tai.[183] The Buwayhids monopolised most temporal (secular)[184] powers

---

[179] Al-Mawardi 1881, 15.

[180] Rosenthal 1962, 345; Lambton 1991a, 91; Muir 1891, 573. This adaptation is not observed in al-Baqillani (1987, 477), who mentioned managing the armies among the duties of the leader.

[181] Negmatov 1998, 86.

[182] Ibn al-Jawzi 1992b, 98.

[183] Rudhrawari and Muhassin 1921, 79.

[184] Bosworth (1962b, 218) and Crone (2004, 146) use secular powers.

such as the vizirate, the army, the land administration, the non-canonical taxation and the coinage, the intelligence service and the postal administration. The caliph retained the religious powers, including the religious taxes, the appointment of judges and the organising of public worship.[185]

The Abbasid caliph lost the financial powers, but more importantly, he lost also the *vizirate*, the institution that had symbolised the Abbasid state tradition.[186] To the Abbasids, no longer having a vizier with temporal powers meant that the caliphate was no longer a *mulk*.[187] Baghdad had two palaces: the palace of the Buwayhid amir in the southern part of city, and the caliph's palace in the upper northern part.[188] The public sphere in Baghdad was almost entirely under the control of the Buwayhids, who decided on relevant matters, like the rules on the carrying of arms.[189] According to Herbert Busse, the Buwayhid ruler, Adud al-Dawla, wanted a division of power between the caliphate and the monarchy, a division that was equivalent to the medieval European theories of Church and Empire.[190]

When we look at what was left to the caliphs as effective means, we see the vesting of diplomas, the collecting of poll-tax and the appointment of judges. As it was nearly impossible to challenge the caliphs' vesting of diplomas, they focused on preventing the Buwayhids from intervening in judicial

---

[185] Kennedy 2011, 364; Lapidus 2002, 114; Donohue 2003, xvi and 54; Rudhrawari and Muhassin 1921, 3, 37 and 140; Levy 1929, 161.

[186] Berkel 2013, 87–9, 94 and 104; Lambton 1991a, 97; Muir 1891, 573.

[187] Adapting to the cohabitation, al-Mawardi (1881, 21 and 25; 1994, 10) defined the vizier appointed by the caliph as a limited (*tanfid*) vizier, unlike the general (*tawfid*) vizier appointed by the Buwayhids. But this is for creating an aura of honour for the Abbasid vizier. Al-Baghdadi 1981, 185. This was parallel with al-Qadir's policy of reviving the prestige of his vizier by issuing strong titles such as *rais al-ruesa* (the head of heads). Kabir 1964, 199.

[188] Strange 1900, 320. Before, bureaucratic offices (*diwan*) had been located next to each other in the vizierial palace in the Mukharrim district, which was close to the caliphal palace. Berkel 2013, 91; al-Ya'qubi 2018b, 82–6.

[189] Rudhrawari and Muhassin 1921, 57–8. Public order in Baghdad was frequently disturbed. Sunnis reacted to the Buwayhids' imposing '10 Muharram' as a day of mourning. In 977, the Buwayhids prohibited scholars' commenting on theological questions, as that triggered sectarian tension. Ibn al-Athir 2002, 79–80; Duri 2007, 37.

[190] Busse 2007, 277.

affairs. For example, when al-Muʿizz attempted to intervene in the appointment of judges, despite it being the beginning of the cohabitation when the caliphs were weak, the caliph resisted.[191] The judges gradually emerged as efficient agents for strengthening the caliph's influence and messages. As an example, in 999, Caliph al-Qadir asked the newly appointed local judge in Jilan (northwestern Iran) to persuade the local people to be obedient to the caliphate.[192] Realising their political impact, the caliphs appointed as many judges as possible.

The poll-tax was the major revenue of the caliphate, as the land taxes were assigned to the provincial states.[193] However, that was contested by the Buwayhids (later also by the Saljuqs). When crises began to erupt between the caliph and the Buwayhids on the poll-tax, as was the case in 1042 when Jalal al-Dawla attempted to confiscate the caliph's share, al-Mawardi took the mediating role in defence of the caliphate's position.[194] It is not surprising that *Ahkam* defines the poll-tax as the caliph's right.[195]

To conclude, unlike in the classical caliphate, the caliphate in the cohabitation was no longer a *mulk* (a political power). It was effectively nothing other than a spiritual leader. The concepts of the separation of temporal and religious powers, or of imaging the caliph as a spiritual leader, might sound to the reader as anachronic statements. To show that this is not the case, the account of someone who lived in that period is helpful. Al-Biruni (d. 1050), who lived in the Abbasid periphery in that period, described this separation of the temporal and the religious powers in *al-Athar* thus:

> At the beginning of that of al-Mustakfi, the empire and the rule had been transferred from the hands of the family of ʿAbbas into those of the family of Buwaihi, so that the authority that remained with the Bani-ʿAbbas was only a juridical

---

[191] Siddiqi 1942, 63.
[192] Tholib 2002, 165.
[193] Berkel 2013, 92.
[194] Rudhrawari and Muhassin 1921, 54; Ibn al-Athir 1998b, 259; 2002, 52.
[195] Al-Mawardi 1881, 28. As Haddad (1996, 172) noted, al-Mawardi is contradictory on poll-tax. This could be due to the different practices in the past, but also to the power-sharing between the Buwayhids and the Abbasids.

and religious one, not a political and secular affair. In fact, [it was] something like the dignity of the Rosh-gulutha with the Jews, [a person] who exercises a sort of religious authority without any actual rule and empire. Therefore the ʿAbbasside prince, who at present occupies the throne of the Khilafa [caliphate], is held by the astrologers to be only the (spiritual) head of Islam, but not a king.[196]

Looking at the Arabic words in the manuscript of *al-Athar*, we get a clearer picture. Al-Biruni wrote that what was left to the Abbasids was the regulation of religious and faith affairs (*amr diniyya wa ʿitiqadi*), not the political authority of worldly power (*la mulkiyya dunyawiyya*). He likens the Abbasids to the Jewish people during Goliath, who had authority only in religious affairs, not a political authority and state (*min gayr-i mulki wa la dawlati*). According to al-Biruni, the caliph was the 'president of Islamdom (*raʾis al-islamiyya*) . . . not a king (*la melik*)'.[197]

The Restoration

There is no doubt that the caliphate was weak in the provincial order. However, while reading al-Mawardi, one observes a confident and demanding approach on various critical subjects. This begs the question of how al-Mawardi was able to make Abbasi-centred demands in such a difficult circumstance.

This brings us to the Abbasid policy of restoration that was initiated by al-Qadir. Al-Mawardi's public service coincided with this policy, which motivated people greatly. That revivalist policy was indeed exciting for the Sunnis who were living under the Buwayhid rule, and witnessing a general Shiʿa dominance of the Muslim world. Behind that confidence was the Ghaznawids' rise to change the balance of power in the provincial order in favour of the Abbasids, and the caliphs' initiation of the ambitious strategy to restore their powers by relying on them. So, this requires the observation of a nuance in our analysis of al-Mawardi. The historical background that affected his political thought consisted of two dynamics. While the Abbasid caliph had no temporal powers, he might now try to revive his influence

---

[196] Al-Biruni, 1879, 129. Al-Biruni studied comparative religion, astronomy and mathematics. His views on the separation of temporal and religious powers were analysed by various scholars. Crone 2004, 221; E. S. Kennedy 2007, 394–5.
[197] Al-Biruni 1000, 45.

by using his religious means, despite that the success of such an initiative was dependent on the Ghaznawids' power. The caliph's temporal powers were not restored, but he could use his political power indirectly. To briefly explain the rise of the Ghaznawids and their impact on Abbasid politics, Sultan Mahmud emerged as an Abbasid partner after he was granted caliphal investiture in 999.[198] The caliphal legitimacy was vital for the Ghaznawids, who were frantically searching for political legitimacy.[199] As mentioned before, Mahmud needed the caliphal legitimacy primarily for his state, as it depended on military activism through expeditions to India.[200] Mahmud similarly needed the caliphal legitimacy in his westward expansion.[201]

In the earlier period of the cohabitation, when the Abbasids had no provincial state behind them, the caliphs were almost the dependents of the Buwayhids. Al-Muti, the first caliph in the cohabitation, was a captive of the Buwayhids, with no power at all.[202] He had once declined to contribute to the holy war because he had no financial resources and no troops under his control.[203] The following caliph, al-Tai, survived by relying on the allowance given by the Buwayhid ruler Muʿizz.[204] Adud al-Dawla, during whose reign the Buwayhid power reached its zenith, once forced the caliph to leave Baghdad for not welcoming him when he returned from expeditions. This was a humiliating situation.[205] In another case, Adud al-Dawla omitted Caliph al-Muti's name from khutba, on the pretext of political tension.[206] But more critical was the Buwayhid intervention in the election of the caliphate: al-Muti was made caliph by Muʿizz al-Dawla, who deposed Caliph al-Mustakfi in 973.[207] The Buwayhids later deposed Caliph al-Tai, and made al-Qadir caliph in 991.[208]

---

[198] Al-Qazwini 1913, 79.
[199] Bosworth 1998, 104; El-Hibri 2021, 200.
[200] Habib 1951, 81; Bosworth 1962a, 54 and 67.
[201] Bosworth 1962a, 57.
[202] Masudi 1989, 242.
[203] Ibn al-Athir 1998b, 456.
[204] Ibn Miskawaihi 1921, 91.
[205] Kabir 1964, 193.
[206] Shaban 1976, 62.
[207] Al-Qazwini 1913, 67; Ibn Miskawaihi 1921, 90; Masudi 1989, 423.
[208] Rudhrawari and Muhassin 1921, 215.

Mahmud's 'touch' radically changed that grim picture in favour of the Abbasids. The Ghaznawids became supporters of the caliph everywhere. In 1001, when Wathiqi, a descendant of Caliph al-Wathiq (d. 847) who had claimed right of succession to the caliphate,[209] arrived in Khurasan, Mahmud imprisoned him in a fortress, where he remained till his death upon the request of al-Qadir.[210] Mahmud supported al-Qadir's appointment of Ghalib as heir by including his name in khutba and on coinage.[211] He backed the Abbasids against the Fatimids.

When al-Hakim, the Fatimid caliph, sent a letter to Mahmud in 1012 to ask that his name be read in khutba in defiance of the Abbasid caliph, he burnt it in public after executing the envoy.[212] This event was celebrated in the caliph's palace.[213] The Ismaili propaganda had stalled in Persia and Khurasan, thanks to the Ghaznawids.[214] The Ghaznawids also counterbalanced the Buwayhids in the western regions like Ray (northern Iran), which made the atmosphere more favourable to the Abbasids.[215]

The Ghaznawid support naturally empowered the caliph against the Buwayhids. For example, al-Qadir felt himself more independent in the appointing of judges.[216] In 1003, when the Buwayhid ruler Baha al-Dawla appointed al-Musawi, a Shi'a jurist, to a key religious post, al-Qadir opposed it, seeing the appointment as an intervention in his jurisdiction.[217] This was the first time that the caliph had put himself at the head of a popular protest, and successfully refused to accept the nomination.[218]

Caliph al-Qadir, a shrewd political actor, wanted to use Ghaznawid support in the ambitious strategy of restoring the influence of the caliphate.[219] He calculated

---

[209] Siddiqi 1942, 92–3; Hanne 2007, 66.
[210] Rudhrawari and Muhassin 1921, 325–6.
[211] Siddiqi 1942, 93.
[212] Ibn al-Jawzi 1992b, 92.
[213] Bosworth 1962a, 60.
[214] Siddiqi 1942, 93.
[215] Bosworth 1970, 76.
[216] Hanne 2007, 65.
[217] Tholib 2002, 254; Hanne 2007, 65–6.
[218] Kennedy 2016, 207.
[219] Lapidus 2002, 141.

that he could mobilise the Sunnis under the banner of protecting the true faith. A call for Sunni restoration against the Shiʻa, rather than a specific Abbasid goal, would be more attractive to the larger Muslim community.[220] Living under the grim psychology of witnessing the Buwayhid rule, and the Fatimid threat, had already developed a disposition among the Sunnis to embrace any policy in this direction.[221] This brings us to a concept in al-Mawardi's *Ahkam*, where he defined one of the duties of the leader as combatting innovations.[222]

Predictably, the Fatimid threat was a usual subject of al-Qadir's restoration policy. In 1001, he convened a council to renounce the Fatimid genealogy.[223] This was only two years after Mahmud of Ghaznawid was given the caliphal diplomas. Al-Qadir systematically developed a policy framed and popularised by symbolic religious issues. Another popular issue was the Qur'an. In 1006, there were ongoing tensions over the codex of Abdullah bin Masud, a variant of the Qur'an that was still used by some groups, and formed a part of the theological debate among various groups. In 1010, al-Qadir appeared in public wearing the veil of the Prophet, accompanied by Abu Hamid al-Isfarayini, a leading scholar, and declared the Uthman codex as the only variant.[224]

In 1018, al-Qadir asked that an epistle on Sunni doctrine be read publicly in mosques. This was an updated version of the Hanbali views that condemned Shiʻism, Muʻtazilism and even Ashʻarism. In 1029, the tenet of the 'created Qur'an', a thesis of Muʻtazile, was also denounced. Known as 'the Qadiri creed' (*al-ʻaqida al-qadiriyya*), al-Qadir's Sunni restoration aimed at ending the theology debates by providing the simple (and populist) formulas drawn from the Hanbali school.[225] That doctrine, a political text in a theological guise, had the aim of drawing a boundary between correct belief and heresy.[226] As Hugh Kennedy put it, 'it was no longer possible to be simply a Muslim'.[227] One had to adhere to the correct school of Islam.

---

[220] El-Hibri 2021, 195–7; Kennedy 2016, 208.
[221] Haddad, 1996, 170–1; Bosworth 2007b, 170. Also see al-Qazwini 1913, 68.
[222] Al-Mawardi 1881, 15.
[223] O'Leary 1923, 166.
[224] El-Hibri 2021, 195.
[225] Mouline 2014, 30; Hanne 2004, 66.
[226] El-Hibri 2021, 196; Black 2011, 82.
[227] Kennedy 2011, 392.

The eleventh century was the age of theological crisis in Islamic societies. It was usual to witness skirmishes among the Hanbalis, Shafis and the Muʿtazila.[228] That theological crisis turned out to be a useful socio-political framework for the Abbasid caliph to instrumentalise his religious powers. Al-Qadir mobilised all religious means at his disposal, such as judges,[229] schools and mosques,[230] to boost his ability to proclaim religious messages in public,[231] to meet pilgrims regularly (particularly from Khurasan) and to transmit messages to the wider Sunni world.[232] The Abbasid caliph, who had no temporal power, effectively founded a doctrine by employing theologians, the *ulama*, scholars and even popular ascetics.[233] A complex network of sermon writers, preachers and imams volunteered to serve al-Qadir's Sunni restoration policy.[234]

As I have noted above, what enabled the caliph to use his religious means in such an effective way was Ghaznawid power. They made the political setting suitable for the Abbasids to pursue such an ambitious agenda. They did not hesitate to place their powers at the caliph's disposal to impose the creed.[235] In Khurasan, the Ghaznawids emerged as agents of al-Qadir's polices, and they persecuted heretics – any group other than the faithful of Sunnism,[236] like the Qarmatians, the Muʿtazile[237] and the Ismailis.[238]

Interests versus *norms*

Having analysed how al-Mawardi reformulated the caliphate according to the political balances of the provincial order and the cohabitation, we can

---

[228] Ibn al-Athir 2002, 79–80, 89 and 102.
[229] Tholib 2002, 7–8.
[230] Black 2011, 82. Al-Qadir constructed a new sultan mosque in the Harbiyya quarter of Baghdad. Ibn al-Jawzi 1992a, 365.
[231] Hanne 2007, 86.
[232] Ibn al-Athir 1998b, 17; Rudhrawari and Muhassin 1921, 419.
[233] Hanne 2004, 50; Kennedy 2016, 207. Also see Bosworth 1962a, 58.
[234] Mouline 2014, 30.
[235] Ibn Isfandiyar 1905, 233; Morgan 2016, 4.
[236] Hanne 2007, 68.
[237] Siddiqi 1942, 98 and 103.
[238] Kennedy 2011, 373.

now proceed to other issues that he elaborates on in *Ahkam*. As the following pages will display, al-Mawardi proposed various arguments on major political issues by taking the Abbasid position as the autonomous dynamic to shape the interpretation of rules. These are examples of his political rationalist stance. In practice, al-Mawardi's pro-Abbasid stance on other issues is a continuation of his policy of reformulating the caliphate to bring it in line with the realities of the provincial order. To illustrate that in this section, I shall analyse al-Mawardi's comments on the election of the caliph, and the relevance of the Quraishi condition.

To begin, the caliph is elected by the electors, *ahl al-aqd wa al-hal*. The electors, who should have qualities such as prudence and knowledge, are procedurally expected to elect someone as caliph on condition that he can deliver justice, is knowledgeable and is physically in good condition, like having healthy hearing.

But this was an idealistic model, far from the actuality. In practice, those who were informed earlier about the cessation of office dictated their choice. Concerns like 'What if there is a better candidate in terms of Islamic norms?' were sacrificed. Al-Mawardi, however, finds this legitimate, because it is done according to 'custom, not religion'.[239] We can easily guess why al-Mawardi has an accommodating view of customary practice: it enabled the Abbasids to hold the election quickly, and in isolation. Since the Abbasids had no power to impose their agenda, being prescriptive on procedure might have prompted third-parties' intervention. In fact, al-Mawardi, as a member of the Abbasid court, witnessed the election of the caliph according to the customary practices, such as the Abbasids' closing of the gateways in 1031, during the election of al-Qaim.[240]

Ironically, when it comes to the condition of Quraishi genealogy, al-Mawardi advocated a strict policy, one that is rather anachronic four centuries after Muhammad.[241] In what appears to be a religious argument, al-Mawardi retains the caliphate exclusively for the Abbasids, not only against the Fatimid challengers (who had their own genealogy) but also against any potential

---

[239] *'Urfan la-shar'an.* Al-Mawardi 1881, 4–5.
[240] Ibn al-Jawzi 1992b, 215.
[241] Al-Mawardi 1881, 5.

Sunni contender.[242] As the caliph had no temporal power, the formal rule of Quraishi genealogy turned out to be the perfect pro-Abbasid argument against any contender. The Quraishi genealogy also helped the Abbasids in their interaction with the wider Muslim community. So, al-Mawardi shares the position of Abu Mansur al-Baghdadi and al-Baqillani on the Quraishi condition.[243] However, as Gibb observes, this is a nuanced position, as it was custom-made for Abbasid interests.[244] Al-Mawardi here did not defend a religious principle, but the Abbasid interest.

The lineage of the Quraysh was a major component of Fatimid–Abbasid competition. This propaganda was dangerously spread by Ismaili missionaries across regions like Syria and Khurasan. The Abbasids felt themselves obliged to counter-challenge the Fatimid propaganda on the Quraishi lineage.[245] Al-Mawardi was a typical Sunni elite who had experienced the common psychology of awareness of the Shi'a threat. His early years in public service coincided with the rule of al-Aziz Billah (r. 975–96), the greatest ruler of the Fatimids.[246]

In 976, three years after al-Mawardi's birth, the Fatimids captured Hejaz, and removed the Abbasid caliph's name from Friday sermons in Mecca and Madina. They took charge of pilgrimage.[247] The trajectory of Islamic history was about to turn into a Shi'a-dominated politics. In 1010, al-Mawardi witnessed Caliph al-Qadir asking the Buwayhids to counter-challenge the Ismaili propaganda, as various local rulers were proclaiming their allegiance to the Fatimid caliph.[248] Al-Mawardi also witnessed the following alarming developments: in 1013, the Fatimid caliph al-Hakim sent a letter to Mahmud of Ghaznawids, requesting that his name be read in khutba.[249] The Ismaili propaganda was strong among the Dailami subjects of the Buwayhids.[250]

---

[242] Kallek 2003, 182.
[243] Al-Baghdadi 1928, 275–6; al-Baqillani 1987, 471.
[244] Gibb 1962, 156.
[245] Berg 2010, 14.
[246] Jiwa 1992, 58.
[247] Al-Qazwini 1913, 68. The Fatimids used their patronage of pilgrimage to exert their influence and prestige. Kennedy 2016, 280.
[248] Tholib 2002, 8–9; O'Leary 1923, 164.
[249] Ibn al-Jawzi 1992b, 92.
[250] Bosworth 1965/6, 147.

Though it lasted only briefly, the Buwayhid ruler Adud al-Dawla's interest in the Fatimid thesis panicked the Abbasids. Abu Kalijar too, the ruler of various Buwayhid provinces, was influenced by Ismailism. This ended only in 1044, when he had the chance to take over Jalal al-Dawla's position, the rulership of Iraq. This was made possible by the Abbasid caliph's approval. However, in the meantime, the Ismailis became influential in Shiraz.[251]

In short, the Fatimid threat was a major motif of the historical background of al-Mawardi's political thought. But, like others, he was right to be worried about it. In 1058, the year when al-Mawardi died, al-Basasiri invaded Baghdad, sent the Abbasid caliph into exile, and read the Friday sermon in the name of the Fatimid caliph.[252]

The semantics of al-Mawardi's framing of the Quraishi lineage display a parallelism with Caliph al-Qadir's 1011 official debunking as a myth of the Fatimid genealogical claim.[253] That policy was the commencement of the genealogy fight between the Alids and the Abbasids of the eighth century. Having a genealogy based on 'daughter of Muhammad', the Fatimids easily discredited the Abbasid genealogy based on 'uncle'. Probably realising that the Fatimid genealogy was more effective in propaganda, the Abbasids decided to debunk it.

The Abbasids' completely debunking the Fatimid genealogy in 1011 was a deviation from the early Abbasid strategy of competing with the Alid thesis, as illustrated in the letter of the first Abbasid caliph al-Mansur in Chapter 1. The cause of this shift was the birth of the Fatimid state. The Alids were no longer a community; they had a state. The traditional narrative of 'mine is better than yours' turned into an argument that could have legitimised the Fatimids. Unsurprisingly, this political manoeuver was immediately sanctioned by scholars. Spotting this, Ibn Khaldun criticised as 'Abbasid partisans' al-Saymari, al-Baqillani and al-Isfarayini, who had supported the 1011 declaration.[254] In this regard, al-Mawardi's stance on the Quraishi condition was an example of his support of the Abbasids against the Fatimids.

---

[251] Howes 2011, 879–85.
[252] Ibn al-Athir 2002, 121; Nishapuri 2001, 42.
[253] El-Hibri 2021, 196.
[254] Ibn Khaldun 1958a, 44–6.

Electing the leader

On the election of the leader, al-Mawardi developed his ideas further by adapting to the Abbasid position. After discussing the various views on how many electors are needed (one, five or six), he concluded that the leader is elected by a number of qualified electors, so there is no need for a large group, nor yet for all the people.[255]

People need not know the name of the elected person; it is satisfactory to know that a qualified person is elected.[256] While framing this argumentation, al-Mawardi develops his arguments by criticising Sulayman bin Jarir (d. 785), a Zaydi scholar.[257] This is yet another case that displays how reasoning in al-Mawardi is affected by the political setting. Sulayman bin Jarir's views (known as Sulaimaniya or Jarirriyya) were influential among the Buwayhids.[258] Thus, by denying that people need to know the elected personally, al-Mawardi provided a political-theological stance to the Abbasids against the Buwayhids.[259] He effectively contributed to the policy of keeping the caliphal election an intra-Abbasid affair.

Al-Mawardi did not propose a religious norm. His is a political reasoning determined by the realities of the cohabitation, particularly the presence of the Buwayhids in Baghdad, the locus of the caliphal elections. He certainly knew about how the Buwayhids had deposed al-Tai, and imposed al-Qadir. *Ahkam* was written during the reign of either al-Qadir or al-Qaim, the two caliphs who pursued the policy of restoring the caliphal powers, given that they were backed by the Ghaznawids.

Al-Mawardi, whose public service coincided with these two caliphs, was a bureaucrat who was expected to contribute to that policy. Otherwise, the idea that people need to know the new leader is an absurd (or normally redundant) argument. Al-Mawardi justified this argument with the weak analogy that people do not know the judges in person; they know only that they are

---

[255] Al-Mawardi 1881, 5. Al-Baqillani (1987, 467–9) has the same view. Abu Mansur al-Baghdadi (1928, 281) is not clear on the required number.
[256] Al-Mawardi 1881, 13.
[257] Al-Shahrastani 1984, 136.
[258] See Bausani 1968, 291; Wolfson 1960, 218; al-Baghdadi 1920, 44.
[259] Lambton 1991a, 94; Kallek 2003, 182.

qualified for the job.[260] There is no way that a person of al-Mawardi's calibre would not know the difference between a political leader and a judge.

Al-Mawardi knew that power had already subdued norms in politics, including those relevant to the leadership.[261] Not long before his birth, al-Mu'tazz (r. 866–9) was elected caliph by soldiers, and later killed by them. As al-Tabari noted, all procedural undertakings of judges and jurists were only a formality in the election of al-Mu'tazz. The whole process was decided by the troops, so much so that he was made caliph when al-Musta'in was still in charge.[262] Neither the electors nor the norms are meaningful if they are not backed by political power.

Put differently, what appeared as formal procedure was in reality a manifestation of power. Fourteen years before al-Mawardi's birth, in 940, the electors, including the elite like the vizier, judges and members of the Abbasid family, gathered to choose al-Muttaqi as the new caliph.[263] In reality, this was possible because the former caliph's sight was destroyed by the Turkish general of the troops. However, later, al-Muttaqi was himself blinded, which meant legally that he was no longer in the condition required of the leadership, so his powers have to be transferred to a new caliph.[264] Blinding symbolised the interplay of power and rules, as the blinding of a man automatically enforces the rule that the blind cannot lead.

The situation was no different during the Abbasid–Buwayhid cohabitation. In 974, the year al-Mawardi was born, Sebuktigin, a Ghaznawid commander whom Caliph al-Muti had co-opted to repel the Fatimid danger, took control of Baghdad, and forced al-Muti to abdicate in favour of his son, al-Tai.[265]

In what was probably the more influential case to al-Mawardi, al-Qadir was imposed by the Buwayhid ruler, Baha al-Dawla, in 992.[266] The caliph, during whose reign al-Mawardi was born, educated and accepted into public

---

[260] Al-Mawardi 1881, 14.
[261] Ibid., 4–5.
[262] Al-Tabari 1985a, 41, 113, 164 and 35.
[263] Ibn Miskawaihi 1921, 1.
[264] Masudi 1989, 415.
[265] Ibn Miskawaihi 1921, 354.
[266] Rudhrawari and Muhassin 1921, 153–5 and 215.

service, was imposed by the Buwayhids. He, Al-Qadir, was the third caliph in a row (after al-Muti and al-Tai) to be elected by the Shiʿite Buwayhid amir who did not qualify on the legal criteria for electorship.[267] Ironically, the power elites, who normally should have been invalidated on religious criteria, determined the election of the caliph.[268]

Given the quandary of the political thought into which he was born, Al-Mawardi developed his views when the Abbasid caliph, who survived through religious powers, ended up bereft of temporal power. We will never know how al-Mawardi would have framed his theory if he had lived during the early Abbasids. The burden of his context forced al-Mawardi to apply modifiers to secure Abbasid interests, even in less significant matters. For example, on what to do if there are two equal and eligible candidates, Al-Mawardi proposed that even if it is better to choose the older, the younger can be elected if he meets the requirements of the time, such as knowledge and courage. Accordingly, courage is preferred when the time is ripe for border protection and insurgencies, and knowledge is preferred when there is a need for the protection of religion in a time of heretics.

But what was the requirement of his time? This cannot have been courage, as the Abbasids had no military power. As we discussed above, al-Mawardi, in perfect accord with this, defined the primary duty of the caliph as protecting the faith, with special reference to the duty to fight heretics.[269] In fact, the two caliphs, al-Qadir and al-Qaim, for whom al-Mawardi worked, proclaimed the policy of fighting heretics. Predictably, this was the only feasible strategy to exert influence, as the caliphs had no temporal powers.

Likewise, al-Mawardi rejected the view that the making of demands pursuant to the duty of leadership is a sign of bad character.[270] He opposed this view despite the fact that being modest and not seeking leadership were normally seen as Islamic virtues. In fact, he rejected this view because it was at odds with the Abbasid policy of monopolising the caliphate. Al-Mawardi

---

[267] Hanne 2004, 60.
[268] March 2019, 30; Gibb 1962, 161.
[269] Al-Mawardi 1881, 6 and 15.
[270] Ibid., 6–7.

also urged that the elected leader should stay even if a better candidate were to appear later. He criticises al-Jahiz (d. 869), a rationalist philosopher who defended the opposite view.[271] Al-Mawardi did not seek the ideal caliph; he proposed solutions based on the empirical reality, which in this case was the Abbasid caliphate. He simply did not imagine politics through idealistic norms. This is not surprising, as al-Mawardi took reason to be the tool for acquiring practical (or religious) knowledge.[272] Apart from logical inferences generated by reason, he held there was no knowledge other than that gained from observation through the senses.[273]

In another pro-Abbasid interpretation, al-Mawardi rejected the coexistence of two caliphs.[274] That was a deviation from the Ash'ari tradition that al-Baghdadi justified, because the essential contingent of the latter's justification was missing in his time. That contingent was 'if the Muslim land is separated by a sea'.[275] Besides, even if that contingency had been present, the al-Baghdadi justification could not be defended by an Abbasid bureaucrat of the time because its defence would serve no purpose other than to justify the Fatimids.[276] This was equally risky in the Sunni context. Al-Mawardi certainly knew relevant precedents, like the Samanids' allegiance to the deposed Caliph al-Tai's rejection of al-Qadir.[277]

Appointing the leader

Al-Mawardi paid close attention to the election of the caliph by appointment, as that provided a secure method for the Abbasids in a period when they had no temporal powers.[278] His position on this subject should be considered

---

[271] Ibid., 6–7.
[272] Fakhry 1994, 160. Al-Mawardi (2012, 134) defines reason as the first virtue. All other virtues exist thanks to reason.
[273] Al-Mawardi 1987, 7.
[274] Ibid., 7. Al-Baqillani (1987, 470) too rejects two imams at the same time, which should be seen as the impact of the political context.
[275] Al-Baghdadi 1928, 274.
[276] Al-Baghdadi 1981, 152; Kallek 2003, 182.
[277] Ibn al-Athir 1998a, 451.
[278] Al-Mawardi 1881, 10.

together with the fact that, while al-Mawardi was in public service, Caliph al-Qadir appointed his son as heir. This was the first appointment since the beginning of the cohabitation. It was indeed one of the most critical events of the period. As importantly, the appointment was seen as a success of al-Qadir's policy of restoring caliphal powers.

In 997, campaigns emerged in regions like Jilan, with the goal of restoring the caliphate of the deposed al-Tai. As another worrying development, in 1001, Wathiqi claimed right of succession to the caliphate, and succeeded in attracting the attention of various local groups, along with several jurists.[279] Amidst these developments, in 1001, Caliph al-Qadir designated his eight-year-old son, Ghalib, as his heir.[280] As a cautious response, the Buwayhid ruler, Baha al-Dawla, did not put al-Ghalib's name on the coinage, even though he did not oppose the appointment.[281] Ghalib, however, died in 1018.

In 1030, al-Qadir appointed another son, Abu Ja'far (who would become Caliph al-Qaim), after consulting with the dignitaries.[282] The Buwayhid ruler Jalal al-Dawla sent a letter to al-Qadir to demand an explanation.[283] In his official response, al-Qadir tended the pretext of his own deteriorating health. However, the appointment was possible thanks to various developments in the provincial order that created a supportive atmosphere for the Abbasids. Besides, the Buwayhid ruler was swamped by domestic problems.[284]

More importantly, the Abbasids secured the Ghaznawid support. That restored the Abbasid caliphate's ability to use political power, even if only indirectly. Al-Qadir informed Mahmud by letter on his appointment of heir, and asked him to put the heir's name in khutba and on the coinage.[285] The appointment of heir was a turning point in the Abbasid policy of restoring the caliphal electoral procedure.[286] Al-Qaim became caliph after the death of al-Qadir, the

---

[279] Rudhrawari and Muhassin 1921, 421–2.
[280] Ibn al-Jawzi 1992b, 26.
[281] Hanne 2004, 67.
[282] Güner 2002, 24; Kabir 1964, 196–7.
[283] Hanne 2004, 61.
[284] Ibn al-Athir 1998b, 185.
[285] Bosworth 1962a, 63.
[286] If the caliph did not appoint a successor, that ground was effectively left open to the power holders. This happened in 847 when Caliph al-Wathiq gave the Turkish soldiers an excellent pretext by not appointing a successor. Mottahedeh 2007, 76.

first caliph to die in office since the beginning of the cohabitation. This was the first time since the beginning of the cohabitation that a caliph had been chosen without the involvement of the Buwayhids.[287]

Looking now at how al-Mawardi justifies the election of the leader by appointment, the reader is reminded of the historical precedent of Umar's and Abu Bakr's appointment of the next caliph.[288] This proof is problematic, at least for the Umar part, for his was not an investiture of an heir. Rather, he gathered a commission to appoint the next caliph.[289] Apparently finding this proof rather unconvincing, al-Mawardi offered the highly unsubstantiated argument that the right to appoint an heir belongs to the leader, because his choice is counted as more worthy of enforcement in this matter.[290]

The practical purpose for al-Mawardi was that he wanted the incumbent caliph to have full authority to designate the next caliph. This was in full harmony with the Abbasid policies of his time. This, however, abandons the procedural rules of the election of the caliph. As if to forestall objection to this riding roughshod over those procedural rules, al-Mawardi stressed that the incumbent caliph should do his best to find a qualified candidate. Thus, the caliph, for al-Mawardi, has the right, even without consulting the electors, to appoint as heir anyone other than a son or father.[291] Al-Mawardi effectively defined political power as the ultimate criterion in the decision on the election of the successor.

But how about the appointing of a son as heir, as Caliph al-Qadir did? On this critical point, al-Mawardi lists alternatives without elucidating his position: the caliph may appoint a son or father with the approval of electors; or he should have the ultimate authority in appointing a son or father. Or the caliph can appoint his father but not son.[292] Gibb interprets al-Mawardi's silence on the appointing of a son as a reflection of the Sunni dilemma according to which no legal argument can be adduced for the

---

[287] Hanne 2004, 77.
[288] Al-Mawardi 1881, 8. This justification has its origin in al-Ashʿari's *Al-Ibanah*. Al-Ashʿari 1940, 135. It reflects the Ashʿari mainstream view.
[289] Rosenthal 1962, 33–4.
[290] Al-Mawardi 1881, 9.
[291] Ibid., 9.
[292] Ibid., 9–10.

validity of appointing a son. However, historical reasons made it impossible to declare it invalid.[293] More dramatically, this appointment issue arose during his public service. Simply, while al-Mawardi endorsed al-Qadir's appointing of his son as heir, he was wary of giving the impression of supporting a practice that resembles hereditary monarchy.[294]

This made al-Mawardi embrace the prospect of a caliph appointing heirs in a line such as 'first X, then Y, then Z'.[295] He first supported this argument by the weak proof of the Prophet appointing three commanders in a chain, so that if one was killed, the other replaces him. This would be a false equivalence, because it equates the appointment of a military servant and the appointment of a political leader. To clarify this, al-Mawardi later reminds us that both are driven by the rationale of public concern.[296] We understand that he did not cite as religious evidence the prophetic example of appointing commanders. (That would have been a false equivalence too, because appointing commanders is not the same as appointing political leaders.) Al-Mawardi chose instead to justify the use of 'public welfare' to legitimate a new reasoning.

Legitimacy by power: theorising the provincial order

As already noted, at the very foundation of the providential order lies power: any actor who has enough power can impose himself as a legitimate ruler. It was the power-oriented mechanism of the provincial order that legitimised the cohabitation in Baghdad and in the provincial states. It is unimaginable that al-Mawardi would have failed to respond to those situations. He categorised the situations imposed by power within the provincial order.

His first category in this regard is *hajr* (custody), where the leader is under the control of an aide who takes over the conduct of state affairs. The leader

---

[293] Gibb 1962, 157.

[294] M. Y. Khan 2001, 76. Such prudency is observed in al-Mawardi on the right to rebel. Though he recognises the right to rebel, even the deposing of an unjust leader, he leaves the subject in darkness by not providing detail. Al-Mawardi 1881, 16 and 55–6. A tolerant view on this subject would contradict the Abbasid interest.

[295] Harun al-Rashid (r. 786–809) appointed his son, al-Amin, as heir, and his other son, al-Ma'mun, to succeed al-Amin. When Harun died, al-Amin attempted to make his son the next heir, thereby replacing al-Ma'mun. This triggered a civil war. Masudi 1989, 146–69.

[296] Al-Mawardi 1881, 12–13.

is recognised as doing his job so long as the custodians act according to the law. Otherwise, the leader should seek the help of aides to end the custody.[297] *Hajr* justified the caliph's position in the cohabitation with the Buwayhids.[298] Accordingly, the caliph's legitimacy (even if this was limited) could not be questioned, as he carries on his work as the law requires. Where he sees a need for them, he can seek the support of aides. And this brings to mind the Ghaznawids.[299]

The second category is captivity (*qahr*), when the leader is relieved of his duties without hope of reprieve. In this case, the electors should elect a new leader.[300] If *qahr* occurs when rebels capture the caliph, and thereby divide the country, the caliph is recognised as functional until the rebels set up a new leader.[301] But if rebels declare a new leader (and there is no hope for the captured leader), a new leader should be elected in a peaceful part of the territory.[302]

With these clauses of *Ahkam*, al-Mawardi developed a theory against the usual case of rebels, on the grounds that the caliph has no temporal power. In fact, this issue had been a problem for the caliphate in various cases, like the Tulunid break-away between 870 and 905, during which time the caliph's nominal recognition continued.[303] As a diplomat, al-Mawardi took roles in several negotiations with the rebels. For example, when a Turkish commander rebelled in 1036, the Buwayhid ruler, Jalal al-Dawla, sent him to the negotiations.[304]

Observing endless cases of rebels, and small or large territorial splits, it became a top priority for the Abbasids to develop a political theory that always secures the caliph's survival, and never leaves open the possibility that others can advance a counterclaim.[305] On this account, al-Mawardi can be seen

---

[297] Ibid., 19.
[298] Crone 2004, 232; Gibb 1962, 159–60; Bosworth 1962a, 68.
[299] Q. Khan 1983, 43.
[300] Al-Mawardi 1881, 19–20.
[301] For al-Baqillani (1987, 470–1), if the country is divided, and people with heretic views hold the leadership, there is *dar al-qahr*, i.e. the rule of tyranny. Obeying the ruler in such a case is not required. Muslims should look for help to get rid of this situation.
[302] Al-Mawardi 1881, 19–20.
[303] Kennedy 2016, 265; Hitti 1937, 455.
[304] Amedroz 1905, 394.
[305] D. Brown 2009, 144.

to have proposed a pre-emptive framework that guaranteed the Abbasids' monopolistic right to continue the caliphate.[306]

Indeed, al-Mawardi also had the Fatimid threat in mind while formulating that pre-emptive framework.[307] Al-Mawardi lived in a period when the Abbasids were being subjected to continuous Fatimid threats. Hypothetically the Fatimids' capturing the Abbasid caliph would be *qahr*. And, as it happened, a short time after al-Mawardi's death, there was a development for which al-Mawardi's *qahr* is a perfect fit: Basasiri, a Fatimid ally, raided Baghdad. He made khutba and coins in the name of the Fatimid caliph, and asked the officials, including the judges, to follow the Fatimid policies. Meanwhile, the Abbasid caliph al-Qaim lived three years as a hostage of the Uqaylids, an ally of the Fatimids.[308] The caliph was able to escape with the help of 'his friend', the Saljuq ruler Tugrul.

Next, al-Mawardi proposed a concept to justify the provincial states' imposing themselves merely by virtue of their power: 'rulership by usurpation/force' (*amir al-'istila*). This justifier concept was, however, conditional on the usurper's recognition of the caliph as the manager of religious affairs. This is the opposite of rulership by appointment (*amir al-istikfa*), where the caliph appoints a ruler to a particular territory, for specific tasks.[309] With this clause, we see that al-Mawardi developed a theory of legitimacy according to the functioning of the provincial order.

With this justifier concept, al-Mawardi had developed a theory of political legitimacy gained by power alone.[310] In fact, reminding us of Machiavelli's *necessita* versus *virtu*, al-Mawardi underlined that there can be no strict rule in rulership by usurpation because power prevails in that context.[311] As Gibb

---

[306] Lambton 1991a, 93–4.
[307] Al-Baghdadi 1981, 170.
[308] Ibn Khallikan 1843a, 173; Daftary 2007, 196.
[309] Al-Mawardi 1881, 28–9. A passage in Jean Bodin (1992, 6) is reminiscent of al-Mawardi's *amir al-istikfa* and *amir al-'istila*: 'I would add that if a sovereign magistrate, whose term is only annual or is for a fixed and limited time, contrives to prolong the power entrusted to him, it must either be by tacit consent or by force. If by force, it is called a tyranny. Yet the tyrant is nonetheless a sovereign, just as the violent possession of a robber is true and natural possession even if against the law, and those who had it previously are dispossessed.'
[310] Also see Mikhail 1985, 42.
[311] Al-Mawardi 1881, 32–3.

spotted, this justification undermines the foundations of all law by closing eyes to the apparent illegality.[312]

Al-Mawardi was not unaware of what he was doing. He first reminds us that a situation is the result of necessity. Next, he provides us with what appears to be a short summary of Islamic political theory by reminding us that necessity annuls the rules, and this should be noted in the public interest (*al-masalih al-'amm*).[313] This is the right context to remember that he highlighted the public interest, at the very beginning of *Ahkam*, as the basis of administrative issues. Thus, in al-Mawardi we see that politics in the provincial order was able to justify itself independently of norms.[314] This is a political order based on power. Religious or philosophical norms are no longer autonomous dynamics to affect politics. Al-Mawardi's stance in this regard also displays that his thought was the outcome of his empirical investigation of politics in the provincial order. It is thus different from the jurists' method of explaining politics by deducing ideas from given principles.[315]

Conclusion: Legitimising Power

Al-Mawardi's political thought reflects the dynamics and realities of the provincial order. Power was shared among the provincial states. The caliphate had no temporal power, due to the separation of temporal and religious powers. Al-Mawardi's referenced caliph was not Ibn al-Muqaffa's al-Saffah. It was al-Qadir, who was a spiritual leader without temporal power. Responding to this historical setting, al-Mawardi systematically incorporated political dynamics into his political thought. His opinions on various subjects are never general prescriptions; they are reflections of the political context. He thought contextually about almost every subject he handled. In this context, al-Mawardi's legitimising of rule by usurpation/power is in significance comparable to Ibn al-Muqaffa's invention of the state. Both posited that the idealistic models are no longer effective or explanatory.

---

[312] Gibb 1962, 162–4. For many, al-Mawardi transformed unlawfulness into legality. Kallek 2004, 239; Al-Baghdadi 1981, 200; Q. Khan 1983, 42–3; Crone 2004, 233. In contrast, for Al-Azmeh (2007, 244), al-Mawardi did not violate any previous rule, as there was no previous constitution in this sense.

[313] Al-Mawardi 1881, 32–3.

[314] Lambton 1991a, 98; Hamid 2001, 8.

[315] Hamid 2001, 7.

Al-Mawardi also proposed also a systemic explanation of the birth of political power and of the institutions in Islamic history. He explained political institutions as phenomena that had emerged in the Muslims' historical transition from personalistic rule to a more sophisticated polity. This narrative deeply influenced the later political rationalists, especially Nizam al-Mulk and Ibn Khaldun.

The Sunni restoration was never a full recovery for the Abbasids. It did not end the cohabitation. In 1031, al-Qadir promised to 'comply with the requirements of support and fidelity' to the Buwayhids.[316] Yet, as the next chapter will demonstrate, the decline of the caliph continued, and it eventually became completely irrelevant. That also meant the end of the provincial order. Logically, a great deal of al-Mawardi's political thought became irrelevant as the historical setting that it referenced disappeared. Most of al-Mawardi's ideas would therefore be irrelevant to Ibn al-Muqaffa, who lived before him, and to Nizam al-Mulk, who lived after him. Seen as an example of Islamic political theory, there is nothing wrong with this, as al-Mawardi's political thought, being historical and empirical, reflected its human context. On the contrary, it is wrong to take his political thought out of its context, and imagine it as if it had been proposed as an idealistic model to remain valid in all times and circumstances.

---

[316] Mottahedeh 1980, 55–6.

3

NIZAM AL-MULK: ISLAMIC POLITICAL THEORY IN THE AGE OF STATES

As concluded in Chapter 2, despite the restoration efforts, the decline of the caliphate continued. The evolution of Islamic societies gradually gave birth to the last generation of provincial states, which would later become completely independent. These states were more sophisticated in terms of institutions, power and legitimacy. In this regard, the post-Mawardi period was the closing of the provincial order. Soon, the caliphate would become completely irrelevant, and the political fragmentation of the Islamic world would be finalised. Independent states would become the sole actors of politics in the Muslim world.

The Saljuqs' was a state of the late period of the provincial order. Having destroyed the Buwayhids, they established an Abbasid–Saljuqid cohabitation in Baghdad. They later dominated the Sunni world. Though they attached importance to their relations with the caliph, the Saljuqs (or Seljuqs) imagined themselves as having a self-established legitimacy. The Saljuq political thought was not caliph centred.

Nizam al-Mulk's political thought, the subject matter of this chapter, reflected this transition. We have in Nizam al-Mulk the first full-blown state-centred political thinker. What made this possible was the Saljuqs' separation of the caliphate and statehood. In Ibn al-Muqaffa, the political leader is the caliph in whom both politics (*dawla*) and religion are bestowed. Al-Mawardi's caliph, who was forced to share his political powers, symbolised the transitory period of overlapping and fluid institutions. In contrast, in Nizam al-Mulk, the sole reference is the Saljuq sultan, who monopolised political power, and separated himself from the caliph.

Saljuqs: From Nomadism to State

In the ninth century, the Oghuz Turks (organised as a federation under a leader, the *yabgu*) lived in the region that expands from the east of the Caspian to the Seyhun river.[1] A group from the Kınık tribe of this federation gradually gathered around Saljuq.[2] Driven mainly by the scarcity of pastures, this group – now called 'Saljuqs' – moved to Jand some time between 825 and 895.[3] This was the region with a warfare culture, at the forefront of jihad.[4] The Saljuqs converted to Islam when they understood that this was required to dominate the region.[5] Islam soon provided them with political opportunities: they declined to pay tax to the *yabgu*, arguing that Muslims cannot be taxed by non-Muslims,[6] and they raided the pagan Turks.[7] The Saljuqs developed economic relations with the Samanid merchants.[8]

The Turks had a nomadic lifestyle where military culture and economic survival were intertwined. Ibn Fadlan (d. 960), visiting the Turks around 921, described them as 'nomads who live in animal-hair tents that they pitch and strike regularly'.[9] The intersection of a nomadic culture and a militarism-conscious economy created a kinetic polity.

The Saljuqs' entry into the Muslim world coincided with the decline of the Samanids, and the rise of the Ghaznawids and Qarakhanids. But neither of the latter groups was able to fulfil the vacuum left by the Samanids, as both affected the region remotely, without strong local support. Furthermore, the Ghaznawids treated Khurasan as a tax-extraction field, and this created resentment.[10]

---

[1] Sevim and Merçil 1995, 1.
[2] Nishapuri 2001, 29; Fazlullah 2010, 70.
[3] Ibn al-Athir 2002, 31; Bar Hebraeus 1976, 195.
[4] Başan 2010, 22–3.
[5] Bar Hebraeus 1976, 195.
[6] Ibn al-Athir 2002, 31.
[7] Bosworth 1968b, 18.
[8] Sümer 1972, 43.
[9] Ibn Fadlan 2017, 10.
[10] Bosworth 1968b, 11–13.

At first the Saljuqs followed a pragmatic policy in their dealings with the two rivals, the Samanids and the Qarakhanids: they defended the Samanid territories against the Qarakhanids, which enabled them to intervene in Khurasani politics.[11] This helped them to counterbalance the Qarakhanids, with whom they competed for local jihadi networks.[12] A fruit of this policy was a pasture in Transoxiana, given by the Samanids in around 990.[13] This was their first serious interaction with the Persio-Islamic political culture.[14] However, the dissolution of the Samanids in 999 changed the regional balances, as the course of the Saljuqs' politics was inevitably to connect to another state: that of the Ghaznawids.

Saljuq died around 1009, and was replaced by his son, Arslan Israel. However, he was imprisoned by Mahmud in 1025, which assisted the rise of Chagri and Tugrul.[15] Mahmud settled some of Arslan's followers in Khurasan, expecting their support.[16] Meanwhile, the population of other Turks, led by Chagri and Tugrul, had already increased, and this created a dire need for pastures. Tugrul and Chagri entered Khurasan in 1035, without the Ghaznawids' consent.[17] When the new Ghaznawid sultan Masud tried to expel the Saljuqs in 1035, this resulted in the Nesa victory, pursuant to which the Saljuqs finally got a small territory of their own.[18] This was the Saljuqs' entrance into the provincial order as the embryonic sub-provincial state of the Ghaznawids. Reflecting this, they used Saljuqid and Ghaznawid symbols.[19] This was the beginning of Saljuq statehood in Khurasan, a region of Persio-Islamic political tradition.

Three years later, the Saljuqs took over Nishapur from the Ghaznawids.[20] As of 1000, Nishapur was the second largest city in the Muslim world, surpassed

---

[11] Ibn al-Athir 2002, 31.
[12] Turan 2008, 70–3.
[13] Fazlullah 2010, 71.
[14] Başan 2010, 23.
[15] Ibn al-Athir 2002, 13; Nishapuri 2001, 34.
[16] Al-Qazwini 1913, 93; Fazlullah 2010, 73 and 81.
[17] Gardizi 2011, 85 and 98.
[18] Turan 2008, 96.
[19] Köymen 1976, 6–9.
[20] Nishapuri 2001, 38.

	The Saljuqs / The Ghaznawids	The Abbasid Caliphs
	Mahmud of Ghazna (999–1030)	Caliph Al-Qadir (991–1031)
	Chagri (d. 1060)	
		Masud of Ghazna (1030–1040)
Nizam al-Mulk (1018–1092)	Tugrul (1037–1063)	Caliph Al-Qaim (1031–1075)
	Alp Arslan (1063–1072)	
	Malik-Shah (1072–1092)	Caliph Al-Muqtadi (1075–1094)

Figure 3.1 Nizam al-Mulk and political actors.

only by Baghdad.[21] In Nishapur, Tugrul sat on Masud's throne, and held *mazalim* court for the first time.[22] These were indications of the embracing of state institutions, and the abandoning of the traditional nomadic culture.

Finally, the Saljuqis destroyed the Ghaznawids in Dandanakan in 1040, which made Khurasan a safe region for them, and opened the gates of the Iranian lands.[23] Their prestige among Muslims increased.[24] Having destroyed the caliph's leading ally, the Saljuqs immediately wrote to Caliph al-Qaim to ask for official legitimacy, and to promise loyalty. Their request was well received. Al-Qaim sent an envoy that included his investitures who were given the mission of supervising whether the Saljuqs rule fairly (that is, without plundering people), and whether they send tribute to Baghdad.[25] The Saljuqs, a nomadic people whose founding leader, Saljuq, had died as recently as in

---

[21] Bulliet 2020, 101.
[22] Bar Hebraeus 1976, 199; Ibn al-Athir 2002, 26.
[23] Peacock 2010, 40–1; Rice 1961, 30.
[24] Fazlullah 2010, 92.
[25] Nishapuri 2001, 39–41; Bar Hebraeus 1976, 201–4.

1009, became a state in the provincial order. Tugrul and Chagri next divided the territories according to the Saljuq principle of collective sovereignty: Tugrul took the western territories; Chagri took Khurasan.[26]

The Abbasid–Saljuqid Cohabitation

Meanwhile, as the Buwayhids weakened, Basasiri, originally a Turkish slave and later the commander of Turkish troops, expanded his power to Basra and Anbar, and finally, took over Baghdad.[27] He forced Caliph al-Qaim to read his name in khutba.[28] Basasiri was the Fatimids' ally. The desperate caliph, who had no option other than to let the Saljuqs fill the vacuum left by the Ghaznawids, invited Tugrul to Baghdad. In al-Mawardi's jargon, the caliph was in *hajr*, thus he called for the help of friends.

After negotiations, Tugrul accepted the invitation, and arrived in Baghdad in December 1055. Basasiri left Baghdad after consulting with the Fatimids.[29] Tugrul's name was read in khutba. Tugrul, under the pretext of quelling the skirmishes between local Turkish and Dailami soldiers, terminated the 110-year Buwayhid rule by deposing their last ruler, al-Malik Khusraw. Ironically, Caliph al-Qaim, the head of the Sunnis, demanded that Tugrul release al-Malik, threatening that he will leave Baghdad if he does not. Tugrul did not back down: he put the Buwayhids' powers, such as taxation, under his management. As appeasement, he increased the caliph's funds, and arranged a marriage between the caliph and Chagri's daughter.[30]

Not seeing the Saljuqs as his equals, the caliph, however, did not meet Tugrul in person during his 13-month stay in Baghdad.[31] He once even warned Tugrul that Baghdad was the throne of the Arab people.[32] When his cousin Ibrahim Yınal revolted, Tugrul left Baghdad in January 1057.[33]

---

[26] Nishapuri 2001, 40; al-Qazwini 1913, 94.
[27] Ibn al-Athir 2002, 127; Daftary 2007, 195.
[28] Ibn Khallikan 1843a, 173.
[29] Ibn al-Athir 2002, 100; Fazlullah 2010, 100.
[30] Ibn al-Athir 2002, 100–2; Bar Hebraeus 1976, 207–9.
[31] Communication was handled by viziers. Bosworth 1968b, 47.
[32] Bar Hebraeus 1976, 207–9; Ibn al-Athir 2002, 108.
[33] Fazlullah 2010, 100.

This was followed by Basasiri's return, who made khutba and coins in the name of the Fatimid caliph. He ordered the officials (including the judges) to follow the Fatimid policies. This continued for three years in what appears as another *hajr*, as the caliph was under Uqaylid custody in Ani.[34] The desperate caliph again asked for Tugrul's help. Tugrul, after killing Ibrahim Yınal, came to Baghdad and restored the caliphate in 1060. Basasiri was killed. The second visit was a victorious one: when the caliph returned from Ani, Tugrul 'rose and took hold of the bridle of his mule, until he reached the gate of his apartments'. Al-Qaim praised Tugrul and assigned new titles to him. They met in person.[35] Tugrul laid down the rules of the Abbasid–Saljuqi cohabitation as he wished.[36] Like in the previous cohabitation, the Saljuqs and the Abbasids divided religious and temporal powers.[37] Paradoxically, the cohabitation of two Sunnis weakened the caliph's autonomy, as he could no longer use the Sunni–Shi'a confrontation card.

The Saljuqs adopted a supportive and respectful stance towards the caliph;[38] Tugrul kissed the ground when he met him.[39] They protected the caliph, and fulfilled other obligations, such as sending gifts and money to him, putting his name on coins, and reading khutba in his name.[40] Meanwhile, Alp Arslan, whose caliphal recognition came late, did not use the titles required pursuant to a caliphal recognition.[41] In the Manzikert war (1071), a caliphal envoy witnessed the Saljuqs' diplomatic correspondence with the Byzantine. The caliph was informed about the victory.[42] When Alp Arslan died, the Saljuqs sent an ambassador to Baghdad to acquire caliphal recognition for the new sultan.[43] In 1087, Malik-Shah asked for caliphal approval to appoint an heir.[44]

---

[34] Ibn al-Athir 2002, 121; Bar Hebraeus 1976, 214; Fazlullah 2010, 99–102.
[35] Nishapuri 2001, 42–3; Ibn al-Athir 2002, 114 and 126–31; Bar Hebraeus 1976, 215.
[36] Fazlullah 2010, 104–5; Nishapuri 2001, 44.
[37] Turan 2008, 307; Cahen 1969, 146.
[38] Hillenbrand 2022, 331.
[39] Ibn al-Athir 2002, 114; Bar Hebraeus 1976, 212.
[40] Hanne 2004/5, 168; Lowick 1970, 241–3.
[41] Köymen 1966, 11–16.
[42] Sevim and Merçil 1995, 63 and 72.
[43] Rizvi 1978, 169.
[44] Ibn al-Athir 2002, 234.

Marriages brought the two sides closer. In 1056, al-Qaim married Khadija Khatun, Chagri's daughter.[45] In 1071/2, al-Qaim's son, the would-be Caliph al-Muqtadi, married Alp Arslan's daughter.[46] Every caliph from the mid-eleventh to the mid-twelfth century had a Saljuq wife.[47]

However, the Saljuqs had absolute power to impose their policies upon the caliphate. In an event described by Ibn al-Athir as unprecedented, the caliph was forced to imprison a man who had sought sanctuary from the Abbasids.[48] The event symbolised the end of the immunity that the Abbasid palace had enjoyed in the previous cohabitation. The Saljuqs re-allocated several estates of al-Qaim to other people in 1073. In 1075, the Saljuqs, facing a financial crisis, collected taxes in Baghdad despite the caliph's opposition.[49] Alp Arslan once limited the caliph's funds to protest against the caliph's vizier.[50] In 1078/9, as part of communal strife between Hanbali and Shafi groups, the Saljuqs managed the dismissal of the caliph's vizier.[51]

However, these developments were the Saljuqs' responses to the political setting, rather than a deliberate policy of weakening the caliphate. Indeed, the Saljuqs imagined themselves as having their own legitimacy that did not necessitate external approval. But, like the Buwayhids, they needed the caliphate in their relations with the Sunni world, as well as to counterbalance the Fatimids.[52] There were also cases where native Saljuqi legitimacy was not enough. When Saljuqs took over Samarqand from the Qarakhanids in 1089, their governor was killed in the turmoil caused by local people.[53] The Saljuqs needed caliphal legitimacy to varying degrees, even after the reign of Malik-Shah.[54]

Baghdad was the locus of the Saljuqid–Abbasid cohabitation, not the Saljuq capital. Sultans did not stay there for long periods. No sultan set foot

---

[45] Ibid., 103–4.
[46] Bosworth 1991, 275.
[47] Peacock 2015, 140–1.
[48] Ibn al-Athir 2002, 115.
[49] Usta 2013, 100–2.
[50] Köymen 1966, 8.
[51] Ibn al-Athir 2002, 196.
[52] Bosworth 1991, 274.
[53] Sevim and Merçil 1995, 119.
[54] Lambton 1968, 206–7.

in Baghdad between 1063 and 1086/7.[55] While Malik-Shah visited Baghdad only three times, Alp Aslan never visited.[56]

The Saljuqs were represented by a *shihna* in Baghdad. The most famous one was Gawharayn, appointed by Alp Arslan.[57] The *shihna* had the duties of keeping public order, the allocation of the caliph's allowances, the levying of taxes in Baghdad (and wider Iraq), and the securing of the inclusion of the sultan's name in khutba.[58] There was, however, a conflict of jurisdiction in Baghdad. Both the Saljuqid and Abbasid officials played roles chaotically in the quelling of communal strife.[59] The caliph had his *diwan* and officials in charge of Baghdad's administration.[60] Through his agents, he also monopolised the moral policing of his domain.[61] For example, in 1076, al-Muqtadi prohibited the selling of wine, and closed down the brothels and other places of entertainment. This was a strategy to revive his influence. But such policies were subject to a supportive political setting.[62] The caliphs sought to prevent the local people becoming attached to the Saljuqs. To achieve this, they employed various tactics, like easing taxation in Baghdad before the visits of Saljuq sultans. Al-Muqtadi, in 1082, initiated construction projects to counterbalance the Saljuqs' constructions that had begun after Tugrul's first visit.[63]

The exception was Tugrul's strategy to make Baghdad the capital during the later years of his rule, when he intended also to declare his grandson Ja'far, Caliph al-Muqtadi's son, as the caliph.[64] As part of this plan, the Saljuqs initiated large constructions in Baghdad. The project, however, failed when Tugrul died in 1092.[65]

---

[55] Peacock 2015, 143.
[56] Hanne 2007, 98; Bosworth 1968b, 60.
[57] Ibn al-Athir 2002, 173–4.
[58] Bosworth 1991, 275.
[59] Hanne 2007, 121.
[60] Renterghem 2011, 119.
[61] Ephrat 2011, 149.
[62] Ibn al-Athir 2002, 236 and 184.
[63] Hanne 2007, 118.
[64] Golden 1992, 233; Hanne 2004/5, 146.
[65] Ibn al-Athir 2002, 250.

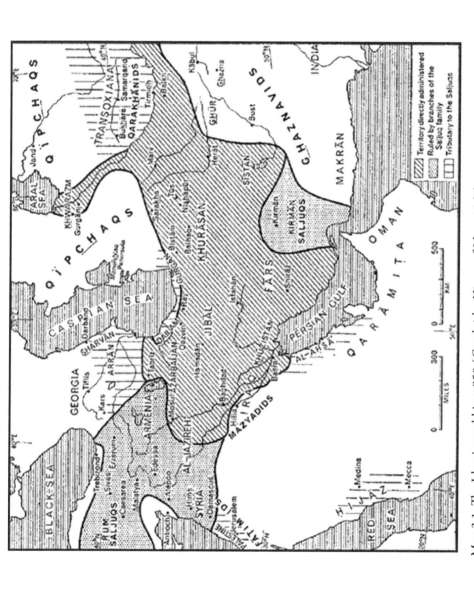

Map 3.1 The Islamic world in c.950 (*Cambridge History of Islam*, 1968).

The Life of Nizam al-Mulk

Nizam al-Mulk was born in 1018 (the year al-Qadir declared his creed), in Tus, Khurasan, as a 'citizen' of the Ghaznawids. His early life coincided with the Ghaznawids' imposition of Sunnism, and persecution of heretics. Mahmud is praised in *Siyasatnama* for fighting against heretics in support of al-Qadir.[66]

Nizam al-Mulk studied Islamic law and traditions. His cultural background provided him with a knowledge of Sasanid culture. He learnt Arabic in his early education.[67] He was taught by the leading Shafi scholar in Nishapur, Imam Muwaffaq (d. 1048),[68] who might have nurtured his enthusiasm for Shafism.[69] Nizam al-Mulk was also taught by others, like Abu'l-Qasim al-Qushayri (d. 1072).[70] He had an interest in the religious sciences.[71]

Nizam al-Mulk had a *dihqan* family.[72] His father later became a tax-farmer in Ghaznawid Tus.[73] He first gained administrative experience as a government official in Ghaznawid Khurasan. This experience was influential: he makes references to Mahmud in *Siyasatnama*. His family later fled to Ghazna when his father failed to deliver the required amount of tax because of the Saljuq attacks on Tus.[74] However, Ghazna, too, failed. After 1040, Nizam al-Mulk started working for Ali ibn Shadan, the ruler of Balkh under Saljuq control.[75] His transition to the Saljuq administration concluded in Marv.[76] Nizam al-Mulk became Alp Aslan's secretary. He later worked for ten years as the vizier of Alp Arslan, and almost twenty years for Malik-Shah.

Nizam al-Mulk was a statesman. Ibn Khallikan described him as ruling the state while Malik-Shah enjoyed the pleasures of the chase.[77] Ibn al-Athir reported

---

[66] Nizam al-Mulk 2002, 65–6.
[67] Lambton 1984, 55.
[68] Rizvi 1978, 2.
[69] Bosworth 1968b, 56.
[70] Safi 2006, 48.
[71] Ibn al-Athir 2002, 257; Ibn Khallikan 1843a, 413.
[72] Al-Bayhaqi 2004, 182.
[73] Lambton 1984, 55.
[74] Paul 2013, 8.
[75] Ibn al-Athir 2002, 256; Ibn Khallikan 1843a, 413.
[76] Yavari 2008a, 352.
[77] Ibn Khallikan 1843a, 413.

	Periods	Processes	Political Model
Nizam al-Mulk (1018–1092)	1000–1028	Emergence of Seljuqs	Provincial system
	1028–1040	Decline of Ghaznawids Rise of Seljuqs	
	1040–1055	Consolidation of Seljuqs	
	1055–1092	Seljuqi–Abbasid cohabitation	

Figure 3.2 Nizam al-Mulk and the historical setting.

to Malik-Shah, saying to him 'I hand over to you all affairs'.[78] After the sultan, he was the main executor of taxation, foreign policy and military operations.[79] He commanded armies in wars like the Manzikert, as well as in the intra-Saljuqi battles like the one between Sultan Alp Arslan and his great uncle Kutalmish.[80] He was even the chief commander of the Fars expedition in 1071/2.[81]

Islamic Political Theory in *Siyasatnama*

Siyasatnama was written in response to Malik-Shah who, in 1086, wanted comments and suggestions on the conditions of the country when policies were observed by the previous kings, but were unknown to the Saljuqs.[82] He later added eleven parts around 1091, shortly before his assassination, to respond to the imminent developments, including the plots against him.[83] *Siyasatnama* is therefore a pragmatic treatise that deals with concrete problems of state management. This is not a work of philosophical idealism or Islamic law.[84] It is along the lines of Ibn al-Muqaffa's *Risala*.[85]

---

[78] Ibn al-Athir 2002, 181.
[79] Lambton 1984, 55; Hillenbrand 2022, 254.
[80] Taneri 1970, 124–5; Rizvi 1980, 111; Nicolle 2013, 23.
[81] Ibn al-Athir 2002, 175.
[82] Nizam al-Mulk 2002, 1.
[83] Meisami 2007, 146; Rizvi 1978, 27.
[84] Simidchieva 2004, 101; Rizvi 1978, 42 and 50; Meisami 2007, 149; Starr 2013, 389.
[85] Lambton 1984, 55–6.

Nizam al-Mulk uses two reference sets to justify his arguments. Firstly, the cases are collected from the political history of various nations, but mainly of the Tahirids, Ghaznawids and Samanids. In effect, he addresses the shared political memory of his times.[86] Secondly, he addresses the ongoing developments and dynamics of Saljuq politics as he observes them.

As Ann K. S. Lambton says, *Siyasatnama* is not a mirror.[87] C. E. Bosworth and Andrew Peacock share this view.[88] In this regard, *Siyasatnama* reminds us of the general problem of seeing mirrors as literary or fiction texts. Erik Ohlander seeks to correct this view of mirrors, arguing that, written in a period of crisis, mirrors reflect the competition of provincial states and the caliphate, when authority and legitimacy is contested. They reflect the changing semantics of the political vocabulary in that context.[89]

When it comes to the developments to which Nizam al-Mulk responded, the first of them was the rise of the Saljuqs in the provincial order, and their replacing the Buwayhids in Baghdad. The second was the domestic developments in the Saljuq society, particularly their transformation from a nomadic culture into a Persio-Islamic statehood. Third was the personal problems Nizam al-Mulk faced because of the various plots against him.

Below, I shall analyse Nizam al-Mulk's political thought by contextualising it in its historical time. *Siyasatnama* includes many subjects, from diplomacy to private drinking parties. I therefore analyse *Siyasatnama* through several subjects that I define as central themes, but I add many other themes to provide a detailed view of Nizam al-Mulk's political thought.

Nizam al-Mulk on state

Nizam al-Mulk lived three centuries after Ibn al-Muqaffa, when the separation of caliphate and state had almost ended, giving way to independent states.[90] He naturally had a strong conception of the state. He lived just after the euphoria caused by al-Qadir's restoration had faded. The caliph

---

[86] Simidchieva 2004, 101; Paul 2018b, 24.
[87] Lambton 1984, 56.
[88] Peacock 2015, 67; Bosworth 1990, 167.
[89] Ohlander 2009, 240–1.
[90] Gibb 1955a, 20.

having been three years (1057–60) in Uqaylid custody, and the imposition of Fatimid politics in Baghdad, virtually destroyed caliph-centred political thought. A new thinking emerged among Muslims that saw the state as the central element.

This was observed even among the jurists. For example, al-Juwayni (1028–95) in *al-Giyathi*, unlike al-Mawardi, no longer required a Quraishi lineage for leadership. He historicised the condition as the creation of past perceptions and circumstances.[91] Unlike al-Mawardi, who contributed to al-Qadir's restoration, al-Juwayni held out no hope for a revival of the caliphate.[92] He was the head of the Nizamiyya College ruled by Nizam al-Mulk, where there was a Turkish-dominated polity in which the Arab/Quraishi lineage was completely irrelevant. But, unsurprisingly, al-Juwayni justified al-Mawardi's rulership by usurpation (*amr 'istila*).[93] This was borrowed, however, only to justify the Saljuqs.[94]

Emphasis on the state is much stronger in Nizam al-Mulk's work, as he was not interested in religious articulations, unlike his employee al-Juwayni. *Siyasatnama* has 'state' as the justifier of political reasoning. Nowhere does he appeal to religious reasoning in *Siyasatnama*.[95] This can be best illustrated by breaking Nizam al-Mulk's conception of the state down into its constituent parts.

The Origin and Nature of the State

Nizam al-Mulk, following al-Mawardi, saw the state as a historical formation that emerged in a later period of Islamic history. State is not ontologically a religious construct for him. The early Muslims had no state. That was a time of faith, when people solved their problems by personal methods, needing no institutions. Even justice was dispensed among them in person, not through

---

[91] Al-Juwayni 2011, 257–8.
[92] Hallaq 1984, 30.
[93] Nizam al-Mulk 2002, 427. Written thirty years after al-Mawardi's *Ahkam*, al-Juwayni's justification of rule by sheer power is not original. Its significance is in that this justification is systematically incorporated into Islamic law. Siddiqui 2019, 252–3.
[94] Crone 2005, 234; Lambton 1991a, 106.
[95] Rizvi 1978, 50.

a delegation. Gradually, Muslim society became complex, and required new methods to transcend the personalistic ways of problem-solving.

However, since they were not skilled in developing advanced institutions, they borrowed them from other nations. Nizam al-Mulk reminds us that the *mazalim* tribune was borrowed from the Persians.[96] This was a turning point in several ways. To begin with, it symbolised the birth of political autonomy as the *mazalim* introduced a new level of administration beyond personalistic methods. Delegations replaced personal ways. People were assigned the powers to be delegated, and this created a distinction between them and other persons. This was the birth of 'the public', where officials act in the name of institutions beyond personal capacity.

Secondly, this narrative saw the state in non-canonical terms. As institutions like the *mazalim* were borrowed from the Persians, they were in origin non-canonical. As a matter of fact, having emerged after the Prophet, they were necessarily non-canonical. This cross-cultural interaction justified the imagining of politics as subject to general rules beyond religious demarcations. This is, as R. Stephen Humphreys remarks, to define political concepts such as 'justice' as 'rationally knowable and advocated by all decent religions, not Islam alone'.[97] A general consequence of this approach is that political reasoning, as its framework of reference goes beyond Islam, cannot be reduced to juristic legal reasoning.

This notion of general laws is detected in Nizam al-Mulk in the form of 'ancient customs and institutions which good kings have laid down'.[98] In that list of wise kings whose names 'will be blessed until the resurrection' are not only Muslim Umar but also the Greek Alexander and the Persian Ardashir.[99] Political differences are similarly meaningless: Mahmud of the Ghaznawids, Ismail bin Ahmad of the Samanids, Umar bin Abd al-Aziz of the Umayyads and Harun Rashid of the Abbasids were wise names whose opinions should

---

[96] Nizam al-Mulk 2002, 42 and 13.
[97] Humphreys 1991, 164–5.
[98] Nizam al-Mulk 2002, 243.
[99] Ibid., 61. Nizam al-Mulk (2022, 32) described Anushirwan almost as a *hanif*: 'When he was a youth his nature was infused with justice right from infancy; he recognized evil things as evil, and he knew what was good.' Also see Tor 2011a, 119–21.

be followed.[100] As Gibb notes, the *Siyasatnama* is not a religious text, as 'its arguments are based on expediency, and its proofs are drawn from history and experience'.[101]

This is a shift from a religious discourse to a neutral, technical discourse in political thought. The ideas and the identities of actors are pushed back: instead, general rules are accepted as affecting everyone, regardless of their religion, nation or political opinion. Politics was imagined in structural terms, such that those terms affect individuals equally, by general rules. This logically reframed culture and religion as no longer a general category, which, though not rejected, is interpreted by general rules.

The Autonomy of the State

In Nizam al-Mulk, the state is the highest authority to unite people at all levels. No actor, not even a jurist, can exercise a right that is not legitimised by the state. Law enforcement is exclusively a function of the state's sovereignty. In what looks like a proto-modern (or a proto-Weberian) analysis, Nizam defines the state as the monopolist agent of violence:

> Whatever concerns the king and falls to him to do or to order, such as castigation, decapitation, mutilation, castration or any other kind of punishment – if anyone does such a thing without the king's permission or command, even to his own servant or slave, the king must not agree to it but have the man punished, so that others may take warning and know their places.[102]

As an extension of this view, Nizam al-Mulk saw judges as administrative organs. The government should have information about every judge, as it is responsible for employing qualified judges. Judges that do wrong are dismissed by the sultan.[103] Nizam al-Mulk also promoted paying the salaries of doctors of religion out of the treasury.[104] For him, the salary is an efficient

---

[100] Nizam al-Mulk 2002, 61.
[101] Gibb 1955a, 21. Also see Lambton 1956, 135.
[102] Nizam al-Mulk 2002, 73.
[103] Ibid., 42 and 47.
[104] Ibid., 59–60.

means of generating political loyalty.[105] The state's monopolistic authority to dominate everything is mostly visible when Nizam al-Mulk quotes the Iranian maxim that kingship and religion are like two brothers.[106] As Lambton clarified, the maxim is quoted not on religious but on political grounds.[107] It symbolises the end of the autonomy of religion in the political field. Religion is still important, but as it is instrumentalised by the state. Correspondingly, heresy is treated as a political concept in many paragraphs of *Siyasatnama*.[108]

Not Transcendental

Nizam al-Mulk wanted the Saljuqs to develop an advanced state in line with the Iranian tradition. However, this never meant that he imagined the state as transcendental, and explained it as a historical formation. That is, he did not idealise it. On the contrary, he even held a sceptical view of state: *Siyasatnama* is full of the mistakes of rulers, including those of the Saljuq sultans. He held that officers at all levels are prone to corruption, and suggested that the king should supervise them, or even the vizier might do that.[109] He warned that there may be 'self-interested and oppressive persons' among officers.[110] Even of the idealised political figures of *Siyasatnama*, many are presented in their human condition, such as being drunk, corrupt or jealous.

Siyasatnama does not glamorise or praise the state. For Nizam al-Mulk the state is subject to social, political and economic dynamics. He witnessed the fall of the Ghaznawids, and how the Saljuqs strived to develop an advanced state. His political career is full of agendas and strategies for fixing problems within the state. Knowing that the state is fraught with problems, Nizam al-Mulk sought to achieve a strong and efficient state. To that end, he suggested the erection of political and institutional solutions, such as giving people easy access to the holders of power to report the injustices they face.[111]

---

[105] Ibid., 64.
[106] Ibid., 60.
[107] Lambton 1968, 211. Immediately after this maxim, Nizam al-Mulk (2002, 60) warns that 'the worst among the learned men is he who seeks the society of the king'.
[108] Nizam al-Mulk 2002, 14–22, 161 and 188.
[109] Ibid., 31 and 47.
[110] Ibid., 21–2 and 14.
[111] Ibid., 61.

He did not promote idealistic problem-solving prescriptions. Not being transcendental, the state for Nizam al-Mulk is a man-made historical construct that corrupts easily. Efforts to fix it should therefore be continuous.

Legitimacy

Nizam al-Mulk explained political legitimacy in a way that makes justice, not religion, the chief element in state–society relations.[112] This was formulated as 'a kingdom may last while there is irreligion, but it will not endure when there is oppression'.[113] He defined justice as a political and administrative manifestation of religion. Religion matters because it contributes to the social order, not because of its abstract truth value.[114] Religion exists to serve a higher goal: justice. Consequently, religion is no longer the most important concept: 'There is nothing better than justice', as it 'is the measure of all good things', even of 'the glory of the faith'.[115] This effectively amounted to the defining of religion in terms of politics, and to the consequent creation of a public/political religiosity: God's most expected act from rulers is to provide justice,[116] while the greatest sins are tyranny and injustice.[117]

Statehood versus the Nomadic Culture

A great deal of Nizam al-Mulk's political thought was a response to the Saljuqs' transformation into a Persio-Islamic state. *Siyasatnama* outlines his views and efforts to help the Saljuqs in this transition.

The Saljuq period, as Carol Hillenbrand puts it, was an encounter between the long-Islamised eastern Iranian provinces and their high level of culture, and the nomadic lifestyle of the newly converted Saljuqs.[118] Ibn Fadlan depicted this encounter thus: the Turks do not clean themselves; they avoid contact with water. He illustrated their limited knowledge of Islam by narrating that a Turk once asked him whether God had a wife.[119] Many Saljuqi

---

[112] Lambton 1984, 56; 1988, 35.
[113] Nizam al-Mulk 2002, 43.
[114] Humphreys 1991, 164–5. Also see Tor 2011a, 119.
[115] Nizam al-Mulk 2002, 49.
[116] Ibid., 12.
[117] Ibid., 43.
[118] Hillenbrand 2022, 182.
[119] Ibn Fadlan 2017, 10–11.

sultans were illiterate.[120] Naturally, they did not speak Arabic. In *Saljuqnama* (written in *c.*1175), Chagri, during the gathering of the troops on the night before the Dandanakan war, asked the meaning of the verses read by a soldier. He did not know them.[121] Knowing the Saljuqs' limited knowledge of Islam, Nizam al-Mulk reframes piety not as 'one's competence' in Arabic grammar, but as 'knowing what one ought to know'.[122] However, the Saljuqs had created a strong empire that was advanced in trade, culture and the arts. An exhibition at the Metropolitan Museum of Art has displayed a brilliant collection of Saljuqid art.[123] Though personal attainments in the arts were not high, the sultans recorded great developments through patronage.[124]

The transition from nomadic to Persian administrative culture divided the early Saljuqs into two groups: the *traditionalists* and the *reformists*. While the former defended the traditional nomadic culture, the latter defended the embracing of the Persio-Islamic institutions. This required that the reformist sultans adopt a policy of appeasing the traditionalists by finding them pastures. But that was not easy, due to their nomadic patterns: Turkmen who had been given pastures developed a new motivation to search for new lands.[125] The movements of the nomadic Turkmen (along with their women, children and livestock), versed in military techniques like archery, was always accompanied by the plundering and attacking of local people.[126] These nomads were critical of the policies that the Saljuqs adopted as part of their adaptation to the provincial order, and saw them as detrimental to their economic lifestyle.[127] When they were not satisfied, they immediately organised themselves into a political opposition. This made Saljuq politics subject to two contending dynamics: the policies of the sultan, and Turkmens' independent activities.[128]

---

[120] Meisami 2007, 141.
[121] Fazlullah 2010, 90; Nishapuri 2001, 37–8.
[122] Nizam al-Mulk 2002, 44 and 61.
[123] See Canby *et al.* 2016, 308–9.
[124] Lambton 1968, 205.
[125] *Hudud al Alam* says of them: 'In summer and winter they wander from place to place.' Minorsky 1982, 94.
[126] A single Turkmen family might have around 100 sheep, which meant that a 3,000-strong army would have 300,000 sheep. Peacock 2015, 45.
[127] Köymen 1970, 6; Bosworth 2011, 16.
[128] Bosworth 1968b, 62.

The Saljuqs could not ignore the Turkmen, as they needed their military contribution. For example, Tutush, supported by irregular Turkmen forces, secured the Saljuq interest in Syria;[129] this ended the Fatimid rule of Damascus that had been in place for more than a century.[130] Besides, they were the demographic basis of an expanding empire to the west, where Turks were the minority.[131] Nizam al-Mulk reported Alp Arslan's warning to the Turks that they are foreigners in western Iran.[132]

The Saljuq political elite pursued a strategy of weakening, but also managing, the nomadic dynamics of the Turkmen in the effort to achieve a Persio-Islamic statehood.[133] This created what Anthony Black describes as a dialectic between the nomadic tribe and the state.[134] To minimise their impact, the Saljuqs encouraged the Turkmen to continue their expeditions for new pastures. This was also relevant in terms of legitimacy: it was not enough to permit the nomads' plundering; the leader was obliged also to actively assist them.[135] After 1045, expeditions to south Caucasia, eastern Anatolia and north-western Iran were authorised. This tactic was used by Tugrul, Alp Arslan and Malik-Shah.[136] These campaigns, having no intention of annexing territory nor even of taxing the inhabitants, helped the Turkmen occupy new pastures, and to attack towns in their vicinity that threatened their control of the pastures.[137]

This intricate dynamic of Saljuq politics gave rise to a moving state.[138] The sultans, particularly Tugrul and Alp Aslan, spent long periods travelling on expeditions.[139] Saljuqs had no fixed capital. Their centre was where the sultan happened to be.[140] Each sultan used a city as their capital for a while:

---

[129] Ibn al-Athir 2002, 197.
[130] Havemann 1989, 234.
[131] Kafesoğlu 1972, 131; Starr 2013, 386.
[132] Nizam al-Mulk 2002, 161.
[133] Cahen 1969, 147.
[134] Black 2011, 92.
[135] Peacock 2005, 225.
[136] Nicolle 2013, 14; Hillenbrand 2007, 6; Brauer 1995, 54.
[137] Peacock 2015, 46.
[138] Divitçioğlu 2000, 104–5.
[139] Lambton 1968, 204–5.
[140] Hillenbrand 2011, 23.

Nishapur was the first capital. Later, Tugrul used Ray[141] and Alp Arslan used Isfahan.[142] Malik-Shah used both Isfahan and Ray.[143] In their collective rule, Chagri and Tugrul used Marv and Ray separately.[144]

Nomadic plundering, however, meant the destruction of cities without ever intending to occupy them.[145] The Turkmen were unfamiliar with the concept of defined frontiers, and with the concept of the sanctity of land as property.[146] Classical resources informed on the Turkmen's plundering of cities and regions like Hamadan, Ray, Kirman, Wasit, Basra, Ahwaz and Ani.[147] The Saljuqs were seen as barbarians by the settled population of the Iranian world.[148] This prevented the formation of strong relations between the local people and Saljuqs, and more importantly, of a stable state in which a regular taxation and administration of land systems could be established. For example, when the Turkmen plundered Sawad in 1055/6, people fled from the cities.[149] The Saljuqs' endless 'conquests' of Muslim cities created a frustration in Baghdad. Having received the Saljuqs' inflated victory communiques after they took over Samarqand, the caliph's vizier, Abu Shuja, complained that this was not a conquest of Byzantine land.[150]

The Saljuqs, particularly the reformists, grasped the necessity of embracing a Persio-Islamic administrative model, for two reasons. Firstly, they were strangers to the business of ruling a territorial state that had the long-established traditions of a Persio-Islamic past.[151] They had first encountered state institutions – mostly left by the Ghaznawids – when they entered the Iranian world.[152] Secondly, the provincial order required states to prioritise

---

[141] Fazlullah 2010, 95.
[142] Lambton 1968, 223.
[143] Fazlullah 2010, 133; Nishapuri 2001, 61; Ibn al-Athir 2002, 82.
[144] Bosworth 1968b, 49.
[145] Peacock 2005, 224–5.
[146] Bosworth 1968b, 20.
[147] Ibn al-Athir 2002, 14–18, 47–51, 131 and 155; Nishapuri 2001, 53.
[148] Peacock 2010, 54; 2015, 1. Bosworth (1968b, 15) writes that the Saljuqs appeared in Transoxiana and Khurasan as marauders and plunderers.
[149] Ibn al-Athir 2002, 51, 102 and 131.
[150] Ibid. 248–9.
[151] Sevim 1998, 158.
[152] Bosworth 1968b, 11 and 21; Kafesoğlu 1972, 143.

power delegation, peace treaties and the protection of urban areas. When Chagri wanted to plunder Nishapur in 1038 according to the nomadic tradition, Tugrul stopped him by reminding him of the caliph's letter, which had warned them against such acts.[153]

Tugrul's stance was not surprising, as he had managed the early correspondence with the caliph, and had met the caliph's envoy, al-Mawardi.[154] Also, he had benefitted from the provincial order: he was recognised by the caliph as *sultan al-dawla*.[155] Tugrul used his relations with the caliph to consolidate himself as a strong ruler.[156] More importantly, Tugrul had taken the Saljuq territories in western Iran when he shared the lands with Chagri after Dandanakan. Tugrul's political destiny, reminiscent of Muʿawiya's Syria, was linked to western Iran.

As the foremost reformist, Tugrul – whom we could dub 'the Saljuqs' Umar' – pursued a synthesis on the Persio-Islamic model. Bar Hebraeus (d. 1286) described Tugrul's wearing of 'the white apparel [made] of cotton',[157] which marked his adoption of Iranian clothes. In Nishapur, he sat on Masud's throne,[158] led the Redress, and gave other indications of adaptation to Persio-Islamic statehood.[159] He asked the advice of a local judge, Abu'l Qasim al-Juwayni, confessing that he did not know the relevant codes of administration.[160]

The Saljuqs later benefitted from the former Samanid and Ghaznawid bureaucrats.[161] Tugrul did not shun diplomacy: in 1048/9, he made a treaty with the Byzantine. In exchange for his help in the release of the king of

---

[153] Ibn al-Athir 2002, 26; Nishapuri 2001, 41.
[154] Bar Hebraeus 1976, 201 and 206.
[155] Qazwini 1913, 95. Tugrul's near-obsession with marrying the caliph's daughter was about the strategy to use his relations with the caliph to help him become a prestigious ruler beyond other provincial states: Makdisi 1970a, 260–1. When the caliph rejected the marriage, Tugrul decreased the caliph's funds, and arrested his men to compel him. The marriage contract was arranged after three years of negotiations. Ibn al-Athir 2002, 137–9; Nishapuri 2001, 44–5.
[156] El-Hibri 2021, 204.
[157] Bar Hebraeus 1976, 201.
[158] Fazlullah 2010, 88.
[159] Bosworth 1968b, 23.
[160] Peacock 2015, 47.
[161] They had a near shortage of qualified and educated officials. Taneri 1970, 118.

Georgia, an ally of Byzantine, he had the small mosque in Constantinople repaired, where his name was read in khutba,[162] which consolidated his fame among Muslims.

Tugrul faced the traditionalists' resistance. When he went to Baghdad in 1055, Turkmen troops devastated the agricultural lands and plundered the villages.[163] The Turkmen, reminiscent of the Arabs who had criticised Umar's *diwan*, resisted Tugrul's new standards because they eroded the Turkmen's nomadic autonomy. Tugrul not plundering Qazvin in 1042/3, due to a contract with the local people, upset the Turkmen.[164] His strategic wars were meaningless to Turkmen, who understood 'war' as 'plundering'. In 1084, the Turkmen, led by Artuk, rejected a peace deal with the local leader of Mosul by asking: 'Do you wish to turn back empty and without spoil?'[165]

The Turkmen's discontent was more dangerous when it was abused by the traditionalist Saljuq royals. Once, Tugrul's cousin, Rasultegin, attacked Hazarasb (a person to whom Tugrul had assigned the tax-farming of Basra, Khuzestan and Shiraz). Tugrul supported Hazarasb's wish to fight with Rasultegin to save this contract.[166] In 1050, Chagri's son marched into Fars from Marv, and plundered several cities in the region, without informing Tugrul. In the apology letter to the Buwayhid ruler Jalal al-Dawla, Tugrul confessed that he could not stop the Turkmen.[167]

One strategy to overcome the resistance was to recruit slave soldiers (*ghulam*). This was another indication of the adoption of Persio-Islamic statehood.[168] It began after Tugrul's visit to Baghdad in 1055, and became a permanent strategy during Alp Arslan's reign.[169] The army came closest to being an exclusively *ghulam* army during the reign of Malik-Shah.[170] Resentful Turkmen naturally reacted to *ghulam*. In 1076, a group of them

---

[162] Ibn al-Athir 2002, 73–5; Kafesoğlu 1972, 35.
[163] Peacock 2015, 50.
[164] Ibn al-Athir 2002, 50.
[165] Bar Hebraeus 1976, 228.
[166] Ibn al-Athir 2002, 115.
[167] Ibid., 23 and 78.
[168] Lambton 1968, 218; Kafesoğlu 1972, 132.
[169] Peacock 2010, 73 and 95–6; Cahen 1969, 142.
[170] Köymen 1970, 8.

shifted to the Fatimids during a military encounter.[171] Several Turkmen leaders entered Arab and Byzantine service.[172]

A more harmful situation, as briefly mentioned above, was the Turkmen's support of the royals who were critical of the Persio-Islamic agenda.[173] This dangerous dynamic was most effective in times of intra-royal fights triggered by collective sovereignty. Sovereignty was collectively held by the Saljuq family (Map 3.1). Any male member had the right to claim rulership, and the lands were divided among royals.[174]

Ibrahim Yinal revolted in 1055. He, presenting himself as a traditional leader, plundered Azerbaijan and eastern Anatolia.[175] He was immediately supported by Turkmen who were annoyed by Tugrul's policies of recruiting *ghulam*, centralisation, and by his strategic wars in western Iran, which did not fit in with the nomadic practices of herding and plundering.[176] They even imposed the condition on Ibrahim Yinal that he may not normalise relations with Tugrul.[177]

Claiming his right to rule, Kutalmish, Arslan's son, revolted in 1061.[178] His role in traditional plunders since the Caucasia expedition in 1038 had already made him popular among Turkmen.[179] As Tugrul had died during the revolt, Kutalmish appeared with a large Turkmen army to confront Alp Arslan.[180] As Bosworth sees it, this was an encounter of two paradigms: the nomadic Turkmen versus the new army in line with the Persio-Islamic rules.[181] The impact of the Turkmen was so huge that Alp Arslan, having quelled the revolt, organised expeditions for plunder to appease the Turkmen.[182]

---

[171] Sevim and Merçil 1995, 86.
[172] Sümer 1972, 107–8.
[173] Peacock 2011, 79.
[174] Turan 2008, 305; Paul 2011, 99.
[175] Ibn al-Athir 2002, 67 and 125; Nishapuri 2001, 42.
[176] Turan 2008, 125; Peacock 2015, 51 and 224; Cahen 1969, 145.
[177] Sümer 1972, 106. This probably left no option for Tugrul other than to kill him.
[178] Nishapuri 2001, 45.
[179] Peacock 2005, 217–20.
[180] Ibn al-Athir 2002, 178.
[181] Bosworth 1968b, 58.
[182] Peacock 2015, 54.

Kavurd revolted in 1073, after the death of Alp Arslan, when Malik-Shah had just taken the throne.[183] Ruling Kirman as part of a collective sovereignty, Kavurd, Malik-Shah's uncle, developed strong connections with Turkmen, who saw him as a traditional leader who might challenge the centralisation plans.[184] He even had supporters within the army.[185] We see Nizam al-Mulk on the side of reformists in the midst of this crisis. He distributed money to Turkmen soldiers to regain their loyalty.[186] Malik-Shah could then defeat Kavurd with the help of Kurdish and Arab troops.[187] Seeing that some troops still supported Kavurd, Malik-Shah executed his uncle on the advice of Nizam al-Mulk.[188]

In search of a state

Al-Kunduri was the first vizier to experience the Saljuqs' transition from nomadism to a state. He had virtually stage-managed the process of the Abbasids' creation of the new cohabitation in Baghdad. He had led negotiations with the caliphate before Tugrul's first visit to Baghdad; he had brokered the marriage of al-Qaim to Khadija Khatun.[189]

Similarly, Nizam al-Mulk contributed to the policy of embracing Persio-Islamic statehood. In the grand intra-Saljuqid debate between the reformists and the traditionalists, Nizam al-Mulk was with the reformists. An indication of this stance is that he had a negative view of Turkmen. 'Turk' is almost the symbol of uncultured behaviour in *Siyasatnama*. In one case this work relates, a man who rejected payment for a good act he did says that acting otherwise would have made him a worse oppressor than a Turk. In another case, a Turkish amir drugged a young woman to rape her. Listing the indications of the times of discord and collapse, Nizam al-Mulk mentions the Turks' adopting titles proper to civil dignitaries, and the latter taking titles that belong to

---

[183] Qazwini 1913, 96; Fazlullah 2010, 126.
[184] Köymen 1970, 5–6.
[185] Nishapur 2001, 57–8.
[186] Sümer 1972, 108.
[187] Peacock 2015, 132.
[188] Fazlullah 2010, 127; Nishapur 2001, 58–9.
[189] Hillenbrand 2022, 162–8 and 271.

Turks.[190] Nizam al-Mulk saw Turkmen as not having the cultural capacity to fit the urban and political standards of Persian-Islamic high culture.

This cultivated a mixed policy of balance and gradualism in Nizam al-Mulk's thinking. He supported the Saljuqs' reforms, but knew that they could succeed only slowly. This is observed in his approach to *ghulam*. Nizam al-Mulk, who had his own *ghulam* army, naturally supported this policy. The Saljuqs preferred the *ghulam* for their loyalty. A *ghulam*, technically a slave, had loyalty only to his master.[191] *Siyasatnama* gives the case of a *ghulam* who did not hesitate to break the law to protect his master.[192] Managing the *ghulam* was easier than managing the free Turkmen.[193] This helped the Saljuqs construct a centralised and efficient administration.

Addressing this point, Nizam al-Mulk reminds us that Caliph al-Muʿtasim, who had 70,000 *ghulam*, 'always used to say there is nobody like the Turk for service'.[194] Picking up a recent shared memory, Nizam al-Mulk quotes Alptigin – a slave general of the Samanids whom Tugrul and Chagri knew personally[195] – saying that 'a worthy and experienced servant or slave is better than a son'.[196] However, *ghulam* should not become a problem for the state.[197] Nizam al-Mulk knew that *ghulam* themselves might become a problem, should a rift occur between their master and the state.[198] The murder of Alp Arslan in front of 2,000 *ghulam* by a man who was brought to sultan's presence as a prisoner[199] is an oft-repeated case in classical resources that might be linked to this double loyalty problem. But, whatever the intention behind the *ghulam* strategy, it appeared as an anti-Turkmen agenda on the social level

---

[190] Nizam al-Mulk 2002, 49, 55 and 139.
[191] Mottahedeh 1980, 84.
[192] Nizam al-Mulk 2002, 50.
[193] Peacock 2010, 95.
[194] Nizam al-Mulk 2002, 56.
[195] Bosworth 1998, 115–16; Köymen 1976, 5.
[196] Nizam al-Mulk 2002, 117.
[197] Unlike the Abbasids, the Saljuqs managed the slave soldiers better. They had smaller revolts. A Turkish *ghulam*, Bilge declared independence in Isfahan after Malik-Shah's death. Sümer 1972, 109.
[198] Tor 2008, 223.
[199] Fazlullah 2010, 123.

and as a deep resentment of them. Reflecting the intricate nature of the problem, Nizam al-Mulk suggested a balanced strategy on the Turkmen:

> Although the Turkmans have given rise to a certain amount of vexation, and they are very numerous, still they have a longstanding claim upon this dynasty, because at its inception they served well and suffered much, and also they are attached by ties of kinship.[200]

The vizier came close here to suggesting a gradual, long-term strategy for the management of the *ghulam* issue by reminding his readers of its complicated sociological consequences in regard of the Turkmen.[201] The keywords in the paragraph are 'kinship' and 'numerous', for they give prominence to what it is that constitutes the problem that is a highly sensitive for one for the Saljuqs: the Turkmen are indispensable. Nizam al-Mulk's stance on this subject reflects a main dilemma of his age: while the professionals are better in performance, their loyalty is never guaranteed. Put another way, though more loyal, tribal fellows are never like the professionals with regards military training and discipline.[202]

The long-term policy made Nizam al-Mulk perform various balancing acts that sometimes appeared to be contradictory. He enrolled a Turkmen group into the service of a sultan at the palace. The plan was to appoint them as local governors after they had benefitted from training in the palace atmosphere, where they would be exposed to high political culture and bureaucratic codes.[203] It was probably also imagined as a public campaign among the Turkmen. However, Nizam al-Mulk agreed with the purge of the Turkmen aristocrats who supported Kavurd.[204]

In reality, despite the apparent contradiction in Nizam al-Mulk's stance, both aspects of it contributed to his policy of making a transition to a centralised administration. When Malik-Shah purged 7,000 Armenian soldiers

---

[200] Nizam al-Mulk 2002, 112.
[201] Ibid., 102.
[202] Kennedy 2011, 363.
[203] Rizvi 1980, 116; Kafesoğlu 1972, 132.
[204] Peacock 2015, 68–9 and 223; Başan 2010, 82.

because he was not satisfied with their condition,[205] and because the *ghulam* behaviour had provoked a similar treatment,[206] Nizam al-Mulk resisted this, warning that the soldiers could soon revolt, as they could not do any other job. Probably, he had calculated that those soldiers would support the traditionalists. Proving him correct, the purged Armenians supported the revolt of Tekesh, Malik-Shah's brother.[207]

Such examples reveal that Nizam al-Mulk, while responding to developments, had the top priority of securing the Saljuqs' transition to a Persian-Islamic statehood. Reflecting this approach, Nizam al-Mulk suggested a multi-ethnic army in which groups like Iranians and Dailamis balance one another. This also would prevent one group's rebellion. He saw having all soldiers of the same race as a potential problem.[208]

Nizam al-Mulk's political career displays the difficulties that face the bureaucrat who handles the Saljuqs during their transition from nomadism to the state.[209] Another important subject in this context is his effort to develop an administrative relationship between the state and the land, which was unknown to the nomadic imagination. Nizam al-Mulk narrates a case of which the message is the significance of a stable and penetrating rule: a woman complains to Mahmud about the problems in her village. Realising that Mahmud does not know the location of her village, she lectured him: 'Take no more territory than what you can know the extent of, and be responsible for, and look after properly.'[210]

Nizam al-Mulk was critical of the mobile nature of the Saljuqid polity. He objected particularly to the excessive mobility of the sultans. He warned that if the king is distracted by expeditions and wars, he will not be able to focus on critical issues that are of importance to the state.[211] The continuous plundering raids were equally problematic. They obstructed the erection

---

[205] Ibn al-Athir 2002, 202.
[206] Sümer 1972, 109.
[207] Ibn al-Athir 2002, 202.
[208] Nizam al-Mulk 2002, 93 and 100.
[209] Hillenbrand 2022, 255.
[210] Nizam al-Mulk 2002, 64.
[211] Ibid., 139.

of regular institutions and rules that organise the land, the people and the state. That caused people to abandon their lands, which created economic and demographic problems.

A central theme of *Siyasatnama* is the ruining of villages.[212] Nizam al-Mulk once prevented Alp Aslan's destruction of a Byzantine castle by persuading him to use it as an established frontier castle.[213] His advice and policies in this area were the result of his experience. He had served Alp Aslan during the latter's incessant campaigns.[214] (Hillenbrand describes his thirty years in Saljuq service as 'working in a travelling court'.[215]) He witnessed how the Saljuqs' nomadic political culture created reactions among the urban groups.[216]

When it came to the inner workings of a government, Nizam al-Mulk wanted the Saljuqs to

i. abandon their nomadic traditions; and
ii. embrace the bureaucratic procedures of the Persian-Islamic statehood.

To examine the first task: the vizier wanted to explain to the Saljuqs the vital importance of the distinction in the administration between the personal and the public/official.[217] He criticised them for not giving people titles according to their rank and importance. Instead, titles granted to scholars and civil dignitaries were used in confusion.[218] Such problems, caused mainly by the fact that the Saljuqs were still living with their nomadic culture, prevented the development of a strong border between the personal and the public.[219] For example, the Turkmen still treated the sultan as a nomadic leader. So, the Sultan worked without a schedule. That resulted in chaos for the people; they would come to see him, but leave without having met him. Nizam al-Mulk therefore proposed rules to regulate the giving of audiences.[220] As another

---

[212] Ibid., 128–9.
[213] Ibn al-Athir 2002, 153.
[214] Peacock 2016, 7.
[215] Hillenbrand 2022, 330.
[216] Tor 2020, 53.
[217] Nizam al-Mulk 2002, 120.
[218] Ibid., 148 and 156–7. Also see Bosworth 1962a, 62.
[219] Peacock 2015, 159.
[220] Nizam al-Mulk 2002, 117–18.

example of his repudiation of nomadic habits, he warned against the reprimanding of officials in public.[221] Reading Nizam al-Mulk on such issues, one must agree with Bosworth, who notes that Nizam al-Mulk sometimes appears to be frustrated because he could not mould people into the exact shape he wished.[222]

Regarding the second task, the vizier was most critical of the irregularities of the Saljuq administration. He wanted the sultan not to write so many letters, because their frequency made them less effective. He wanted the couriers to have a regular time schedule.[223] The vizier criticised the sultans for making quick and arbitrary decisions. He warned that hastiness – a merit in the nomadic setting – is a sign of weakness, not of strength, in a bureaucratic order.[224] Nizam al-Mulk wanted the Saljuqs to acquire the bureaucratic decision-making procedure of which the staple is patience and professionalism. He thus highlighted the importance of the division of professions and expertise, and suggested that the king should make use of the knowledge of experts.[225]

As importantly, criticising the personalistic techniques of communication within the state, the vizier introduced the concept of 'administrative hierarchy'. Soldiers should demand the supply of their needs through their leaders, not directly themselves, as this would make them think their leaders useless.[226] The absence of a hierarchical and departmental bureaucracy must have bothered him a lot. When an old woman came to voice a problem to the vizier, he expressed his anger to his chamberlain for this direct contact by saying: 'It is for people like this woman that I have employed you.'[227] But the vizier knew the difficulty of social and administrative change; he noted that the new protocol rules would become habitual in time.[228]

The Saljuqs' transition to a Persian-Islamic statehood did not occur in a vacuum: there were two political/spatial dynamics to effect this complex change. Firstly, it happens within the Saljuq state's 'socialisation' in the

---

[221] Ibid., 91, 121 and 129.
[222] Bosworth 1968b, 22.
[223] Nizam al-Mulk 2002, 72 and 87.
[224] Ibid., 91, 121 and 129.
[225] Ibid., 91.
[226] Ibid., 121.
[227] Ibn al-Athir 2002, 182.
[228] Nizam al-Mulk 2002, 117–18.

provincial order, and secondly, mostly within the context of Saljuq political activism in western Iran. Logically, like any reformist, Nizam al-Mulk imagined the caliphate as an important factor in the Saljuqs' transition to an advanced state. The caliphate should thus be respected: *Siyasatnama* cites the Saffarid ruler as a negative case on disobedience to the caliph. As an indication of Nizam al-Mulk's valuing of the rules of the provincial order, he asked for additional respect for judges, because they represent the caliph.[229]

The vizier knew the benefits of the caliphate in giving prestige to the Saljuqs. He mentions Malik-Shah as the 'right hand of the Caliph', a title given him by the caliph.[230] In a critical passage of *Siyasatnama*, Nizam al-Mulk warns Malik-Shah against various people in the Saljuq establishment, for they are hatching a plot to persuade the sultan to overthrow the caliphate.[231] Given the timing of this warning, we understand that he opposed Malik-Shah's plan to make Baghdad the capital by destroying the caliphate. In harmony with this background, Nizam al-Mulk had close relations with the caliph. He took a role in Malik-Shah's daughter's marriage to the caliph in 1087.[232] When his daughter died, displaying his good relations with the caliphate, she was buried in the graveyard of the caliphal palace.[233] In conclusion, Nizam al-Mulk pursued a more cooperative and balanced relationship between the Saljuqs and the caliphate.[234] That balanced policy could not endure after his death.[235]

Last, but not least, *iqta* was another component of Nizam al-Mulk's strategy of developing an efficient bureaucratic administration. *Iqta* was an administrative subject for Nizam al-Mulk. He imagined it as a distilled administrative model that would be successful if operated according to the rules.[236] This

---

[229] Ibid., 15 and 44.

[230] Ibid., 1.

[231] Ibid., 188.

[232] Ibn al-Athir 2002, 201–3. Also see Safi 2006, 64–5.

[233] Ibn al-Athir 2002, 195.

[234] Safi 2006, 55 and 58. Naturally, Nizam al-Mulk had sometimes political issues with the caliph. In 1079, he had the caliphal vizier Fakhr al-Dawla dismissed, and tried to impose his son, Muayyad al-Mulk, as the caliphal vizier. Bosworth 1968b, 99–100.

[235] Sevim and Merçil 1995, 132.

[236] Starr (2013, 390) reminds us that *Siyasatnama* barely touches on the economic sphere.

formalist approach saw *iqta* in terms of the rules concerning the collection of taxes on time, and in due amount.[237]

Nizam al-Mulk, unlike Ibn al-Miskawayh (d. 1030), did not broach the various economic problems that *iqta* may produce. As they lived in different political contexts, their approaches on *iqta* are naturally different. For example, Nizam al-Mulk suggested the changing of *iqta* holders every two or three years, to pre-empt various problems.[238] This would have seemed a scandalous item of advice to Ibn al-Miskawayh, as his main criticism of *iqta* was that the system brought in people whose knowledge of agriculture and local conditions was weak.[239] But Ibn al-Miskawayh criticised *iqta* within the Buwayhid context, where it was initiated to overcome the financial problems that were part of the tenth-century monetary crisis.[240] Practised excessively during the reign of Mu'izz al-Dawla, *iqta*, proving Ibn al-Miskawayh right, decreased agricultural production because the troops who had been assigned lands had no knowledge of cultivation.[241] Later Adud al-Dawlah attempted to abolish *iqta*.[242]

In contrast, Nizam al-Mulk wrote on *iqta*, when it was initiated by the Saljuqs, that state control should be extended over the new territories, as well as among the military.[243] While *iqta* was a result of the Buwayhids failure to pay salaries, it was a normal payment system for the Saljuqis.[244] They, who had faced problems like the Turkmen in their transition to the Persio-Islamic state, saw *iqta* as an efficient method to consolidate a network of central rule across the country.[245] Nizam al-Mulk's *iqta* was therefore used in the service of the state to maintain control.[246]

---

[237] Nizam al-Mulk 2002, 22–3 and 32.
[238] Ibid., 41–2.
[239] Ibn Miskawaihi 1921, 98–9, 131–2.
[240] Mottahedeh 1980, 36–7; Shaban 1976, 63.
[241] Nadvi 1971, 261.
[242] A. R. Lewis 1969, 50.
[243] Starr 2013, 388; Safi 2006, 89.
[244] Turan 2008, 309.
[245] Divitçioğlu 2000, 122; Turan 2008, 309–10.
[246] Cahen 1969, 158.

The case of *iqta* recalls my warnings of Chapter 1: political practices linked to the Persian influence should not be imagined as essential constructs that operate with the same outcomes in all contexts. Context matters. As Lambton says, under a strong ruler, *iqta* may well contribute to the strength and cohesion of the state.[247]

Fine-tuning the Persian Impact

Nizam al-Mulk is usually said to have had an Iranian concept of sacral leadership.[248] This is defended by statements in *Siyasatnama* like 'in every age and time God chooses one member of the human race'.[249] I find this argumentation an overinterpretation. *Siyasatnama* has no serious articulation on divine kingship.[250] As my first counter-argument, I propose that it is better to understand such statements as a cultural reflection of Ash'ari understanding, to which Nizam al-Mulk adhered. In Ash'arism, there is nothing God does not will.[251]

Nizam al-Mulk follows this Ash'ari theology as the general background when explaining historical events. Black calls this 'a fatalistic' tenet of Nizam al-Mulk, according to which states are overtaken, governments change, or pass one house to another, by celestial causality.[252] Confirming this, in *Siyasatnama* it is God who 'caused you to be defeated', 'he preserved our family', grants success, takes away realms from one and gives to another, orders the affairs of people, sends healing, grants people's requests, and rules over prosperity and power.[253] Nizam al-Mulk freely applies this tenet to political events. He justifies Mahmud's fights against heretics, and his support of al-Qadir's Sunnism policy, by arguing that he was created and appointed for this purpose.[254] He believed that God 'favored the Turks,

---

[247] Lambton 1968, 239.
[248] Simidchieva 2004, 105–8.
[249] Nizam al-Mulk 2002, 9.
[250] Kafesoğlu 2021, 15; Köymen 1976, 71; Divitçioğlu 2000, 127; Humphreys 1991, 166.
[251] Al-Ash'ari 1953, 35.
[252] Black 2011, 93.
[253] Nizam al-Mulk 2002, 9, 17, 20, 47, 53, 76 and 78.
[254] Ibid., 66.

and gave them dominion' over the Fatimids.[255] These examples display that Nizam al-Mulk's God is the final arbiter of politics, which is just another aspect of human affairs. Divine ordainment is not referred to in any sense of the term.[256] As noted above, they should be read as a reflection of the general Ash'ari cultural setting.

Secondly, the Saljuqid system was a synthesis of the steppe tradition and the Iranian-Islamic tradition.[257] Collective sovereignty, a component of the steppe tradition, contradicts the Iranian sacral kingship theory. Collective sovereignty limited the Saljuq sultan's superiority over other royal members, preventing his becoming an absolute ruler like the Roman or Persian kings.[258] No sitting sultan was able to develop a theory, be it divine or temporal, that would prevent others' right to claim leadership.[259] Sulayman, who had been declared the new ruler by al-Kunduri, was replaced by Alp Arslan.[260] Even if he recognised Alp Arslan, Kavurd always had issues with him in power sharing. That caused no fewer than three incursions.[261]

Unliked the Roman and Persian concept of indivisible sovereignty, the Saljuqid sovereignty was divisible: sovereignty was divided; the country was divided. The Saljuqs were a composition of overlapping authorities.[262] Ibn al-Athir describes the Saljuqs' lands in 1040 as ruled collectively, mainly by Tugrul and Chagri, but also by other princes.[263] It was a period with two overlapping non-hierarchical administrations.[264] Once, Tugrul and Chagri appointed rival governors in Sistan.[265] In 1042/3, when Tugrul attempted a

---

[255] Ibid., 161.
[256] Rizvi 1978, 49; 1981, 132–3.
[257] Kafesoğlu 1972, 115; Köymen 1970, 37; Hillenbrand 2022, 331. For Peacock (2016, 9–10), the Saljuq political system was more Turkish and less Iranian.
[258] Turan 2008, 306.
[259] Cahen 1969, 161; Bosworth 1968b, 67.
[260] Ibn al-Athir 2002, 145; Qazwini 1913, 96; Bar Hebraeus 1976, 216.
[261] Peacock 2015, 53.
[262] Lambton 1968, 218; Bosworth 1968b, 78 and 82; Golden 1992, 231; Meisami 2007, 141.
[263] Ibn al-Athir 2002, 30.
[264] Köymen 1976, 19–20.
[265] Peacock 2015, 42–3.

unification, he was threatened by the other royals.[266] Collective sovereignty affected the Saljuqs until as late as the period after the reign of Malik-Shah.[267]

Last but not least, an Iranian sacral kingship is a theoretical contradiction, given that the Saljuqs recognised the caliph. The sacral kingship concept requires the rejection of any contender. For example, the Fatimids rejected the Abbasid caliphate for ontological reasons. Thus, while it was unimaginable that the Fatimid caliph would kiss the floor in front of the Abbasid caliph, that was usual for the Saljuq sultans.

Wine and Political Rationalism

Siyasatnama has a special chapter on wine. More interestingly, throughout the book Nizam al-Mulk insistently mentions people, whom he narrates for different reasons, drinking wine. On just one reading of the book, the reader comprehends that wine-drinking was a usual part of daily life.[268] To cite a few references to this: Nizam al-Mulk begins the story of a man with Alp Arslan, in the chapter on the inadvisability of hastiness in affairs, with: 'One day during a drinking bout he said in front of the sultan. . .' In another chapter, which is about not giving two appointments to one man, Nizam al-Mulk narrates a case about Caliph Suleyman ibn Abd al-Malik that includes the remark 'they settled down to their drinking'. The story of Caliph al-Mu'tasim's three victories carries the introductory sentence, 'One day al-Mu'tasim was sitting at a drinking party. . .'[269]

A jurist would categorically prohibit wine-drinking. Nizam al-Mulk was not a jurist. His interest in wine centred on his intention to resolve the problems caused by the excessive drinking of the Saljuq political elite. He had to look for solutions where judicial idealism (that is, reminding about the prohibition of wine) is not in place. In this regard, Nizam al-Mulk's views on drinking wine were an integral part of his advice, as a high-class educated Persian, to Turks with problems of adaptation to urban life and state protocol.

---

[266] Ibn al-Athir 2002, 50.
[267] Tetley 2009, 24.
[268] Koch 2014, 224.
[269] Nizam al-Mulk 2002, 130, 176 and 236.

The drinking of wine was widespread among the Saljuqs.[270] According to *Saljuqnama*, Arslan was fond of wine.[271] Alp Arslan is reported to have been drunk during the siege of Aleppo.[272] In *Jami al-Tawarikh*, Alp Arslan drank with his prisoner, Romanus Diogenes, the Byzantine emperor.[273] *Saljuqnama* makes known that the two emperors drank red wine while listening to music.[274] Nizam al-Mulk confirms that Alp Arslan liked wine.[275] The poet Muʿizzi (d. *c*.1127) said of Malik-Shah that 'he sat on the banks of the Tigris with a cup in hand'.[276] Sultan Barkyaruq, Malik-Shah's son, was addicted to wine.[277] Wine was also popular among the members of Nizam al-Mulk's family, who occupied important official posts. His son, Jamal al-Din, liked drinking.[278] Another son, Izzat al-Mulk, even had alcoholism problems that caused various troubles.[279]

Wine was an integral part of the Saljuq court.[280] The Saljuq palace had a cellar.[281] Along with hunting and polo, drinking and feasting were the sultans' favourite ways of relaxation.[282] There were regular *bar-ı hass* (royal drinking parties) where only select, and usually high level, people drank with the sultan. The Saljuqs employed a *sharabdar-ı hass*, a royal official for winery and cellars.[283]

---

[270] In *Oğuznama*, Oghuz Khan asked for wine when he was a small child. Ağca 2016, 1–2.
[271] Nishapuri 2001, 31. It was observed among the Ghaznawids. Nizam al-Mulk (2002, 45) describes Mahmud drinking all night. Ibn al-Athir (2002, 39) also recorded that Mahmud drank wine.
[272] Hillenbrand 2022, 139.
[273] Fazlullah 2010, 77 and 118.
[274] Nishapuri 2001, 51.
[275] Nizam al-Mulk 2002, 130.
[276] Peacock 2015, 177.
[277] Hillenbrand 2020, 15.
[278] Ibn al-Athir 2002, 206.
[279] Taneri 1970, 94-95.
[280] Hillenbrand 2020, 15.
[281] Nizam al-Mulk 2002, 88.
[282] Peacock 2015, 172; Canby *et al.* 2016, 73. Also see Fazlullah 2010, 132; Nishapuri 2001, 60; Qazwini 1913, 97.
[283] Köymen 1966, 32-3 and 59; Turan 2008, 210–11; Nizam al-Mulk 2002, 119.

What prompted Nizam al-Mulk to write on the subject was the various problems he observed, like the sultan making decisions on critical issues in a state of drunkenness. Absurd situations created by drunken sultans were equally problematic in terms of political prestige and bureaucratic discipline. Palace officials, not knowing what to do, usually called the sultan's wife, the *khatun*, to take care of the drunken sultan. For instance, Alp Aslan ordered the dismissal and execution of Vizier al-Kunduri at a royal drinking party. The authorities sometimes had to work hard to dissuade the sultan from implementing the decisions he made while he was drunk. When Alp Arslan got drunk in the Aleppo region, he decided to kill Mahmud, the ruler of the Mirdasid vassal state, who was normally given protection through a treaty. To stop Alp Arslan, Nizam al-Mulk had to ask for the help of the *khatun* to take the sultan to bed.[284]

To propose a solution, Nizam al-Mulk included sections in *Siyasatnama* concerning: 'the rules and arrangements for drinking parties', the arrangements for setting a good table, and on 'being careful with messages in drunkenness and sobriety', where wine is treated in the context of how to consume it properly. Nizam al-Mulk, knowing that the juristic/idealistic view was useless in his context, suggested a pragmatic blueprint, from an administrative perspective, for propriety while drinking wine. He did not preach against wine-drinking by reminding of religious norms; he proposed the best available solution.

In chapter 15 of *Siyasatnama*, 'On being careful about messages in drunkenness and sobriety', Nizam al-Mulk lays down a strategy for damage-control made necessary by the decisions of drunk sultans. He first defined the problem: 'It may be that some of these commands are [given] in a state of merriment.' A decision taken in the state of merriment might be wrong, and people may abuse this situation. The vizier described the problem as a delicate matter that needs the utmost caution. He first warned that those decisions not be executed until a report on them is made by the *diwan*. He next required that all those correspondences on such matters be conducted personally, and never through a deputy, so that others do not abuse the situation.[285]

---

[284] Köymen 1966, 61–6. This problem is observed in other officials, including even those of the madrasa. For example, Nizam al-Mulk dealt with problems of Abu Zakariya, the librarian at his madrasa who drank wine. Taneri 1970, 120.

[285] Nizam al-Mulk 2002, 88.

Next, Nizam al-Mulk proposed a structural solution, a code for the royal drinking party, where the political elites, including the sultan, can drink wine as they wish, without harming state affairs. Accordingly, court officials would organise royal drinking parties, but for only a limited number of special guests. Nobody was allowed to bring his own wine. All details of the party should be managed by court officials. They would see to it that the sultan drinks only with his boon company, and not with nobles, generals and civil governors.[286] The vizier did not want the royal party to become a venue for the making of political decisions. Also, the sultan should not spend time at the party with pages.[287] This aimed at preventing the pages or the *ghulam*s disseminating information or orders given by a drunk sultan. Nizam al-Mulk underlined that the sultan should consult with his vizier on all matters of administration. This was a clear warning that no one may use royal parties as opportunities for obtaining approval from the sultan on a political issue.[288]

On the pretext that always talking about state issues might 'increase his fatigue and anxiety, and torture his spirit', Nizam al-Mulk suggested that the sultan should have boon-companions at royal drinking parties who set his spirit free.[289] He made clear also that 'people who are employed in any official capacity should not be admitted as boon companions, nor should those who are accepted for companionship be appointed to any public office'.[290] This was a well-thought-out tactic for isolating the drunk sultan in the company of people without official power.

Nizam al-Mulk did not make any reference to religion. No one knew better than he that there is no judge who would impose those rules on a sultan like Alp Arslan. The vizier's approach to wine would be shocking to a pious modern Muslim. In another passage, after reminding that the King [Malik-Shah] 'should not drink wine for the sake of intoxication', he concludes that:

> Let him not be constantly jocular, nor altogether austere. If occasionally he occupies himself with entertainment, hunting and drinking, let him also

---

[286] Ibid., 119.

[287] Ibid., 74.

[288] Ibid., 119.

[289] Ibid.

[290] Ibid., 88. As Nizam al-Mulk reminds his readers, having boon-companions was also a practice of Ghaznawids and Samanids.

sometimes devote himself to thanksgiving, almsgiving, nocturnal prayer, fasting and charitable works; then he will possess both worlds. In all things he should take the middle course, for the prophet said, the best of things is the middle of them.[291]

We see Nizam al-Mulk, a devoted Shafi and towering political figure who affected the history of Sunnism, quoting a tradition to seek a middle-course life, the balanced consumption of wine. While Nizam al-Mulk wrote of alcohol in this way, the curriculum he imposed in madrasas led to the canonisation of al-Buhari's *Sahih*.[292] There is, however, no contradiction here, as Nizam al-Mulk was a political actor, not a scholar; he proposed his opinions as responses to problems. *Siyasatnamah* is a text of Islamic political theory, not a treatise on doctrinal idealism. Meanwhile, he did not need to be afraid of jurists. He was the employer of al-Ghazali. In his *al-Giyathi*, al-Juwayni, the major jurist of the time, provided Nizam al-Mulk with a suitable religious interpretation by justifying with political reasons that the vizier is prevented from making a pilgrimage.[293]

Nizam al-Mulk's views are political suggestions without any allusion to the religious prohibition of wine.[294] They illustrate how Islamic political theory is different from the religious view of politics on a controversial subject. The same approach is observed in his contemporaries who had a similar political perspective. Kai Kaus's *Qabusnama* has a chapter on 'the regulation of wine drinking'. He, who normally prefers that people not drink, says that he neither urges anyone to drink, nor does he tell anyone not to drink, because 'young men never refrain from an action at anyone's bidding'. His solution is simple: 'Know how to drink.'[295]

---

[291] Ibid., 244.
[292] Brown 2007, 3–4.
[293] Al-Juwayni 2011, 456 and 460–5.
[294] He does not question the wine prohibition. While describing the Khurramiyya as heretical, Nizam al-Mulk (2002, 237) writes that they do not recognise the principle of forbidding wine. But this is mentioned in *Siyasatnama* in a completely different context.
[295] Kai Kaus ibn Iskandar 1951, 57–8.

Women and Politics

While listing the indications of the times of collapse, which is a criticism of the Saljuqs under Malik-Shah, Nizam al-Mulk mentions that 'the king's wives will issue orders'.[296] But this only generates harm, because women have no direct access to politics, and this makes them reliant on others' reports.[297]

This generalisation about women was the vizier's response to a series of events around him.[298] Those responses are expressed in chapter 42, a later-added section of *Siyasatnama* that reflects the final part of Nizam al-Mulk's career when he was being purged from politics as part of a defamation campaign led by Terken Khatun, Malik-Shah's wife.

Terken Khatun led an anti-Nizam al-Mulk faction that included influential people like Taj al-Mulk, Majd al-Mulk, Abu'l-Mahasin Muhammad and Sadid al-Mulk.[299] At the core of the feud between Terken Khatun and Nizam al-Mulk was that while she supported her son Mahmud as heir, the vizier supported Barkyaruq.[300] However, the faction led by Terken Khatun was just another example of the anti-Nizam al-Mulk feelings shared by many because of the vizier's fortune, private army, his grip on the religious network, and many of his sons and other relatives' holding key positions. Even before Terken Khatun, people had complained about Nizam al-Mulk. Ibn al-Athir narrates that a letter of malicious report concerning the vizier was left in front of Alp Aslan.[301]

Originally a Qarakhanid princess, Terken Khatun married Malik-Shah in 1066. Having her *diwan*, she was an influential figure with a large private army

---

[296] Nizam al-Mulk 2002, 139.
[297] Ibid., 179–82.
[298] Safi 2006, 71.
[299] Lambton 1984, 64; De Nicola 2017, 34; Yavari 2008b, 49; Hillenbrand 2022, 194. Terken Khatun was not the only woman with whom Nizam al-Mulk had issues. He confiscated Gawhar Khatun's property because she supported Kavurd against Malik-Shah. The vizier later had her killed. Turan 2008, 173; Taneri 1970, 123.
[300] Qazwini 1913, 97. The feud continued even after the death of Nizam al-Mulk, this time between his *ghulam* and Terken Khatun. Fazlullah 2010, 144.
[301] Ibn al-Athir 2002, 178.

of *ghulam*.³⁰² A madrasa was financed by her endowments.³⁰³ She took a role in the negotiation of the marriage of the caliph and Malik-Shah's daughter. As the mother-in-law of Caliph al-Muqtadi, she had strong contacts in Baghdad. The caliph's son from this marriage, Jaʿfar, stayed mostly in his grandmother's court. Terken Khatun, after Malik-Shah's death, asked the caliph to recognise Mahmud as the new sultan, and threatened that otherwise, she would declare Jaʿfar as an alternate caliph in Isfahan.³⁰⁴

The apogee of Nizam al-Mulk coincided with the period before the marriage of Malik-Shah to Terken Khatun.³⁰⁵ Terken, along with her private vizier Taj al-Mulk, emerged as challengers of Nizam al-Mulk.³⁰⁶ Backed by Terken Khatun, Taj al-Mulk gained multiple positions related to the treasury, harem, and even the control of armies in several regions.³⁰⁷ This is criticised by Nizam al-Mulk in *Siyasatnama* in a chapter on 'not giving two appointments to one man', where he writes that enlightened kings have never given two appointments to one man. Probably disturbed by Taj al-Mulk's growing power, he warned that one appointment to two men would always cause administrative inefficiency. In a direct assault on Taj al-Mulk, Nizam al-Mulk wrote that incapable men hold ten posts; yet they would get additional posts even by bribing, if necessary.³⁰⁸

The negative campaign led by Terken Khatun was particularly effective during Nizam al-Mulk's last period of tenure.³⁰⁹ They systematically campaigned on the accusation that the vizier helds the main power, a tactic meant to provoke Malik-Shah. They faulted him also for other reasons, such as his excessive expenditure and nepotism.³¹⁰ Nizam al-Mulk defended himself by submitting that his fortune belongs to Malik-Shah, and he spends it

---

[302] Sevim and Merçil 1995, 510; Kafesoğlu 1972, 118.
[303] Arjomand 1999, 270.
[304] El-Azhari 2019, 288.
[305] Safi 2006, 63.
[306] Loewe 1923, 308; Simidchieva 2004, 99; Paul 2011, 109.
[307] Safi 2006, 69.
[308] Nizam al-Mulk 2002, 158–9 and 178.
[309] Başan 2010, 70.
[310] Rizvi 1978, 22; Sevim and Merçil 1995, 129–30.

on religious endowments.[311] Nizam al-Mulk, who was experienced in dealing with statesmen and caliphs, had trouble, however, in counter-challenging this asymmetrical opposition.[312] His rivals were better at intricate dealings. Taj al-Mulk is described by Nishapuri as a person 'who understood both the surface and the inner nature of things'.[313]

Beyond the personal feud, this was also a clash of political paradigms on various issues. Nizam al-Mulk's rivals defended downsizing the army from 400,000 to 70,000, an idea which Malik-Shah seemed to have bought. Nizam al-Mulk opposed the plan, arguing that it would ruin the country.[314] For him, such ideas underestimated the Ismaili threat.[315]

The rivals intensified their campaign, particularly around the year 1088. The relationship between the vizier and the sultan was all but paralysed.[316] Meanwhile, Malik-Shah, who was mature and fairly experienced in politics, became annoyed with Nizam al-Mulk holding too much power.[317] According to Ibn Khallikan, Malik-Shah was fatigued by seeing him live so long.[318] This triggered several crises. The first crisis came to a peak in an indirect problem in 1088: Malik-Shah's jester, Ja'farak, circulated satirical stories about Nizam al-Mulk at court. His resented son, Jamal al-Mulk, killed the jester. Malik-Shah responded harshly by poisoning Jamal al-Mulk.[319] The execution was a turning point, as it illustrated the sultan's decision to assert his authority, and give up on Nizam al-Mulk.[320]

In another crisis, Nizam al-Mulk's son, Shams al-Mulk, the governor of Marv, arrested the *shihna* appointed by the sultan. Malik-Shah wrote a letter

---

[311] Ibn al-Athir 2002, 211–12. According to Lambton (1968, 261), Nizam al-Mulk admitted to taking one-tenth of Malik-Shah's wealth, which he said he had spent on the standing army, on alms, gifts and endowments.
[312] Safi 2006, 67.
[313] Nishapuri 2001, 61.
[314] Nizam al-Mulk 2002, 165.
[315] Ibid., 188.
[316] Taneri 1970, 96.
[317] Safi 2006, 65.
[318] Ibn Khallikan 1843a, 415.
[319] Ibn al-Athir 2002, 206.
[320] Safi 2006, 65.

to Nizam al-Mulk to remind him of his limits.[321] As a more complex and perpetual problem, the sultan and the vizier were at odds over *iqtas*. The sultan was unhappy about the numerous fiefs the vizier held in his possession.[322] Once, Malik-Shah had killed Ibn Allan, a fief-holder promoted by Nizam al-Mulk. The event seriously offended Nizam al-Mulk, as Malik-Shah had been provoked to the action by his rivals.[323]

In what could be seen as the final crisis, the provoked Malik-Shah criticised the vizier for favouring his sons.[324] The accusation was not baseless, as Nizam al-Mulk's sons and other relatives had become a political clan prioritising its own interests.[325] He accused Nizam al-Mulk of exceeding his boundaries by sharing the sultan's authority. Despite Nizam al-Mulk responding to the sultan politely, the mediators – who had probably connected themselves to Terken Khatun – purposefully reported to Malik-Shah that the vizier's response was not submissive. The tension led to the murder of Nizam al-Mulk by Fatimid assassins provoked by Taj al-Mulk.[326]

To conclude, Nizam al-Mulk's ideas on women reflected the particular context. They were never general opinions that represent a philosophical or religious perspective.[327] A frameless reading of Nizam al-Mulk on women would give only a negative picture of the status of women in Saljuq society. Ironically, Nizam al-Mulk's opinions were a reflection of women's influential

---

[321] Ibn al-Athir 2002, 252.

[322] Ibn Khallikan 1843a, 415.

[323] Ibid., 201.

[324] Nizam al-Mulk's sons held critical posts. Shams al-Mulk was a governor of Marv; Jamal al-Mulk was a governor of Balkh; Muʿayyid al-Mulk was a high-level bureaucrat who once ruled Tikrit. Taneri (1970, 94) calculated that one-third of all Saljuqi viziers are Nizam al-Mulk's offspring or relatives. On the impact of his offspring who survived after Nizam al-Mulk's death, al-Bayhaqi (2004, 184–5) provides a long list of those who worked in various positions after his death. Indeed, this period was even known as *al-dawla al-Nizamiyya*.

[325] Peacock 2015, 207–8.

[326] Nishapuri 2001, 62; Fazlullah 2010, 134. Ibn Khallikan (1843a, 415) wrote that 'it is said that the assassin was suborned against him by Malik-Shah'. Contemporary scholars also opine that Malik-Shah and Taj al-Mulk were behind the murder. Hillenbrand 2022, 126; Yavari 2008b, 55; Safi 2006, 49.

[327] Cortese and Calderini 2006, 102.

[328] El-Azhari 2019, 285–348. Women's influential role in Saljuq society was also linked to Turkish culture. Ibn Fadlan (2017, 10) noted with interest that the Turks' womenfolk do not cover themselves in the presence of a man, whether or not it is one of their menfolk.

role among the Saljuqs. The era of Saljuq politics is even dubbed by several scholars as the golden age of the *khatuns*.[328] Royal women had viziers, *diwan* and troops.[329] To present a number of examples: Safia Khatun, an influential actor within the ruling dynasty, held a large number of fiefs. She occupied Mosul with her son after the death of Malik-Shah.[330] The wife of Caliph al-Mustazhiriyya, who was the sister of Sultan Sanjar, was another influential woman who offered patronage to prominent scholars like al-Ghaznawi.[331] Mahsati (d. 1159), a female poet, became a scribe at Sanjar's court.[332] Sanjar's mother also had her *diwan*.[333] Similarly, Tugrul's wife, Altunjan Khatun, and Alp Arslan's sister, Jawhar Khatun, had their *diwans*, *iqtas* and troops.[334] When Tugrul was besieged in Hamadan during the fight with Basasiri, Altunjan Khatun marched from Baghdad in person with the army, despite the caliph's opposition.[335] Jawhar Khatun acted as a mediator between Alp Arslan and Kavurd when the latter revolted.[336]

Religion as Politics

Nizam al-Mulk survived thirty years at the apex of political power, thanks to a loyal network that included religious agents. As I have mentioned before, a major accusation against him was that he spent public money to establish a political grip over religious foundations. When Nizam al-Mulk was accused of corruption, he defended himself by arguing that he spent the money on religious endowments.[337]

Nizam al-Mulk had openly promoted the idea of paying the salaries of doctors of religion from treasury funds.[338] He also implemented a parallel strategy of using religious actors and networks to strengthen his political agenda. He, a Persian with a Shafi-Ash'ari background, lived among the Saljuqs who favoured

---

[329] Başan 2010, 19; Ibn al-Athir 2002, 276.
[330] Sanaullah 1938, 13–14 and 23. Bar Hebraeus (1976, 2015) describes Tugrul's *khatun* as administrating all the business of the kingdom.
[331] Ephrat 2011, 147.
[332] Davies 2019, 7.
[333] Sevim and Merçil 1995, 510.
[334] Turan 2008, 311.
[335] Ibn al-Athir 2002, 119–20.
[336] El-Azhari 2019, 290.
[337] Ibn al-Athir 2002, 211–12.
[338] Ibid., 59–60.

Hanafism. Hanbalism was already monopolised by the Abbasid caliphate in the Sunni restoration policy. He thus developed a policy through the Shafis, his natural constituency.

To put this into a historical setting: the Shafis had already embraced a political awareness as a result of the al-Qadiri creed, and later the Hanafism implemented by the Saljuqs in Nishapur. (The al-Qadiri creed was explained in Chapter 2.) To briefly explain the latter: when the Saljuqs took over Nishapur, which became their first big city where they experienced the early transition to statehood, they imagined the city as their power base.[339] The vizier al-Kunduri pursued a Hanafi policy to monopolise the administration, as well as to create a local constituency and legitimacy in Nishapur.[340] In 1053, Ash'arism was cursed from the Khurasan pulpits.[341] In 1054/5, al-Qushayri wrote a petition to defend Ash'arism. He defined the persecution of the Shafis as the second inquisition after the Abbasid inquisition in 833.[342] Facing political risk, prominent Shafi scholars, including al-Juwayni, left Nishapur and sought refuge in Iraq or Hejaz.[343] The exodus helped the Saljuqs fill those posts with Hanafis.[344]

After he took office, Nizam al-Mulk abolished al-Kunduri's anti-Ash'ari policy, and brought back prominent scholars such as al-Juwayni.[345] Naturally, this made him a Shafi hero. Increasing his popularity further, he pursued a policy that favoured Shafi scholars such as al-Juwayni, al-Qushayri and al-Farmadhi,[346] as well as one of financing Shafi students and scholars by various means, such as funding a *khan*, a multiple-use space where students stayed and had religious training.[347]

Probably inspired by the Ghaznavid madrasa, Nizam al-Mulk later decided to establish his own madrasa.[348] Though the Saljuqs already had madrasas in

---

[339] Peacock 2010, 111.
[340] Madelung 1985, 124–5 and 139–40; Melchert 2015, 24; Peacock 2010, 111; Bulliet 1978, 50.
[341] Madelung 1985, 128.
[342] Siddiqui 2019, 46–7.
[343] Ibn al-Athir 2002, 148; Widigdo 2021, 170; Saflo 2000, 12–13.
[344] Bulliet 1978, 47–50.
[345] Ibn al-Athir 2002, 195 and 257.
[346] Ibid., 257.
[347] Makdisi 1981, 24.
[348] Bulliet 2008, 73.

Marv and Nishapur, Nizam al-Mulk decided on a personal madrasa, expecting that this would better serve his strategy of building a strong power base.[349] Other reasons, such as the need to counterbalance the Ismaili threat, also had an impact on his decision.[350] The Saljuq rulers' failure to understand the scope of the Fatimid threat (as he laments in *Siyasatnama*) might have persuaded Nizam al-Mulk to prefer personal strategies.[351] Probably, the Saljuq sultans, who were staunch Hanafis, cautiously tolerated their vizier promoting Shafis against the Hanbali, as this would help the consolidation of their rule in Baghdad. As a matter of fact, Nizam al-Mulk imagined the Hanbalis as antagonistic to the Saljuq political interests. He defined Shafi and Hanafi as two legitimate schools, and all the rest vanity and heresy.[352] He suggested that the sultan employ only people, including the vizier, with a Hanafi or Shafi background.[353]

The Nizamiyya Madrasa was opened in October 1067, with Abu Ishak al-Shirazi as professor.[354] Madrasas were also opened in other cities, such as Nishapur, Mosul, Herat, Damascus, Balkh, Ghazna, Basra and Marv. As those cities were all Shafi zones, not only the instructors but also staff like librarians were Shafi.[355] The Nizamiyya Madrasa was a project of Nizam al-Mulk and his family. The college was designed to remain under Nizam al-Mulk's personal influence.[356] He was the de facto administrator. His son, Muʿayyid al-Mulk, was his main representative as the trustee.[357] Muʿayyid even stayed in a house that was part of the madrasa complex in Baghdad.[358] Nizam

---

[349] Makdisi 1961, 51; Bulliet 1978, 52.
[350] Bosworth 1968b, 70.
[351] As a critical note, Cahen (1969, 154) says that the Saljuqs extended madrasas into Buwayhid domains.
[352] Nizam al-Mulk 2002, 96–7.
[353] Ibid., 159, 173 and 180.
[354] Ibn al-Athir 2002, 157 and 161.
[355] Dargahani 2019, 570 and 596; Bosworth 1968b, 72; Makdisi 1981, 302; Lambton 1968, 216.
[356] Arjomand 1999, 270.
[357] Dargahani 2019, 574. Though there is no doubt that Nizam al-Mulk secured the madrasas' funding, it is not technically easy to ascertain the source of this money. While Makdisi (1990, 158) and Ephrat (2011, 142) argue that the madrasa was financed by Nizam al-Mulk's endowments, Köymen (1975, 83) and Tibawi (1962, 232) believe that this money was indirectly state money.
[358] Ibn al-Athir 2002, 195.

al-Mulk had absolute authority in academic appointments: in 1090, Abu Abd Allah al-Tabari came to Baghdad to teach at the madrasa with the approval of Nizam al-Mulk. Later in the same year, al-Shirazi was also appointed by the vizier.[359] Similarly, Nizam al-Mulk brought al-Ghazali to Baghdad in 1091.[360] The vizier sometimes rejected the appointment of professors.[361] He involved himself even in the appointment of secondary positions, such as the trustee and financial staff.[362]

Nizam al-Mulk's policy of promoting Shafism occurred in the larger context of the Hanbali–Shafi rivalry that had already culminated. As part of the theological debates, the Hanbalis did not refrain from cursing the Ashʿaris as heretics for their concept of God that deviated from orthodoxy.[363] Protests triggered by theological differences frequently paralysed Baghdad.[364] Thus, when Nizam al-Mulk initiated his policy of promoting Shafism/Ashʿarism, it was competing with the ultra-traditional Hanbalism, which was at the centre of Caliph al-Qadir's creed. The Hanbali protests began immediately after Nizam al-Mulk brought the exiled Shafi scholars back to Baghdad.[365] The Hanbalis were not happy to see the Shafis gaining power in Baghdad. When Abu Nasr taught in Baghdad in 1076/7 upon the invitation of Nizam al-Mulk, his disparaging comments about the Hanbalis triggered an assault on the Nizamiyya madrasa.[366] His lectures were cancelled. In 1083, when Abu Qasim al-Bakri al-Maghrebi, who was appointed by Nizam al-Mulk, harshly criticized Ahmad ibn Hanbal, he almost brought chaos to Baghdad. He was expelled from Baghdad.[367]

During the above-mentioned crisis in 1076/7, in a letter responding to a Shafi scholar who asked his support against the Hanbalis, Nizam al-Mulk

---

[359] Ibid., 247.
[360] Bosworth 1968b, 72.
[361] Ibn Khallikan 1843a, 10–11.
[362] Dargahani 2019, 573.
[363] The concept of God in *Lumʿa al-Adillah* of al-Juwayni (2000, 239–40) clearly shows how Ashʿarism differs from Hanbali.
[364] Ibn al-Athir 2002, 79–80, 89 and 102.
[365] Renterghem 2011, 125; Peacock 2016, 27.
[366] Ibn al-Athir 2002, 193, footnote 59. Also see Hanne 2007, 112.
[367] Ibn al-Athir 2002, 207.

underlined that the state has no policy of imposing an official religious school, as this would cause communal strife.[368] As this letter confirms, Nizam al-Mulk's policy of promoting Shafi madrasas was not a general Saljuq strategy for effecting a Sunni revival.[369] It was a political strategy. In any case, he had no ability to impose Shafism and persecute others, like the Hanafi al-Kunduri did before, as the Saljuq sultans were staunch Hanafis. As Madelung notes, even the vizier had to pursue his Shafi policy secretly during Alp Arslan's rule.[370] Alp Arslan was a devoted Hanafi who had Hanafi jurists with him even during battles.[371] Nizam al-Mulk confessed in *Siyasatnama* that he lived in constant fear of Alp Arslan, whom he described as a fanatical Hanafi disprover of Shafi who lamented that his vizier was a Shafi.[372]

The Nizamiyya was just another college in the league of Saljuq madrasas promoted by different people with different purposes. In 1067, when Nizam al-Mulk was the grand vizier, Abu Sa'd al-Mustawfi, Alp Arslan's top official in financial matters, founded the Shrine College of Abu Hanifa, an exclusively Hanafi madrasa.[373] It was therefore not possible to label any madrasa as the official Saljuqi project. Even Nizam al-Mulk failed to monopolise the Shafi domain, as his rival Taj al-Mulk had founded a Shafi madrasa in Baghdad, the Tajiyya Madrasa.[374]

Conclusion: Embracing Independent States

Siyasatnama's originality is in its state-centred perspective of politics and society. This links naturally to the historical fact that Nizam al-Mulk lived in the latter part of provincial order, when independent states had formed.

---

[368] Bulliet 1978, 47; Brown 2007, 4; Tibawi 1962, 237–8.
[369] Makdisi 1961, 51; Bulliet 1978, 52; Turan 2008, 313; Peacock 2010, 5.
[370] Madelung 1985, 131.
[371] Tor 2011b, 51; Safi 2006, 94.
[372] Nizam al-Mulk 2002, 96.
[373] Ibn al-Athir 2002, 161; Makdisi 1970b, 263.
[374] Ibn al-Athir 2002, 244. According to Makdisi (1961, 30), the reputation of the Nizamiyya madrasas as monopolistic institutions was due mainly to the fact that Nizam al-Mulk was a public figure whose life was known about in detail.

Nizam al-Mulk's political rationalism produced radical views on controversial issues like alcohol. He was equally radical when he defined religion in politics as a function of justice, another major product of his state-centred political thought. Nizam al-Mulk was even not interested in the Sunni theories of leadership. He approached religion from an instrumentalist perspective. Religion was incorporated into political thought in the terms of the Saljuq states' policies and priorities. The ultimate power that united people and the law was the Saljuq state.

Reflecting a major feature of Islamic political theory, Nizam al-Mulk approached political issues by contextualising them in their social and political setting. He explained social and political phenomena as they happened. He was an empiricist in this regard. Idealistic solutions did not attract his attention. Not advancing the idealistic solutions of political philosophy or religion, Nizam al-Mulk proposed practical solutions within the limits of the available means. Reflecting this, he employed a bureaucratic (or technocratic) vocabulary composed of words like order, hierarchy, titles, positions, schedule, rules and responsibilities. Predictably, such a technocratic vocabulary automatically excluded philosophical and religious precepts from his political analysis.

With Nizam al-Mulk's state-centred political thought, the evolution of Islamic political theory that had begun with Ibn al-Muqaffa reached its climax. But this trajectory of Islamic political theory was limited to the societies in the Muslim East, where Turks, Arabs and Persians dominated the scene. It excluded the Muslim West, which evolved on its own trajectory. The analysis of Islamic political theory in the Muslim West will be the subject matter of the following chapters.

4

IBN TUFAYL: POLITICAL RATIONALISM IN AN ELITIST ORDER

In the eleventh century, while the Seljuqs (or Saljuqs) were rising in the Muslim East at the expense of the Ghaznawids, the Almohads were on the ascendent in the Muslim West, and destroying the Almoravids.

The Almohads had become major players in European politics. In 1212, King John of England sent a delegation to the Almohad court to ask for support. Matthew Paris (d. 1259), in *Chronica majora*, wrote that 'King John offered to transfer the entire kingdom of England to the Almohad caliph, and to embrace Islam'.[1] Though that offer is inconceivable, the reference illustrates the image of the Almohads in the chronicles of England, as well as their role in European affairs.[2] The Almohads are seen as the 'golden age' of Maghribi civilisation.[3]

This chapter studies political rationalism in the Muslim West through Ibn Tufayl. The Almohads, as they did not recognise the Abbasid caliph, are a case to justify the study of politics outside the Abbasid caliph-led order. In this regard, the Almohads were a continuation of the Maghrib's autonomy, which had emerged between the early Berber resistance and the expansion of Islam and the Khariji-Berber Revolt in 741.[4] This autonomy created a dichotomy

---

[1] Shoval 2016, xviii.
[2] Fromherz 2009, 47–8.
[3] Le Tourneau 2008, 225.
[4] Dale 2015, 46.

between the Muslim East and the Muslim West that went beyond the geographical descriptions of cultural, political and religious differences.[5] The Muslim West was an independent and somewhat self-sufficient political, economic and cultural zone with its own local dynamics.[6] Like the Muslim East, the Muslim West imagined itself to be the religious centre. The Almohad traveller Ibn Jubayr (d. 1217), who visited the Muslim East around 1184, wrote in his *Rihla* that 'there is no Islam save in the Maghrib lands'.[7]

Like the Abbasids', the Almohad state was created by the revolution in which the Masmuda Berbers destroyed the Almoravid regime. Ibn Tufayl lived in this revolutionary context, and in the subsequent period of regime consolidation.

The Almohad Revolution

The Almohads were another chapter of Muslim politics in the Maghrib, a term that entails Muslim Spain (al-Andalus) and North Africa. If we imagine the expansion of Islam in the region as the first phase, the second is the Umayyad rule in al-Andalus. The period of the *ta'ifa* kings, the third period, began in the early tenth century, when the Umayyads had weakened. This had similarities with the rise of provincial states in the Muslim East, when the Cordoban caliph, Suleyman al-Musta'in, gave concessions to the local authorities that enabled them to continue their influence indirectly.[8] The fourth period is the Almoravids', a Berber state with North African origins. When the al-Andalus Muslims asked for the help of the Almoravids in 1085, the gates were opened to Berber rule in al-Andalus. After the 1140s, a period known as the second *ta'ifa*s, the Almoravid decline was followed by the emergence of tiny states. Then comes the age of the Almohads, another Berber empire that came to dominate the whole of the Maghrib, as the sixth period.

Ibn Tumart

Almohad history begins with Ibn Tumart, the man behind both the revolution and the doctrine that made the Almohads. He was born at some time

---

[5] Calasso 2021, 37.
[6] Fromherz 2010b, 10.
[7] Ibn Jubayr 2020, 93.
[8] García-Sanjuán 2020, 67.

between 1076 and 1081, in Igilliz, in the Sus valley (according to the Anti-Atlas of Morocco), among the Hargha, a division of the Masmuda Berbers.[9] His early education was in Cordoba.[10] Around the year 1106, he travelled to the Muslim East to learn the sciences, and he visited Cairo, Damascus and Baghdad.[11] He met Abu Bakr al-Sashi, who taught him Islamic law.[12] Various classical authors claim that Ibn Tumart met al-Ghazali.[13] This is, however, rejected by others, such as Ibn al-Athir.[14] Probably, the al-Ghazali meeting was added for the purposes of legitimacy.[15] For example, the pro-Almohad al-Marrakushi (d. 1250) claimed that during their meeting, al-Ghazali had miraculously informed Ibn Tumart about future developments.[16]

After returning to the Maghrib in 1119, Ibn Tumart began his religious activism in Mallala with the promise of revitalising religion by destroying the innovations. There, he met Abd al-Mu'min, who would become his caliph.[17]

In 1121, Ibn Tumart proclaimed himself the *Mahdi*.[18] The next phase was the revolutionary period when Ibn Tumart and his followers, now called 'the Almohads', challenged the Almoravid regime.[19] Following the method of enjoining good and forbidding evil, Ibn Tumart destroyed the shops that sold musical instruments, and broke the vessels that contained wine.[20] He criticised the non-Islamic taxes.[21] In a more direct attack on the Almoravids, he condemned their practice of men veiling themselves (*litham*).[22] He accused

---

[9] Ibn al-Athir 2016a, 215; Ibn Abi Zar' 1972, 172.
[10] Laroui 1977, 175.
[11] Ibn Khallikan 1868, 206.
[12] Al-Marrakushi 1881, 128.
[13] Ibn Abi Zar' 1972, 172; al-Zarkashi 1998, 8; Ibn Khallikan 1868, 206.
[14] Ibn al-Athir 2016a, 215.
[15] Griffel 2005, 754. For an opposite view, see Fletcher 1997a, 307–9 and 317.
[16] Al-Marrakushi 1881, 128–9.
[17] Ibn al-Athir 2016a, 215; Ibn Khallikan 1868, 207; al-Zarkashi 1998, 11. Not a Masmuda Berber, Abd al-Mu'min was a member of Kumiya, Zenata Berbers. Al-Marrakushi 1881, 246.
[18] Ibn Abi Zar' 1972, 173; al-Zarkashi 1998, 14.
[19] Musa 1991, 39.
[20] Al-Marrakushi 1881, 128; al-Baydaq 1971, 24.
[21] Buresi 2020, 116.
[22] Al-Baydaq 1971, 13 and 27.

them of being dominated by women.[23] However, as the gist of his propaganda, Ibn Tumart castigated the Almoravids' concept of God for being anthropomorphic. This licenced the Almoravids' destruction.

In a debate organised by the Almoravid ruler Ali bin Yusuf (r. 1106–43), Ibn Tumart challenged the Maliki scholars.[24] The Almoravids, having realised Ibn Tumart's ability to influence people, attempted to kill him. In what was interpreted as *hijra* by his followers, Ibn Tumart escaped to Aghmat. This region, to which he originally belonged, became his stronghold, and his movement flourished there.[25] The Almoravids' expeditions against Ibn Tumart failed, for it was impossible to operate effectively in the high mountains.[26] Also, they faced financial and man-power shortages because they were conserving a large amount of their resources to deal with problems in Spain, like the local rebellions and the campaigns of the Christians.[27]

The Masmuda Berbers were behind Ibn Tumart's movement. The Sanhaja, mostly nomadic, lived in the Western Sahara. The Masmuda, a sedentary confederation, lived in the High Atlas Mountains and in the Sus valley, and were dependent on agriculture, as the valleys and terraces of the mountains supported that activity.[28] The Sanhaja, who founded the Almoravid state, were historical competitors of the Masmuda. That historical competition became the bedrock of Ibn Tumart's movement, as it emerged immediately after a period when the Masmuda were seriously undermined by the Sanhaja expanding their territory.

That expansion was in reality the Sanhaja's march to Almoravid statehood by means of spreading from their desert plains into the nearby areas.[29] In 1055 – the year Tugrul arrived in Baghdad – the Almoravids took over Sijilmasa, the regional trade centre.[30] Sijilmasa was contested by various Berber tribes,

---

[23] Kennedy 2004, 612. Almoravid tribes were matriarchal; women were not veiled, and held relatively strong social status, while men wore veils over their mouths. Gómez-Rivas 2020, 96.

[24] Ibn al-Athir 2016a, 216; al-Marrakushi 1881, 132.

[25] Ibn Khallikan 1868, 210; al-Zarkashi 1998, 16; al-Baydaq 1971, 28.

[26] Kennedy 2014, 183.

[27] Bennison 2016, 57.

[28] Irwin 2018, 23.

[29] Ibn Khaldun 1958a, 296.

[30] Kennedy 2014, 157. Sijilmasa was the main port of entry for Sudanese gold coming into North Africa. Messier 1974, 38.

including the Masmuda.[31] The Sanhaja Berbers next captured Marrakesh, Fez and Tlemcen, key cities between the desert and the Mediterranean Sea.[32] Soon, the Almoravids completely dominated the regional economic network.[33] In 1058, the Almoravids took over Aghmat, a Masmuda town.[34] Several Masmuda tribes were put under Almoravid taxation.[35] The Almoravid expansion put the Masmuda in a precarious balance between survival and extinction: they were a mountain people whose survival depended on their control of the outposts on the plains to the north and south of their habitat. Any disruption of this control would have left them deprived of vital staples, such as grains and salt, and of their seasonal movements to the foothills.[36]

This situation created a reaction among the Masmuda that provided the necessary milieu for Ibn Tumart to hatch his political movement.[37] He simply provided them with a politico-religious ideology that justified war against the Almoravids. This was not unlike what their contemporaries, the Seljuqs, had done to the Ghaznawids. For the Seljuqs, as for the Masmuda, religion no longer symbolised political unity when two Muslim states were at war, each determined to wrest power from the other.

In 1128, Ibn Tumart purged (*tamyiz*) various old supporters by introducing a new power hierarchy in Tinmal.[38] This created an embryonic bureaucracy that would later become the core of the Almohad state.[39] The Council of Ten as the core group, and other councils with less critical roles, such as the Council of Fifty, were also created.[40] This was in practice the merger of religious and tribal hierarchies: while the former group was composed of Ibn Tumart's close followers, the latter was composed mostly of tribal leaders.[41]

---

[31] Bigon and Langenthal 2022, 3788.
[32] Viguera-Molins 2010, 24.
[33] Lacoste 1984, 18.
[34] Gómez-Rivas 2020, 96.
[35] Le Tourneau 1969, 5.
[36] García 1991, 4.
[37] Ibn Abi Zar' 1972, 176; Hopkins 1986, 958.
[38] Ibn al-Athir 2016a, 220. Also see al-Sanhaji 1971, 36. *Tamyiz* was a Berber tradition of forming alliances among tribes before wars. Fromherz 2010a, 96.
[39] Abun-Nasr 2012, 90; Hopkins 1986, 958.
[40] Al-Marrakushi 1881, 132; Ibn Abi Zar' 1972, 177.
[41] Al-Sanhaji 1971, 32–5; Hopkins 1954, 93.

The incorporation of Berber networks into the political structure was inevitable, given that the Berbers lived a nomadic life based on tribal loyalty and customs.[42]

Ibn Khaldun would later explain Ibn Tumart's success as the result of the tribal support he got from the Masmuda Berbers.[43] This, however, made Almohad politics operate on two sets of legitimacy: Ibn Tumart's doctrine and Berber tribalism.[44] The success of this model was always dependent on keeping the balance between those two factors.[45] As that was never easy, the dual legitimacy model, paradoxically, exposed the Almohads to an incessant legitimacy risk.

Having created an embryonic state, Ibn Tumart next made military advances against the Almoravids.[46] At this bloody revolutionary stage, the Almoravids were killed and their property plundered.[47] Ibn Tumart, however, would not see the final victory. He died after the battle of Buhayra in 1129/1130, when they were defeated by the Almoravids.[48]

The foundation of the Almohad state

Abd al-Mu'min became the first Almohad caliph in 1132. Tactically, Ibn Tumart's death had been kept secret for two years.[49] The new caliph continued the revolutionary agenda. For a while, he refrained from military contact with the Almoravids. This was a strategy to gain time for accumulating a larger support base.[50] He succeeded in securing the support of influential Masmuda leaders, including Abu Hafs 'Umar, the leader of the richest tribe, the Hintata.[51] Abd al-Mu'min besieged Tlemcen in 1143.[52] In 1145/6, he

---

[42] Ibn Khaldun 1958b, 266–7.
[43] Ibn Khaldun 1958a, 55.
[44] Miranda 2004, 93; Fromherz 2009, 45.
[45] Fromherz 2010a, 8.
[46] Ibn Abi Zar' 1972, 177; al-Baydaq 1971, 35–9.
[47] Ibn al-Athir 2016a, 218.
[48] Al-Zarkashi 1998, 17.
[49] Ibn al-Athir 2016a, 221; Ibn Abi Zar' 1972, 184.
[50] Le Tourneau 1969, 51.
[51] Fromherz 2010a, 107.
[52] Ibn al-Athir 2016a, 222; al-Zarkashi 1998, 19.

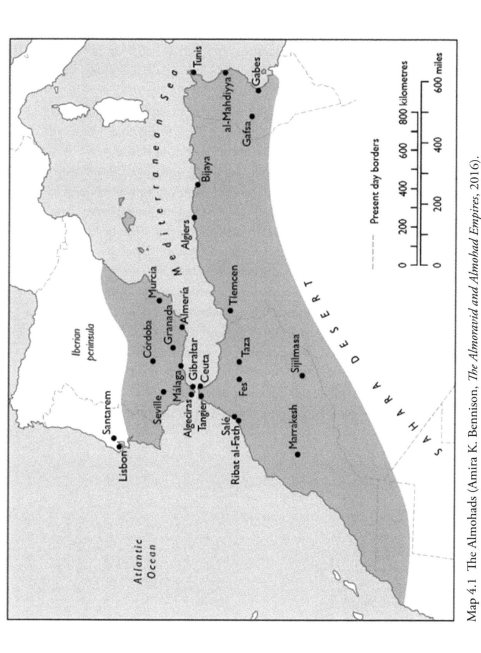

Map 4.1 The Almohads (Amira K. Bennison, *The Almoravid and Almohad Empires*, 2016).

earned the loyalty of the Zenata and the Masufa tribes, which consolidated the Almohads against the Almoravids. Many tribes, having realised the growing power of the Almohads, were on course to distance themselves from the Almoravids.[53] In 1145, the Almohads stepped into al-Andalus.[54] This was the second *ta'ifa* period of small states declaring their autonomy when the Almoravids were in crisis.

In the following stage, Caliph al-Mu'min worked towards full control of Morocco.[55] The Almohads conquered Fez, Seville and Marrakesh in 1146/7.[56] The capture of Marrakesh, the Almoravid capital, was critical, as it symbolised the consolidation of Abd al-Mu'min's rule.[57] He left his son, Abu Ya'qub Yusuf, as governor in Seville.[58] Next came the total purge of the Almoravids: in 1152/3, Abd al-Mu'min defeated the Sanhaja troops, and the various revolt-prone Arab tribes.[59] Many Almoravids, including members of the dynasty, were executed. The local population of Marrakesh were brutally purged during hree days of plunder after the city's conquest.[60] As of 1157, the Almohads had captured all critical cities and regions in al-Andalus, thereby ending the Almoravid presence.[61] The whole of the Maghrib, as far as Tripoli, was under their control by 1163.

Ibn Tumart laid the foundations of the Almohad political movement; but the conquests were achieved by Abd al-Mu'min.[62] It was he who created a state on Ibn Tumart's legacy.[63] He was the first non-Arab caliph in history,[64] but only if this term is used in a strict Almohad ecumenism as he was the

---

[53] Bennison 2016, 71 and 59.
[54] Ibn Abi Zar' 1972, 188; Bennison 2016, 74.
[55] Al-Marrakushi 1881, 163.
[56] Ibn Abi Zar' 1972, 189; al-Marrakushi 1881, 151.
[57] Ibn al-Athir 2016a, 225.
[58] Buresi and El Aallaoui 2013, 44.
[59] Ibn al-Athir 2016b, 43 and 62.
[60] Levi-Provençal 1986, 79.
[61] Ibn al-Athir 2016b, 91.
[62] Ibn Khallikan 1868, 215.
[63] Ibn Khallikan 1843b, 183. Makki (1992, 72) finds Abd al-Mu'min 'a great statesman'. Miranda (2004, 200) likens him to Charlamagne.
[64] Abun-Nasr 2012, 94.

caliph/successor of Ibn Tumart rather than of Muhammad.[65] Still, the Almohads claimed the leadership of all Muslims. To justify this, they used various arguments, such as attributing to Abd al-Mu'min a lineage to Qays 'Aylan, an Arab tribal federation.[66]

Abd al-Mu'min appointed his son as heir in 1156/7, and this transformed the state into a Mu'minid dynasty. His other sons were appointed as local governors.[67] He recruited Arabs into the army to counterbalance the Berbers.[68] This shift was not smooth: Abd al-Mu'min killed several brothers and other relatives of Ibn Tumart who had resisted his changes.[69] However, this was not an abandonment of Ibn Tumart's doctrine but a transition to a formal administration to meet the social expectations that rose with the expansion of the state.[70]

The Almohads' purge of the Almoravids affected the greater Muslim society, as the latter recognised the Abbasid caliphate. During the reign of Yusuf bin Tashfin (r. 1061–1116), the Almoravids sent an envoy to the caliph with a diploma for investiture;[71] the Almoravid coins were still carrying the Abbasid caliph's name.[72] However, the Almohads, who never recognised the Abbasid caliph, emerged as another competing caliphate, like the Fatimids. The Almohad revolution thus redefined the status of the Maghrib within the wider Muslim world.

Ibn Tumart's Doctrine

Ibn Tumart's doctrine was the ideological pillar of the Almohad state. I shall now summarise the doctrine, for its knowledge is required not only to understand the historical context but also Ibn Tufayl's political thought.

---

[65] See Ibn Khaldun 1958a, 472; Balbale 2018, 4.
[66] Garcia-Arenal 2006, 188. Also see Ibn al-Athir 2016a, 216.
[67] Al-Marrakushi 1881, 164; al-Baydaq 1971, 69–72 and 76–7; Ibn al-Athir 2016b, 81.
[68] Baadj 2020, 164–84.
[69] Ibn Abi Zar' 1972, 195.
[70] Kennedy 2004, 619; Addas 1993, 29.
[71] Ibn al-Athir 2016a, 109; Ibn Khaldun 1958a, 470.
[72] Armada 2017, 80.

Tawhid

As the most significant component of the doctrine, *tawhid*, which literally means 'unity', is belief in God without attributing incorporeality to him. The term gave the state its name: 'Almohads' in English and 'al-Muwahhidun' in Arabic.

In *A'azzu ma yutlab*, Ibn Tumart underlines that God does not resemble his creatures.[73] In *Murshida*, he states that no intelligence can comprehend him, and no imagination can characterise him.[74] Any attempt to conceptualise God is to attribute corporeality to him, that is, *mucessima*.[75] The Almohad *tawhid* defined the political and religious orthodoxy: other people were '*mujassimun*' (anthropomorphists).[76]

Ibn Tumart's *tawhid* is clear on the explication that God is trans-conceptual; he cannot be defined and conceptualised. However, it is never clear when it comes to imagining God properly. It is a deadlock that allows the minimalist conclusion that human knowledge of God is confined to the mere fact that he exists, and any reasoning that goes beyond this – like speculating on what he is like – unavoidably leads into anthropomorphism.[77]

Ibn Tumart's developing of a political ideology through a theological debate was in line with the general trends of the Muslim world. While he 'excommunicated' the Almohads for their conception of God, Hanbalis and Ash'aris – as discussed in Chapter 3 – fought each other in Baghdad, aroused by differences in their conceptions of God. The Almohad *tawhid* was therefore a continuation of a grand intra-Islamic debate in the Maghrib. Accordingly, the Mu'tazila imagined God almost as an intellect without a body.[78] On the opposite pole was Hanbali, which recognised God as a body, and accepted him as having hands and other corporeal features, as explained in the scripture. The Ash'ari held the middle ground: in al-Ash'ari's *al-Ibanah*, God is still known as having a face and throne, but that is never understood to be a human face and throne.[79] However, this was still a weak

---

[73] Ibn Tumart 2007, 216–18.
[74] Ibid., 226.
[75] Ibid., 217.
[76] Al-Baydaq 1971, 90.
[77] Thiele 2022, 218.
[78] Fakhry 2004, 59.
[79] Al-Ash'ari 1940, 50.

theology that might easily lead to anthropomorphism.[80] Thus, Ibn Tumart, who imagined God not as a body but as an abstraction, appears closed to the Muʿtazila.[81] (The Muʿtazila also named themselves *ahl al-tawhid*.) As a matter of fact, Ibn Tumart was criticised later by Hanbali scholars like Ibn Taymiyya for rejecting the divine attributes, a criticism levelled also at the Muʿtazila.[82] Nevertheless, the Muʿtazili rejection of an ontological contact between God and his creatures was also unacceptable to Ibn Tumart.[83] Among other reasons, Mahdism necessitates a contact between God and nature.[84] It is thus better to imagine Ibn Tumart as a follower of neo-Ashʿari theology, which was a form updated by borrowings from Ibn Sina. According to Griffel, Ibn Tufayl was inspired by the neo-Ashʿari paradigm in Baghdad, at a time when al-Juwayni's students dominated the Nizamiyya network.[85]

The Almohad *tawhid* had serious outcomes: Ibn Tumart used *tawhid* in the sense of 'faith'.[86] He asked his followers to learn and memorise *tawhid* because whoever is not cognisant of it is not a believer. Among his followers, *tawhid* became like the Qurʾan.[87] He was 'almost as a new prophet',[88] and the Almohad *tawhid* was a new Berber monotheistic religion.[89] It was described as a general religion that had been professed by all previous prophets.[90] To enhance this, Biblical names such as Yaʿqub (Jacob) and Yusuf (Joseph) were preferred.[91] Islam, like other religions, was downgraded to being a historical representation of the Almohad *tawhid*.

---

[80] Thiele 2022, 220.
[81] Hawi 1975, 66.
[82] Griffel 2005, 800–1. The Almohad period coincided with the rise of the Muʿtazila impact in al-Andalus. Stroumsa 2019, 63.
[83] Fierro 1999, 229.
[84] Similarly, on free will, Ibn Tumart is unsurprisingly closed to the Ashʿari. Ibn Tumart 2007, 219–20.
[85] Griffel 2005, 802. Classical authors like Ibn Khaldun (1958a, 471) linked Ibn Tumart's *tawhid* to Ashʿarism.
[86] Al-Najjar 1984, 257.
[87] Ibn Abi Zarʿ 1972, 177.
[88] Fierro 2016, II/3.
[89] Buresi 2020, 128–9.
[90] Bennison 2016, 247.
[91] Fierro 1999, 227.

Logically, this required the replacing of the existing forms of Islam with the Almohad *tawhid*. All non-Almohads were deprived of their status as believers.[92] All people, including the Muslims, were invited to accept the new faith. In *Akhbar al-Mahdi*, written by Ibn Tumart's official historian al-Baydaq (d. 1164), we read accounts of Muslims becoming unitarian, that is, *muwahhid*, by converting to the Almohad faith.[93] That critical stance towards other Muslims was observed in the *Rihla* of medieval traveller Ibn Jubayr. Ibn Jubayr, a scribe to the Almohad governor of Ceuta, expressed his disapproval of Muslims in Hejaz, whom he defined as holding schismatic views, by wishing that God may soon purify them with the Almohads' swords.[94]

Tawhid required the refusal of everything inherited from the 'anthropomorphist' Almoravids. The Almohads minted square coins, replacing the round ones.[95] The traditional Kufic calligraphy was replaced by Nakshi. The *qibla* of mosques were re-oriented ('purified'), and new ways of calling to prayer were established.[96] They even discouraged pilgrimage to Mecca.[97] *Tawhid* also required an Almohad ecumenism that rejected the Abbasid caliphate. Their coins defined Ibn Tumart as the leader of all Muslims.[98] As *tawhid* equalised all people, including the Muslims, the Almohads abolished the status of *dhimma*.[99]

Christians and Jews who did not convert to the Almohad *tawhid* became infidels. They faced either forced conversion or exodus.[100] When Abd al-Mu'min captured Ifriqiyya, he gave the Jews and Christians the choice

---

[92] Garcia-Arenal 2006, 157.

[93] Al-Baydaq 1971, 67.

[94] Ibn Jubayr 2020, 93.

[95] Ibn Khaldun 1958b, 57. The coins had no date, symbolising Ibn Tumart's Mahdism in the latter days.

[96] Hebert 1991, 125; Garcia-Arenal 2006, 157; Ibrahim and Pliego 2020, 182.

[97] The Spanish Umayyads once prohibited people from going abroad to fulfil their pilgrimage duty as part of their competition with the Abbasids. Ibn Khaldun 1958b, 100.

[98] Armada 2017, 82. The coins include *al-hamdu lillah wahdahu* meaning 'praise be to God alone'. Lane-Poole 1873, 154; Ibrahim and Pliego 2020, 182.

[99] Stroumsa 2009, 56; Fierro 2016, ix.

[100] Aranda 2012, 68; Garcia-Arenal 2010, 596; Fierro 2019, 114.

of conversion to Islam or death.[101] Al-Marrakushi wrote that there was no longer a *dhimmi*, nor even a church or synagogue, in the Maghrib during the rule of the second caliph, Abu Ya'qub bin Yusuf.[102]

As another decisive outcome, *tawhid* justified jihad against the Almoravids, whom Ibn Tumart saw as infidel anthropomorphists.[103] The section of *A'azzu ma yutlab* on 'anthropomorphists and their indicators'[104] was in fact a critique of the Almoravids. Ibn Tumart invited the Almoravids to his faith.[105] Otherwise, *tawhid* justified killing them, confiscating their property, and enslaving their women.[106]

The Almohad *tawhid* automatically challenged Malikism, the official law of the Almoravids.[107] Malikism was the ideological and legal glue in the transportation of the Sanhaja Berbers into the Almoravid state. Around the year 1035, Yahya bin Ibrahim, ruler of the Gudala (Judala) tribe of the Sanhaja confederation,[108] looked for a religious scholar to instruct his tribesmen.[109] The networks in Qayrawan connected him with Abdullah bin Yasin, a Maliki jurist.[110] Malikism thus became the paradigm that moved the Sanhaja Berbers from tribal customary law into a sophisticated administrative law.[111] This

---

[101] Ibn al-Athir 2016b, 104. As the works of Fierro (2010c, 86) and Corcos (2010, 279–83) show, the violence was limited to the early Almohad period. This was linked to the fact that the early period witnessed state formation through military expeditions, as well as political purges. Bennison 2016, 71.

[102] Al-Marrakushi 1881, 223.

[103] Ibn Abi Zar' 1972, 181–2.

[104] Ibn Tumart 2007, 242.

[105] Al-Marrakushi 1881, 137.

[106] Albarrán 2021, 2.

[107] The Maliki school became widespread in al-Andalus, even in the lifetime of Malik (d. 795). Abd al-Rahman III (r. 912–61) declared Malikism as the official doctrine of the Cordoban Umayyad caliphate. A relationship between al-Maghrib and Malikism reminiscent of Transoxiana and Maturidism/Hanafism can be proposed. R. Idris 2017, 85–6; Glick 2005, 156–7.

[108] The Sanhaja confederation included almost seventy tribes, including the major ones: Gudala, Massufa and the Lamtuna. Ibn Abi Zar' 1972, 120.

[109] The Almoravids were more connected to western Africa. Their origin was connected to the intra-tribal affairs in Ghana and Mali. Lange 1996, 313–51.

[110] Ibn Abi Zar' 1972, 122–4; Viguera-Molins 2010, 36.

[111] Bennison 2016, 53.

paved the way for an entente between Maliki scholars/jurists and the Sanhaja Berbers. This entente later became the pillar of the Almoravid regime.[112]

Maliki jurists assumed the role of legitimisers by providing the legal reasonings that accommodated the Almoravid policies. When the Almoravids took over al-Andalus, scholars like Abu Bakr ibn al-Arabi (d. 1148) and Ibn Abdun articulated an Almoravid theory of government and legitimacy.[113] Maliki jurists also legitimised various Almoravid policies during the times of the *ta'ifa* kings.[114] Their role was equally significant in the Almoravids' rivalry with Ismailism.[115] Finally, they sided with Almoravids to quell the early Almohad opposition. Qadi Iyad (d. 1149) challenged Ibn Tumart's Mahdism as heresy, and even organised a political movement against the Almohads.[116]

The Maliki school was based on the Islamic practices of the early Madina Muslims. It regarded the consensus of the Madina scholars as the superior of all others. This looked to the Almohads as a local interpretation that distorted Islam's message. Ibn Tumart criticised the Malikis for prioritising case law based on Maliki scholars' opinions.[117] According to Ibn Tumart, personal opinions and analogies should be avoided in legal reasoning because they cause a plurality of opinions, which is unacceptable, as there is one true interpretation of religion.[118] The Almohads prohibited personal opinions (*ra'y*) in legal reasoning, and threatened holders of them with punishment.[119] The repercussions on the Almohad belief were that *tawhid* is the final and perfect method that provides legal unity, and puts an end to inconsistent legal opinions.[120] The Almohads saw personal opinion as the distortion of the truth with local elements.

As importantly, the Almohads used theological debates around *tawhid* to exert influence on the judiciary.[121] Dismantling or re-organising the Maliki

---

[112] Abun-Nasr 2012, 84; Casewit 2017, 46.
[113] Gómez-Rivas 2020, 102–6.
[114] Bennison 2016, 48.
[115] Gómez-Rivas 2014, 4; Messier 2001, 61.
[116] Al-Zarkashi 1998, 23; Kassis 1983, 510–11.
[117] Cornell 1987, 93; Messier 2010, 140.
[118] Ibn Tumart 2007, 166. Also see Stroumsa 2019, 129.
[119] Fierro 1999, 237.
[120] Fierro 2010a, 159; Garcia-Arenal 2006, 178.
[121] Serrano 2014, 270.

judiciary was a primary task for the Almohads, whose political survival required a new concept of legitimacy. However, since the dismantling of the Maliki establishment was virtually impossible, they created a religious class, the *talaba*. The *talaba* (the student) was invented by Ibn Tumart to preach his doctrine.[122] This was a new class of religious agent for the defence and development of Ibn Tumart's doctrine, and for the legitimising of the state.[123]

Mahdism

Ibn Tumart's Mahdism was incorporated into the state ideology.[124] Mahdism made his leadership and doctrine binding on all people. It generated the ultimate authority to interpret religion. He was not just another scholar, but a divine person seen to be *maʿsum*, infallible.[125]

Reminiscent of the Abbasids, Mahdism was framed within an Alid (or Shiʿa) narrative.[126] For many contemporary scholars, Ibn Tumart's was the middle ground between Sunnism and Shiʿism,[127] or closer to the latter.[128] Ibn Tumart's use of *jafr* (the science of the symbolic meanings of the letters used to discover future events) was a typical Alid practice.[129] Also, the Almohads paid enormous attention to the Alid genealogy for legitimacy.[130] Though this was a later invention, as Ibn Khallikan wrote,[131] it reflected a political intention to acquire legitimacy through Ali.

In retrospect, the region was open to the Alid impact. The Idrisids, who dominated some parts of Maghrib, had an Alid theory of rulership.[132] Their founder, Idris bin ʿAbdallah (r. 789–91), was a Zaydi.[133] The Idrisids were

---

[122] Al-Baydaq 1971, 30.
[123] Fierro 2010b, 166.
[124] Fierro 2016, VI/9; Ghouirgate 2015, 43; Fromherz 2009, 47.
[125] Ibn Abi Zarʿ 1972, 177; al-Baydaq, 1971, 12.
[126] Ibn Khaldun 1958a, 471.
[127] Bennison and Gallego 2010, 145.
[128] Fierro 2010c, 82.
[129] Miranda 2004, 36.
[130] Al-Zarkashi 1998, 6; al-Marrakushi 1881, 128.
[131] Ibn Khallikan 1868, 206.
[132] Fenwick 2022, 34; Ibn Khaldun 1958a, 47–8.
[133] Dale 2015, 52.

dominant in the Sus Valley, where Ibn Tumart was born. Naturally, Shiʿism affected Sus.[134] Another conduit of the Alid impact were the Fatimids who dominated Ifriqiyya in 909.[135] The Fatimid caliph Abu Abd Allah (d. 934) declared himself the *Mahdi* there. Later, in 972, the Fatimid caliph Muʿizz announced North Africa as a dependent unit under the rulership of Ibn Ziri, a Sanhaja Berber.[136] Sanhaja tribes like Talkata and Kutama became supporters of the Fatimid *daʿwa*.[137]

Kitab al-Ansab, the major Almohad text on genealogy, traces Ibn Tumart's origin to Muhammad through Fatima, via an Idrisid ruler.[138] Ibn Khaldun accepted this Fatimid descent as authentic.[139] The attribution of Alid origins to other Almohads, like Abd al-Mu'min in *Kitab al-Ansab*,[140] reinforced the idea that those legitimation tactics are sound. Yet the Almohads had never claimed to be Shiʿis.[141] Indeed, *Rawd al-Qurtas* defines Abd al-Mu'min as a Sunni.[142] Furthermore, the Almohads used the Uthman's codex of political legitimacy, which was an anti-Shiʿa symbol because the codex came from the Umayyads, the arch-enemies of the Shiʿis.[143]

Almohad Mahdism was also connected to the traditional elements of charismatic leadership: the magic and miracles of the Berber culture.[144] It was a perfect match for the holy personages of North African religious life.[145] Ernest Gellner, who shaped this explanation, opened the chapter on North

---

[134] Morrow 2021, 99 and 256; Fierro 2010c, 66. As Maddy-Weitzman (2011, 23) reminds, religious praxis in North Africa was highly syncretic, combining elements of Judaism, Christianity and paganism. A reason for the local presence of syncretism was that the Muslim West was the shelter for various groups, like the Kharijites. R. Idris 2017, 86.

[135] Baadj 2014, 22. Laroui (1977, 174) saw Ibn Tumart as under Fatimid esoterism.

[136] Brett 2010, 49. Also see Ibn Abi Zarʿ 1972, 102–8.

[137] Baadj 2014, 13 and 22.

[138] Al-Sanhaji 1971, 12–13. According to Makki (1992, 69) and Fierro (2010b, 173), the Fatimids might have influenced Ibn Tumart in Cairo.

[139] Ibn Khaldun 1958, 55.

[140] Al-Sanhaji 1971, 13.

[141] Fierro 2020, 6.

[142] Ibn Abi Zarʿ 1972, 204.

[143] Buresi 2020, 132.

[144] Fierro 2016, III/5. Also see Ibn Khaldun 1958b, 202.

[145] Fletcher 1997b, 236 and 240; Watt and Cachia 1996, 108.

Africa in his *Muslim Society* by defining the saint (the holy personage) as the most characteristic social institution of North African religious life.[146] For example, the Barghawa and the Ghumara branch of Masmuda had their own prophets.[147] Ibn Tumart fitted this holy personage profile. He was reported to carry a *jafr* book with him.[148] He used other occult symbols too, such as the passing of the year 500 according to the Islamic calendar (1106/7 on the Gregorian calendar).[149]

The motif of the latter days is a major theme in *A'azzu Ma Yutlab*.[150] Ibn Tumart gives the impression that his life is similar to Muhammad's.[151] He wore simple clothes, such as palm branches and sandals.[152] He called his family *ahl al-dar*, like Muhammad's *ahl al-bayt*.[153] His escape to Tinmal was called *hijra*; he spent three months in a cave there, which is reminiscent of Muhammad's Hira.[154]

As a matter of fact, Ibn Tumart incorporated the Berber culture into his doctrine. *Rawd al-Qurtas* presents Ibn Tumart as a man who came from the Berbers. He preached and wrote in Berber.[155] For the first time, the Qur'an was translated into Berber. The call to prayer was sometimes made in Berber.[156] Berber became the language of liturgy.[157] In this regard, Ibn Tumart's doctrine was another phase in the Berbers' historical cultural resistance to the Arabs, which had begun as early as Islam's expansion during the time of Uqba bin Nafi (i.e. *c.*680).[158] They had rebelled continuously, and even apostatised,

---

[146] Gellner 1984, 131.
[147] Fierro 2010c, 68.
[148] Ibn Khallikan 1843b, 182. According to Ibn Abi Zar' (1972, 180), before he died, Ibn Tumart gave that book to Abd al-Mu'min.
[149] Ibn Khallikan 1843b, 188.
[150] Ibn Tumart 2007, 243.
[151] Bennison 2010, 209.
[152] Al-Marrakushi 1881, 138.
[153] Bennison 2016, 68.
[154] Al-Baydaq 1971, 33.
[155] Ibn Abi Zar' 1972, 181.
[156] Lázaro 2013, 278; Fierro 1999, 227.
[157] Jones 2013, 76–7; Maddy-Weitzman 2011, 31.
[158] Le Tourneau 2008, 213. As an important detail, Ibn Abd al-Hakam (1858, 34) wrote that the first Berber insurrection against Arabs happened in Sus.

even after Islam was established among them.[159] That resistance, which was in effect a cultural negotiation between the Berbers and the Arabs, gave way to the North African form of Islam:[160] a Berberised Islam.[161]

This historical encounter created a mythic narrative among the Berbers – similar to that of *mawali* during the Abbasid revolution – according to which they saw themselves as the people destined to revive Islam, a religion that the Arabs had betrayed.[162] Ibn Tumart had in effect allowed the Berbers to imagine them as the main actors of Islamic history.[163]

Finally, Mahdism, for its connection to mysticism, was relevant against Malikism. In fact, Ibn Tumart's movement emerged in the context of the 'Sufi revolt', when the various Sufi movements turned out to be a military-religious opposition to the Almoravids.[164] These groups problematised the Maliki jurists' entente with the state, and their dry legalistic method.[165] For example, the *muridun* movement led by al-Qasi (d. 1151), who had declared himself the *Mahdi*, led a revolt in 1141.[166] Having become a military organisation, they captured various cities, and supported the Almohads.[167] Ibn Barrajan (d. 1141), known as the 'al-Ghazali of al-Andalus', was another representative of the Sufi opposition.[168] He wrote a spiritual interpretation of the Qur'an, *Idah*, in which he developed the doctrine of the return of the *Mahdi*.[169] He captured several villages, but was later executed by the Almoravids.[170]

The magnitude of this threat forced the Almoravids to implement radical policies, like the persecuting of the Sufis. Also, seeing that al-Ghazali's opinions justified the Sufis' esoteric knowledge, they burnt his books in 1109

---

[159] Ibn Khaldun 1958a, 333.
[160] Brett 2017, 190; Le Tourneau 2008, 216.
[161] Rodd 1925, 730.
[162] Sánchez 2010, 175–9.
[163] Bennison 2016, 131; Sánchez 2010, 186.
[164] Ben-Zaken 2011, 25.
[165] Dale 2015, 61; Fletcher 1997b, 253; Bellver 2020, 330; Casewit 2012/13, 119.
[166] Gómez-Rivas 2020, 107; Guichard 1997, 698; Fierro 2016, III/1.
[167] Dudgeon 2018, 97–8; Ibn Khaldun 1958a, 323; Messier 2010, 163.
[168] Casewit 2012/13, 111–42.
[169] Ibn Barrajan 2015, 908.
[170] Bellver 2013, 671 and 661; Casewit 2017, 48. The Almohads later restored his reputation.

and 1143.[171] Al-Ghazali, whose opinions represented the status quo in the Muslim East, became a symbol of opposition in the Muslim West.[172]

Elitism

The Almohad *tawhid* envisaged a society composed of the elite and the average people. According to Ibn Tumart, there is no third category that can be added to 'those who know', and 'those who are ignorant'.[173] The average people are the ignorant. They cannot know truth because culture and language distort it. The Almohad *tawhid*, which promises understanding the truth beyond cultural distortions, belongs to the elite because they can understand the truth without falling into corporality.[174] The Almohads' view of society was therefore a pessimistic one.

Language occupied a major place in Ibn Tumart's critique of society. Ibn Abi Zar' defines him as a master of language.[175] Some passages of *A'azz Ma Yutlab* give Ibn Tumart an image of a scholar of semantics. As his main argument, he rejects the view that language is a neutral means of transmitting the truth. For him, language inevitably distorts the truth because it operates in a cultural context. This inevitably leads to anthropomorphism when it comes to the conception of God.[176] Ibn Tumart imagined the truth as being beyond language and culture. This is reflected in his metaphor of understanding God at the day of one's birth.[177] He saw culture and language as the distorters of communication, whereas the truth is frameless and does not change according to context.[178]

Reflecting his distrust of society, Ibn Tumart wanted his followers to see themselves as strangers. A tradition (that is, Islam), 'began as a stranger (*gharib*) and shall return to being a stranger just as it began; thus, blessed be

---

[171] Ben-Zaken 2011, 25; Safran 2014, 164–5.
[172] Viguera-Molins 2010, 38; Fletcher 1997a, 305.
[173] Ibn Tumart 2007, 43.
[174] Urvoy 1974, 37–9.
[175] Ibn Abi Zar' 1972, 181.
[176] Ibn Tumart 2007, 45, 53 and 56–7.
[177] Fromherz 2010a, 160.
[178] Ibn Tumart 2007, 293.

the strangers', was his motto.[179] Paradoxically, while the 'stranger' narrative elevates his followers, it reveals their limits too; since it is not possible to stop the impact of culture and language on the average people, the agents of truth will be few and isolated.[180] This is significant from the perspective of Islamic political theory: 'a perfect society' is an oxymoron for Ibn Tumart, as society is naturally a distorter of the ideal.

Eclecticism

Ibn Tumart's doctrine was hyper-eclectic. Al-Marrakushi describes it as Ash'ari with borrowings from the Mu'tazila and the Shi'a.[181] In what could be seen as the best summary of Ibn Tumart's eclecticism, Pascal Buresi and Hicham El Aallaoui define the Almohad doctrine as drawing from almost all the theological currents that had seen the day since the beginnings of Islam.[182]

The reason behind this is Ibn Tumart's method that employs both rational and mystical strands. Accordingly, the search for truth begins in nature, and is discoverable by rational-empirical methods. This is then followed by the higher stage, where one experiences the truth in its incorporeality by mystical methods. While the empirical methods of philosophers like Ibn Sina are applied at the first stage, al-Ghazali's mystical methods are applied at the second stage.[183]

Ibn Tufayl: His Life

Ibn Tufayl was born in 1116 in Wadi-Ash (Guadix), four years before Ibn Tumart declared himself the *Mahdi*.[184] His childhood and youth coincided with the time when the Almoravids were first weakened, and later destroyed, by the Almohads. He was born into social turmoil, and grew up in the midst of a political transition.[185] He was educated under the Almoravid regime. He

---

[179] Ghouirgate 2015, 45.
[180] Fierro 2000, 232.
[181] Al-Marrakushi 1881, 132.
[182] Buresi and El Aallaoui 2013, 27.
[183] Hopkins (1986, 959) and Le Tourneau (1969, 28) do not find Ibn Tumart as original. According to Watt (1985, 115), Ibn Tumart's theology would hardly be worthy of mention, had it not become the official theology of the Almohads. Fromherz (2010a, 46) appreciates Ibn Tumart's intellectual contribution.
[184] Conrad 1996a, 5.
[185] Ben-Zaken 2011, 16.

studied with leading scholars such as Abu al-Fad al-Sharaf (d. 1140), a man of letters. His father was a scholar.[186]

In 1147, he went to Marrakesh with Ahmad bin Milhan, the Almoravid ruler of Guadix during their collapse, to undertake an assignment from the Almohads.[187] This was his transition to the new regime. Ibn Tufayl became the secretary of the Almohad governor of Granada. Later, in 1157, he became the secretary of the Almohad governor of Ceuta and Tangiers, Abu Said Uthman, the son of Abd al-Mu'min.[188]

He began to work for the Almohads in their critical period of state formation. In 1163, he was appointed adviser and physician to the court of Abu Ya'qub Yusuf, the second Almohad caliph. Ibn Tufayl kept this position until 1182, when he resigned from the post in favour of Ibn Rushd.[189] *Rawd al-Qurtas* describes Ibn Tufayl as Abu Ya'qub Yusuf's doctor, a man knowledgeable in medicine.[190] Al-Marrakushi added that Ibn Tufayl became interested in metaphysics (the divine sciences) during the latter part of his life. He noted that he spent long hours with Abu Ya'qub, during which they discussed political developments.[191] He was paid by the government.[192] He contributed also to the education of caliph's son, Abu Yusuf Ya'qub.[193]

Ibn Tufayl's breadth of scholarship was encyclopedic. Apart from medicine, he was versed in mathematics, philosophy and poetry.[194] But he was not a philosopher by training.[195] He was given the honorific title of vizier, but that was not meant to be understood in the usual sense as an executive power.[196] However, he was always at the centre of political life as an advisor.[197]

---

[186] Fierro 2020, 8–9.
[187] Conrad 1996a, 5–6.
[188] Fierro 2020, 9–10.
[189] Cornell 1996, 134–5.
[190] Ibn Abi Zar' 1972, 207.
[191] Al-Marrakushi 1881, 172.
[192] Conrad 1996a, 18–19.
[193] Fierro 2020, 11.
[194] Corbin 1993, 237–8.
[195] De Rande 2019, 210.
[196] Conrad 1996a, 3–4.
[197] Richter-Bernburg 1996, 90.

The Political Context: The Almohads' Legitimacy Crisis

The reign of Caliph Abu Yaʻqub bin Yusuf (henceforth Abu Yaʻqub), a period that covered almost all of Ibn Tufayl's public service, was a period of crisis in both prosperity and legitimacy. Abu Yaʻqub became caliph when his father, Abd al-Mu'min, died in 1163.[198] Several Almohad elites, including various members of the Council of Ten, had reservations about him.[199] As a matter of fact, he was not the original heir to the throne. The original heir was his half-brother, Muhammad. However, the latter was ousted from the succession by Abu Hafs Umar, Abu Yaʻqub's brother, during Abd al-Mu'min's illness. This paved the way for a duumvirate.[200]

Abu Yaʻqub first quelled the various tribes that had revolted after the death of the first caliph.[201] In 1070/1, he set out on a major campaign to al-Andalus, where he had not visited for years.[202] Al-Marrakushi reported him allocating money to scholars, expecting that they would collect traditions (*hadith*) on jihad before this campaign.[203] The campaign was presented to the public amid great feasts.[204] The aim of the campaign was to consolidate public legitimacy, as well as to show the power of the caliph to rivals, including the Muslims who opposed Ibn Tumart's doctrine. The army moved slowly across the cities to demonstrate the caliph's power. However, when it came to a military encounter with Christians in Huete, the Almohad army lost its order and disbanded. The campaign had failed, but for a few small military gains.[205] In 1071, while the Manzikert victory against Christians provided huge legitimacy to the Seljuqs, the new Almohad caliph was not able to achieve that. He later spent time in Huete, where he began construction projects. He returned to Marrakesh in 1078.[206]

---

[198] Ibn Khallikan 1843b, 184; Ibn al-Athir 2016b, 139; al-Marrakushi 1881, 169. The Almohad caliphs were buried in Tinmal near Ibn Tumart's grave, a state cemetery. Ibn Abi Zarʻ 1972, 202; al-Zarkashi 1998, 30 and 36.

[199] Fierro 2010c, 74.

[200] Bennison 2016, 92–4.

[201] Ibn al-Athir 2016b, 154–5; al-Zarkashi 1998, 30.

[202] Al-Marrakushi 1881, 178.

[203] Ibid., 183.

[204] Kennedy 2014, 223.

[205] Bennison 2016, 95–8; Kennedy 2004, 618.

[206] Ibn Abi Zarʻ 1972, 211; Fierro 2010c, 75.

	Political Actors	Political Dynamics
	Ibn Tumart's revolt (1121–1130)	Decline of the Almoravids and rise of Almohads (The Almohad Revolution)
	Caliph Abd al-Mu'min (1130/3–1163)	
Ibn Tufayl (1110–1185)		Almohad state formation
	Caliph Abu Ya'qub (1163–1184)	
		Transformation of Almohads
	Caliph al-Mansur (1184–1199)	

Figure 4.1 Ibn Tufayl in political history.

Abu Ya'qub later organised expeditions against the revolt of the Sanhaja tribes.[207] In 1180, the Almohads organised a campaign to reinstate their power over Gafsa, where the Portuguese and Castilians had renewed their attacks on Muslim settlements.[208] The Almohad administration again presented those activities to the public as policies that display the caliph's power.[209] The purpose of Abu Ya'qub's final military expedition was to recapture Santarem, held by the Portuguese for almost forty years.[210] Probably, the Almohads expected that recapturing Santarem would give them strong popular legitimacy. The caliph, however, was not well-prepared against the military strategies of the Portuguese.[211] The clash ended in failure in 1184. The caliph was wounded, and this injury led to his death at the hands of the Christians.[212]

Caliph Abu Ya'qub failed to deliver the crucial victory that was needed to consolidate his political legitimacy. Unlike his father, he was an indecisive leader whose administration was interrupted by his long periods of illness.[213] After him, his son, Abu Yusuf Ya'qub (hereafter Abu Yusuf), managed to defeat a Christian coalition in 1184, which earned him the title al-Mansur, the victorious.

[207] Bennison 2016, 99.
[208] Ibn al-Athir 2016b, 273; Ibn Abi Zar' 1972, 212.
[209] Bennison 2016, 99.
[210] Ibn al-Athir 2016b, 299; al-Marrakushi 1881, 185–7; Ibn Abi Zar' 1972, 214.
[211] Al-Zarkashi 1998, 31.
[212] Ibn Abi Zar' 1972, 215.
[213] Kennedy 2014, 217.

However, later developments during the reign of Abu Yusuf, particularly the capture of Bijaya by Ali bin Ishaq bin Ghaniya (the ruler of the Balearics on the coast of Ifriqiyya) in 1884, again triggered a legitimacy problem, as the Ghaniyya tribe claimed the Almoravid political legacy.[214] In 1184, the caliph organised a huge parade to show his empire's splendour, and to convey messages about its legitimacy.[215] Ibn Tufayl was by this time in the late period of his public service. Meanwhile, the Ghaniya threat continued over a long period.[216] Abu Yusuf spent four years dealing with this problem.[217] To prevent Ali bin Ishaq penetrating the tribes, he travelled to Tunis in 1186. The Almohads defeated Ali bin Ishaq in 1187.[218]

The Almohads' continuous search for legitimacy had structural reasons. Their country was composed of two regions separated by a sea: the Maghrib and al-Andalus. Abu Yusuf did not visit al-Andalus between 1184 and 1190.[219] This resulted in political instability in al-Andalus.[220] Similarly, the government's contact became weak when the caliph was in al-Andalus. Sometimes, when they faced problems in both regions, the Almohads prioritised one part. For example, when the Christians intensified their attacks in al-Andalus, and local communities failed to deliver the caliph's financial share, Caliph Abu Ya'qub preferred to focus on the Maghrib.[221] Similarly, when Abu Yusuf faced resistance in Maghrib in the early period of his reign, he paused the military fight with the Christians in al-Andalus. This was exploited by Alfonso VIII of Castile, who took over various cities between 1184 and 1186, and plundered the Muslim territories.[222]

Another factor was the urban–rural dichotomy. Since political legitimacy was based on Ibn Tumart's doctrine and Berber tribalism, it turned into a mechanism in continuous crisis, for the urban, both in al-Andalus and the Maghrib, were under the impact of Malikism, and did not find Ibn Tumart's doctrine convincing, his Mahdism especially not. It is one thing to accept

---

[214] Al-Zarkashi 1998, 33.
[215] Bennison 2016, 99–100.
[216] Ibn al-Athir 2016b, 310.
[217] Makki 1992, 73.
[218] Bennison 2016, 105; Ibn al-Athir 2016b, 310–12.
[219] Bennison 2016, 106.
[220] Kennedy 2014, 233.
[221] Bennison 2016, 99–100; Ibn al-Athir 2016c, 21–2.
[222] Oliva 2017, 173.

Mahdism in theory, but quite another thing to accept that someone is the *Mahdi*. Mahdism became a burden for the urban and educated people.[223] Similarly, other components of Ibn Tumart's doctrine, such as changes to the rituals, and the presenting of *tawhid* as a new religion, did not achieve uptake. Ibn Tumart's doctrine, which had worked perfectly in the tribal locale, fell short of convincing other people. The expanding empire was in need of new formulas to consolidate legitimacy.[224]

To overcome this problem, the Almohads developed other strategies. For example, al-Ghazali's thought was incorporated as a mean of establishing legitimacy.[225] Another strategy was to claim a Quraishi and pro-Alid genealogy for Ibn Tumart and Abd al-Mu'min.[226] Similarly, the Almohads used the codex of Uthman, a leftover of the Umayyads, along with the Qur'an left by Ibn Tumart, in their ceremonies.[227] The Uthman codex was an important symbol of legitimacy under the Umayyads of Spain. Ibn al-Qutiya (d. 987) wrote in *Tarikh* that the Umayyad officials take oaths on this codex.[228] All these strategies aimed at persuading people that the Almohads were another usual representative of Islam. They were examples of rapprochement with the mainstream religio-political culture of al-Andalus and the Maghrib.[229]

However, such strategies had natural limits, due to the rigid nature of Ibn Tumart's doctrine. The doctrine, which ruled that Ibn Tumart's thought was divinely correct, and all existing religious interpretations were wrong, was a hard one that could not be easily reconciled with other views. Reconciliation seemed to the Almohad elites as yielding to local cultures, which only distorts the truth. At some point, either the Almohads or other people had to give up their faith. This made a strange political order in which state ideology was denied full legitimacy. There was a constant legitimacy crisis.[230] Ibn Tumart's doctrine was the cause of both strength and weakness.[231]

---

[223] Watt and Cachia 1996, 110.
[224] Ghouirgate 2015, 42.
[225] Fletcher 1997b, 238.
[226] Fierro 2016, V/8–11.
[227] Al-Marrakushi 1881, 181.
[228] Ibn al-Qutiya 2009, 110.
[229] Bennison 2007, 154.
[230] Watt 1964, 28; Laroui 1977, 185.
[231] Laroui 1977, 188.

In 1229, Caliph Idris al-Ma'mun (r. 1229–32), exhausted by the continuous crises of legitimacy, finally renounced the Ibn Tumart doctrine. References to Ibn Tumart on coins and in khutba were removed.[232] This decision, however, triggered secessionist movements. Ibn 'Allan, governor of Tlemcen, declared independence as a reaction to al-Ma'mun's decision. Though he was sacked, the crisis led to the process of the splitting of the region under the name of the Zayyanids. More importantly, another part immediately split from the Almohads under the name of the Hafsids.[233]

The Hafsids presented themselves as the inheritors of the Almohad *tawhid*. Abu Zakariyya, the Hafsid leader, established a school to teach the Almohad doctrine.[234] The originator of the Hafsids was Abu Hafs 'Umar, whom I cited above as the leader of the rich Hintata tribe. He was among the group that pledged alliance to Ibn Tumart when he declared Mahdism in 1121.[235] Abu Hafs protected Ibn Tumart when he was an Almoravid target.[236] The Almohad politics had long had the Hafsids, the sons of Abu Hafs 'Umar, and the Mu'minids, the sons of Abd al-Mu'min, as two major political clans. But, when the Mu'minids abandoned the doctrine, expecting that this would permanently assure the loyalty of urban people, they effectively shattered the tribal basis of the state. This became apparent with the Hafsids' split.

Ibn Tufayl: a talaba

Ibn Tufayl worked at the centre of the Almohad court. As a special circumstance, the illness of Caliph Abu Ya'qub had developed a close relationship between him and the caliph.[237] Al-Marrakushi counts Ibn Tufayl among the caliph's friends.[238] They discussed philosophical questions at length.[239] Logically, his close contact with the court exposed Ibn Tufayl to political developments.[240]

---

[232] Ibn Abi Zar' 1972, 251. Also see Balbale 2018, 8.
[233] Al-Zarkashi 1998, 53–5; Ibn Khaldun 1979, 11.
[234] Al-Najjar 1984, 379.
[235] Al-Zarkashi 1998, 15.
[236] Abun-Nasr 2012, 118; Thiele 2020, 302.
[237] Bennison 2016, 95.
[238] Al-Marrakushi 1881, 172.
[239] Bennison 2016, 260.
[240] Bashier 2011, 41.

More importantly, Ibn Tufayl was a *talaba* assigned with the mission of defending and promoting the Ibn Tumart doctrine. But this was never an abstract intellectual activity. The *talaba* were expected to perform this duty amid the current political problems. The difficulties that the Almohad state faced determined their agenda. In fact, the *talaba* and *huffaz* (the guardians) – another group created by the Almohads for similar purposes – formed the core of the bureaucracy.[241] While the former were the ideologues (or the theorists) of the regime, the latter, as they were trained in horsemanship, shooting and swimming, were the indoctrinated bureaucrats made ready for civil and military positions.[242] For example, each Almohad ship of the fleet was commanded by a *talaba* or *hafiz*.[243]

The *talaba* status was a main component of 'the Almohad political and cultural project', the purpose of which was to create a new political and religious elite under the control of the Almohad caliph. These elites were expected to extend the Almohad doctrine to the common people.[244] Having learnt Ibn Tumart's doctrine by heart, they had expertise in different disciplines, such as dialectics and the natural sciences.[245] Though created by Ibn Tumart, the status of the *talaba* was reformed by Abd al-Mu'min. These reforms increased their impact on education, the judiciary, and even military affairs.[246] Certain delicate and symbolic duties, such as minting coins with strict Almohad features, were assigned to them.[247]

As part of his reforms, Abd al-Mu'min created a special group: *Talaba al-hadar* (students who are present). In Marrakesh he established a school for their training with a curriculum that included the religious and non-religious sciences.[248] Being present at court, they were in the service of the

---

[241] Buresi 2020, 126.
[242] Laroui 1977, 179; Abun-Nasr 2012, 95.
[243] Buresi and El Aallaoui 2013, 184. Ibn Khaldun (1958b, 43) described the Almohad fleet as organised in the most perfect manner ever known, and on the largest scale over observed. The Almohad fleet was established by Abd al-Mu'min. Ibn Abi Zar' 1972, 201.
[244] Fierro 2009, 177–8; 2016, x
[245] Hopkins 1954, 108.
[246] Fricaud 1997, 331–87; Buresi and El Aallaoui 2013, 58.
[247] Fierro 2010c, 85.
[248] Stroumsa 2019, 132–4.

caliph, unlike the *talaba al-muwahhidin*, who were employed in cities by local governors.[249] The *talaba al-hadar* were a prestigious component of the caliph's entourage who even accompanied him on his travels. They sometimes assumed diplomatic roles.[250] For example, Ibn Sahib al-Salah (d. *c.*1199), a *talaba*, mediated the negotiations between Abu Ya'qub and Abu Hafs 'Umar. Al-Salah defined the Almohads as the sole legitimate state in the Muslim West, and justified the violence against Ibn Mardanish, the ruler of a *ta'ifa* kingdom who resisted the spread of the Almoravids.[251]

Caliph Abd al-Mu'min considered the *talaba al-hadar* as partners in key decisions: for example, when he burnt various books, they were notified.[252] The *talaba* continued to be influential during Caliph Abu Ya'qub's reign. The preserved manuscripts of Ibn Tumart were copied by the *talaba* during his reign in 1171.[253] Their impact survived even later: Ibn al-Qattan (d. 1230), the head of the *talaba* during the reign of Abu Yusuf, became in practice the second in command of the state during the reign of the next caliph, al-Nasir (r. 1198–1214).[254] On the Almohad doctrine, the *talaba*'s studies were to be supervised by the caliph, who joined them in discussions, and managed their activities.[255] In this regard, the Almohad caliph, like the Fatimid caliph, was an imam-caliph, the authority in the defining of religious orthodoxy.[256] Judges were required to call on the caliph for difficult cases.[257] That spiritual authority enabled them to make decisions like the burning of the Maliki books by Abu Yusuf.[258]

The contribution of the *talaba* was particularly decisive in education, where one purpose was the indoctrinating of the people according to Ibn

---

[249] Fricaud 1997, 332 and 348.

[250] Ibn Abi Zar' 1972, 194; Fierro 2020, 10. Like the Seljuqs, the Almohad court was mostly a mobile state in the early period with no standard capital. Kennedy 2014, 208.

[251] Jones 2008, 793–829.

[252] Ibn Abi Zar' 1972, 195.

[253] Fierro 1999, 235.

[254] Maghen 2007, 348.

[255] Fierro 2010b, 168–9; Miranda 2004, 300.

[256] Buresi 2020, 127.

[257] Buresi and El Aallaoui 2013, 203–4.

[258] Safran 2014, 162.

Tumart's doctrine.[259] As the Almohads relied on a new concept of faith that saw the existing forms of religious practices as anthropomorphistic, regime survival was linked to disseminating that new faith to the people.[260] As early as Ibn Tumart's time, people were expected to memorise his works like *Aqida* and *Murshida*.[261] The Almohad continued to promote, even to enforce, Ibn Tumart's doctrine. The knowing and the memorising of the Almohad doctrine was obligatory for both the elite and the ordinary people.[262] The state used every means to bring the doctrine to the people: a typical Almohad khutba always reminded them of Ibn Tumart's views.[263] City walls, bridges, mosques and palaces were built in a way that reflected the doctrine.[264] Abd al-Mu'min put together a book in which the basics of *tawhid* were explained. That book was sent to every conquered city.[265]

Despite its intricate relationship to philosophy, Almohad elitism appealed to scholars. It proved to be protection for the elite against the average people. The Almohads not only dismissed the average people for not having the ability to grasp the incorporeal truth. They deplored traditional interpretations of religion too, many of which were antagonistic to philosophy. Subsequently, the Almohad claim that they possessed the final and perfect paradigm justified the critique of all existing religious or philosophical traditions.

This generated a strong relationship between the Almohads and the scholars. For example, *The Guide for the Perplexed* of Maimonides (d. 1204), who lived under Almohad rule between 1148 and 1165, reflects Ibn Tumart's doctrine.[266] On the Ibn Tumartian view, Maimonides explained that he wrote that book 'to explain certain obscure figures that occur in the Prophets', as they are taken literally by ignorant and superficial readers.[267] The chapters from

---

[259] Buresi and El Aallaoui 2013, 7.
[260] Fierro 2016, III/6.
[261] Stroumsa 2019, 131–2; Le Tourneau 1969, 63.
[262] Olson 2020, 40; Fromherz 2009, 46.
[263] Jones 2013, 74.
[264] Buresi 2020, 133.
[265] Fletcher 1991, 113; Ilahiane 2006, 4.
[266] Stroumsa 2009, 70, 83, 341. For Fierro (2010a, 163), Maimonides was an Almohad thinker.
[267] Maimonides 2002, 2.

the fifty-first to the sixty-first[t] are directly linked to Ibn Tumart's doctrine.[268] Maimonides shared in the Almohad elitism: he complained about the descriptions of God that imply corporeality, and attributed those descriptions to the inability of the multitude to comprehend an existence that is not connected with a body.[269] And he rued the fact that ignorant people believed that teaching the incorporeality of God was contrary to the teachings of the scripture.[270]

Another, and more significant, case is Ibn Rushd, who might have been a *talaba*.[271] His works were composed under the patronage of the Almohad caliphs. He was encouraged by the Almohads to comment on Aristotle, in order to make the work more understandable. As Fierro notes, the intended readership of those works must have been the *talaba*.[272] Several other scholars, like Walzer and Black, confirm the supportive connection between Ibn Rushd's works and the Almohad regime.[273] According to Rosenthal, Ibn Rushd was in full agreement with the religious policy of the two caliphs whom he served.[274] His various works, like his commentary on Ibn Tumart's *Aqida*, aimed to promote a better understanding of the Almohad doctrine.[275]

Similarly, Ibn Rushd wrote *Bidayat al-Mujtahid* as a legal codification to help the Almohad in the fields of legal doctrine and practice.[276] The book reflects the evolution of the Almohad doctrine in the context of the political necessities that had arisen since the death of Ibn Tumart.[277] *Bidayat al-Mujtahid* explains the differences between the various schools of law, as well as the methodological reasons that underpin them.[278] This method reminds us of the Almohad

---

[268] Ibid., 67–89.

[269] Ibid., 35.

[270] Ibid., 199.

[271] Fierro 1999, 235; Stroumsa 2019, 142–3.

[272] Fierro 2009, 183.

[273] Walzer 1962, 26; Black 2011, 120. Thiele (2022, 220–1) contends that Ibn Rushd was forced to revise some of his works to accommodate the Almohad doctrine.

[274] Rosenthal 1953, 256.

[275] Conrad 1996a, 21; Griffel 2005, 794.

[276] Fierro 2010c, 84; Stroumsa 2019, 147; Urvoy 1997, 870–1; Omar 2019, 147.

[277] Fierro 1999, 243 and 248.

[278] To provide a sample to illustrate the method in *Bidayat al-Mujtahid*: on children's pilgrimage, Ibn Rushd (2000, 374–5) wrote that the Malik and the al-Shafi'i accept it, while Abu Hanifa prohibited it. He later explains the methodological reasons behind their different opinions.

caution against being the *ghayr muqallid* who adheres to a perspective without seeking evidence of its merit. Importantly, as Dutton spotted, a main feature of the book is Ibn Rushd's frustration with the *ulama*, particularly in regard of *qiyas* (the process of deduction by analogy in jurisprudence) for it causes confusion. He was frustrated also by the *ulama*'s strong attachment to the opinions of their predecessors.[279] This is another similarity with Ibn Tumart's methodology. Rosenthal asserts that Ibn Rushd must be in agreement with Ibn Tumart on the disparaging of personal opinion in legal reasoning.[280]

Commitment to Ibn Tumart's doctrine is also observed in Ibn Rushd's *Fasl al-Maqal*.[281] This book appears to be party to the policy of revising Ibn Tumart's doctrine during the reigns of the second and third caliphs, when the regime faced problems of legitimacy.[282] The book seeks a middle way for the Almohad ideology.[283] Ibn Rushd reintroduces the Aristotelian theory of the three basic methods of demonstration: scientific demonstration, rhetorical demonstration and dialectical demonstration.[284] But he is always loyal to the Almohad policy, which is observed in his warning that interpretations must be confined to writings accessible only to specialists.[285] He saw the elite as capable of formulating the truth, while the masses should be satisfied with other explanations like metaphors.[286]

As a middle-ground solution, Ibn Rushd justifies *ta'wil*, an allegorical interpretation, *ipso facto* at odds with Ibn Tumart's doctrine, which may lead to anthropomorphism. He warns that this interpretation is not suitable for the masses. Yet he adds that the risk of misleading people is valid in the other sciences.[287] Such revisions of method illustrate the Almohad policy of adapting their doctrine to the social and political setting: the Almohads were no longer in the times of Ibn Tumart.[288]

---

[279] Dutton 1994, 193.
[280] Rosenthal 1953, 257.
[281] Ibid., 256.
[282] Rosenthal 1962, 181.
[283] Stroumsa 2019, 143; Black 2011, 121.
[284] Mahdi 1957, 92.
[285] Ibn Rushd 2011, 91.
[286] Taylor 2009, 231; Irwin 2018, 68; Rosemann 2013, 132.
[287] Ibn Rushd 2011, 80–2.
[288] See Fierro 2020, 13–14.

In this regard, in *The Incoherence of the Incoherence*, Ibn Rushd's harsh critique of al-Ghazali for his conception of God as 'a tyrannical prince'[289] needs attention. In this Aristotelian critique, Ibn Rushd denounces al-Ghazali's conception of God for its rejection of the laws and order in nature that exclude causality. Ibn Rushd attacks al-Ghazali because his theory of motion requires a personal God. This critique reflects the precepts of Ibn Tumart's doctrine that criticised al-Ghazali for imagining God as a person.

However, though Ibn Rushd and al-Ghazali are presented as being intellectual polar opposites, they are similar in their positions *vis-à-vis* the rulers. They both justified the political regimes under which they lived. Like al-Ghazali, who attacked the rivals of the Seljuqs and the Abbasids, Ibn Rushd, in *Commentary on Plato's Republic*, attacks the Almoravids for corruption, hedonism and tyranny.[290] Ironically, when Ibn Rushd is described in the literature as being opposed to al-Ghazali, he is usually imagined as the symboliser of the neutral philosophical truth. That is a frameless interpretation.

Turning back to Ibn Tufayl, he was most likely another leading *talaba al-hadar*. As part of his mission to defend the regime, he wrote a poem on Uthman's codex, and another poem to urge the tribes to jihad for the Almohads against Ibn Mardanish in al-Andalus. The latter poem boosts the linage of the Qays tribe, and was later attributed to Ibn Tumart as a legitimation strategy. Ibn Tumart did write such poems in other cases, like the Almohad conquest of Qafsa. It was thought Ibn Tufayl wrote these poems between 1170 and 1180, when he was a paid advisor.[291] He was an official who disseminated Ibn Tumart's doctrine.[292] He, for example, took roles in the inspection of books in processes where the authorities approved books for dissemination to the public.[293] Ibn Tufayl's intellectual activism occurred within Caliph Abu Yaʿqub's policy of developing strategies to expand the social basis of Almohad political legitimacy. His contribution was to frame the Almohad ideology in a persuasive way for the public. *Hayy bin Yaqzan*

---

[289] Ibn Rushd 1987, 325.
[290] Ibn Rushd 1974, 124. Also see Butterworth 1992, 187–202.
[291] Conrad 1996a, 19–22; Fierro 2020, 10–12.
[292] Ben-Zaken 2011, 27.
[293] Conrad 1996a, 20–4.

was written some time between 1177 and 1182 as part of this mission when he was in the Almohads' service.[294]

Ibn Tufayl's Political Thought: *Hayy bin Yaqzan*

Hayy Ibn Yaqzan, which can be translated as *Alive, Son of Aware*, is Ibn Tufayl's only surviving work.[295] The book reflects the Almohad policy of consolidating legitimacy by providing a persuasive narrative of Ibn Tumart's doctrine. However, this work is usually read as if it were a contribution to the general literature on philosophy. That results in frameless interpretations that ignore its political nature.

In an earlier article, Albert Hourani highlighted this problem when he asked, 'what is this book [*Hayy bin Yaqzan*] primarily about?' However, the various alternate explanations he provides, like the book was written to show 'the ascent of unaided human reason to mystical knowledge', or 'the harmony of religion and philosophy',[296] are frameless conclusions, as the historical and political context of the work is still not acknowledged. Likewise, conclusions by other scholars present *Hayy bin Yaqzan* as the deliverer of messages like:

- 'Islam is a valid revealed religion, but at the same time, it proposes that philosophy can achieve the same end';[297]
- 'philosophy and revealed religion can be reconciled';[298]
- 'perfectly reasonable men are held to be able to know theological truth by the light of unaided reason';[299]
- 'emphasizing freedom of choice and tolerance';[300]
- showing 'the practical limits of ideals like friendship and hospitality',[301] or
- 'an intellectual labor that culminates in a science-based mysticism'.[302]

---

[294] Ibid., 7.
[295] The first Latin translation, published in Oxford in 1671, changed the title to *Philosophus Autodidactus*.
[296] Hourani 1956, 40.
[297] Gerli 2013, 422.
[298] Hitchcock 2014, 148.
[299] Fletcher 1991, 123.
[300] Attar 2007, 63.
[301] M. Idris 2011, 100–1.
[302] Hawi 1976, 90.

All the above are frameless interpretations in different ways. In what Aravamudan formulated as 'the *Hayy* problem in English',[303] this book has been interpreted as representing different perspectives since its first discovery in the West. This 'problem' is mainly the result of missing the political context that shaped Ibn Tufayl's perspective in the work.

In contrast, the works of scholars like Ben-Zaken, Conrad, Urvoy and Fierro, not seeing *Hayy bin Yaqzan* as a general book on philosophy, interpret it as a work written to contribute to the Almohad's legitimation strategy.[304] According to Ben-Zaken, the work is a response to the various disturbances of the time, such as the Sufi disorders, as well as to the revolt in Granada, and the persecution of Muslims by Christian rulers. According to him, Ibn Tufayl wrote *Hayy bin Yaqzan* to contribute to the Almohad policy of consolidating legitimacy, particularly the rule of Caliph Abu Ya'qub.[305] Slightly differently, Fierro interprets *Hayy bin Yaqzan* in the context of efforts to develop a post-Messianic orientation that would preserve the loyalty of Berbers, but also attract urban people and the scholarly elites. Fierro, reminding us of the apparent absence of any reference to Mahdism in this work, interprets *Hayy bin Yaqzan* as an Almohad strategy of propagating the doctrine, but in a completely different context. Accordingly, the work symbolises the Almohad efforts to propagate Ibn Tumart's doctrine outside its original Berber context.[306] According to Conrad, after Ibn Tufayl's long discussions at the Almohad court, he decided to communicate not to a select circle of philosophers, but to large audiences of diverse intellectual capacities and interests.[307]

In what follows, I shall basically expand the methods of the above-mentioned scholars by providing a detailed account of the relationship between *Hayy bin Yaqzan* and Almohad politics and doctrine.

---

[303] Aravamudan 2014, 207.
[304] Ben-Zaken 2011, 27; Conrad 1996a, 22; 1996b, 245–58; Urvoy 1996, 40–8; Fierro 1999, 228. Examples of others who support this method are Watt (1964, 28), Le Martire (2022, 82) and Ben (2016, 34–4).
[305] Ben-Zaken 2011, 28–9
[306] Fierro 2020, 3 and 12–15.
[307] Conrad 1996a, 245.

The prologue

Hayy bin Yaqzan begins with a prologue in which the author explains his purpose by referencing a number of scholars. The prologue is not Ibn Tufayl's engagement with scholars in the general discussion of philosophy. He engages with them on the presumption of their suitability to support his goal of defending the Ibn Tumart doctrine.

The prologue is committed to elitism. A friend asked Ibn Tufayl to explain the secrets of oriental wisdom. However, that requires the state of experiencing the abstract truth, which natural language cannot explain (*bi-haythu la yasifuhu lisan*). Some who attempted to explain it without the required intellectual capacity, could talk only about their experience in general terms, without detail. Even the educated, who observed that experience correctly, confessed the limits of language. Al-Ghazali, for example, wanted others to not ask about his experience, as that was beyond the limits of description.[308] Ibn Tufayl quoted al-Ghazali as confirming the Almohad elitism.

Commenting on the prologue, Hawi criticises Ibn Tufayl for rejecting on one page what he had accepted before on another page.[309] This critique is fair if we judge Ibn Tufayl's consistency only from the perspective of general philosophical debates. But Ibn Tufayl had the political purpose of defending the Almohad doctrine in the prologue. A book written to defend the Almohad doctrine requires the rejection of any other solution as a completely correct one. As a matter of fact, Ibn Tufayl makes clear that the method he defends is different from all existing methods, be they mystical or rational.[310]

This is not surprising, since an Almohad *talaba* has to be *ghayr muqallid*.[311] But of course, a *talaba* would appreciate others who approve the Almohad doctrine, as they can serve only to promote the Almohad legitimacy. Thus, an Almohad view, that Ibn Tufayl represents perfectly, would reject any other paradigm that purports to deliver a perfect solution. But it selectively

---

[308] Ibn Tufayl 1964, 55–7.
[309] Hawi 1974, 60. Similar criticism is raised by other scholars. See Richter-Bernburg 1996, 92; Gonzales-Ferrin 2015, 31.
[310] Ibn Tufayl 1964, 60–1.
[311] Maghen 2007, 349.

appreciates people who live with other paradigms on various subjects, provided that they have confirmed the Almohad doctrine.

Watt summarised the above by noting that Ibn Tufayl selected a number of unrelated and apparently incompatible points that had been adopted because of some immediate practical relevance to the context of Ibn Tumart's doctrine.[312] This requires the evaluation of Ibn Tufayl's consistency from the perspective of the Almohad doctrine, not upon general philosophical paradigms. It is thus wrong to present Ibn Tufayl as representing an Aristotelian or Avicennan perspective.[313] He cannot be an Aristotelian or Ghazalian; he can endorse some parts of their views, but never the entirety of them.

Ibn Tufayl's underlining of the limits of language is indeed another Almohad tenet. He repeats Ibn Tumart on this subject: truth cannot be framed by language. Any attempt to frame truth in language or a book would only distort it.[314] As Somma pointed out, Ibn Tufayl cannot voice outright even the topic of his own text.[315] This ambiguity illustrates that Ibn Tufayl obeys the Almohad political principle of not discussing the truth publicly, because that may lead average people into anthropomorphism.[316] Correspondingly, Ibn Tufayl reminds us that a discursive representation of truth is as rare as 'red sulphur' because the law of the land and the people prohibit it. As the political setting did not allow discursive and intellectual demonstration of the truth, Ibn Tufayl concludes that this can be done only in isolation.[317]

This sounds like the rationale behind his choice of a narrative that centres on a young man on an island. No less importantly, Ibn Tufayl refers to his people as the *al-milla al-hanifiyye*.[318] *Hanif* is a person who adheres to a monotheistic (*muwahhid*) faith that preceded Islam. His description in the twelfth century of his society as *hanif* is unusual. It evokes the Almohads' identification of their *tawhid* as a general religion that temporally and spatially

---

[312] Watt 1964, 27.
[313] For example, according to Kruk (1991, 76) the prologue proves Ibn Tufayl's Neoplatonism.
[314] Ibn Tufayl 1964, 60–1.
[315] Somma 2022, 337.
[316] Hernandez 1992, 789.
[317] Ibn Tufayl 1964, 61.
[318] Ibid., 61.

transcends Islam. Like the Almohad *tawhid*, *hanif* is the belief in God's unity across history and above cultures.

Ibn Tufayl's critique of Ibn Bajja reflects his commitment to Almohad doctrine similarly: Ibn Bajja was mistaken because he did not go beyond reason, nor did he dissociate himself from people.[319] Ibn Bajja is criticised for offering the possibility of all people's union with the reality.[320] This violates Almohad elitism. Ibn Tufayl's critique of Ibn Bajja on reason reflects another tenet of Ibn Tumart: though rational observation is important, it is never enough to reach the truth that cannot be framed in popular language (*alfaz*), nor in the specialised terminology of experts (*istilah*). Thus, rational observation should be followed by a mystical method, as that alone can frame the absolute truth.[321] So Ibn Tufayl promised a method that combined rational and mystical elements.[322]

Having an ideal method in mind, Ibn Tufayl is naturally not satisfied by the works of Aristotle, al-Farabi or Ibn Sina. To begin with al-Farabi, Ibn Tufayl criticises him for accepting the possibilities of happiness in this world and in society, and of attaining truth by using logic.[323] As a man of practical politics, Ibn Tufayl repudiates al-Farabi's theory of state, and particularly his idealist method of attaining happiness. This argument is a structural refutation of political philosophy. It thus seeks to disprove the categorising of *Hayy bin Yaqzan* as a work of utopia, or on political philosophy like al-Farabi's *The Virtuous City*.[324] But *Hayy bin Yaqzan* is not interested in the philosopher-king, a major element of the utopias, and the plot has no society at all.[325] In fact, ideal society is an oxymoron for the Almohads.[326]

The Almohad philosophy accepts that society and culture distort ideals. Symbolising the Almohad elitism, Ibn Tufayl attacks al-Farabi for putting

---

[319] Ibid., 58–68.
[320] Fierro 2016, I/32.
[321] Ibn Tufayl 1964, 58–60.
[322] Miguel and Vilchez 2012, 651.
[323] Ibn Tufayl 1964, 62.
[324] For the several scholars who categorise *Hayy bin Yaqzan* as utopia, see Malti-Douglas 1991, 84; Regnier 2018, 18; Lauri 2013, 23.
[325] Marmura 1979, 320–3.
[326] See Radtke 1996, 167.

the wicked on the same level as the good.[327] At this point, I disagree with Hawi's evaluation that Ibn Tufayl's criticism of al-Farabi is not correct, or correct only sometimes.[328] Ibn Tufayl's is an Almohad critique of al-Farabi. As Mahdi notes, Ibn Tufayl's concern was not with the truth of al-Farabi's radical position as he formulated it, but with its moral, political and religious implications.[329]

When it comes to Ibn Sina, Ibn Tufayl finds his works less than ideal because they cannot bring one to the supreme realm where one can experience the ultimate truth in its incorporeality. To show the limits of Ibn Sina's method, Ibn Tufayl engages the blind-man metaphor. The main message is that to observe the absolute truth we need quite different means.[330] But Ibn Sina is given credit because his rational methods bring one to a state where one develops empathy with the incorporeal truth by intuition.[331] This is not al-Ghazali's mystical experience. Instead, it is a liminal stage where one, though still in the phase of rational observation, grasps the abstract truth. So Ibn Tufayl actually appreciated Ibn Sina for providing a rational explanation of man's ability to articulate the timeless and frameless truth.[332]

As I noted above in reference to Griffith, this sort of interpretation of Ibn Sina was developed by al-Juwayni, who incorporated Ibn Sina's thoughts into theology. Accordingly, al-Juwayni grasped the gaps in classical Ash'arism from a philosophical and scientific perspective.[333] The early Ash'ari scholars, having a limited understanding of the physics of time and space, proposed a theology which failed to successfully define God and his actions as being out(side) of time and space. This led to conceptions of God where he was imagined as a personal God acting in space/time, and thus created a lot of problems. To solve such problems, al-Juwayni incorporated Ibn Sina (and indirectly Aristotle) into Ash'ari thought. The outcome was post-classical

---

[327] Ibn Tufayl 1964, 62.
[328] Hawi 1995, 298.
[329] Mahdi 1990, 98.
[330] Ibn Tufayl 1964, 59.
[331] Ibid., 64. Also see Gutas 2000, 160.
[332] Ibn Tufayl 1964, 58. Also see Germann 2008, 283.
[333] Griffel 2005, 756–75.

Ash'arism. Al-Juwayni's contribution appealed to Ibn Tumart, who was searching for a method that situates God timelessly and framelessly, but does not reject rational observation.

Again, the argument advanced by various scholars that Ibn Tufayl misunderstood or overinterpreted Ibn Sina's thought,[334] which might be a valid point at the general philosophical level, is, however, frameless because he did interpret and incorporate Ibn Sina in line with his pro-Almohad stance. Ibn Tufayl's position on other philosophers was political.

Ibn Tufayl also applies his pro-Almohad stance to al-Ghazali. The Almohads could not dispense with al-Ghazali, for he legitimised the mystical method, and that forms the most critical part of Ibn Tumart's method.[335] But al-Ghazali cannot be thought perfect, as that would contradict the uniqueness of the proposition of the Almohad doctrine. As a solution, Ibn Tufayl effectively reframed al-Ghazali for the Almohads. He claimed that there are various inconsistencies in al-Ghazali's thought. But he later apologised for that move. Accordingly, al-Ghazali confessed that there are different types of opinion: those commonly held by the masses, and those held privately. Al-Ghazali said also that he would be satisfied if his works were to shake people's traditional faith that they learned from their families.[336] It was effectively through al-Ghazali that Ibn Tufayl justified the Almohad principles of elitism and the critique of society.

Ibn Tufayl puts great effort into exonerating al-Ghazali. He reacted against some people who claimed that al-Ghazali's work, *Mishkat al-Anwar*, includes the grave error of ascribing to God an attribute incompatible with his oneness. This is a sensitive point, as al-Ghazali was blamed for violating the major Almohad principle. Ibn Tufayl defends al-Ghazali by reminding us that he was among those who reached this sublime goal and enjoyed the ultimate bliss (*sa'd al-sa'adah*) of experiencing the truth of the incorporeality tenet. But the truth as al-Ghazali observed it was 'veiled by light'. That truth lost its uniqueness when it was put in a frame.[337]

---

[334] Gutas 1994, 230; Bashier 2011, 14; Hawi 1974, 58.
[335] Fierro 2010c, 69.
[336] Ibn Tufayl 1964, 58.
[337] Ibid., 64–5.

To conclude, the prologue is not a doxography. Its subject matter is limited.[338] Ibn Tufayl engaged with philosophers with the purpose of framing the Almohad doctrine within general Islamic thought, and also to show how it was better than all other doctrines. This is a typical legitimation strategy, and it is in line with Almohad politics. Otherwise, one would have to take seriously the possibility that Ibn Tufayl intended, in a few pages of discourse, to challenge the giants of Islamic philosophy, including al-Farabi, Ibn Sina, Ibn Bajja and al-Ghazali. This was never his goal. That is supported also by the fact that he seems to have relied on memory, not on systematic notes and collections of books.[339] Ibn Tufayl probably had not seen the works of Ibn Bajja and some of the others.[340] He himself confessed that not all the books of al-Ghazali had reached him.[341]

The prologue was a typical Almohad text. As Maghen observes in the case of Ibn al-Qattan (d. 1230), who was a *talaba*, a typical Almohad text claims originality, unlike other Muslim scholars who modestly begin their discourses by reminding that they are but the follower of others.[342] An Almohad *talaba* was always *ghayr muqallid* because his paradigm rests on the rejection of the others' paradigms. This always forced the *talaba* to be in contrary engagement with others. An Almohad scholar can benefit from others, so long as they fit the Almohad doctrine. But benefitting may never result in the complete endorsement of another paradigm.

As Ibn Tufayl explained, *Hayy bin Yaqzan* follows Ibn Tumart's method: seeing the truth first by observation and reasoning, and later by actual experience.[343] He includes or excludes philosophers' opinions accordingly: he borrows from Ibn Sina while using rational methods at the rational-empiricist stage. When it comes to experiencing the truth in a mystical state, Ibn Tufayl borrows from al-Ghazali. This eclectic method, if read in a frameless way, may justify the presentation of Ibn Tufayl as a rationalist, an Avicennan, a

---

[338] Somma 2022, 333–53.
[339] Hawi 1976, 92. Also see Adamson 2016, 478.
[340] Conrad 1996a, 13–14.
[341] Ibn Tufayl 1964, 62–3.
[342] Maghen 2007, 346.
[343] Ibn Tufayl 1964, 65.

Neoplatonist, or a mystic.[344] But when Ibn Tufayl is read in the historical and political context, all those presentations are irrelevant, as he was an Almohad.

The plot

The plot of *Hayy bin Yaqzan*, the story of a boy on an isolated island, was designed as a demonstration of the Almohad doctrine. The plot is a pedagogical tool to facilitate communication with others.[345] Conrad explains this as the 'socialization of knowledge' where the purpose is to provide a text that speaks to a broad continuum of interests, convictions and intellectual abilities.[346] The deliberate preference for the fiction genre is another indicator of Ibn Tufayl's break with the philosophical tradition.[347]

The plot begins with the rise of baby Hayy on an isolated island. Two accounts are provided on his birth: spontaneous generation without father or mother, and standard generation with parents. The standard generation was meant for the public, the spontaneous generation was for the elites.[348] Hayy is attributed a noble lineage in the standard generation account.[349] The spontaneous generation seems to be the ideal option to demonstrate the Almohad doctrine because it requires zero contact with society. According to Ibn Tufayl, human nature can attain abstract truth if its capacity becomes strong enough.[350] But this is possible only if there is no distortion by society.[351]

Hayy meets a doe who becomes like his mother. He learns how to survive, and the knowledge of things, by imitating the doe. He learns how things occur in nature in this period. When he is seven years old, he begins to make

---

[344] For example, according to Kukkonen (2009, 97), Ibn Tufayl differs from al-Ghazali as he values rational inquiry. This however can only be proposed for earlier stages of Ibn Tufayl's method.

[345] Hawi 1974, 34.

[346] Conrad 1996b, 258.

[347] Stroumsa 2021, 28. As Conrad (1996b, 238–66) notes, since the plot was designed as a story to prove an idea, some contradictions or coincidences are allowed. For example, there are no predatory animals on islands. Ibn Tufayl 1964, 73.

[348] Le Martire 2022, 87–8. Also see Richter-Bernburg 1996, 97.

[349] Fierro 2020, 16.

[350] Ibn Tufayl 1964, 71.

[351] De Rande 2019, 208–17.

judgements based on his observation of nature, mainly animals, such as covering his sexual organs with leaves. This period symbolises the rational observation stage of Ibn Tufayl's method as inspired by Ibn Tumart. Ibn Tumart defined knowledge in terms of the senses, reasoning and hearing.[352] Observing the empiricist nature of Ibn Tumart's method, Urvoy posits a kinship between Ibn Tumart and Aristotelian naturalistic empiricism.[353] This contention is partially informative, since, unlike Aristotle, Ibn Tumart's empiricism is limited to the earlier part of his method. He gives no credit to empirical methods in the later part of his method.

The next theme in the plot is Hayy's dissection of the doe after her death, expecting that he will find the reason behind the death. In Ibn Tufayl's method, the dissection symbolises the stage where Hayy realises that there is a truth in a different form beyond the physical world. It proves that the body, that is, the physical world, is not a source of the absolute truth. Without that truth, the body is a machine without motion, a simple tool like the stick he uses.[354] Thus, the truth cannot be attained by bodily means like the senses.

The dissection also demonstrates the limits of rational observation. It proves that humans have the natural ability to connect with the truth, as Hayy attributes this ability to the empty chamber in the doe's heart, which he thought to be abandoned by something.[355] Hayy is no longer interested in the body. Questioning this gone thing, Hayy steps into a stage where truth is analysed in a frameless way. After the dissection, Hayy encounters a fire, another designed theme in the protagonist's voyage that shows that there are things that affect us, but we cannot touch them.[356]

Hayy is now poised to find the truth beyond this world. He discovers many other proofs of the existence of a superior and abstract truth. For example, analysing the similarities and differences among the various species, and the human organs, Hayy understands that beyond those differences is the oneness of spirit. In what appears as a typical Ibn Tumartian reasoning, Hayy

---

[352] Ibn Tumart 2007, 30.
[353] Urvoy 1996, 41.
[354] Ibn Tufayl 1964, 79.
[355] Ibid., 78–9. We understand that Hayy/Ibn Tufayl has the cardiocentric view. Kukkonen 2011, 198–9.
[356] Ibn Tufayl 1964, 79–80.

concludes that the truth is formless, without any quality or attribute. In this passage, Ibn Tufaly defines the absolute truth without a body (*jism*), strongly alluding to anthropomorphism (Arabic *mujassima*). Besides, any attempt to frame it is inevitably a distortion.

The relationship between truth and the context is demonstrated by Ibn Tufayl as the difference between the weight of a thing and the abstract concept of heaviness (mass). While weight is in the state of corporeity, heaviness is something else, symbolising the incorporeal; it is later added to the corporeal things. This later-added thing determines movement and the nature of a thing. Ibn Tufayl likens it to power. Importantly, Hayy realises that he has discovered the incorporeal element, not through his senses but by reasoning. Ibn Tufayl defines this as Hayy's entry into the stage of practising the mystical or spiritual science. This is his first glimpse into the spiritual world, as he has discovered that a non-corporeal element exists beyond the bodies of things. From now on, Hayy explains everything from this perspective, abandoning the corporeality of things.[357]

Therefore, Hayy's observation of everything else, like fire, water, air and solids, gives the same message, which is that there is a dimension that goes beyond the corporeality of everything. For example, he detects that the shape of clay changes because the concept of mass is distinct from it.[358] Each metaphor in the plot underlines the same message: there is one incorporeal power that affects all things in the universe. That power is, however, reflected in the forms of objects with distortions. The celestial power does not pass on the forms.[359] Though each object reflects that incorporeal power, we never grasp its true nature by observation. Ibn Tufayl likens this to the *hyle* in metaphysics: the matter devoid of forms.[360]

Hayy develops the habit of seeing everything in its incorporeal truth, which cannot be observed by the senses. He realises that this incorporeal power is attributed to objects through an agency. They, the objects, exist thanks to that agency.[361] Logically, Hayy decides to get to know this agent,

---

[357] Ibid., 85–8.
[358] Ibid., 90–1.
[359] Kruk 1996, 89.
[360] Ibn Tufayl 1964, 91.
[361] Ibid., 92–3.

God, in his incorporeal state. From now on, truth for Hayy means God's incorporeal conception. Ibn Tufayl intervenes here, and informs us that Hayy is aware also that knowing God in his incorporeality is different from how God is imagined in society.[362] Hayy is now an embodiment of the Almohad doctrine.

At this stage, Hayy comprehends that everything is a consequence of God, but they are not subsequent to God in time, as God is outside of time.[363] This paragraph demonstrates the voyage of Aristotelian physics, as interpreted by Ibn Sina, into the Ash'ari theology through al-Juwayni. Since the incorporeal God is outside of time and space, rational observation is no longer effective. Even imagining God is not possible, because imagination is a projection based on our experiences in space and time.[364]

We can now see Hayy as a *muwahhid*: he has developed the correct faith without the intervention of religion or prophet. Ibn Tufayl makes his protagonist speak almost as a summary of the Almohad *tawhid*: the creator of the universe should be incorporeal, entirely devoid of corporeal attributes. Having now realised that bodies distort the truth even though they represent it, Hayy abandons his analysis of the objects in the universe.[365] He ends up in a cave, in deep contemplation of God's incorporeality.[366]

Ibn Tumart, too, had a cave experience. The cave symbolises a state where the senses are irrelevant. Thus, Ibn Tufayl introduces the term 'intimacy', a state that is beyond the limits of language. In fact, raised alone on an island, Hayy does not know a language. Ibn Tufayl again intervenes, and warns that it is not possible to provide more detail on this experience, as that may create danger.[367] The reference is directly to the Almohad policy that prohibits the public demonstrations of such knowledge, as it may mislead the public. As Hayy is now in the stage of mystical experience, Ibn Tufayl's vocabulary changes correspondingly: Hayy's intimacy is a kind of intoxification.[368] This

---

[362] Ibid., 96.
[363] Ibid., 96.
[364] Ibid., 97.
[365] Ibid., 98–101.
[366] Ibid., 115.
[367] Ibid., 116. Also see Mahdi 1990, 95.
[368] Ibn Tufayl 1964, 116.

is a Ghazalian lexicon. Avicennan methods and vocabulary are meaningless, as Hayy has grasped that the physical dimension of objects distorts the incorporeal truth.[369]

Finally, Hayy reaches the celestial level, where he realises the truth in its incorporeal state. He has seen the lower world as a place of distortion of the truth.[370] This Neoplatonic narrative of lower and upper worlds is found also in Ibn Tumart.[371] The physical world is the shadow of the superior one. Though they are connected, the upper world does not need the lower one.[372] Ibn Tufayl warns against asking for information about this experience; that is impossible to provide.[373]

Hayy reaching the point of experiencing God in his incorporeal reality is the last stage of the method that Ibn Tufayl propagates. As De Rande notes, if the work's mere purpose had been to present the philosophical system of Avicennism, or the mystical possibilities of a special human being to the ruler, Ibn Tufayl could have ended his account here.[374] But, the plot continues with a section on Hayy's encounter with normal people, where the political dimension of the plot is more visible.[375]

Absal came from an island where there is 'a true faith based upon the teachings of one of the ancient prophets'.[376] Logically, that faith is Islam, and the prophet is Muhammad.[377] Ibn Tufayl's design of Absal, who represents the distorted form of truth, is a Muslim man, the typical contradiction of the Almohad stance of seeing their *tawhid* as the perfect faith, beyond even Islam. This is more visible in his condescending attitude to the religion on the second island: there, reality is presented with symbols and various allegories.[378]

Absal, who has expertise in languages, is eager to learn the inner meanings of the scripture. His brother Salaman, however, stays on their second-island

---

[369] Ibid., 117.
[370] Ibid., 118.
[371] Ibn Tumart 2007, 30.
[372] Also see Bashier 2011, 1; Miguel and Vilchez 2012, 657.
[373] Ibn Tufayl 1964, 121.
[374] De Rande 2019, 217; Adamson 2016, 490.
[375] Le Martire 2022, 89.
[376] Ibn Tufayl 1964, 122.
[377] Bürgel 1996, 125.
[378] Ibn Tufayl 1964, 122.

home, satisfied with the symbolic representation of religion. When Hayy and Absal meet, they realise that they have the same faith. The message is that the Almohad doctrine is legitimate, as it is not different from what true and educated Muslims find in the scripture. However, Absal, having listened to Hayy, comprehends that all he knows about religion is things like angels, hell, heaven, prophets, and scriptures . . . all mere symbolic representations. He concludes that Hayy's method is the supreme one.[379] Now the message is the superiority of the Almohad *tawhid* to the religion as practised by the people.[380] Though Hayy respects Absal's religion, he could not figure out why their prophet used allegories to present the divine world, as this allows people to fall into the grave error of conceiving God corporeally, that is, anthropomorphism. And Hayy could not understand a number of other teachings of the prophet, such as the rituals.

Ibn Tufayl, in what appears to be a summary of Almohad elitism, intervenes and reminds us that Hayy wrongly imagined all men as having outstanding characters, brilliant minds and resolute spirits. But in fact, they can be stupid, inadequate, thoughtless and weak willed.[381] This intervention summarises the Almohad view of other religions, including Islam: they are never perfect at avoiding the distorting truth, but that is inevitable, given that their followers have no ability to grasp the truth in its incorporeal form.

Hayy later went to Absal's island to enlighten the people. However, Hayy failed to persuade the people, not even the elite.[382] The failure proves the Almohad elitism: that truth, particularly God's incorporeality, cannot be grasped by society.[383] An ideal society is an impossibility from an Almohad perspective.[384] In what could be seen as one of the most radical Almohad stances in the book, Hayy saw the people on the second island as being in the state of unreasoning animals (*aktharahum bimanzilati-l-hayawan*).[385] Hayy

---

[379] Ibid., 123–6.
[380] Urvoy 1996, 41.
[381] Ibn Tufayl 1964, 127.
[382] Ibid., 127–8.
[383] Bashier 2011, 58.
[384] See Le Martire 2022, 98.
[385] Ibn Tufayl 1964, 129.

is now the ultimate pious Almohadi.[386] He thus advised people to observe the rules of their religion, without delving into complex things, by submissively accepting even the problematic elements. Not to be misguided by those people, Hayy returned to his isolated island.[387]

Short Debate

We can now easily discern how Ibn Tufayl contributed to the Almohad policy of consolidating legitimacy. Firstly, the lack of reference to Mahdism symbolises the adaptation to the political realities during the reign of the second and third caliphs. It denoted the weakening among the Almohad elites of their commitment to Mahdism. Secondly, the absence of Mahdism (and of the supernatural) symbolises the search for an interpretation that would attract urban people. Ibn Tufayl did not have Berbers in mind when he wrote this work. Instead, the work has the main goal of rationalising the Almohad doctrine. Thirdly, the work reframed Almohad elitism. Though it repeats the strong Almohad critique of average people, there is a nuance: society has Absal, not only Salaman, symbolising the possibility of a change, all be it limited. Fourthly, the argumentation throughout the work is not set in an intra-Almohad narrative. The work has a strategy of legitimising the Almohad doctrine by engaging with the great names of Islamic thought. These names were thus reframed as conforming to the Almohad doctrine. This was an attempt to normalise the Almohad *tawhid* for urban people. Finally, engagement with a number of Islamic scholars from various backgrounds, including even the Almoravid Ibn Bajja, was also a strategy to fine-tune the earlier Almohad narrative of positioning *tawhid* as radically hostile to other Muslims.

On this account, Ibn Tufayl symbolises a transition to Islamic political theory based upon Ibn Tumart's idealism, a doctrine that is mostly an example of Islamic political philosophy. This idealism, which required a revolutionary change in society, was, however, to fail. During the time of the second and the third caliphs, the Almohads realised that they should adapt to the social dynamics of their society. Legitimacy was no longer formulated in

---

[386] Ben-Zaken 2011, 28–9.
[387] Ibn Tufayl 1964, 130.

terms of Ibn Tumart's idealistic framework; social realities were incorporated in that formulation. Ibn Tufayl's political thought symbolises that transition. Thus, even if they used similar narrative, unlike Ibn Tumart's opinions, which referred to idealistic norms, Ibn Tufayl's opinions had social dynamics as a point of departure.

Logically, my approach is critical of works that interpret Ibn Tufayl from alternate, particularly general philosophical, perspectives. I have already addressed several examples of such works throughout this chapter. But I want to elaborate that subject further, shortly after I have finished my analysis of *Hayy bin Yaqzan*. My expectation is that this elaboration will make my argument clearer.

Arguing that 'Hayy has no religion. He is not a Muslim, a Christian, or a Jew. He is not white or black', Attar presents him as the prototypical cosmopolitan visionary who deems it essential to disregard name, family, history, religion and language as ingredients in the makeup of personal identity.[388] On the contrary, I propose that Hayy had in him the Almohad *tawhid* whose political programme does not refrain from oppressing Muslims, Christians and Jews. Hayy's critique of existing religions is done in the name of the Almohad *tawhid*, not in the name of cosmopolitanism.

Malti-Douglas's interpretation of *Hayy bin Yaqzan* as a male utopia[389] is problematic, unless that argument is explained with reference to the Almohads, particularly to Ibn Tumart's critical views of women in the context of their opposition to the Almoravids. In the same way, defining *Hayy bin Yaqzan* as a book that works as the beginning of the scientific method[390] is highly problematic: there are scholars like Ibn al-Haytham (d. 1040) who, well before Ibn Tufayl, developed what can be called 'the scientific method'. Hayy's use of the rational method is instrumental. As a matter of fact, Hayy, abandoning rational observation, later embraces a mystical method, which is alien to the scientific method.

---

[388] Attar 2007, 239 and 64.
[389] Malti-Douglas 1991, 69. Lauri (2013, 27–8) criticises Malti-Douglas for proposing a weak argument.
[390] Cerda-Olmedo 2008, 161–2.

Conclusion: Politics as Legitimacy

Ibn Tufayl wrote on political subjects under philosophical influence.[391] *Hayy bin Yaqzan* is thus a significant case in which to observe political thought in the Almohad context where philosophical issues affect political legitimacy and survival.[392]

Ibn Tufayl instrumentalised philosophy in the service of politics. That was part of the Almohad's strategy of consolidating their legitimacy. He endorsed or rejected various philosophical opinions from a political perspective. What Ibn Tufayl did is not essentially different from what al-Mawardi had done. The difference in Ibn Tufayl's thought is in his focus on philosophy which appears to have been made necessary by Ibn Tumart's doctrine that categorically denounces other religious interpretations. The Almohad legitimation required a complex engagement primarily with philosophy, not with legal methodology.

The main problem of the Almohads was the very legitimacy of their political project, not only the legitimacy of their rulers. For example, they were not like the Seljuqs whose goal was to legitimise their rule through the existing legal and political frameworks. Nor were they like the Shi'a Buwayhids, who ruled a Sunni Iraq through a cohabitation that allowed the coexistence of two groups that did not recognise each other theologically. The Almohad project first required the conversion of people to a new religious paradigm on which the Almohad state would acquire its legitimacy. Meanwhile, until this goal was achieved, the Almohads appealed to elitism, which, however, meant an exhaustive fight over orthodoxy, and more importantly, the erecting of a wall between the political elite and the people. *Hayy bin Yaqzan* was a work on a political model where the rulers could not transform their people, nor could they develop a model on which both sides saw each other as different but politically legitimate.

---

[391] Crone 2005, 167.
[392] Pennell 2003, 56.

5

IBN KHALDUN:
A PROTO-MODERN ISLAMIC
POLITICAL THEORY

With the demise of the Almohads, political unity in the Muslim West ended. The Muslims had their last stronghold, the Granada Amirate in Spain, while the Christians had already consolidated their power. Three Muslim states emerged in the politically disunited Maghrib: the Marinids in the western Maghrib (approximately today's Morocco), the Hafsids in Ifriqiyya (modern day Tunisia and its surroundings) and the Zayyanids (or Waddadids) in between them. Ibn Khaldun (1332–1406) lived in this setting, where states and tribes struggled for power in the post-Almohad crisis of legitimacy in the medieval Maghrib.[1]

As this chapter will illustrate, we find in Ibn Khaldun a crystal-clear perspective, mostly not in need of further explanation, and even sounding as if a modern man were speaking to us. That fits the nature of Islamic political theory. Ibn Khaldun contributes to the evolution of Islamic political theory by bringing a second dynamic into the calculation: his political rationalism, which had previously been framed mostly in reference to the state's autonomy, by incorporating social (or 'sociological') dynamics. This provides a theoretical paradigm that explains politics and society completely by reference to autonomous dynamics exclusive of religious norms. He categorically rejected

---

[1] Fromherz 2016, 196.

the non-empirical knowledge (i.e. of political philosophy and religion) as a source to explain political affairs. He openly asks that religious scholars to be excluded from administrative roles.

However, this splendour of Ibn Khaldun's ideas, along with his own intellectual creativity, is the flavour of the period he lived in. Ibn Khaldun lived six centuries after Ibn al-Muqaffa. While Ibn al-Muqaffa's *Risala* was the first prose text in Arabic, Ibn Khaldun's *Muqaddima* has a chapter on prose theory. In Western periodisation, Ibn Khaldun lived in the Late Middle Ages, that is, in the early modern period. Seventy years before his birth, in 1258, the Mongols had invaded Baghdad and killed Caliph al-Musta'sim. Ibn Khaldun was the coeval of Orhan, Murat I and Bayezid I, the sultans of the Ottoman state, for whom the caliphate was completely irrelevant. In other words, he wrote after several trends in the Muslim world had already culminated, making early institutions and ideas surrender to the rules imposed by realpolitik.

The Post-Almohad Maghrib

The post-Almohad Maghrib was Ibn Khaldun's primary historical context.[2] Two dynamics were formative upon his political thought: the competition among the Marinids, the Zayyanids and the Hafsids; and the complex relations between the nomads and the urban people in the whole of the Maghrib. Ibn Khaldun developed his political thought while he was involved in the politics at both levels. At inter-state level, he was a major actor in the various developments among the states. He was probably the only person who met all the leaders of the times, from those of the Hafsids, Marinids and Zayyanids, to Peter, the King of Castille, the Mamluk Sultan Barquq, and the Mongol Emperor Timur. At domestic level, he was an actor coveted by rulers for his knowledge of the tribes. That knowledge made him of strategic importance in the rallying of the tribes to particular political positions. He worked with tribal leaders, and even lived among the tribes. He negotiated with them on many issues, such as taxation and other political matters.

---

[2] Toynbee's (1955, 322) reading of Ibn Khaldun in the context of the interregnum (*c*.975–1275), which had been the sequel to the breakup of the Umayyad and Abbasid caliphates, seems not directly relevant.

We can analyse the political setting in the Maghrib by briefly examining three competing states in the region. To begin with, the Hafsids, whom I discussed briefly in the previous chapter. They broke away from the Almohads when they enunciated Ibn Tumart's doctrine in 1229. The Hafsids continued the Almohad political and administrative tradition.[3] Al-Zarkashi's *Tarikh al-Dawlatayn* (The History of Two States) narrates the Almohads and the Hafsids as a historical continuity.

In 1207, Abd al-Wahid – the son of Abu Hafs, the Hintata leader to whom the Hafsids' origins traced back – became the governor of Almohad Ifriqiyya. This was effectually the beginning of the Hafsid state. He ruled the region until 1221. Tunis under the Hafsids was the destination of those who left Spain because of the Christian takeover.[4] This changed not only the local demography, but it also affected the Hafsid bureaucracy, as there were newcomer bureaucrats and scholars among them who had brought their Almohad culture with them.[5] The Hafsids claimed the caliphate during the reign of Muhammad I (r. 1249–77).[6]

In 1337, Hafsid Tunis was invaded by the Marinids. However, they left the region having faced tribal resistance in 1348. When Abu Ishaq (r. 1350–69) became the ruler, the Hafsids were in political and social turbulence. As he was so young, Ibn Tafragin emerged in practice as the ruler, and dominated Hafsid politics for fourteen years. Ibn Tafragin was the first ruler who, in 1350, appointed Ibn Khaldun to an official post. The young Ibn Khaldun worked for the Hafsids when they were contending with serious internal and external problems. An endemic problem of the Hafsids was the difficult relations between the centre (including the administrators and urban people) and the tribes. In 1357, the Marinids again invaded the region, but their failure came quickly. The Hafsid regime was, however, almost destroyed by the Marinids. There was a Hafsid restoration as late as the reign of Abu'l Abbas (r. 1370–94).[7] Meanwhile, the tribes' role in the restoration increased their leverage, complicating relations

---

[3] Mediano 2010, 106.
[4] Thiele 2020, 302.
[5] Irwin 2018, 25; Simon 1999, 83–4.
[6] H. Idris 1986, 66.
[7] Ibn Khaldun 1958b, 17.

Map 5.1 Ibn Khaldun's historical context: the post-Almohad Maghrib (Allen James Fromherz, *Ibn Khaldun, Life and Times*, 2010).

between the government and them.[8] Annoyed by this, Abu'l Abbas pursued a policy of easing the tribal pressure on urban centres.[9]

The Marinids' was also a split state gained from the Almohads in wars between the 1240s and 1260s.[10] Their capture of Marrakesh in 1269 brought

---

[8] Abun-Nasr 2012, 129.
[9] H. Idris 1986, 68.
[10] Ibn Abi Zar' 1972, 283–4; Baizig 2020, 1.

the end of the Almohads. The Marinids, who benefitted from the control of regional gold outlets, were strong also in the grain trade.[11] Sijilmasa, a trade hub, was a Marinid city connecting them to the African trade as far as to Mali. Like the Hafsids, the Marinids could not become centralised because of the autonomy of the tribes that protected them. During the reign of Abu Said Uthman (1310–31), the Marinids organised expeditions to tribal areas to restore the administration eroded by tribal revolts.[12] As an illustration of the tension between the Hafsids and the tribes, Ibn Khaldun informs us of the Marinids' security guards who were charged with protecting the ruler from the common people.[13] To secure tribal alliances, the Marinids organised strategic marriages with tribal families.

The autonomy of the tribes, and the inadequacy, both numerically and in terms of power, of the Marinid army, prevented the establishment of a central rule.[14] Arabs and Turks were therefore added to their armies.[15] Besides, they lacked a strong religious theory of legitimacy, which was another obstacle to attaining effective rule. They compensated for this by other means, such as tribal dynamics,[16] and the instrumentalising of the madrasa by creating a state-controlled Berber-speaking *ulama*.[17] They developed a network of madrasas in cities like Fez, Sale and Marrakesh, with the particular purpose of reaching out to the urban populace.[18]

The Marinids, however, had the ambitious goal of uniting the Maghrib after Abu Yusuf Ya'qub ibn Abd al-Haq (r. 1259–86). But the champions of this strategy were Abu'l Hasan and Abu Inan.[19] In 1337, when the 100 Years War broke out in Europe, Abu'l Hasan (r. 1331–48) took over Hafsid Tunis, and imported a group of scholars to be there with him. The Marinids reached the pinnacle of their epoch under Abu'l Hassan. Fez became the richest city

---

[11] Shatzmiller 2009, 24–5; Mediano 2010, 122.
[12] Ibn Abi Zar' 1972, 398–9.
[13] Ibn Khaldun 1958b, 17.
[14] Pennell 2003, 64; Le Tourneau 2008, 232.
[15] Shatzmiller 2009, 14.
[16] Bennison 2014, 195–216.
[17] O'Kane 2017, 593.
[18] Ilahiane 2006, 89–90.
[19] Enan 1941, 9.

of the region.[20] A vibrant intellectual milieu emerged in Tunis, where Ibn Khaldun had been taught. However, the Marinid strategy in Tunis failed, because they could not secure local support. That possibility was thwarted by the tribes, who saw external powers as threats to their autonomy.[21] Also, their policy of reducing the Bedouins' revenues triggered a reaction that led to the Marinid defeat.[22] The Marinid policy of central government in Tunis had failed.[23] The defeat sealed Abu'l Hassan's career. He died in exile in the High Atlas, having been driven out by his son, Abu Inan.[24] Later, Abu Inan re-invaded Tunis, and pursued the same centralisation policy between 1352 and 1357; but he was similarly obstructed by the tribes.[25] With Abu Inan's defeat, the Marinid decline had set in.[26]

Finally, the Marinids had complex relations with the Granada Emirate. However, I shall be satisfied to mention only a particular issue in this context, for it gave rise to important consequences in Ibn Khaldun's life. Muhammad V (r. 1354–59 and 1362–91), the Granada emir, was hosted in Fez when he was exiled in 1360. As this coincided with Ibn Khaldun's stay there, they developed close relations. When Ibn Khaldun later faced political threat, he was able to find refuge in Spain, thanks to this acquaintance.[27]

When it comes to the Zayyanids, Ibn Khaldun described them as the least developed group, without even a government institution, because of their Bedouin character and insufficient power.[28] To a large extent, they pursued a policy of using their geographical position to play their neighbours against one another.[29] Like the Hafsids, they claimed independence as a reaction to the Almohads abandoning Ibn Tumart's doctrine. Ibn 'Allan, the governor

---

[20] Mediano 2010, 113.
[21] Simon 1999, 87.
[22] Al-Zarkashi 1998, 172–3. Also see H. Idris 1986, 68.
[23] Shatzmiller 2009, 7.
[24] Al-Zarkashi 1998, 184. The Marinids intervened in Spain, and framed it as jihad, as part of a legitimation strategy. O'Callaghan 2011, 60.
[25] H. Idris 1986, 68.
[26] Al-Zarkashi 1998, 183; Ibn Khaldun 1979, 54.
[27] Abun-Nasr 2012, 113–14.
[28] Ibn Khaldun 1958b, 18.
[29] Fromherz 2010b, 18–19.

of Tlemcen, had preserved his allegiance to the doctrine. The Almohads dismissed him. But the new governor, Jabir bin Yusuf, enjoyed more autonomy as he was backed by the local tribes. When, in 1234, local power was transferred to the Zayyanid tribe, which was part of the Abd al-Wad confederation, the separation from the Almohads was complete.[30]

The Zayyanids had a similar problem with the control of the tribes. Given the weakness of their governmental structure, the Zayyanid politics operated mostly on an endless bargaining basis (in peace or at war) with the tribes. They were invaded by the Hafsids and Marinids several times.[31] As part of the unification strategy, Abu'l Hasan invaded Tlemcen in 1337.[32] Later, Abu Inan invaded Tlemcen.[33] The Zayyanid sultan was taken captive and killed. It was the local tribes, mainly the Dawawda, that restored the Zayyanid rule in 1359.

This brief examination of the post-Almohad Maghrib has pointed out that there were three states in the region, and they were at war with one another. The tribes, which enjoyed a high degree of autonomy, played key roles in these wars, as well as in domestic politics. None of these states' institutional capacities were strong enough to consolidate a firm central authority that was able to discipline the tribes. In brief, this was a region where politics were determined by the interplay of legitimacy and power, which it turn was contested by the states and tribes.

Ibn Khaldun's Life

Ibn Khaldun begins his *Ta'rif* (or Autobiography) with his familial origins. Banu Khaldun (the House of Khaldun), the origin of which is Hadramout, Yemen, settled in Seville in the eighth century. It was an influential family in political and intellectual life. The family served the Umayyads, the Almoravids and the Almohads. Alarmed by the expanding Christian threat, they left Spain, and settled in Hafsid Tunis in 1248.[34]

---

[30] Ibid., 18–19.
[31] Abun-Nasr 2012, 134–5.
[32] Pennell 2003, 63–4.
[33] Al-Zarkashi 1998, 191.
[34] Ibn Khaldun 1979, 3–10; Irwin 2018, 24.

Waliyyuddin Abdurrahman Ibn Khaldun was born in 1332. He spent his childhood under the Hafsids, who still followed Ibn Tumart's doctrine.[35] His father, a scholar of Islamic jurisprudence, was the most influential person in his early life, as he provided a rich educational programme for his son.[36] Standard religious instruction formed a major part of his early education. However, various leading names also taught him other subjects, including grammar and poetry. Ibn Khaldun in *Taʿrif* writes that he had pursued knowledge since his birth.[37]

Meanwhile, scholars who migrated from Spain to Tunis enriched the intellectual environment there.[38] Abul Hasan's invasion in 1337 was particularly transformative for Ibn Khaldun, as the scholars who came with the Marinid ruler shaped his intellectual formation.[39] Among them was Muhammad ibn Ibrahim al-Abili (d. 1356), who deeply influenced Ibn Khaldun by teaching him the rational sciences, like philosophy and mathematics.[40] Al-Abili connected Ibn Khaldun with Ibn Sina, al-Farabi, Ibn Rushd and al-Razi, the key figures of Greco-Islamic thought.[41]

In 1350, Ibn Tafragin, the de facto ruler of the Hafsids, appointed Ibn Khaldun to the job of finalising the letters of the ruler, Abu Ishaq, by adding signatures and other components.[42] It was his first administrative experience.[43] But Ibn Khaldun left the Hafsids for the Marinid Fez when al-Abili returned

---

[35] Ibn Khaldun 1979, 14. Ibn Khaldun (1958a, 53) had a high opinion of Ibn Tumart. We see several but certainly limited elements that might be interpreted as Ibn Tumartian tenets in his thought, like a prudent approach to God's nature. Ibn Khaldun 1958c, 44 and 63.

[36] Pišev 2019, 3.

[37] Ibn Khaldun 1979, 17–19 and 57.

[38] Ibn Khaldun 1958b, 24.

[39] Al-Zarkashi 1998, 168–71.

[40] Ibn Khaldun 1979, 21–4, 45 and 57. As he lamented in this part of *Taʿrif*, many of these scholars and his family members perished in the Black Death. For detailed information on various leading scholars who taught Ibn Khaldun, see Dhaouadi 2005, 586; Rosenthal 1958a, xxxviii–xxxix; Alatas 2012, 3.

[41] Nassar 1964, 109–14; Dale 2006, 432. Simon (1999, 86) describes al-Abili as the propagandist of the Andalusian-Maghribian Averroism.

[42] Ibn Khaldun 1979, 57; al-Zarkashi 1998, 165.

[43] Enan 1941, 7.

there upon the request of the Marinids.[44] He resumed his education with al-Abili and other scholars at Abu Inan's court.[45] Meanwhile, Fez had become a hub of economic and cultural activism as a result of Abu Inan's reforms. He brought Muslim architects from al-Andalus to rebuild his capital.[46] He was surrounded by scholars, a Marinid legitimation strategy. During his eight-year stay there, Ibn Khaldun was given official duties by Abu Inan, which enabled him to observe the problems that plagued the Marinids, like the factions of the tribes.[47]

In 1357, Abu Inan arrested Ibn Khaldun for cooperating with Abu Abdullah, the former Hafsid ruler of Bougie, whom he had met before he arrived in Fez. He stayed in prison almost for two years.[48] He was released after Abu Inan's death in 1358. However, Ibn Khaldun's interest in intra-Marinid politics continued. He supported Abu Salim, a contender against the incumbent ruler. As part of this campaign, he persuaded the tribes to support Abu Salim. Abu Salim later rewarded him with the duty of keeper of his secret correspondence. This position required him to deal with the tribal issues. But when Abu Salim gave him the oversight of *mazalim*, the vizier, Ibn Marzuq, became jealous. Ibn Khaldun decided to return to Tunis, but the Marinids prevented this, fearing that he might share his expertise with their rival Zayyanids. He decided on an alternative, and arrived in Spain in 1362.[49] This was possible thanks to his acquaintance with the Granada Amir.

In Granada, Ibn Khaldun worked under the vizier Lisan al-Khatib, whom he had also known previously. As an important experience for him, Muhammad V sent him as an envoy to Peter, the Castille ruler, in 1363.[50] However, the environment became depressive for Ibn Khaldun, due to the deterioration of his relations with al-Khatib. This affected his relations with Muhammad V negatively. In 1365, he asked for permission to go to Bougie, as Abu Abdullah had finally become the ruler there, having been appointed by the Marinid

---

[44] Ibn Khaldun 1979, 60.
[45] On scholars who taught Ibn Khaldun in Fez, see Rosenthal 1958a, xlii.
[46] Mahdi 1957, 23.
[47] Alatas 2012, 5; Irwin 2018, 29.
[48] Ibn Khaldun 1979, 69 and 102.
[49] Ibid., 70–2, 79–80 and 84.
[50] Ibid., 82–3, 88–9 and 167.

ruler Abu Salim. (Back in 1357, Ibn Khaldun had been arrested for collaborating with Abu Abdullah.) Abu Abdullah promised him the position of *hajib* (chamberlain), the most important official after the ruler. It was the *hajib* who managed the relations of the ruler with others.[51]

As part of his job, Ibn Khaldun dealt with the tribes, sometimes even visiting them in their mountainous regions to discuss various issues, particularly taxation. This was an opportunity to observe the tribes' social and political behaviours, such as their resistance to Abu Abdullah's centralisation policies.[52] Marko Pišev writes that this was Ibn Khaldun's first experience of major fieldwork. In the course of it, he came to know the tribal people, and their political, economic and cultural attitudes.[53]

When Abu Abdullah was killed by Abu'l Abbas in 1366, Ibn Khaldun wanted to leave Bougie. But Abu'l Abbas forced him to continue his job. He managed to settle in Biskra. Meanwhile, Abu Hammu, the Zayyanid ruler, attacked Abu'l Abbas and claimed Bougie.[54] Abu Hammu, who desperately needed expertise to rally the tribes to his politics, offered Ibn Khaldun the opportunity to become his *hajib*. Ibn Khaldun declined to take that job, concerned about its dangers, and because of his desire to focus on scholarly works.[55] Though he tried to isolate himself from politics, Ibn Khaldun still worked for Abu Hammu. He once persuaded his protector, Ibn Muzni, the Amir of Biskra, to support Abu Hammu. In another case, he rallied tribes for Abu Hammu. However, the regional fights between Abu Hammu and Abu'l Abbas became a full regional war when the new Marinid ruler, 'Abd al-Aziz, organised an attack on the Zayyanid capital, Tlemcen, knowing that Abu Hammu was busy with his fights. To escape from the chaos, Ibn Khaldun headed again for Spain, but found himself stuck because of the ongoing war.[56] Worse, 'Abd al-Aziz arrested him, expecting to employ him in the rallying of

---

[51] Ibid., 96–9 and 103–4. Reflecting its importance, Ibn Khaldun (1958b, 15–18) gives detailed information on the status of *hajib*.
[52] Ibn Khaldun 1979, 105–6.
[53] Pišev 2019, 4.
[54] Ibn Khaldun 1979, 102 and 106.
[55] Ibid., 109–12.
[56] Ibid., 143.

the Arab tribes to the Marinid side.[57] He took Ibn Khaldun to task for having abandoned the Marinids in the past. Having persuaded ʿAbd al-Aziz that he was not at fault in the abandonment incident, Ibn Khaldun escaped to a Sufi shrine, where he took refuge. However, he occasionally worked for the Marinid sultan in rallying the tribes to him.[58]

Ibn Khaldun had observed Marinid politics at a time of wars complicated by tribal complexities that affected the state's relations with the people.[59] Coincidentally, his growing influence on the Arab tribes like the Dawawida had become a matter of concern for Ibn Muzni, his protector in Biskra. Meanwhile, the Marinid ruler ʿAbd al-Aziz died, and Abu Hammu recaptured Tlemcen from the Marinids. Ibn Khaldun, now a Zayyanid target, escaped to Fez, and managed once again to reach Spain in 1374. However, he was extradited in 1375, which left him defenceless against Abu Hammu, who wanted him to rally the Dawawida tribe to his side.[60] Once more, Ibn Khaldun took refuge in the same Sufi shrine that had sheltered him previously. He later obtained the protection of Awlad Aʿrif, who controlled Qalʾat ibn Salama, where he would stay four years and begin writing the *Muqaddima*.[61]

In 1378, Ibn Khaldun returned to Hafsid Tunis and took work in the service of Abuʾl Abbas, but there he encountered the envy of the local jurists.[62] In what Irwin interprets as a 'pious stratagem' of retiring from a fraught environment,[63] Ibn Khaldun asked permission to go on pilgrimage.[64]

Ibn Khaldun entered Cairo in 1382. He was received by the Mamluk sultan Barquq, and he began to teach there.[65] Being from Circassia originally, the appointment of Barquq had already changed the Mamluks from a Turkish to a Circassian dynasty. Barquq had appointed many loyalists to consolidate

---

[57] Fromherz 2010b, 80–1.
[58] Ibn Khaldun 1979, 144; Rosenthal 1958a, lii.
[59] See Titaw 2010, 83, 122 and 545–6.
[60] Fromherz 2010b, 83.
[61] Ibn Khaldun 1979, 141–4 and 244–5.
[62] Ibid., 221.
[63] Irwin 2018, 85.
[64] Ibn Khaldun 1979, 262–3.
[65] Ibid., 266.

his regime. Also, he recruited Circassian soldiers to balance the Turks. These policies were naturally criticised by the Egyptian elites as a disruption of the traditional order.[66] Barquq had faced various other problems, including minor rebellions.[67] Ibn Khaldun might thus have appeared to Barquq, who aimed at creating a strong entourage, as a potential partner.[68] However, when Barquq was temporarily deposed in 1389 by his governors, Ibn Khaldun supported his deposition. When he regained his powers, Barquq dismissed him from the madrasa. But the Mamluk sultan had never intended his complete purge.[69]

Ibn Khaldun's career in Cairo included various posts in madrasas and Sufi lodges (*khankah*).[70] However, his appointment as the chief Maliki judge, despite his reservations, was a critical turning point.[71] In *Ta'rif*, he complains about the complex problems of the judiciary, like corruption.[72] Meanwhile, his increasing influence provoked the local jurists, and scholars like Ibn Hajar al-Asqalani (d. 1449) and his student al-Sakhawi (d. 1497), against him. They criticised Ibn Khaldun in strong terms, accusing him of not having a satisfactory depth of religious knowledge, of being ill-mannered, and even of sexual immorality.[73] He dismissed these accusations as malicious fabrications.[74]

At a later time of his life, in 1401, Ibn Khaldun had a historic meeting with the Mongol ruler, Timur, in Damascus. This happened when he, though unenthusiastically, accompanied the Mamluk ruler, Faraj, who went to Syria to stop the Mongols. The meetings took place under Timur's tent, and were interpreted by a Hanafi scholar from Khwarazm. Ibn Khaldun briefed Timur on his work, the political and social conditions in the Maghrib, and on other general issues of the human societies.[75] Ibn Khaldun died in Cairo in 1406.

---

[66] Levanoni 2010, 259–67.
[67] Irwin 2018, 90.
[68] Rosenthal 1958a, lix.
[69] Levanoni 2010, 259.
[70] Ibn Khaldun 1979, 343–4. Also see Sato 2021, 399 and 408.
[71] Ibn Khaldun 1979, 273. Ibn Khaldun was appointed as judge several times, as he was dismissed or had resigned several times.
[72] Ibid., 273–6.
[73] Irwin 2018, 105–6; Kosei 2002, 127–9; Simon 1999, 18.
[74] Ibn Khaldun 1979, 277–8.
[75] Ibid., 406–11.

Expanding Islamic Political Theory: Ibn Khaldun on Human Organisations

Ibn Khaldun describes society and politics by a rational methodology based on empirical observation.[76] He explains the birth and evolution of human organisations from their simplest form to statehood, and their later collapse, as determined by general causes. Below, I shall illustrate the rational-empirical method in Ibn Khaldun's hands by examining the major subjects that constitute his thought.

ʿAsabiyya

Ibn Khaldun used ʿasabiyya to explain how human organisations emerge, evolve and collapse. The term symbolises his explanation of social phenomena as determined by autonomous dynamics.

Franz Rosenthal's translation of ʿasabiyya as 'group feeling' has become standard usage. Though its meaning is not clear, ʿasabiyya is usually imagined as a social bond that measures the strength and stability of a social grouping.[77] When it comes to its emergence, the Bedouins, because they have no tradition of constructions like walls to protect them, trust in a respected chieftain's protection. The chieftain controls people, so an order is created, and that ends the egalitarian system in the group.[78] The Bedouins accept this, driven by their psychological bonds – that is, a group feeling implanted by various dynamics, particularly blood ties (kinship).[79] But ʿasabiyya is never a synonym of 'kinship'. Kinship is decisive, but it is just another element of ʿasabiyya.[80] ʿAsabiyya is functional, not genetic.[81]

---

[76] Andic and Andic 1985, 455–6; Hassan 1998, 146; Dale 2015, 3; Issawi 1950, 14; Lelli 2021, viii; Arslan 2014, 7; Qadir 1941, 120; Rosenthal 1962, 84. Considering this empirical aspect, Ibn Khaldun is usually recognised within the Greco-Islamic tradition. Dale 2006, 431; Alatas 2014, 26; Fromherz 2010b, 123.

[77] Baali 1988, 44. According to Fromherz (2016, 198), 'Ibn Khaldun may have preferred to keep the exact meaning imprecise'.

[78] Lacoste 1984, 110 and 184; Arslan 2014, 96, 168.

[79] Ibn Khaldun 1958a, 262–3.

[80] Lacoste 1984, 106.

[81] Kayapınar 2008, 384. Ibn Khaldun (1979, 3, 4) treats genealogies as mostly fabricated for political purposes. In his *Autobiography*, he even criticises his own family genealogy for its deficits. For him (1958a, 265), a genealogy, no matter if it is correct or wrong, is meaningful

'*Asabiyya* appears as a social law in Ibn Khaldun.[82] It produces certain outcomes in a given context. For example, when it emerges among the Bedouins, its imminent impact is to generate a chieftain hierarchy and tribal order. But it later transforms into a dynamic that pushes them to attain statehood. In this regard, its goal is the state. Once the state is created, *asabiyya* tends to decline.[83] It is a feeling that binds people. It emerges spontaneously when the supporting conditions are present, and autonomously determines all social and political phenomena, such as institutions and political power. In this regard, it is a general cause, or law, that explains the cohesion among people, as well as the evolution of their organisations.[84] Thus, Ibn Khaldun's model explains all social and political phenomena, including religion, in terms of *asabiyya*. It equalises all people, whether Muslim or not, by putting them under a general law of causation. Reflecting this, Ibn Khaldun uses a neutral and technical vocabulary composed of terms like *asabiyya*, urban, Bedouin, crafts, state, population and power, where the subjective religious terminology is irrelevant.[85] Politics and society are thus explained from a mechanical perspective. For example, as Gellner underlines, *asabiyya* is therefore not a personal virtue, it is a mechanical solidarity.[86]

Logically, Ibn Khaldun explains religion within the general causation power of *asabiyya*, without giving it an autonomous power. This is most visible when he writes that Muhammad's success was also owed to *asabiyya*.[87] Religion is important, but only as an additional support of *asabiyya*.[88] Ibn Khaldun thus explains Islamic history, as well as Islamic institutions, as subject to the general dynamics and laws of human history.[89] There is no difference between Muslims and non-Muslims in this regard. For example, he explains

---

if it motivates people. Otherwise, attempts to prove a genealogy based on historical and scientific proof does not automatically motivate people. Thus, Ibn Khaldun (1958a, 270) is critical of the use of various genealogies for legitimacy in urban societies like the Abbasids.

[82] Ibn Khaldun 1958a, 264–5.
[83] Ibid., 284 and 286; Ibn Khaldun 1958b, 291.
[84] Baali 1988, 46; Gellner 1975, 203; Goodman 1972, 257.
[85] Kayapınar 2008, 382; Hopkins 1990, 10.
[86] Gellner 1975, 205.
[87] Ibn Khaldun 1958a, 414–15.
[88] Ibid., 320.
[89] Kerr 1966, 29; Togan 1985, 163.

the birth of the provincial order as the result of the decline of *asabiyya* during the reign of al-Muʿtasim (r. 833–42) and his son, al-Wathiq (r. 842–7). This led them to rule with the help of the Persians, and the Turkish and Dailami soldiers. But this later generated provincial states, like the Tahirids and Saffarids, on the periphery where the Abbasids could not impose their rule. This causal explanation is valid for Spain: as the Arab *asabiyya* declined, small princes (*taʾifa*) seized power.[90] The rise and fall of dynasties in the Maghrib was similarly determined by the causal dynamics generated by *asabiyya*.[91]

Asabiyya was Ibn Khaldun's adaptation to the political realities of his time, when Islam was no longer the supra-political identity, as politics was determined by states that defined themselves primarily in terms of their cultural identities, be it ethnic or tribal, such as Persian, Berber, Turkish, Masmuda or Zenata. Religion was still significant, but it no longer symbolised political unity. Instead, it was interpreted according to the political interests of the states, the political legitimacy of which was linked primarily to their cultural identities.

Symbolising how culture causes differentiation at a political level, Ibn Khaldun emphasised the variety of titles, flags, seals, outfits and institutions among Muslims.[92] His *asabiyya* had simply replaced religion. He believed that a ruler can achieve power only with the help of his people. He had learned that it is difficult to rule states composed of many tribes.[93] He no longer believed in Islam's traditional claim to unite people politically. Thus, unlike the previous political rationalists like Nizam al-Mulk, according to Ibn Khaldun it is the armies with one *asabiyya* that are better than those that have many soldiers with different *asabiyya*. It is in such mixed armies that soldiers tend to defect.[94] For Ibn Khaldun, an army of many nations is only a proof of declining *asabiyya*, which signals the approach of a state's collapse.[95]

---

[90] Ibn Khaldun 1958a, 314–16; 1958b, 129.
[91] Ibn Khaldun 1958a, 316.
[92] Ibid., 465–72; Ibn Khaldun 1958b, 12–13 and 51.
[93] Ibn Khaldun 1958b, 332 and 372.
[94] Ibid., 87.
[95] Ibn Khaldun 1958a, 342–3 and 372–6.

The state

Another significant concept in Ibn Khaldun's lexicon is *'umran*. He defined it as a science, for it has an independent subject: human civilisation and social organisation. *'Umran* is to explain all the conditions that construct 'human civilization'.[96] He uses the term to denote the totality of human civilisation (or culture) of which the constructive elements include economic, social and cultural activities.[97] Similar to *'asabiyya*, *'umran* symbolises the explaining of social and political phenomena within the general scheme of causation.

There are two types of *'umran*: bedouin (*badawi*) and urban (*hadari*). While the former is 'found in outlying regions and mountains, in the hamlets and pastures, and on the fringes of sandy deserts', the latter is the 'sedentary civilization as found in cities, villages, towns, and small communities'.[98] Any group living in countryside, that is, out of urban centres, fits Ibn Khaldun's 'bedouins'. It includes all countryfolk, no matter how their lifestyles may differ.[99] Though Rosenthal suggests 'civilization' for Ibn Khaldun's *'umran*, the term – at least from a modern view – is problematic in the case of the Bedouins, as they cannot have a civilisation. But Rosenthal clarifies that *'umran* applies to any settlement above the level of individual savagery.[100] These concerns justify 'culture' as the better alternative.[101]

Bedouin culture is a minimalist form of social organisation. It is society almost without institutions. Bedouins live in simple and bare forms. They do not have crafts and sciences, for they are interested only in their primary and natural needs.[102] *'Asabiyya* is strong among Bedouins, which makes them embrace and practice values by heart. *'Asabiyya* motivates Bedouins. They have no need of institutions. Since they can achieve virtues like order and security without external institutions like education, Bedouins are morally good in character and brave.[103] Every state was a bedouin culture at its outset.

---

[96] Ibid., 77; Ibn Khaldun 1958c, 285.
[97] Corbin 1993, 279; Lacoste 1984, 151; Chabane 2008, 332.
[98] Ibn Khaldun 1958a, 84–5.
[99] Sivers 1980, 71; Dale 2015, 174.
[100] Rosenthal 1958b, lxxvi–lxxvii.
[101] Dale 2015, 28; Mahdi 1957, 8.
[102] Ibn Khaldun 1958b, 347–8.
[103] Ibn Khaldun 1958a, 259–61.

As this culture lacks institutions, the ruler and people were enclosed together, not separated by institutions and intermediaries.[104]

Societies are in natural transition from bedouin to urban culture where the motor is *'asabiyya*. By nature, *'asabiyya* brings bedouins to urban culture, which is the last stage of social organisation.[105] When this last stage is attained, *'asabiyya* declines, and urban culture turns toward corruption and senility.[106] Urban people depend on 'walls' – symbolising institutions – for their security. Their reliance on such structures illustrates their weakness of character. Gradually, urban culture degenerates into luxury and cultural decadence.[107] According to Ibn Khaldun, the transition from bedouin to urban culture occurs within four generations, and *'asabiyya* is completely lost at the end.[108]

The state emerged within this transition from bedouin to urban. As stated above, the bedouins have their chieftain who obtains loyalty through others' veneration. This is a psychological relationship. Other than that, a chieftain has no means of imposing obedience. However, over time, one group of bedouins gains power over all the others and, eventually, brings them under its sway. The state that emerges at this stage is linked by this group's *'asabiyya*. The outcome is the gradual foundation of institutions that enable state institutions to impose their will, no matter whether the people concede or not. The ruler is now separated from the people because there are now intermediary actors, rules and institutions, the typical features of urban culture.[109] The emergence of the political power that institutions embody symbolises the birth of the state. Paradoxically, *'asabiyya* now tends to decline.

The superiority of urban culture in terms of its sciences and crafts does not alter the bedouins' superiority in morality and intelligence. This is because urban superiority in the sciences and crafts is the product of institutions that transform sciences and crafts into habits. Habit is not intelligence; it is created by demand. If there is no demand for a particular craft, for example, no one is

---

[104] Ibn Khaldun 1958b, 111.
[105] Ibn Khaldun 1958a, 253–4.
[106] Ibn Khaldun 1958b, 295–6.
[107] Ibn Khaldun 1958a, 253–8.
[108] Ibid., 279, 287, 343–5.
[109] Ibid., 284, 336–7 and 383; Ibn Khaldun 1958b, 111–13 and 118.

interested in learning it.¹¹⁰ On this account, Ibn Khaldun's model is a process where *'asabiyya* is gradually replaced by urban institutions. This transition is necessarily an advancement in institutions, but a regresssion in morality.

Ibn Khaldun's view of the state has three major consequences, the first of which is its autonomy. The state is separate from the people because it imposes its will through institutions. It has destroyed the personalistic component of group administration.

The second consequence is that political power is the state's central dynamic. The nature of political power is that it is won by competition. Political power is rarely handed over voluntarily to the self-entitled entity. That means that neither the religious nor the philosophical entities' power can override state power. Power struggles define everything, including the leader.¹¹¹ Concepts like 'legitimacy', and even 'the law', are defined by the political power. The state instrumentalises everything else. Logically, the state is never primarily a moral phenomenon. The centrality in it of political power makes it naturally unjust.¹¹²

The third consequence is that the state becomes a historical formation. It is now the natural habitat of mankind, and that emerges from human need.¹¹³ It is not required, nor yet dictated, by a religious or philosophical framework. Political institutions are bound by human history.¹¹⁴ Religious rules are never the general rules of *'umran*.

Ibn Khaldun's explanation of the emergence of state as the human evolution from a moral society to an advanced stage with institutions was inspired by al-Mawardi. Imagining the earlier period of humanity as moral societies without institutions, where affairs are managed in personalistic ways, was a narrative that al-Mawardi had proposed. His explanation of politics and the state as being within the general causation principle results in the radical but inevitable consequence of setting the subjective rules of religion aside. Ibn Khaldun thus separated the caliphate from leadership. While leadership is

---

[110] Ibn Khaldun 1958b, 351 and 433.
[111] Ibn Khaldun 1958a, 313, 339 and 380.
[112] Al-Azmeh 1982, 29–31 and 83.
[113] Ibn Khaldun 1958a, 380.
[114] Ra'ees 2004, 178.

based on the rational argument that all humankind needs a social organisation where a leader restrains the people, the Islamic caliphate is not based on a general rational necessity, as there are nations without it.[115] As a logical consequence of that reasoning, Ibn Khaldun rejected jurists and scholars having executive powers in administration:

> State and government authority are conditioned by the natural requirements of civilization. Thus, the nature of civilization does not require that jurists and scholars have any share in authority. Executive authority belongs only to the person who controls the *'asabiyya* (meaning political power) and is by it enabled to exercise authority, to do things or not do them. These who do not have group feeling, who have no control over their own affairs, and who cannot protect themselves, are dependent upon others. How, then, could they participate in councils, and why should their advice be taken into consideration? Their advice as derived from their knowledge of the religious laws is taken into consideration only in so far they are consulted for legal decisions. Advice on political matters is not their province, because they have no *'asabiyya* and do not know the conditions and laws which govern *'asabiyya*.[116]

This paragraph is a crystal-clear definition of Islamic political theory. It defines politics in terms of power, and assigns the executive role only to those who have political power. It eloquently displays how Islamic political theory is different from Islamic political philosophy, and from the religious view of politics. It is also a later confirmation of what Ibn al-Muqaffa had argued centuries before. In fact, Ibn Khaldun remembers Ibn al-Muqaffa as a person who previously touched upon many of the problems he (Ibn Khaldun) discusses.[117]

Having defined the state as a historical phenomenon, Ibn Khaldun explains the birth of the state among Muslims from the same perspective of human needs and dynamics. He repeats the mainstream narrative on the birth of the Islamic state as it was invented by al-Mawardi: the early Islamic community was composed of good individuals who could carry out any given task. There were no crafts, sciences and institutions, not even the educational,

---

[115] Ibn Khaldun 1958a, 389–90.
[116] Ibid., 459–60.
[117] Ibid., 82–3.

and no ranks to symbolise political stratification. Such institutions developed only later, replacing early personalistic methods with professionalism.[118] Ibn Khaldun's early Islamic community was as a bedouin culture (*'umran badawi*) order with a strong *'asabiyya*, so morally strong individuals carried out all tasks without institutions.

That early Islamic community, which was in origin a moral society, later embraced political institutions.[119] But, when exactly did the state emerge? Ibn Khaldun set it off with the establishment of *diwan* during the time of Caliph Umar.[120] We thus understand that the early idealistic society where Muslims solved their problems in personal ways, without institutions, had already ended before the classical caliphate.[121] Next, he not only refers to the period that begins with Mu'awiya, but he mentions also the Persian impact. He narrates how Caliph Umar tolerated Mu'awiya organising his equipment and retinue to imitate the Persians. Ibn Khaldun interprets this as an approval of statehood.

Unsurprisingly, he mentions *mazalim* because it combines elements both of governmental power and judicial discretion.[122] And he addresses the reign of Abd al-Malik to explain how many other intermediaries and institutions emerge between ruler and people.[123] His account of the birth of political institutions is in parallel with the mainstream narrative of the birth of the Islamic state as defined in Chapter 1. As a matter of fact, he wrote that he borrowed this narrative from al-Mawardi.[124]

Following Ibn Khaldun, we understand why Muslims imitated other nations. In the beginning, the Islamic community was institutionally underdeveloped. It was only later, in cities like Basra, Kufa and Baghdad, that Muslims developed crafts. In the meantime, the gap was filled by transfers from other nations like the Persians and the Byzantines. This was possible

---

[118] Ibn Khaldun 1958b, 8–9 and 59–60; 1958c, 311.
[119] Ibn Khaldun 1958a, 428.
[120] Ibn Khaldun 1958b, 21.
[121] Ibn Khaldun 1958a, 78; 1958b, 137–9.
[122] Ibn Khaldun 1958a, 417 and 455–6.
[123] Ibn Khaldun 1958b, 9 and 22.
[124] Ibn Khaldun 1958a, 455.

because sedentary culture is transferable.[125] Ibn Khaldun's explanation normalises the Islamic experience within the general course of human history. Institutions, including that of Muslims, are not given or fixed. They evolve through history.[126] He illustrates this by analysing a popular medieval practice, the oath. Showing how it evolved across societies, he concludes that institutions and practices have different meanings in different times and environments.[127] The fact that they belong to Muslims does not make them exceptional, nor immune from the general rules of human organisations, because 'differences of condition among people are the result of the different ways in which they make their living'.[128]

The Consequences of Political Rationalism

Ibn Khaldun's *'umran*, explaining social and political institutions as the result of general causal dynamics, provides a strong autonomy for the political. The normative explanations of religion and political philosophy are left aside. Political events are created by general causal dynamics. Religion is not rejected, but it is no longer a general dynamic that dictates political events. Its role is limited to demanding good governance. But this is an advisory role, not a general factor in the determination of historical events.[129]

Ibn Khaldun criticises the classical authors for a meaningless act when they explain the rise of statehood among Muslims – particularly linked to the developments with Muʿawiya – as moral decadence. He wanted them to grasp that the state among Muslims is a natural consequence of the general rules that affect all people, and religion had no impact on that. Islam can only endorse or reject a political model in moral terms. It cannot propose rules that affect human societies as general causal laws. This automatically invalidated the imagining of social and political phenomena (such as power, state or richness) as inherently good or bad. For example, richness is not naturally good or bad. There were rich people among the companions of Muhammad

---

[125] Ibn Khaldun 1958b, 50, 350 and 384.
[126] Ibn Khaldun 1958a, 57.
[127] Ibid., 434.
[128] Ibid., 249.
[129] Also see Ziya and Fahri 1940, 65; Mufti 2009, 408.

who were not spoiled by it.[130] The message is clear: one should not explain political events as good or bad. Social and political phenomena should be explained as determined by general causal dynamics.[131]

Ibn Khaldun demonstrates his views in the provocative example of the rivalry between Ali and Muʿawiya. Both the Sunnis and the Shiʿas see Ali as the moral superior of Muʿawiya, who is described as a pragmatist and was corrupt. He expounds upon this case from the general causal dynamics in reference to ʿasabiyya. No matter what their moral qualities and intentions, the struggle between Ali and Muʿawiya was determined by the rules of politics. Both had the right to demand power.[132] But Muʿawiya was the winner, because he acted according to the rules. The fight took place when the Arab ʿasabiyya was weakened and replaced by the state (or political power), and this served Muʿawiya. The morally inferior Muʿawiya was the 'superior' for complying with the political realities. This example gives the message that the fate of political rivalry – even if it goes against Ali, a mostly venerated Islamic figure – is determined by the rules of ʿasabiyya. With this, Ibn Khaldun effectively smashed the religious theories of political legitimacy.[133]

Ibn Khaldun gives other examples to prove that politics is determined by power (meaning general laws) and not by religious norms: Caliph Umar bin Abd al-Aziz, despite publicly praising the moral superiority of Qasim Muhammad, did not appoint him as heir because Qasim had no ability to compete with the Umayyad political power. The appointment of Qasim would have only brought weak government that would give way to political disorder. Similarly, Muʿawiya appointing his son, Yazid – another figure that both the Sunnis and Shiʿas vilified – was normal, given that no other person could rally the Umayyad political power. Any other person, even a morally superior one, would bring chaos, for he could not mandate the needed political power. Thus, Yazid, despite his wicked behaviour, was the correct candidate, for he could secure the public interest and social order, thanks to Umayyad power.[134]

---

[130] Ibn Khaldun 1958a, 416 and 420.
[131] Issawi 1950, 13.
[132] Ibn Khaldun 1958a, 421–2.
[133] Al-Azmeh 1982, 86. Also see Farooq 2019, 87–106.
[134] Ibn Khaldun 1958a, 422, 432 and 435. Also see Kerr 1966, 174.

In yet another provocative case, Ibn Khaldun explains, within the same rules of political power, the murder of Husayn, Prophet Muhammad's grandson, by Yazid. Husayn, the moral superior, made a wrong move when he framed his fight as a religious duty given Yazid's wickedness. However, he was powerless against Yazid, who had the Umayyad power behind him. After reminding us that the religious perspective is different from the political one, and that it cannot explain a worldly matter, Ibn Khaldun concludes that Husayn did not err in religious terms; he erred in a worldly matter.[135]

Another case, which is critical to demonstrate Ibn Khaldun's complete departure from the jurists' religious view of politics, is the Quraishi condition for the caliphate. He asserts that the condition was not required in the beginning as a kinship condition. It was proposed because the Quraish possessed the political power. Thus, when the Quraish (or another dynasty that claims Quraishi origin) no longer hold political power, the lineage condition is meaningless. In other words, what was formulated in the beginning as a Quraishi condition was a contextual and practical formulation of political power. There was a public interest in making that condition a law. No other tribe could unite the Arabs like the Quraish. Thus, any other tribe's claim for leadership would unleash political chaos. That correspondence between the Quraish and political power gradually disappeared when non-Arabs gained political superiority.[136]

The Refutation of Political Philosophy

In Ibn Khaldun's political thought, the explaining of society and politics through general rules, stands as the opposite of al-Farabi's *The Virtuous City* and Plato's *Republic*. Ibn Khaldun refutes idealistic political models of philosophical

---

[135] Ibn Khaldun 1958a, 443–4. Several scholars explain Ibn Khaldun's pragmatic behaviour, like frequently shifting his loyalty, as a reflection of his understanding of politics. Accordingly, he did what politics required. Fromherz 2016, 202; Lelli 2021, 1.

[136] Ibn Khaldun 1958a, 397–401. In Chapter 3, I noted that al-Baqillani had also dropped the Quraishi condition. But, according to Ibn Khaldun (1958a, 398), al-Baqillani did that in a presentist method by observing that it was no longer effective in his time, not to develop a systematic methodology as Ibn Khaldun was doing.

or religious paradigms.[137] The ideal state is certainly not his subject.[138] He studied society as it is.[139] Gellner, in what appears as a modernist but informative framing, defines Ibn Khaldun as 'a sociologist rather than a moralist' because he offers no advice. Instead, he is satisfied to understand things as they are.[140]

In the *Muqaddima*, Ibn Khaldun clearly writes that *'umran*, his science of culture, is different from the political philosophy (*siyasah al-madaniyyah*) represented by al-Farabi. According to him, political philosophy is the administration of home or city in accordance with ethical and philosophical requirements. It is a search for the ideal city, where people with good soul and character can dispense with rulers. If their laws are not determined by the common interest, they are external to society. Disagreeing with the political philosopher al-Farabi, Ibn Khaldun's rational politics explains society and politics in terms of the interaction of causes and people. Its rules are determined by rulers' or by the public's interest. Neither determiner is external to society. Thus, for Ibn Khaldun, rational politics emerges when politics is affected by rules that represent the interest of rulers, or the interest of the public. He does not count political philosophy as rational politics because it is based on religious rules.

Putting it differently, a rational politics is possible with rules that arose in human history. Ibn Khaldun posits the Persians,[141] and the early classical caliphate, as the first type of rational politics, that is, where the main determinant is the public interest, but there is some space for the rulers' interest. All of the later period is the second type of rational politics, where the rulers' interest is the primary dynamic, and there is some space for the public interest.

---

[137] Lana 1987, 153–4; Goodman 2019, 749; Alatas 2012, 49–50; Al-Azmeh 1982, 84; Hassan 1998, 311. As a nuance, Mahdi (1957, 126–32) argues that Ibn Khaldun accepted the al-Farabian concept in his later years, after he had failed politically. But this seems more like giving philosophers some role in a corrupt society. Mahdi is, however, criticised by various scholars like Lacoste (1984, 161) for putting Ibn Khaldun into a political philosophy framework.

[138] Lacoste 1984, 60.

[139] Walzer 1963, 42–3; Gibb 1933, 27.

[140] Gellner 1975, 203.

[141] It is highly significant that Ibn Khaldun, a Berber who was never an agent of the Persian impact on Islam, revered Persian politics as the equal of the early Islamic caliphate.

This is the general model. The politics of non-Muslims are also second-type rational politics.[142]

As part of his refutation of political philosophy, Ibn Khaldun criticises philosophers for imagining happiness as a matter of the soul's perfection in its having arrived at a perception of all existing things, including both the sensual and the beyond-sensual.[143] This is in effect to believe in the power of the human mind to achieve happiness in logical ways.[144] Ibn Khaldun posits that the explaining of happiness by logical argument is a fraudulent method that must be rejected.[145] As an empirical person, who understood happiness in the human context, connecting happiness to various states of the soul or mind was unacceptable to Ibn Khaldun.[146] We remember this argument from Ibn al-Muqaffa and Ibn Tufayl.

Ibn Khaldun saw politics as a practical field. He therefore did not see philosophers as good political actors because they overthink on political issues. But politics is not an act of philosophising. An average person, therefore, has a better chance in politics. To support this argument, Ibn Khaldun shows that the philosophers' method is not applicable in politics. He says that philosophers first discover universal ideas by intellectual speculation; then, in their minds, they make these ideas conform to the facts of the outside world. The problem is that the only procedure that philosophers have at their disposal to give their cogitations existential import is analogical reasoning. Analogy, however, cannot make the facts of the outside world fit what philosophers develop in their minds.

Philosophers are simply wrong to imagine that there are universal ideas that are applicable everywhere. This is impossible, because social and political events have a particular nature even when they share several structural similarities. Being empirical, politics requires the development of ideas on the basis of observing and collecting facts about the real world.[147]

---

[142] Ibn Khaldun 1958a, 78; 1958b, 137–9.
[143] Alatas 2012, 86; Asatrian 2003, 122; Korkut 2008, 557.
[144] Ahmad 2003, 95.
[145] Ibn Khaldun 1958c, 253–4.
[146] Rosen 2005, 596.
[147] Ibn Khaldun 1958a, 385; 1958c, 308–10. Also see Dale 2006, 436; Issawi 1950, 8.

Reflecting this, Ibn Khaldun developed his arguments through the analysis of actual situations, not by analogical and philosophical reasoning.[148] Muhsin Mahdi counted 405 historical examples in the *Muqaddima*.[149] The observations he made through his personal involvement in regional and tribal politics were equally formative. This made his political thought a derivative of his interaction with the human contexts in which he lived. He therefore did not imagine his findings as universally applicable.[150] This case-based empiricism splits Ibn Khaldun from the normative certainty of religion and political philosophy.[151] He did not explain politics on the mould of *a priori* philosophical or religious arguments. Instead, his ideas are his syntheses of what he had experienced in a place and at a specific time, mostly in the Maghrib.[152]

Finally, his empirical method made Ibn Khaldun break away from the Almohad elitism in particular, and the traditional Islamic elitism in general. As Charles Issawi writes, individuals' ability to affect the general causal dynamics is not significant in Ibn Khaldun's model.[153] Explaining society and politics as determined by general rules, he equated all people. Even prophets are subject to the same rules because their success requires ʿ*asabiyya*.[154] Ibn Khaldun's split from Islamic elitism is particularly noteworthy, given that he lived just after the Almohads, the foremost representatives of elitism.

In fact, the exodus of scholars from Spain brought Almohad elitism to the Hafsid lands via scholars like Muhammad al-Sakuni (d. 1317), who wrote commentaries on Ibn Tumart's books. He wrote a book in Tunis that aimed to explain theological issues to the common people (*al-ʿamma*), and the 'ignorami' (*al-juhhal*).[155] Continuing the Almohad elitism, his son,

---

[148] Lacoste 1984, 160–1; Ogunnaiki 2017, 14.

[149] Al-Azmeh 1982, 61.

[150] Irwin 1997, 470; Lacoste 1984, 5, 103–4; Mahdi 1957, 256; Qadir 1941, 118; Weiss 1995, 34; Al-Azmeh 1982, 145. Thus, I disagree with Mojuetan (1981, 93–108), who is not satisfied that Ibn Khaldun's thought was ultimately based on the examination of the particular, and considers him to be a fatalist. Mojuetan was challenged by scholars like Rosen (2005, 596).

[151] Mufti 2009, 392.

[152] Lacoste 1984, 160–2. Also see Korkut 2008, 550.

[153] Issawi 1950, 7.

[154] Ibn Khaldun 1958a, 324.

[155] Thiele 2020, 303–5.

Abu Ali al-Sakuni, wrote various books for average people to protect them from anthropomorphism.[156] In *Uyun al-Munazarat*, he explains 160 theological problems, under separate headings, in easy formulas for the common reader.[157] Having a critical narrative on philosophers, the book, as a typical elitist method, sometimes suggests to the average people that they stay silent, for they are not able to frame complex things correctly.[158] But that elitist period was closed by Ibn Khaldun, who believed that any actor who secures political power can dominate politics. On this account, Ibn Khaldun's mechanical model was a blow also to the religious/normative theories of leadership, which were by nature elitist, given to requiring of the aspirant leader that he be just, or other such banalities.

The Theoretical Explanation of Ibn Khaldun's Political Thought

Ibn Khaldun was an Ash'ari orthodox Muslim. His causal model, despite his Ash'ari background, of which the main tenet is the need to reject Aristotelian causality, is therefore seen as an aberration/ambivalence.[159] Below, I shall try to discuss this view by analysing the three major areas of Ibn Khaldun's thought: his views on causality, his separation of the empirical and the non-empirical knowledge/sciences, and finally, his explanation of religion.

Causality

Ibn Khaldun's model explains social and political phenomena through causality.[160] According to him, man has an intellectual ability to understand things in the outside world so that he may arrange them into an order.[161] This

---

[156] Olson 2020, 47.
[157] Al-Sakuni 1976, 14. Al-Sakuni (ibid., 13 and 45) notes that a major subject of his book is the 'science of unity', which is the Almohad *tawhid*. He tries to explain how to understand difficult issues, such God having a face. But al-Sakuni (ibid., 247) sometimes cannot save himself from using a complex discourse.
[158] Al-Sakuni 1976, 19, 176. Naturally, the book is harsh about what is regarded as a heretic group, such as the Rafidis and the Kharijites. Al-Sakuni 1976, 20–2.
[159] Dale 2015, 101; Irwin 2018, 18; Lacoste 1984, 186.
[160] Spengler 1964, 287; Amri 2008, 353; Togan 1985, 160; Issawi 1950, 7; Muhammad 1980, 196.
[161] Ibn Khaldun 1958b, 412–13.

reminds us of the classical rationalist assumption, observed in other medieval Muslim rationalists like Ibn Rushd or the Muʿtazila, that there is an intelligible order in nature, thanks to natural causes.[162]

First, to briefly explain Ibn Khaldun's causal model: according to him, when a man intends to create something, he must understand the reason or cause of that thing, that is, the conditions governing it. However, reasons and causes are interconnected as a chain. Any sequence of reasoning must have another chain to which its own existence is posterior. This requires that a man begin his work with the last principle/cause known to him. He begins with the first thing in the causal chain, which thinking reaches last.[163]

Ibn Khaldun's causal model can be interpreted as both compatible with and different from Ashʿari causality (or occasionalism).[164] Like Ashʿarism, Ibn Khaldun explains the principle that makes natural events interconnected, where God is the ultimate cause, that is, the cause of the causes. So, what appears as causality is in fact God's customs.[165] But given the solid causal foundation of his approach, further explanations can be proposed.

The first explanation is that Ibn Khaldun, not problematising the contradictions with Ashʿarism, submitted a model that pragmatically employs an Aristotelian interpretation.[166] As Dale says, Ibn Khaldun was not a philosopher.[167] He was not educated in a madrasa.[168] Though he had good teachers, his learning was always connected with practice. As already noted, he was critical of overthinking, and of analogical methods. He rebuffed philosophers for imagining consistency as a mental effort. There is even a passage in the *Muqaddima* where he complains that the human quest for knowledge is impeded by the works available on the subject, the complex terminology and the numerous methods.[169]

---

[162] Çaksu 2007, 53; Issawi 1950, 7.
[163] Ibn Khaldun 1958b, 414–15.
[164] It is useful to remember here that Ibn Khaldun sees Muʿtazila as a heretic. Ibn Khaldun 2017, 11.
[165] Wolfson 1959, 586–7 and 595; Al-Azmeh 1982, 106.
[166] Enan 1941, 98–9; Lacoste 1984, 183–6 and 193.
[167] Dale 2015, 254.
[168] Fromherz 2010b, 50.
[169] Ibn Khaldun 1958c, 288.

Ibn Khaldun was a practical man. In this regard, he reminds us of my discussion of Nizam al-Mulk's relations with Ash'arism. To repeat what I said there: Ash'arism – as long as its contradictions are ignored – is a useful legitimiser, for it argues that it reconciles God's sovereignty, causality and man's free will. But an external critic – this might be a medieval Mu'tazila or a modern rationalist – is never persuaded by the Ash'ari arguments on how this reconciliation is sustained.

As a second explanation, Ibn Khaldun is imagined as synthesising al-Ghazali and Ibn Rushd.[170] Supporting this argument, Ibn Khaldun writes that he imagines Ash'arism as the mediator of different approaches.[171]

As a third explanation, which I prefer, Ibn Khaldun suggested a different concept of causation. To achieve this, he first proposes that God created things with certain natures, and these natures create certain types of behaviour.[172] To illustrate this, he quotes verses of the Qur'an, like 'God gave everything its natural characteristics, and guided it'.[173] This reminds us of the Maturidi strategy of referring to nature (taba'i) to justify free will and causality. Al-Maturidi recognised that events in nature are ordered by established rules that originate in the very nature of things.[174] Similarly, Ibn Khaldun explains general dynamics as the result of the natures that God created in things. For example, God created man in a form that can live and subsist only with the help of food, which requires him having a natural desire for food. Similarly, since God fashioned their natures so, the strength of the horse is much greater than the strength of man.[175] Based on this, Ibn Khaldun concludes that the world has a certain order: there are nexuses between cases and things caused.[176] The term 'nexus' or connection, which is never causality, secures that the order is sustained by God. For example, according to him, there are seven zones on earth and each affects

---

[170] Arslan 2014, 356 and 369–72.

[171] Ibn Khaldun 1958c, 49.

[172] Ibn Khaldun 1958a, 94–6. Also see Dale 2015, 153; Ra'ees 2004, 161. For example, Ibn Khaldun (1958a, 330) wrote that 'this is how God proceeds with his creatures'.

[173] Ibn Khaldun 1958a, 92.

[174] Al-Maturidi 2018, 100–1. Also see Dhanani 1984, 65–7; Frank 1974, 138.

[175] Ibn Khaldun 1958a, 89–90.

[176] Ibid., 194.

the way of life there. So, civilisation is more advanced in some zones than the others. This is because geography and climate affect (or 'cause') the quality of civilisations.[177] As a result, civilisation flourishes in the middle zones with moderate climates.[178] That causal interaction is so strong that climate and the social context affect even who is more or less religious. For example, while religiosity is weak in cities, it is strong among bedouins.[179] But this is all because of 'God's plan for civilization (*'umran*)'.[180] So Ibn Khaldun defines God rather like the creator who makes general rules. This indeed brings him closer to Ibn Rushd.[181]

Meanwhile, however, Ibn Khaldun redefines causality as a more complex phenomenon that fits his analysis of human organisations. This is never like the linear and clear-cut causality of the natural sciences. Ibn Khaldun's causality is tailored for social events. As Charles Issawi points out, Ibn Khaldun's laws were sociological, and 'not a mere reflection of biological impulses, or physical factors'.[182]

Ibn Khaldun also detaches himself from Ibn Rushd and al-Ghazali, as their notion of causality, even when they discuss social issues, is a linear one suitable only in the natural sciences. They imagine causation as '*x* causes *y*'. To remind: the burning of cotton case in al-Ghazali's *The Incoherence of Philosophers* was the main example through which he explains his idea of causation.[183] Like other physical events, the burning of cotton can be distilled or decontextualised.

The idea of using such examples is that what we discover in one instance is applicable everywhere. But can social phenomena be distilled and decontextualised like the burning of cotton? As the answer is simply 'no', we should accept that the causal framework of a social event is more complex and vaguer. A social event is never a burning of cotton. Unlike physical events like burning cotton, social events are always contextual. Reflecting this, Ibn Khaldun

---

[177] Ibid., 103–4.
[178] Ibid., 167.
[179] Ibid., 179–80.
[180] Ibid., 110.
[181] Also see Dale 2015, 103.
[182] Issawi 1950, 8–9.
[183] Al-Ghazali 2000, 167.

proposed a constitutive causality that is an intersection of the 'natures' that generate standard outcomes and local conditions. This requires taking the conditions and realities of the time into consideration.[184] One cannot distil a social event from its context like one can the physical experience of burning cotton. Thus, one should always know that a causal framework of a social event is contextual.

To demonstrate how Ibn Rushd failed to grasp this critical point, Ibn Khaldun criticises him for not understanding several issues because he lived in an urban culture where people have weak *'asabiyya*.[185] Put differently, Ibn Rushd failed because he did not understand how social events operate in a causation that is susceptible to local and temporal conditions. He thus wrongly imagined that social causation occurs similarly in societies with different degrees of *'asabiyya*.

In another example, Ibn Khaldun criticises al-Turtushi, who suggested that the military strength of a state is identical to the size of its army that receives a monthly salary. But he 'generalized the condition observed by him' within the part of Spain where local rulers (*ta'ifa*) dominate. Thus, his argumentation could not be proposed for all societies.[186]

According to Ibn Khaldun, Ibn Rushd and al-Turtushi failed to grasp that there can be no general causality independent of local dynamics. Having failed to realise this, Ibn Rushd and al-Turtushi proposed anachronic explanations. In fact, Ibn Khaldun's grand debate on historical methodology at the beginning of the *Muqaddima* is mainly about this problem, as he finds previous historians like al-Masudi wrong because they narrated past events without checking them with the principles underlying historical/particular situations.[187] The correct way of checking the authenticity of an item of news or a report is to analyse them within their historical contexts. This is necessary because every event possesses a nature peculiar to its essence, as well as to the accidental conditions that may attach themselves to it.[188] Ignoring that

---

[184] Ibn Khaldun 1958a, 75–6.
[185] Ibid., 275–6.
[186] Ibid., 316–17.
[187] Ibid., 16. Also see Ardıç 2008, 452.
[188] Ibn Khaldun 1958a, 72.

peculiar nature of an event, and proposing a general causation to explain all events, is for Ibn Khaldun only to generate wrong conclusions.

Ibn Khaldun meant here that even though there are general dynamics that affect historical events, their interaction with their contexts may generate different effects. His ʿasabiyya is a good referent, as it operates differently in the different contexts and times. For example, its impact is different at the beginning of a dynasty and in the later times.[189] On this account, Ibn Khaldun used the Aristotelian notion of causes, which are usually fixed, but showed them as changing according to their spatial and temporal contexts. This is a flexible, dynamic, dialectical and context-related causality.[190]

By this account, even if we have sufficiently constant laws of causality for social events, which follow regular patterns and sequences, those constants are never the absolutes that govern natural phenomena. Thus, the only available method is to search for those laws with a meticulous collection of facts about human history by observing the existing events, and analysing their historic counterparts.[191] This requires the discovery of the causes of events, and that is endless effort, because social events are never distillable from their context. We can never define that effort and its borders like a physical event. This logically makes Ibn Khaldun accept that (i) one may not be able to know all the causes of an event, or (ii) one may frame a wrong causal nexus in the effort to explain an event.

As an example of point (i), we may never grasp all causal elements in war because there are hidden factors, such as trickery.[192] For (ii), Ibn Khaldun reminds us of the high food prices in Spain when the Christians were attacking the Muslims' lands. Many believed that the high prices were due to the shortage of foodstuffs in the country. But that was wrong, for the local people were advanced in agricultural production. The real reason was that many people had come to Spain to join the jihad, and the local ruler factored their allowances into his pricing, and that created demand inflation.[193] But, Ibn

---

[189] Pišev 2019, 13; Weiss 1995, 30.
[190] Çaksu 2007, 49 and 62.
[191] Issawi 1950, 7–8.
[192] Ibn Khaldun 1958b, 85.
[193] Ibn Khaldun 1958b, 279.

Khaldun, unlike al-Ghazali, is not alarmed by the limits of the human senses. We never see a critique of rationalist and empirical knowledge in Ibn Khaldun. Instead, given that there is a chain of causality, he suggests that man advance in that chain, and act accordingly.[194] For Ibn Khaldun, even though it is never perfect, empirical knowledge is the only means of explaining society and politics.

The separation of the empirical and non-empirical sciences

Ibn Khaldun strictly separates empirical and non-empirical knowledge (and sciences).[195] He does not refute the non-empirical sciences. But for him, only the empirical sciences can explain social and political issues.

According to his classification – which displays a strong impact of Ibn al-Muqaffa – the philosophical sciences depend on man's ability to think and verify through human perceptions and observations.[196] The knowledge of these sciences is provided and verified (or repudiated) by empirical observation. These are natural to a man; not restricted to any particular religious group. They are studied by all people (irrespective of their religion) who are all equally qualified to learn and research them. They are thus transferable to any nation.

In contrast, the conventional sciences (or religious sciences) depend on knowledge provided by religion. Their knowledge comes from religion, that is, the Qur'an and the traditions. Even if analogical methods are used in religious knowledge, they are also derived from the knowledge provided by religion. Therefore, the knowledge provided by conventional/religious sciences cannot be verified or refuted by empirical observation. As a main comparison, the philosophical sciences, because they are empirical, are general; conventional/religious sciences are restricted to Muslims. They are not transferable.[197] To prove himself, Ibn Khaldun reminds us that there are many

---

[194] Ibn Khaldun 1958b, 414.

[195] Also see Ahmad 2003, 36; Mahdi 1957, 73; Hassan 1998, 132 and 137.

[196] We have in this group logic, physics, metaphysics and mathematics, which have sub-branches of geometry, arithmetic, music and astronomy. Ibn Khaldun 1958c, 111–12.

[197] Ibn Khaldun 1958b, 350, 420 and 436–8. Ibn Khaldun (2017, 22) repeats this categorisation in his work on Sufism, *Shifa*: 'Revelation and acquired learning are two obvious matters: acquired learning is obtained through the senses, whereas revelation comes necessarily through religion.' Also see Mahdi 1957, 74–6; Fischel 1961, 112 and 114.

people without a revealed religion, but they have order, and they create dynasties and states. Their success proves how the rules of human organisations are sustained by general laws that are shared by different nations.[198]

Having separated the empirical and the non-empirical sciences, Ibn Khaldun, in yet another example of where he was inspired by Ibn al-Muqaffa, next underlines that confusing them is wrong, as each group is different in nature for having different subjects.[199] Any subject requires its own special science. But the Sufis and theologians confuse this by using their conventional sciences to prove their arguments in rational terms. For example, philosophers attempt to give logical proof of the existence of prophecy.[200] However, their methods are conventional, and have no ability to rationally prove such ideas. Knowledge of the conventional sciences is accepted as true only by Muslims because they recognise Muhammad as a prophet. Otherwise, there is no rational and empirical method to prove any religious knowledge. According to Ibn Khaldun, 'the intellect has nothing to do with the religious law and their views'.[201]

To illustrate Ibn Khaldun on this subject: even if he recognises Sufi knowledge, he rejects the rationalising of it. Sufi ideas cannot be expressed in a solid language, as language expresses commonly accepted concepts, most of which apply to the *sensibilia*.[202] Sufi experience is formed with a subjective and symbolic language. But this knowledge, as it was not verified through empirical factors, cannot be rationally proved. Reminding that the trend of rationalising Sufi knowledge is a recent phenomenon, Ibn Khaldun repulsed it as a meaningless attempt at transforming Sufism into a science. Traditional Sufis like al-Qushayri never did that. They were satisfied within their mystical domain, not much interested even in the supernatural.[203] In his work on

---

[198] Ibn Khaldun 1958a, 92–3.
[199] Ibn Khaldun 1958c, 155.
[200] Ibn Khaldun 1958a, 79 and 92–3.
[201] Ibn Khaldun 1958c, 154.
[202] Ibid., 78–81, 86–8 and 101.
[203] Ibn Khaldun 1958b, 101 and 186; 1958c, 102–3. Also see Mahdi 1957, 102; Mufti 2019, 684. According to Ibn Khaldun (1958c, 80), Sufism became a systematically treated discipline after al-Ghazali.

Sufism, *Shifa*, Ibn Khaldun similarly criticised the later Sufis for mistakenly using their methods as another science.[204]

Ibn Khaldun similarly repulses the philosophers who attempt to rationalise their ideas. This leads only to the mistaken belief that one may discover the essence and conditions of the whole of existence by various speculative reasonings that are beyond the perceivable. Philosophers similarly claim that the articles of faith can be proven rationally. For him, both are methodologically impossible.[205] According to him, philosophy, which relies on hypothesis and suppositions, cannot determine its arguments, as it is not possible to observe them through an empirical method.[206] Similarly, philosophers claim to have grasped the knowledge of the beyond by their various abstractions and mental speculation, and that is problematic.[207]

As he did Sufism, Ibn Khaldun also criticises the 'later' (*muta'ahhirun*) names who wanted to update religious sciences by proposing methods to rationalise religious knowledge. For example, he criticises al-Baqillani for bringing logic into Ash'arism. But he admires the 'earlier' Ash'aris (*aqdamun*), as they were not interested in the methods of logic and did not seek to rationalise their arguments. According to him, the later introduction of logical methods into theology was burdened by the methodological necessity of validating philosophy on a theological perspective. This resulted, as we observed in al-Ghazali, in the declaring of certain philosophers as the enemies of faith. However, this is again to confuse theology and philosophy.[208] This

---

[204] Ibn Khaldun 2017, 59. Beyond his critique of the Sufis for philosophising, and for their intellectual tendencies in later Sufi thought, Ibn Khaldun (2017, 63, 68, 71, 77–8 and 254–7) criticised them in *Shifa* for various reasons, such as their adopting of the *Mahdi* figure; recognising various people as poles of humanity (*qutb*) to lead people; influencing people with their deluded prediction of future events and promoting laziness and weakness; and a problematic piety which detached people from active, intelligent participation in the wider socioeconomic and political life of society.

[205] Ibn Khaldun 1958c, 246–7 and 251–3. Also see Al-Azmeh 1982, 116–17.

[206] Rosenthal 1962, 105; Hassan 1998, 143.

[207] Ibn Khaldun appears to rebuff philosophy for methodological reasons rather than totally reject it: 'Philosophy is dangerous when it goes beyond its boundaries.' Ahmad 2003, 97; Mahdi 1957, 106.

[208] Ibn Khaldun saw al-Ghazali as having made this methodological mistake.

confusion, according to Ibn Khaldun, has its origin in the grave mistake of believing that both disciplines share the same subject. In consequence, the two disciplines became no longer distinguishable from one another.[209]

Religion

For Ibn Khaldun, the prophets are ordinary people with a natural ability to receive divine messages.[210] This is possible as a result of the chain of creation that starts with minerals and passes through animals, and reaches into the spiritual world.[211] The most advanced of each species is connected with the link in the chain above, so it has the ability to acquire its knowledge. As the most advanced humans, the prophets have the natural ability to connect with the spiritual world. Thus, in principle, humans are able to connect with the celestial worlds.[212] This view, which has its origins in Ibn Sina, probably passed from the Almohads to Ibn Khaldun through the scholars he met in Fez.[213] To recap, Ibn Tufayl likewise accepted that human nature has an ability to receive celestial messages.

Ibn Khaldun also accepts that the prophets have a standard method for bringing celestial knowledge to our world as objective content.[214] This differentiates them from the Sufis, who also have the ability to connect with the celestial world, but they could never transfer metaphysical knowledge in an objective way. Unlike the prophets, the Sufis have contending and personal methods that always distort the message.[215] In *Shifa*, Ibn Khaldun writes

---

[209] Ibn Khaldun 1958c, 51–3 and 153.
[210] Ibn Khaldun 1958a, 184–8; 1958c, 75.
[211] Ibn Khaldun 1958b, 423.
[212] Ibn Khaldun 1958a, 199; Asatrian 2003, 79.
[213] Thiele 2020, 315; Mahdi 1957, 85.
[214] Ibn Khaldun 1958b, 424.
[215] Ibid., 421–2; Ibn Khaldun 1958c, 101. According to Ibn Khaldun (1958a, 203), if human nature has the ability of connecting with the supernatural, this 'logical classification requires that there must be another kind of human beings, as inferior to the first as anything that has something perfect as its opposite, must be inferior to that perfect opposite'. These are the soothsayers. However, Ibn Khaldun relegated the influence of the supernatural to a realm outside of, or beyond, the ordinary course of human affairs. Rosenthal 1958b, lxxiii.

that the different and contradicting schools of thoughts and methods among the Sufis cause obscure explanations that make it impossible even to grasp their more vehemently heretical doctrines. In contrast, prophets' knowledge is more complete than that of the gnostic or the saint. Otherwise, there is essential similarity in the nature of the Sufis' and the prophets' knowledge.[216] However, remembered that Ibn Khaldun had already categorised religious knowledge as non-transferable; prophetic knowledge is never general like maths or medicine. This applies even to various items of medical information within the traditions of the prophets: they are Arab customs, not universal knowledge/science. Ibn Khaldun reminds us that Muhammad came to teach religion, not medicine, or any other ordinary matter.[217]

On this account, Ibn Khaldun sees the early Islamic period as ruled by religious law, not by the law of *'asabiyya*, but only for a short and exceptional period.[218] However, he does not imagine that exceptional period as completely autonomous, that is, independent of the general rules of history. For example, he underlines that for the prophets to succeed, they needed *'asabiyya*, as no religious propaganda can have existential import without it. He reminds us of the various historical cases where religious leaders failed because they lacked *'asabiyya*.[219] Ibn Khaldun simply made of religion a dependent variable. That meant that it was no longer an autonomous and monopolistic dynamic to affect society and politics.[220]

---

[216] Ibn Khaldun 2017, 57–9.

[217] Ibn Khaldun 1958c, 150.

[218] Ibn Khaldun 1958a, 426 and 449. Also see Spengler 1964, 287. Ibn Khaldun's concept of miracle is also complex, reflecting both orthodox and critical views. For example, events are named as miracle because they are impossible for other humans to achieve. This insinuates that miracles might have their origin in the differences in the development of human societies. He adds that miracles are rare, as they happen in cases of advanced challenge. Ibn Khaldun 1958a, 188. As an important case in this regard, though he recognises the Qur'an as a miracle, he treats its history in historical terms. According to him, the early companions, because they lacked an advanced ability in the craft of writing, made mistakes in the text. This is to contextualise the history of the Qur'an in the theory of culture/ *'umran*, according to which the early Muslims could not have had crafts like good writing, as they were not of an urban culture. Ibn Khaldun 1958b, 382–4.

[219] Ibn Khaldun 1958a, 322–7; Ibn Khaldun 1958b, 195.

[220] Chapra 1999, 25.

Conclusion: Bringing Society In

In concluding Chapter 3, I said of Nizam al-Mulk that he was at the apex of Islamic political theory. I described him so because Nizam al-Mulk's political thought achieved a full-blown state-centred political perspective. If we evaluate political rationalism in Ibn Khaldun's thought from a state-centric perspective, he did not contribute anything to Islamic political theory at that level. In this regard, Ibn Khaldun repeated what previous political rationalists had proposed since Ibn al-Muqaffa.

However, the revolutionary dimension of Ibn Khaldun in the evolution of Islamic political theory is in his incorporation of social dynamics (or society) into the equilibrium. Going beyond the state and the political elite, Ibn Khaldun constructed a theory that explains politics as a function of the general laws that determine the evolution of societies.

In fact, the subject of 'people' was considered and problematised by previous names, mainly Ibn al-Muqaffa and Ibn Tufayl. However, none of them had achieved what Ibn Khaldun did. He used society to detect the general laws of history that are behind anything that politics is interested in, such as legitimacy and institutions. Ibn Khaldun explained the state as the result of the evolution of societies from the initial stages to the advanced stage of urban culture. In so doing, he provided an objective foundation for Islamic political theory. Though previous political rationalists had accepted the state as a historical construct, they, however, explained it only within Islamic history. Thus, until Ibn Khaldun, the main argument on the state of Islamic political theory was that it was a later, thus a non-canonical, construct. Ibn Khaldun went beyond this by providing a universal explanation, which shows that state is by nature a historical construct, as there are general social laws that determine the evolution of human societies, no matter whether they are or are not Muslim.

Ibn Khaldun left a proto-modern theory to Muslims. This is a rationalist-empiricist analysis of history, politics and society based on general laws. He excluded non-empirical knowledge (of religion and philosophy) from political and social analysis. He demanded that religious scholars have no power in the administrative executive. However, while doing this, his perspective never required the challenging of religion. He proposed a model where religious and empiricist views continue to analyse societies as two disciplines indifferent to each other.

CONCLUSION
POLITICAL RATIONALISM FROM PAST TO PRESENT

By studying the evolution of political rationalism in Islamic history in five cases/periods, this book has demonstrated that there is an Islamic political theory that explains and justifies politics by invoking autonomous variables completely or partially independent of religious and philosophical norms. This perspective is recommended for its efficacy at overcoming the various problems caused by the overlapping approach, which arbitrarily references religious, philosophical and political perspectives in Islamic political thought.

If we make synoptic re-evaluation of this book's content, a number of issues can be highlighted as concluding remarks.

This book has exhibited that there was an established methodology of non-religious political reasoning in Islamic history. However, this was mainly justified in the name of 'the autonomy of power'. Despite clear evidence of it over the five periods that this book engages, political rationalism in Islam has not been identified to be the referencing of people as the source that legitimises non-religious (or 'secular') reasoning. Islamic political theory was mostly about political power and the state. This point is critical in contemporary debates, particularly on the relationship between Islam and democracy. To put it in a nutshell, as this book demonstrates, the records of Islamic political history cannot straightforwardly be used to justify popular legitimacy, the foundation of democracy. But those records can easily be used to justify non-religious reasoning in the name of political power. In other words, to introduce popular sovereignty into the contemporary discourse on Islam requires a new and radical reasoning. This has not yet happened. Yet, as a matter of fact, the concept of popular legitimacy was introduced into Muslim communities during the modernisation period, in the form of imitating the Western practice. Nonetheless, despite the various practices, a neat religious reasoning that establishes the absolute right of people to legislate (i.e. popular sovereignty) does not exist in Islamic theory.

The analysis in this book demonstrates that the state was mostly imagined as a non-religious phenomenon by the early Muslim authors. Political rationalists did not see the origins of the state in the 'canonical' period of Islam, that is, in the earliest period when the Prophet and the first Muslims laid down the foundations of Islam. This is a major point of contention between the many Muslims who interpret Islam as having introduced a practice and theory of state, and the Islamists who do not agree, For the classical Muslim political rationalists, the state was non-religious, as it was adopted late from non-Muslims, mainly the Persians and the Romans.

By defining the state as a later and non-religious phenomenon, the classical Islamic political rationalists justified a field of political reasoning where religion has no impact. As importantly, they defined empirical knowledge as the primary (and many times the sole) authority to explain that non-religious field. In this regard, it is fair to argue that classical Islamic political theory recognised a kind of separation of the religious and the political. Unlike the modern Muslims, medieval Muslim political rationalists were more successful in contextualising Islam within human history. As a result, political rationalists explained Islam within the general causality of human history. They therefore did not treat the state, for example, as an ahistorical religious artifact that was injected into human history. They explained the Islamic laws in political fields like taxation as similarly a product of Muslims' interaction with the historical context.

As another point, the Islamist thesis of a spiritual caliphate to unite the Muslims is not completely baseless, given this book's findings. The caliphate was mostly a spiritual institution during the Muslim medieval provincial order. Despite being a spiritual actor, the caliphate did generate a huge impact on the Muslim community, as was the case during the reigns of Caliphs al-Qadir and al-Qaim. Islamic history provides evidence to justify a spiritual caliphate without temporal power.

The details of Islamic political history, with which this book has engaged in detail, reminds us that contemporary Muslim societies are mostly affected by popular history. The Saljuqi sultan Alp Aslan, who made erroneous decisions because he was frequently drunk, is reincarnated in today's Turkey as a pious figure, comparable to a holy man. Many Muslims cannot comprehend that Muslims were fighting one another as late as the twelfth century because of the use of a different codex of the Qur'an. It is equally difficult today to be reminded that Hanbalis declared the Shafis infidels in the twelfth century. The chapters of this book underline the point that popular history should be addressed as a major problem, as the many key arguments of the various Islamic political movements, including the Islamists', are generated through it. There is a deep and complex 'history' problem among Muslims.

Islamic history is just another chapter of human history. The causal dynamics that affected wars, state-formations and other events operated similarly among Muslims. Islam was also overtaken by this grand causal mechanism. Gradually, Islam was practically 'deconstructed' by political dynamics. That 'deconstruction' inevitably contextualised Islam within the course of historical periods and developments. The Almohads and the Almoravids killed one another by referencing Islam like the Saljuqs, who similarly justified the killing of the Ghaznawid Muslims by referencing Islam. While Qadi Iyad, defending the Almoravid regime, declared Ibn Tumart's Mahdism a heresy, his contemporary, Ibn Barrajan, not only challenged the legitimacy of the Almoravids, but also laid down a theory of Mahdism. Ibn Barrajan was thus executed by the Almoravids. But the Almohads restored his reputation. Naturally, these political dynamics and enmities shaped Islamic political thought. Islam was deeply politicised, regionalised and even 'nationalised' by the continuously unfolding political dynamics. However, the impact of these human contexts was later mostly ignored, and nurtured a frameless reading of Islamic history. This was the fatal cost of approaching that human history dimension as religious precepts.

The literature on Islamic political history is full of references to the influence of Persia. In many books, we are informed that such-and-such viziers or authors were under the Persian impact. However, this 'Persian influence' is usually cited without further explanation, which causes the reader to imagine it as a purely cultural impact. That sort of cultural framing of the Persian influence inevitably nurtures a negative connotation. But why should so many people be under the influence of Persian culture? Though the role of culture cannot be completely ignored, the Persian impact was more an administrative efficiency issue. Simply, many people embraced the Persian institutions because they saw them as the most sophisticated of their time and region. It was not primarily a matter of cultural impact. For the Turkish nomads, the Persian-inspired institutions of the Samanids and the Ghaznawids were the sole models to imitate. Politics is often the imitating of the better.

Medieval Muslims imitated the Persian (and sometimes the Roman) laws and institutions because they were the best available models known to them. It is better to imagine them first as going after the models that they deemed as better, rather than as people who went after the Persian culture. In this regard, Muslims incorporating Persian institutions is one of the three major historical adoptions of external patterns and institutions, along with the reception of Greek philosophy in medieval times, and the modernisation of Muslim societies after the eighteenth century.

Islam's first grand interaction with another civilisation occurred through the Muslims' borrowing of Greek philosophy. Islamic philosophical rationalism, which was produced by this grand interaction, was later challenged in the twelfth century by a new generation of Muslim scholars who represented the nascent Sunni orthodoxy. However, political rationalism, which is a product of Islam's second grand interaction with another civilisation, the Persian, survived. Muslim scholars like al-Ghazali, who challenged the Aristotelian influence on the Muslims, tolerated political rationalism. Thus, as late as 1387, more than 150 years after the death of al-Ghazali, Ibn Khaldun could write that society and politics should be explained only by empirical knowledge, and no sort of mystical (nor even religious) knowledge has any role in this task.

The survival of political rationalism was thanks to various reasons, like it never appearing as a theological challenge to the Sunni scholars, and its intellectual agents having the state's support. But, later, during the Muslims' resistance to modernisation (or Westernisation), they parted ways with classical Islamic political rationalism. Reminiscent of the grand change after the twelfth century, a general revivalism in Muslim communities in contemporary times reframed Islam, and the 'secularising' tenets of medieval Muslim political rationalists were no longer welcome. Those rationalists were either selectively read or interpreted framelessly. The outcome was the illusionary (and indeed, anachronic) conclusion that they wrote in line with the contemporary Sunni revivalist paradigm. Thus, with this later purge of political rationalism in modern times, as philosophical rationalism had already been purged after the twelfth century, Islam was reduced to legal reasoning and methodology.

Finally, if we impose an external logic of progress on the history of Islamic political theory, we may imagine Ibn Khaldun as the culmination of that trajectory. He proposed an almost proto-modern theory that separates politics and religion, and more importantly, he rejected all forms of knowledge other than empirical knowledge as an authority in explaining politics and society. Ironically, Muslims, who are always proud of Ibn Khaldun for various reasons, such as his being the founder of sociology or the inventor of causality in the social sciences, are not much interested in the proto-modern dimension of Ibn Khaldun's thought. If we imagine Ibn Khaldun's *Muqaddima* as a political agenda, the contemporary Muslims' orientation is the opposite of that book's recommendations.

Except for their being proud of Ibn Khaldun (which is probably a strong feeling that became popular because it is useful for challenging Western intellectual superiority), mainstream Muslim political and intellectual traditions today fit what might be called an anti-Ibn Khaldunian trajectory. Unlike Ibn Khaldun, no major Islamic intellectual or political tradition today is inclined to defend the tenet that empirical knowledge is the only reliable authority in explaining politics and society, nor that religious scholars should be completely excluded from political decision-making. Not only the Shi'a clerics and the Sunni Islamists, but also a large group of other Muslims, would find those Ibn Khaldunian opinions inappropriate. Ironically, modern Muslims are much more 'religious' than were the medieval Muslim political rationalists who defined the relationship between religion and politics.

In regard of the foregoing considerations, a major conclusion of this book is that Muslim scholars or political actors in medieval times imagined themselves as having a strong agential authority in interpreting Islam. This is clearly observed in the practices of Umar or Tughrul, as well as in the books of Ibn al-Muqaffa and al-Mawardi. That strong agential claim has been abandoned by the contemporary Muslims. Today, many Muslims claim an agential authority only in secondary issues. Unlike medieval Muslims who did not refrain from changing Islamic theory, the contemporary Muslims are the first to protect it. While classical Muslim political rationalists detected the gaps in Islamic thought, and filled them with new reasonings, modern Muslims almost cannot imagine that there could be gaps in Islamic thought. Contemporary Muslims, by moving Islam above history, have thus largely self-eroded their agential authority in interpreting it.

BIBLIOGRAPHY

Abdel Razek, Ali. 2012. *Islam and the Foundations of Political Power*. Edinburgh: Edinburgh University Press.

Abu-Zayd, Nasr. 2004. *Rethinking the Qur'an: Towards a Humanistic Hermeneutics*. Utrecht: Humanistic University Press.

Abun-Nasr, Jamil M. 2012. *A History of the Maghrib in the Islamic Period*. Cambridge: Cambridge University Press.

Adamson, Peter. 2016. *Philosophy in the Islamic World: A History of Philosophy Without Any Gaps, Vol. 3*. Oxford: Oxford University Press.

Addas, Claude. 1993. *Quest for the Red Sulphur*. Cambridge: The Islamic Text Society.

Adhami, Siamak. 2003. 'A Question of Legitimacy: The Case of Ardasir I (Denkard IV)', *Indo-Iranian Journal* 46(3): 223–30.

Ağca, Ferhat. 2016. *Uygur Harfli Oğuz Kağan Destanı*. Ankara: Türk Kültürünü Araştırma Enstitüsü.

Agha, Saleh Said. 1999. 'The Arab Population in Hurasan during the Umayyad Period: Some Demographic Computations', *Arabica* 46(2): 211–29.

Agha, Saleh Said. 2003. *The Revolution Which Toppled the Umayyads: Neither Arab Nor 'Abbasid*. Leiden: Brill.

Ahmad, Zaid. 2003. *The Epistemology of Ibn Khaldun*. London: Routledge.

Ahmed, Shahab. 2016. *What is Islam? The Importance of Being Islamic*. Princeton, NJ: Princeton University Press.

Al-Alwani, Shaykh Taha Jabir. 2005. *Issues in Contemporary Islamic Thought*. London: International Institute of Islamic Thought.

al-Ash'ari, Abu Hasan. 1940. *Al-Ibanah 'An Usul Ad-Diyanah [The Elucidation of Islam's Foundation]*. Translated by Walter C. Klein. New Haven: American Oriental Society.

al-Ash'ari, Abu Hasan. 1953. *Kitab al-Luma' [The Luminous Book]*. Translated by Richard J. McCarthy. Beirut: Imprimerie Catholique.

Al-Attas, Naquib. 1993. *Islam and Secularism*. Kuala Lumpur: ISTAC.

Al-Azmeh, Aziz. 1982. *Ibn Khaldun: An Essay in Reinterpretation*. London: Frank Cass.

Al-Azmeh, Aziz. 2007. *Times of History: Universal Topics in Islamic Historiography*. Budapest: Central European University Press.

al-Baghdadi, Abu-Mansur. 1920. *Moslem Schisms and Sects [Al-Fark Bain al-Firak] Part 1*. Translated by Kate Chambers Seelye. New York: Columbia University Press.

al-Baghdadi, Abu Mansur. 1928. *Usul al-Din*. Istanbul: Matba'at al-Dawla.

Al-Baghdadi, Ahmad Mubarak. 1981. 'The Political Thought of Abu Al-Hasan Al-Mawardi.' PhD thesis, University of Edinburgh.

al-Baladhuri, abu-l 'Abbas Ahmad ibn-Jabir. 1916. *The Origins of the Islamic State: Being a Translation from the Arabic Accompanied with Annotations Geographic and Historic Notes of the Kitab Futuh al-Buldan Part I*. Translated by P. K. Hitti. New York: Columbia University Press.

al-Baladhuri, abu-l 'Abbas Ahmad ibn-Jabir. 1924. *The Origins of the Islamic State: Being a Translation from the Arabic Accompanied with Annotations Geographic and Historic Notes of the Kitab Futuh al-Buldan Part II*. Translated by Francis Clark Murgotten. New York: Columbia University Press.

al-Baqillani, Abu Bakr. 1987. *Kitab Tamhid al-awail wa talhis al-dalail*. Prepared by I. Ahmad Hamid. Beirut: Muassasa Kitab al-Saqafa.

al-Baydaq, Abu-Bakr Ibn Ali. 1971. *Akhbar al-mahdi Ibn Tumart wa bidayat dawlat al-muwahhidin*. Edited by Abdelwahab Benmansur. Rabat: Dar al-Mansur.

al-Bayhaqi, Ali bin Zayd. 2004. *Tarikh-i Bayhaqi*. Translation by Y. al-Hadi. Damascus: Dar Ikra.

al-Biruni, Muhammad ibn Ahmad. 1000. *Al-Athar al-baqiya 'an al-qurun al-khaliya*. Original manuscript available at https://archive.org/details/BIRUNI-Btv1b8406161z.

al-Biruni, Muhammad ibn Ahmad. 1879. *The Chronology of Ancient Nations: An English Version of the Arabic Text of the Athar-ul-Bakiya of Albiruni*. Translated by C. Edward Sachau. London: W. H. Allen & Co.

al-Farabi, Abu Nasr. 1995. *Kitab ara' ahl al-madina al fadila wa-mudaddatiha*. Edited by 'Ali Abu Mulhim. Beirut: Dar Wa-Maktabat Al-Hilal.

al-Ghazali, Abu Hamid. 1964. *Council for Kings [Nasihat al-Muluk]*. Translated by F. R. C. Bagley. London: Oxford University Press.

al-Ghazali, Abu Hamid. 2000. *The Incoherence of the Philosophers [Tahafut al-falasifa]*. Translated by Michael E. Marmura. Utah: Brigham Young University Press.

al-Hakam, Ibn Abd. 1858. *Dhikr Fath Al-Andalus [History of the Conquest of Spain]*. Edited by John Harris Jones. Gottingen: Dieterich.

al-Jabri, Mohammed Abed. 2009. *Democracy, Human Rights and Law in Islamic Thought*. London: I. B. Tauris.

al-Jabri, Muhammad Abed. 2011. *The Formation of Arab Reason: Text, Tradition and the Construction of Modernity in the Arab World*. London: I. B. Tauris.

al-Juwayni, Abd al-Malik ibn Yusuf. 2000. 'Lumʿa al-Adillah.' In Mohammad Moslem Adel Saflo (ed.), *Al-Juwayni's Thought and Methodology: With a Translation and Commentary on Lumaʿ al-Adillah*, 216–67. Berlin: Klaus Schwarz.

al-Juwayni, Abd al-Malik ibn Yusuf. 2011. *Ghiyath al-Umam fi Tiyath al-Zullam*. Jidda: Dar al-Minhaj.

al-Marrakushi, Abd al-Wahid. 1881. *Kitab al-mujib fi talkhis akhbar ahl al-Maghrib*. Edited by R. Dozy. Leiden: Brill.

al-Maturidi, Abu Mansur. 2018. *Kitabü't-Tevhid [Kitab al-Tawhid]*. Translated by Bekir Topaloğlu. Ankara: ISAM.

al-Mawardi. 1881. *Al-Ahkam al-Sultaniyyah w'al-Wilayat al-Diniyyah*. Cairo: Matbuʿat al-watan.

al-Mawardi. 1987. *Adab al-dunya wa al-din*. Beirut: Dar al-Kutub al-ʿilmiyya.

al-Mawardi. 1994. *Adab al-Wazir*. Cairo: Maktabat al-Khanci.

al-Mawardi. 2012. *Tashil al-Nazar wa al-Taʾjil al-Zafar fi Ahlak al-Melik wa Siyasati-l- Mulk*. Prepared by Ridwan al-Sayyid. Beirut: Markaz Ibn al-Azraq Li Tadrisat al-Siyasiyya.

al-Nadim, Muhammad bin Ishak. 2019. *Al-Fihrist*. Edited by Abdulkadir Coskun. Ankara: Türkiye Yazma Eserler Kurumu Başkanlığı.

al-Najjar, Abd al-Majid. 1984. *Al-Mahdi Ibn Tumart: Hayatuhu, wa arauhu, wa thawraut al-fikriyya wa al-ijtimaʿiyya wa athru bil-maghrib*. Beirut: Dar al-Gharb al-Islami.

al-Nuʿman, al-Qadi. 2006. *Founding the Fatimid State: The Rise of an Early Islamic Empire. An Annotated English translation of al-Qadi al-Nuʿman's Iftitah al-Daʿwa*. Translated by Hamid Haji. London: I. B. Tauris.

al-Qadi, Wadad. 2019. 'The Myriad Sources of the Vocabulary of ʿAbd al-Hamid al-Kaatib (d. 132/750)', *Arabica* 66(3/4): 207–302.

al-Qazwini, Hamdullah al-Mustawfi. 1913. *Tarikh-i Guzida Part II*. Abridged by E. G. Browne. Leiden: Brill.

al-Sakuni, Abu 'Ali 'Umar. 1976. *'Uyun al-munazarat*. Edited by Sa'd Ghurab. Tunis: al-Jami'a al-Tunisiyya.

Al-Salimi, Abdulrahman. 2005. 'Makramid Rule in Oman', *Proceedings of the Seminar for Arabian Studies* (Papers from the thirty-eighth meeting of the Seminar for Arabian Studies held in London in 2004): 247–53.

al-Sanhaji, Abu Bakr. 1971. *Al-Muqtabas min Kitab al-Ansab fi Ma'rifat al-Ashab*. Edited by Abd al-Wahhab bin Mansur. Rabat: Dar al-Mansur.

al-Shafi'i. 1997. *al-Shafi'i's Risala: Treatise on the Foundations of Islamic Jurisprudence*. Translated by Majid Khadduri. London: The Islamic Text Society.

al-Shahrastani, Muhammad b. Abd al-Karim. 1984. *Muslim Sects and Divisions: The Section on Muslim Sects in Kitab al-Milal wa'l-Nihal*. Translated by A. K. Kazi and J. G. Flynn. London: Kegan Paul.

al-Shahrastani, Muhammad b. Abd al Karim. 1992. *Al-Milal wa al-Nihal*. Beirut: Dar al-Maktab al-'ilmiyya.

al-Suyuti, Jalal al-Din. 2015. *History of the Umayyad Caliphs: From Tarikh al-Khulafa*. Translated by T. S. Andersson. London: Taha.

al-Tabari, Muhammad Ibn Jarir. 1985a. *The History of al-Tabari Vol. 35: The Crisis of the 'Abbasid Caliphate*. Translated by George Saliba. New York: State University of New York.

al-Tabari, Muhammad Ibn Jarir. 1985b. *The History of al-Tabari Vol. 27: The 'Abbasid Revolution*. Translated by John Alden Williams. New York: State University of New York.

al-Tabari, Muhammad Ibn Jarir. 1987a. *The History of al-Tabari Vol. 37: The 'Abbasid Recovery*. Translated by Philip M. Fields. New York: State University of New York.

al-Tabari, Muhammad Ibn Jarir. 1987b. *The History of Al-Tabari Vol. 18: Between Civil Wars: The Caliphate of Mu'awiyyah*. Translated by Michael G. Morony. New York: State University of New York Press.

al-Tabari, Muhammad Ibn Jarir. 1989a. *The History of al-Tabari Vol. 26: The Waning of the Umayyad Caliphate*. Translated by Carole Hillenbrand. New York: State University of New York Press.

al-Tabari, Muhammad Ibn Jarir. 1989b. *The History of al-Tabari Vol. 22: The Marwanid Restoration*. Translated by Everett K. Rowson. New York: State University of New York Press.

al-Tabari, Muhammad Ibn Jarir. 1989c. *The History of al-Tabari Vol. 13: The Conquest of Iraq, Southwestern Persia, and Egypt*. Translated by Gautier H. A. Juynboll. New York: State University of New York Press.

al-Tabari, Muhammad Ibn Jarir. 1990. *The History of al-Tabari Vol. 19: The Caliphate of Yazid b. Muʿawiyah*. Translated by I. K. A. Howard. New York: State University of New York Press.

al-Tabari, Muhammad Ibn Jarir. 1992. *The History of al-Tabari Vol. 12: The Battle of al-Qadisiyyah and the Conquest of Syria and Palestine*. Translated by Yohannan Friedmann. New York: State University of New York Press.

al-Tabari, Muhammad Ibn Jarir. 1993. *The History of al-Tabari Vol. 10: The Conquest of Arabia*. Translated by Fred M. Donner. New York: State University of New York Press.

al-Tabari, Muhammad Ibn Jarir. 1994. *The History of al-Tabari Vol. 14: The Conquest of Iran*. Translated by G. Rex Smith. New York: State University of New York Press.

al-Tabari, Muhammad Ibn Jarir. 1995. *The History of al-Tabari Vol. 28: Abbasid Authority Affirmed*. Translated by Jane Dammen McAuliffe. New York: State University of New York Press.

al-Tabari, Muhammad Ibn Jarir. 1996. *The History of al-Tabari Vol. 17: The First Civil War*. Translated by G. R. Hawting. New York: State University of New York Press.

al-Tabari, Muhammad Ibn Jarir. 1997. *The History of al-Tabari Vol. 8: The Victory of Islam*. Translated by Michael Fishbein. New York: The State University of New York Press.

al-Tabari, Muhammad Ibn Jarir. 1999. *The History of al-Tabari Vol. 5: The Sasanids, the Byzantines, the Lakhmids, and Yemen*. Translated by C. E. Bosworth. New York: State University of New York Press.

al-Waqidi. 2005. *The Islamic Conquest of Syria [Futuh al-Sham]*. Translated by M. Sulayman al-Kindi. London: Ta-ha.

al-Yaʿqubi, Ibn Wadih. 2018a. *The Book of the Adaptation of Men to Their Time and Their Dominant Characteristics in Every Age [Mushakalat al-nas li-zamanihim wa-ma yaglibu ʿalayhim fi kull ʿasr]*. In Matthew S. Gordon, Chase F. Robinson, Everett K. Rowson and Michael Fishbein (eds), *The Works of Ibn Wadih al-Yaʿqubi Volume 1: An English Translation*, 29–60. Leiden: Brill.

al-Yaʿqubi, Ibn Wadih. 2018b. *The Geography [Kitab al-Buldan]*. In Matthew S. Gordon, Chase F. Robinson, Everett K. Rowson and Michael Fishbein (eds), *The Works of Ibn Wadih al-Yaʿqubi Volume 1: An English Translation*, 61–199. Leiden: Brill.

al-Yaʿqubi, Ibn Wadih. 2018c. *The History (Taʾrikh): Adam to Pre-Islamic Arabia*. In Matthew S. Gordon, Chase F. Robinson, Everett K. Rowson and Michael Fishbein (eds), *The Works of Ibn Wadih al-Yaʿqubi Volume 2: An English Translation*, 259–594. Leiden: Brill.

al-Yaʿqubi, Ibn Wadih. 2018d. *The History (Taʾrikh): The Rise of Islam to the Reign of al-Muʿtamid*. In Matthew S. Gordon, Chase F. Robinson, Everett K. Rowson and Michael Fishbein (eds), *The Works of Ibn Wadih al-Yaʿqubi Volume 3: An English Translation*, 595–1293. Leiden: Brill.

al-Zarkashi, Abu Abdullah Muhammad ibn Ibrahim. 1998. *Tarikh al-dawlatayn al-Muwahidiyah wa-al-Hafsiyah*. Edited by Husayn al-Yaʿqubi. Tunis: Al-Maktab al-ʿatika.

Alatas, Syed Farid. 2012. *Ibn Khaldun*. Oxford: Oxford University Press.

Alatas, Syed Farid. 2014. *Applying Ibn Khaldun: The Recovery of a Lost Tradition in Sociology*. London: Routledge.

Albarrán, Javier. 2021. 'The Almohads and the "Qurʾanization" of War Narrative and Ritual', *Religions* 12(10): 876. https://doi.org/10.3390/rel12100876.

Amedroz, H. F. 1905. 'The Assumption of the Title of Shahansah by Buwayhid Rulers', *The Numismatic Chronicle and Journal of the Royal Numismatic Society* 5: 393–9.

Amri, Laroussi. 2008. 'The Concept of Umran: The Heuristic Knot in Ibn Khaldun', *The Journal of North African Studies* 13(3): 351–61.

Andic, Fuat M., and Suphan Andic. 1985. 'An Exploration into Fiscal Sociology: Ibn Khaldun, Schumpeter, and Public Choice', *FinanzArchiv/Public Finance Analysis* 43(3): 454–69.

Anthony, Sean W. 2012. 'Chiliastic Ideology and Nativist Rebellion in the Early Abbasid Period: Sunbadh and Jamasp-nama', *Journal of the American Oriental Society* 132(4): 641–55.

Aranda, Mariano Gómez. 2012. 'The Jew as Scientist and Philosopher in Medieval Iberia.' In Jonathan Ray (ed.), *The Jew in Medieval Iberia: 1100–1500*, 60–101. Boston: Academic Studies Press.

Aravamudan, Srinivas. 2014. 'East-West Fiction as a World Literature: The Hayy Problem Reconfigured', *Eighteenth-Century Studies* 47(2): 195–231.

Ardıç, Nurullah. 2008. 'Beyond "Science as a Vocation": Civilizational Epistemology in Weber and Ibn Khaldun', *Asian Journal of Social Science* 36(3/4): 434–64.

Arjomand, Said Amir. 1994. 'Abd Allah Ibn al-Muqaffa and the Abbasid Revolution', *Iranian Studies* 27(1/4): 9–36.

Arjomand, Said Amir. 1999. 'The Law, Agency, and Policy in Medieval Islamic Society: Development of the Institutions of Learning from the Tenth to the Fifteenth Century', *Comparative Studies in Society and History* 41(2): 263–93.

Arjomand, Said Amir. 2022. *Messianism and Sociopolitical Revolution in Medieval Islam*. Oakland, CA: University of California Press.

Armada, Almudena Ariza. 2017. 'The Coinage of al-Andalus', *Shedet* 4: 68–90.

Arslan, Ahmet. 2014. *İbni Haldun*. Istanbul: Istanbul Bilgi Üniversitesi Yayınları.

Asatrian, Mushegh. 2003. 'Ibn Khaldun on Magic and the Occult', *Iran & the Caucasus* 7(1/2): 73–123.

Attar, Samir. 2007. *The Vital Roots of European Enlightment: Ibn Tufayl's Influence on Modern Western Thought*. Lanham: Lexington Books.

Azmeh, Wayel. 2016. 'Misconceptions About the Caliphate in Islam', *Digest of Middle East Studies* 25(2): 186–209.

Baadj, Amar S. 2014. *Saladin, the Almohads and the Banu Ghaniya: The Contest for North Africa (12th and 13th centuries)*. Leiden: Brill.

Baadj, Amar S. 2020. 'Evidence for the Ayyubid Iqta in Ifriqiyya and a Reconsideration of the Almohad Iqta', *Al-Masaq* 32: 169–84.

Baali, Fuad. 1988. *Society State, and Urbanism: Ibn Khaldun's Sociological Thought*. New York: State University of New York Press.

Bachrach, Peter, and Morton S. Baratz. 1962. 'Two Faces of Power', *The American Political Science Review* 56(4): 947–52.

Bacik, Gokhan. 2019. *Islam and Muslim Resistance to Modernity in Turkey*. Cham: Palgrave Macmillan.

Bacik, Gokhan. 2021. *Contemporary Islamic Rationalism: The Religious Opposition to Sunni Revival*. London: I. B. Tauris.

Baizig, Salah. 2020. 'The *'ulama* and the Hafsid Caliphate', *The Journal of North African Studies*, online. doi:10.1080/13629387.2020.1763104.

Balbale, Abigail Krasner. 2018. 'Affiliation and Ideology at the End of the Almohad Caliphate', *Al-Masaq* 30(3): 1–18. doi:10.1080/09503110.2018.1525241.

Bar Hebraeus. 1976. *The Chronography of Bar Hebraeus*. Translated by Ernest A. Wallis Budge. Amsterdam: APA-Philo Press.

Barthold, W. 1968. *Turkestan Down to the Mongol Invasion*. Translated by T. Minorsky. London: Lowe and Brydone.

Başan, Aziz. 2010. *The Great Seljuqs: A History*. London: Routledge.

Bashier, Salman. 2011. *The Story of Islamic Philosophy: Ibn Tufayl, Ibn al-'Arabi, and Others on the Limit Between Naturalism and Traditionalism*. New York: State University of New York Press.

Bausani, A. 1968. 'Religion in the Saljuq Period.' In J. A. Boyle (ed.), *The Cambridge History of Iran Volume 5: The Saljuq and Mongol Period*, 283–302. Cambridge: Cambridge University Press.

Becker, C. H. 2012. 'The Content of the Papyri on Taxation Practices.' In Fred M. Donner (ed.), *The Articulation of Early Islamic State Structures*, 187–215. London: Routledge.

Bell, H. I. 2012. 'The Administration of Egypt under the Umayyad Khalifs.' In Fred M. Donner (ed.), *The Articulation of Early Islamic State Structures*, 217–25. London: Routledge.

Bellver, José. 2013. '"Al-Ghazali of al-Andalus": Ibn Barrajan, Mahdism, and the Emergence of Learned Sufism on the Iberian Peninsula', *Journal of the American Oriental Society* 133(4): 659–81.

Bellver, José. 2020. 'Ascetics and Sufis.' In Maribel Fierro (ed.), *The Routledge Handbook of Muslim Iberia*, 318–43. London: Routledge.

Ben, Hardman. 2016. 'The Mahdi and the Autodidact: Ibn Ṭufayl's Hayy ibn Yaqẓan as a Challenge to Almohad Doctrine', *The International Journal of Critical Cultural Studies* 14(2): 33–45.

Ben-Zaken, Avner. 2011. *Reading Hayy Ibn-Yaqzan: A Cross-Cultural History of Autodidacticism.* Baltimore: The Johns Hopkins University Press.

Bennison, Amira K. 2007. 'The Almohads and the Qur'an of Uthman: The Legacy of the Umayyads of Cordoba in the Twelfth Century Maghrib', *Al-Masaq: Journal of the Medieval Mediterranean* 19(2): 131–54.

Bennison, Amira K. 2009. *The Great Caliphs: The Golden Age of the 'Abbasid Empire.* New Haven: Yale University Press.

Bennison, Amira K. 2010. 'Almohad Tawhid and its Implications for Religious Difference', *Journal of Medieval Iberian Studies* 2(2): 195–216.

Bennison, Amira K. 2014. 'Drums, Banners and Baraka: Symbols of Authority during the First Century of Marinid Rule, 1250–1350.' In A. K. Bennison (ed.), *The Articulation of Power in Medieval Iberia and the Maghrib*, 195–216. Oxford: Oxford University Press.

Bennison, Amira K. 2016. *The Almoravid and Almohad Empires.* Edinburgh: Edinburgh University Press.

Bennison, Amira K., and Maria Angeles Gallego. 2010. 'Religious Minorities under the Almohads: An Introduction', *Journal of Medieval Iberian Studies* 2(2): 143–54.

Berg, Herbert. 2010. 'Abbasid Historians' Portrayal of al-Abbas b. Abd al-Muttalib.' In John Nawas (ed.), *Abbasid Studies II*, 13–38. Leuven: Peeters.

Berkel, Maaike van. 2013. 'The Bureaucracy.' In Maaike van Berkel, Nadia Maria El Cheikh, Hugh Kennedy and Letizia Osti (eds), *Crisis and Continuity at the Abbasid Court: Formal and Informal Politics in the Caliphate of al-Muqtadir (295–320/908–32)*, 87–110. Leiden: Brill.

Berkel, Maaike van. 2014. 'Abbasid "Mazalim" between Theory and Practice', *Bulletin d'études orientales* 63: 229–42.

Berkel, Maaike van, Nadia Maria El Cheikh, Hugh Kennedy and Letizia Osti. 2013. 'Introduction.' In Maaike van Berkel, Nadia Maria El Cheikh, Hugh Kennedy and Letizia Osti (eds), *Crisis and Continuity at the Abbasid Court: Formal and Informal Politics in the Caliphate of al-Muqtadir (295–320/908–32)*, 1–12. Leiden: Brill.

Berkey, Jonathan P. 2003. *The Formation of Islam: Religion and Society in the Near East, 600–1800*. Cambridge: Cambridge University Press.

Berlin, Isiah. 1964. 'Does Political Theory Still Exist?' In Peter Laslett and W. G. Runciman (eds), *Philosophy, Politics and Society*, 1–33. Oxford: Basic Blackwell.

Bigon, Liora, and Edna Langenthal. 2022. 'Tracing Trade and Settlement Infrastructures in the Judaic Material Culture of Tafilalt, Southeastern Morocco', *Heritage* 5: 3785–3818.

Biwar, A. D. H., and S. M. Stern. 1958. 'The Coinage of Oman Under Abu Kalijar the Buwayhid', *The Numismatic Chronicle and Journal of the Royal Numismatic Society* 18: 147–56.

Black, Anthony. 2008. *The West and Islam: Religion and Political Thought in World History*. Oxford: Oxford University Press.

Black, Anthony. 2011. *The History of Islamic Political Thought: From the Prophet to the Present*. Edinburgh: Edinburgh University Press.

Blankinship, Khalid Yahya. 1988. 'The Tribal Factor in the Abbasid Revolution: The Betrayal of the Imam Ibrahim b. Muhammad', *Journal of the American Oriental Society* 108(4): 589–603.

Bligh-Abramski, Irit. 2012. 'Evolution versus Revolution: Umayyad Elements in the Abbasid Regime 133/750–320/932.' In Fred M. Donner (ed.), *The Articulation of Early Islamic State Structures*, 389–406. London: Routledge.

Bodin, Jean. 1992. *On Sovereignty: Four Chapters from The Six Book of the Commonwealth*. Translated by Julian H. Franklin. Cambridge: Cambridge University Press.

Bogue, Donald J. 1952. 'The Quantitative Study of Social Dynamics and Social Change', *American Journal of Sociology* 57(6): 565–8.

Bonner, Michael. 2011. 'The Waning of Empire, 861–945.' In Chase F. Robinson (ed.), *The New Cambridge History of Islam Volume 1: The Formation of the Islamic World Sixth to Eleven Centuries*, 305–59. Cambridge: Cambridge University Press.

Bosworth, C. E. 1962a. 'The Imperial Policy of the Early Ghaznawids', *Islamic Studies* 1(3): 49–82.

Bosworth, C. E. 1962b. 'The Titulature of the Early Ghaznavids', *Oriens* 15: 210–33.

Bosworth, C. E. 1965/6. 'Military Organization under the Buyids of Persia and Iraq', *Oriens* 18/19: 143–67.

Bosworth, C. E. 1968a. 'The Armies of the Saffarids', *Bulletin of the School of Oriental and African Studies* 31(3): 534–54.

Bosworth, C. E. 1968b. 'The Political and Dynastic History of the Iranian World (A.D. 1000–1217).' In J. A. Boyle (ed.), *The Cambridge History of Iran Volume 5: The Saljuq and Mongol Period*, 1–202. Cambridge: Cambridge University Press.

Bosworth, C. E. 1969. 'The Tahirids and the Persian Literature', *Iran* 7(1): 103–6.

Bosworth, C. E. 1970. 'Dailamis in Central Iran: The Kakuyids of Jibal and Yazd', *Iran* 8(1): 73–95.

Bosworth, C. E. 1973. 'The Heritage of Rulership in Early Islamic Iran and the Search for Dynastic Connections with the Past', *Iran* 11: 51–62.

Bosworth, C. E. 1983. 'The Persian Impact on Arabic Literature.' In A. F. L. Beeston, T. M. Johnstone, R. B. Serjeant and G. R. Smith (eds), *Arabic Literature to the End of the Umayyad Period*, 483–96. Cambridge: Cambridge University Press.

Bosworth, C. E. 1990. 'Administrative Literature.' In M. J. L. Young, J. D. Latham and R. B. Serjeant (eds), *Religion, Learning and Science in the 'Abbasid Period*, 155–67. Cambridge: Cambridge University Press.

Bosworth, C. E. 1991. 'Malik-Shah.' In C. E. Bosworth, E. Van Donzel, B. Lewis and Ch. Pellat (eds), *The Encyclopedia of Islam Volume VI*, 273–5. Leiden: Brill.

Bosworth, C. E. 1998. 'The Ghaznawids.' In M. S. Asimove and C. E. Bosworth (eds), *History of Civilizations of Central Asia Volume IV: The Age of Achievement A.D. 750 to the End of the Fifteenth Century*, 102–4. Paris: UNESCO.

Bosworth, C. E. 2000. 'Legal and Political Sciences in the Eastern Iranian World and Central Asia in the Pre-Mongol Period.' In C. E. Bosworth and M. S. Asimov (eds), *History of Civilizations of Central Asia Volume IV: The Age of Achievement: A.D. 750 to the End of the Fifteenth Century*, 133–41. Paris: UNESCO.

Bosworth, C. E. 2007a. 'The Tahirids and Saffarids.' In R. N. Frye (ed.), *The Cambridge History of Iran Volume 4: The Period from the Arab Invasion to the Saljuqs*, 90–135. Cambridge: Cambridge University Press.

Bosworth, C. E. 2007b. 'The Early Ghaznawids.' In R. N. Frye (ed.), *The Cambridge History of Iran Volume 4: The Period from the Arab Invasion to the Saljuqs*, 162–97. Cambridge: Cambridge University Press.

Bosworth, C. E. 2011. 'The Origins of the Seljuqs.' In Christian Lange and Songül Mecit (eds), *The Seljuqs: Politics, Society and Culture*, 13–21. Edinburgh: Edinburgh University Press.

Bowen, Harold. 1929. 'The Last Buwayhids', *The Journal of the Royal Asiatic Society of Great Britain and Ireland* 2: 225–45.

Boyce, Mary. 1968. 'Introduction.' In Tansar, *The Letter of Tansar*, 1–24. Translated by Mary Boyce. Rome: Instituto Italiano Per Il Medio Ed Estremo Oriente.

Boyce, Mary. 1979. *Zoroastrians: Their Religious Beliefs and Practices*. London: Routledge & Kegan.

Brauer, Ralph W. 1995. 'Boundaries and Frontiers in Medieval Muslim Geography', *Transactions of the American Philosophical Society* 85(6): 1–73.

Brett, Michael. 1996. 'The Realm of the Imam: The Fatimids in the Tenth Century', *Bulletin of the School of Oriental and African Studies* 59(3): 431–49.

Brett, Michael. 2010. 'The central lands of North Africa and Sicily, until the beginning of the Almohad period.' In Maribel Fierro (ed.), *The New Cambridge History of Islam Volume 2: The Western Islamic World, Eleventh to Eighteenth Centuries*, 48–65. Cambridge: Cambridge University Press.

Brett, Michael. 2017. 'Conversion of the Berbers to Islam/Islamisation of the Berbers.' In A. C. S. Peacock (ed.), *Islamization: Comparative Perspectives from History*, 189–98. Edinburgh: Edinburgh University Press.

Brockelman, C. 1991. 'al-Mawardi.' In C. E. Bosworth, E. Van Donzel, B. Lewis and Ch. Pellat (eds), *The Encyclopedia of Islam Volume VI*, 869. Leiden: Brill.

Brosius, Maria. 2006. *The Persians: An Introduction*. London: Routledge.

Brown, Daniel. 2009. *A New Introduction to Islam*. Oxford: Wiley-Blackwell.

Brown, Jonathan. 2007. *The Canonization of Al Bukhari and Muslim: The Formation and Function of the Sunni Hadith Canon*. Leiden: Brill.

Browne, Edward G. 1951. *A Literary History of Persia Vol. I: From the Earliest Times Until Firdawsi*. Cambridge: Cambridge University Press.

Brunner, Christopher. 1983. 'Geographical and Administrative Divisions: Settlements and Economy.' In Ehsan Yarshater (ed.), *The Cambridge History of Iran Vol. 3(2): The Seleucid, Parthian and Sasanian Periods*, 747–77. Cambridge: Cambridge University Press.

Bryson, Valeri. 2007. *Gender and the Politics of Time: Feminist Theory and Contemporary Debates*. Bristol: Bristol University Press.

Bull, Hedley. 1977. *The Anarchical Society: The Study of Order in World Politics*. London: Macmillan.

Bulliet, Richard W. 1978. 'Local Politics in Eastern Iran under the Ghaznavids and Seljuks', *Iranian Studies* 11(1/4): 35–56.

Bulliet, Richard W. 2008. *The Patricians of Nishapur: A Study in Medieval Islamic Social History*. Cambridge, MA: Harvard University Press.

Bulliet, Richard W. 2020. 'Why Nishapur?' In David Durand-Guédy, Roy P. Mottahedeh and Jürgen Paul (eds), *Cities of Medieval Iran*, 100–24. Leiden: Brill.

Buresi, Pascal. 2020. 'Berber Rule and the Maghribi Caliphate.' In Maribel Fierro (ed.), *The Routledge Handbook of Muslim Iberia*, 114–44. London: Routledge.

Buresi, Pascal, and Hicham El Aallaoui. 2013. *Governing the Empire: Provincial Administration in the Almohad Caliphate (1224–1269) Critical Edition, Translation, and Study of Manuscript 4752 of the Hasaniyya Library in Rabat Containing 77 Taqadim ('Appointments')*. Translated by Travis Bruce. Leiden: Brill.

Bürgel, J. Christoph. 1996. 'Symbols and Hints: Some Considerations Concerning the Meaning of Ibn Tufayl's *Hayy bin Yaqzan*.' In Lawrence I. Conrad (ed.), *The World of Ibn Tufayl: Interdisciplinary Perspectives on Hayy Ibn Yaqzan*, 114–32. Leiden: Brill.

Busse, Herbert. 2007. 'Iran Under the Buyids.' In R. N. Frye (ed.), *The Cambridge History of Iran Volume 4: The Period from the Arab Invasion to the Saljuqs*, 250–304. Cambridge: Cambridge University Press.

Butterworth, Charles E. 1987. 'Medieval Islamic Philosophy and the Virtues of Ethics', *Arabica* 34(2): 221–50.

Butterworth, Charles E. 1992. 'The Political Teaching of Averroes', *Arabic Sciences and Philosophy* 2: 187–202.

Cahen, Claude. 1969. 'The Turkish Invasion: The Shelchukidis.' In Marshall W. Baldwin (ed.), *A History of the Crusades Vol. I: The First Hundred Years*, 135–76. Madison: University of Wisconsin Press.

Cahen, Claude. 1997. 'Kharadj.' In E. Van Donzel, B. Lewis and Ch. Pellat (eds), *The Encyclopedia of Islam Volume IV*, 1030–3. Leiden: Brill.

Cahen, Claude. 2007. 'Tribes, Cities and Social Organization.' In R. N. Frye (ed.), *The Cambridge History of Iran Volume 4: The Period from the Arab Invasion to the Saljuqs*, 305–28. Cambridge: Cambridge University Press.

Caie, Graham D. 2008. 'The Manuscript Experience: What Medieval Vernacular Manuscripts Tell Us About Authors and Texts.' In Graham D. Caie and Denis Renevey (eds), *Medieval Texts in Context*, 10–27. London: Routledge.

Caie, Graham. D., and Denis Renevey. 2008. 'Introduction.' In Graham D. Caie and Denis Renevey (eds), *Medieval Texts in Context*, 1–9. London: Routledge.

Çaksu, Ali. 2007. 'Ibn Khaldun and Hegel on Causality in History: Aristotelian Legacy Reconsidered', *Asian Journal of Social Science* 35: 47–83.

Calasso, Giovanna. 2021. 'Constructing the Boundary between Mashriq and Maghrib in Medieval Muslim Sources.' In Maribel and Mayte Penelas (eds), *The Maghrib in Mashriq: Knowledge, Travel and Identity*, 35–78. Berlin: De Gruyter.

Campanini, Massimo. 2004. *An Introduction to Islamic Philosophy*. Edinburgh: Edinburgh University Press.

Campanini, Massimo. 2011. 'In Defense of Sunnism: Al-Ghazali and the Seljuqs.' In Christian Lange and Songül Mecit (eds), *The Seljuqs: Politics, Society and Culture*, 228–39. Edinburgh: Edinburgh University Press.

Campopiano, Michele. 2009. 'Irrigation and taxation in Iraq 6th to 10th Century.' Unpublished working paper, University of Utrecht.

Campopiano, Michele. 2012. 'State, Land Tax and Agriculture in Iraq from the Arab Conquest to the Crisis of the Abbasid Caliphate (Seventh-Tenth Centuries)', *Studia Islamica* 107(1): 1–37.

Campopiano, Michele. 2018. 'Land Tenure, Land Tax and Social Conflictuality in Iraq from the Late Sasanian to the Early Islamic Period (Fifth to Ninth Centuries CE).' In Alain Delattre, Marie Legendre and Petra M. Sijpesteijn (eds), *Authority and Control in the Countryside from Antiquity to Islam in the Mediterranean and Near East (6th–10th Century)*, 464–500. Leiden: Brill.

Canby, Sheila R., Deniz Beyazit, Martina Rugiadi and A. C. S. Peacock. 2016. *Court and Cosmos: The Great Age of the Seljuqs*. New York: The Metropolitan Museum of Art.

Canepa, Matthew P. 2009. *The Two Eyes of the Earth: Art and Ritual of Kingship between Rome and Sasanian Iran*. Berkeley: University of California Press.

Casewit, Yousef. 2012/13. 'A Reconsideration of the Life and Works of Ibn Barrajan', *Al-Abhath* 60/61: 111–42.

Casewit, Yousef. 2017. *The Mystics of al-Andalus: Ibn Barrajan and Islamic Thought in the Twelfth Century*. Cambridge: Cambridge University Press.

Cerda-Olmedo, Enrique. 2008. 'Ibn Tufayl (Abentofail) and the Origins of Scientific Method', *European Review* 16(2): 159–67.

Chabane, Djamel. 2008. 'The structure of *'umran al-'alam* of Ibn Khaldun', *Journal of North African Studies* 13(3): 331–49.

Chapra, M. U. 1999. 'Socioeconomic and Political Dynamics in Ibn Khaldun's Thought', *American Journal of Islam and Society* 16(4): 17–38.

Choksy, Jamsheed K. 1988. 'Sacral Kingship in Sasanian Iran', *Bulletin of the Asia Institute* 2: 35–52.

Cobb, Paul M. 1999. 'Al-Mutawakkil's Damascus: A New 'Abbasid Capital?', *Journal of Near Eastern Studies* 58(4): 241–57.

Cobb, Paul M. 2001. *White Banners: Contention in 'Abbasid Syria, 750–880*. New York: State University of New York.

Conrad, Lawrence I. 1996a. 'Introduction: The World of Ibn Tufayl.' In Lawrence I. Conrad (ed.), *The World of Ibn Tufayl: Interdisciplinary Perspectives on Hayy Ibn Yaqzan*, 1–37. Leiden: Brill.

Conrad, Lawrence I. 1996b. 'Through the Thin Veil: On the Question of Communication and the Socialization of Knowledge in *Hayy Ibn Yaqzan*.' In Lawrence I. Conrad (ed.), *The World of Ibn Tufayl: Interdisciplinary Perspectives on Hayy Ibn Yaqzan*, 238–66. Leiden: Brill.

Corbin, Henry. 1993. *History of Islamic Philosophy*. Translated by L. Sherrard and P. Sherrard. London: Kegan Paul.

Corcoran, Simon. 2011. 'Observations on the Sasanian Law-Book in the Light of Roman Legal Writing.' In A. Rio (ed.) *Law, Custom, and Justice in Late Antiquity and the Early Middle Ages: Proceedings of the 2008 Byzantine Colloquium*, 77–113. London: Centre for Hellenic Studies, King's College.

Corcos, David. 2010. 'The Nature of the Almohad Rulers' Treatment of the Jews', *Journal of Medieval Iberian Studies* 2(2): 259–85.

Cornell, Vincent J. 1987. 'Understanding is the Mother of Ability: Responsibility and Action in the Doctrine of Ibn Tumart', *Studia Islamica* 66: 71–103.

Cornell, Vincent J. 1996. 'Hayy in the Land of Absal: Ibn Tufayl and Sufism in the Western Maghrib During the Muwahhid Era.' In Lawrence I. Conrad (ed.), *The World of Ibn Tufayl: Interdisciplinary Perspectives on Hayy Ibn Yaqzan*, 133–64. Leiden: Brill.

Cortese, Delia, and Simonetta Calderini. 2006. *Women and the Fatimids in the World of Islam*. Edinburgh: Edinburgh University Press.

Crone, Patricia. 2004. *God's Rule: Government and Islam*. New York: Columbia University Press.

Crone, Patricia. 2005. *Medieval Islamic Political Thought*. Edinburgh: Edinburgh University Press.

Crone, Patricia. 2015. 'Traditional Political Thought.' In Gerhard Bowering (ed.), *Islamic Political Thought: An Introduction*, 238–51. Princeton, NJ: Princeton University Press.

Daftary, Farhad. 1998a. 'Sectarian and National Movements in Iran, Khurasan and Transoxiana During Umayyad and Early 'Abbasid Times.' In M. S. Asimove and C. E. Bosworth (eds), *History of Civilizations of Central Asia Volume IV: The Age of Achievement* A.D. *750 to the End of the Fifteenth Century*, 48–65. Paris: UNESCO.

Daftary, Farhad. 1998b. *A Short History of the Ismailis: Traditions of a Muslim Community*. Edinburgh: Edinburgh University Press.

Daftary, Farhad. 2007. *The Isma'ilis: Their History and Doctrines*. Cambridge: Cambridge University Press.

Daftary, Farhad. 2013. 'Qarmatians.' In Gerhard Bowing (ed.), *The Princeton Encyclopedia of Islamic Thought*, 445–6. Princeton, NJ: Princeton University Press.

Dale, Stephen Frederic. 2006. 'Ibn Khaldun: The Last Greek and the First Annaliste Historian', *International Journal of Middle East Studies* 38(3): 431–51.

Dale, Stephen Frederic. 2015. *The Orange Trees of Marrakesh: Ibn Khaldun and the Science of Man.* Cambridge, MA: Harvard University Press.

Daniel, Elton L. 1979. *The Political and Social History of Khurasan under Abbasid Rule 747–820.* Minneapolis: Bibliotecha Islamica.

Danner, Victor. 2007. 'Arabic Literature in Iran.' In R. N. Frye (ed.), *The Cambridge History of Iran Volume 4: The Period from the Arab Invasion to the Saljuqs*, 566–94. Cambridge: Cambridge University Press.

Dargahani, Shahab D. 2019. 'The Social Network of Nizamiyyah School System Under Nizam Al-Mulk Administration (456–485/1063–1092)', *Ondokuz Mayıs Üniversitesi İlahiyat Fakültesi Dergisi* 47: 567–91.

Daryaee, Touraj. 2008. 'Kingship in Early Sasanian Iran.' In Vesta Sarkhosh Curtis and Sarah Stewart (eds), *Religion in the late Sasanian Period Volume III*, 60–70. London: I. B. Tauris.

Daryaee, Touraj. 2009. *Sasanian Persia: The Rise and Fall of an Empire.* London: I. B. Tauris.

Davaran, Fereshteh. 2010. *Continuity in Iranian Identity: Resilience of a Cultural Heritage.* London: Routledge.

Davies, Dick. 2019. *The Mirror of My Hearth: A Thousand Years of Persian Poetry.* London: Penguin.

De Blois, François. 1986. 'The Abu Sa'idis or So-Called Qarmatians of Bahrayn', *Proceedings of the Seminar for Arabian Studies* 16: 13–21.

De Nicola, Bruno. 2017. *Women in Mongol Iran: The Khatuns, 1206–1335.* Edinburgh: Edinburgh University Press.

De Rande, Raissa A. Von Doetinchem. 2019. 'An Exceptional Sage and the Need for the Messenger: The Politics of *Fitra* in a 12th Century Tale', *Arabic Sciences and Philosophy* 29: 207–26.

Demirci, Abdullah. 2005. 'Emevilerden Abbasilere Geçiş Sürecinin Bir Tanığı: Abdullah İbnü'l-Mukaffa ve Risaletü's-Sahabesi', *D.E.Ü. İlahiyat Fakültesi Dergisi* 21: 117–48.

Dhanani, Alnoor. 1984. *The Physical Theory of Kalam: Atoms, Space, and Void in Basrian Muʿtazili Cosmology.* Leiden: Brill.

Dhaouadi, Mahmoud. 2005. 'The Ibar: Lessons of Ibn Khaldun's Umran Mind', *Contemporary Sociology* 34(6): 585–91.

Divitçioğlu, Sencer. 2000. *Oğuz'dan Selçuklu'ya (Boy, Konat ve Devlet).* Istanbul: YKY.

Djaït, Hichem. 2007. 'Kufa.' In C. Edmund Bosworth (ed.). *Historic Cities in the Islamic World*, 290–8. Leiden: Brill.

Donner, Fred M. 1986. 'The Formation of the Islamic State', *Journal of the American Oriental Society* 106(2): 283–96.

Donner, Fred M. 2012a. 'Introduction: The Articulation of Early Islamic State Structures.' In Fred M. Donner (ed.), *The Articulation of Early Islamic State Structures*, xiii–xliv. London: Routledge.

Donner, Fred M. 2012b. 'The Formation of the Islamic State.' In Fred M. Donner (ed.), *The Articulation of Early Islamic State Structures*, 1–14. London: Routledge.

Donohue, John J. 2003. *The Buwayhid Dynasty in Iraq 334H./945 to 403H./1012*. Leiden: Brill.

Dressler, Markus, and Arvind-Pal S. Mandair. 2011. 'Introduction, Religion-making, and the Post-secular.' In Markus Dressler and Arvind-Pal S. Mandair (eds), *Secularism and Religion-Making*, 3–36. Oxford: Oxford University Press.

Dudgeon, Hamza A. 2018. 'The Counter-current Movements of Andalusia and Ibn Arabi: Should ibn Arabi be considered a Zahiri?', *Journal of the Muhyiddin 'Arabi Society* 64: 89–108.

Duke, George. 2014. 'Hobbes on Political Authority, Practical Reason and Truth', *Law and Philosophy* 33(5): 605–27.

Duri, Abd al-Aziz. 2007. 'Baghdad.' In C. Edmund Bosworth (ed.). *Historic Cities in the Islamic World*, 30–47. Leiden: Brill.

Duri, Abd al-Aziz. 2011. *Early Islamic Institutions: Administration and Taxation from the Caliphate to the Umayyads and Abbasids*. London: I. B. Tauris.

Dutton, Yasin.1994. 'The Introduction to Ibn Rushd's "Bidayat al-Mujtahid"', *Islamic Law and Society* 1(2): 188–205.

Eaton, Richard M. 2005. *A Social History of the Deccan, 1300–1761: Eight Indian Lives*. Cambridge: Cambridge University Press.

El-Azhari, Taef. 2019. *Queens, Eunuchs and Concubines in Islamic History, 661–1257*. Edinburgh: Edinburgh University Press.

El-Hibri, Tayeb. 2004. *Reinterpreting Islamic Historiography: Harun al-Rashid and the Narrative of Abbasid Caliphate*. Cambridge: Cambridge University Press.

El-Hibri, Tayeb. 2021. *The Abbasid Caliphate: A History*. Cambridge: Cambridge University Press.

Elad, Amikam. 2010. 'The Struggle for the Legitimacy of Authority as Reflected in Hadith al-Mahdi.' In John Nawas (ed.), *Abbasid Studies II Occasional Papers of the School of 'Abbasid Studies Leuven 28 June–1 July 2004*, 39–96. Leuven: Peeters.

Elisséeff, N. 2007. 'Damascus.' In C. Edmund Bosworth (ed.), *Historic Cities in the Islamic World*, 107–24. Leiden: Brill.

Emetan, Aturpat-I, and Shaul Shaked. 1979. *The Wisdom of the Sasanian Sages (Denkard VI)*. Boulder: Westview Press.

Enan, Muhammad Abdullah. 1941. *Ibn Khaldun: His Life and Work*. Lahore: Sh. Muhammad Ashraf.

Ephrat, Daphna. 2011. 'The Seljuqs and the Public Sphere in the Period of Sunni Revivalism: The View from Baghdad.' In Christian Lange and Songül Mecit (eds), *The Seljuqs: Politics, Society and Culture*, 139–56. Edinburgh: Edinburgh University Press.

Esmailpour, Abolqasem. 2007. 'Manichaean Gods and Goddesses in a Classical Arabic Treatise: *Kitab al-Radd-i 'la'l-Zandiq al-la'in Ibn al-Muqaffa*', *Central Asiatic Journal* 51(2): 167–76.

Fakhry, Magid. 1994. *Ethical Theories in Islam*. Leiden: Brill.

Fakhry, Magid. 2004. *A History of Islamic Philosophy*. New York: Columbia University Press.

Fakhry, Majid. 2002. *Al-Farabi, the Founder of Neo-Platonism: His Life, Works and Influence*. Oxford: Oneworld.

Farooq, Mohammad Omar. 2019. 'Ibn Khaldun's Defense of Mu'awiya: The Dynamics of 'Asabiyya, Mulk and the Counter-Revolution According to the Muqaddima', *Journal of Islamic and Muslim Studies* 4(1): 87–106.

Fazlullah, Reşidü'd-din. 2010. *Cami'ü't-Tevarih: Selçuklu Tarihi*. Translated by Erkan Göksu and H. Hüseyin Güneş. Istanbul: Selenge.

Fenwick, Corisande. 2022. 'How to Found an Islamic State: The Idrisids as Rivals to the Abbasid Caliphate in the Far Islamic West.' In Maakie van Berkel and Letizia Osti (eds), *The Historian of Islam at Work: Essays in Honor of Hugh N. Kennedy*, 91–116. Brill: Leiden.

Fierro, Maribel. 1999. 'The Legal Policies of the Almohad Caliphs and Ibn Rushd's *Bidayat al-mujtahid*', *Journal of Islamic Studies* 10(3): 226–48.

Fierro, Maribel. 2000. 'Spiritual Alienation and Political Activism: The *Guraba* in al-Andalus during the Sixth/Twelfth Century', *Arabica* 47(2): 230–60.

Fierro, Maribel. 2009. 'Alfonso X "The Wise": The Last Almohad Caliph?', *Medieval Encounters* 15: 175–98.

Fierro, Maribel. 2010a. 'Conversion, Ancestry and Universal Religion: The Case of the Almohads in the Islamic West (Sixth/Twelfth–Seventh/Thirteenth Centuries)', *Journal of Medieval Iberian Studies* 2(2): 155–73.

Fierro, Maribel. 2010b. 'The Almohads and the Fatimids.' In Bruce D. Craig (ed.), *Ismaili and Fatimid Studies in Honor of Paul E. Walker*, 161–75. Chicago: Middle East Documentation Center.

Fierro, Maribel. 2010c. 'The Almohads (524–668/1130–1269) and the Hafsids (627–932/1229–1526).' In Maribel Fierro (ed.), *The New Cambridge History of Islam Volume 2: The Western Islamic World Eleventh to Eighteenth Centuries*, 66–105. Cambridge: Cambridge University Press.

Fierro, Maribel. 2016. *The Almohad Revolution: Politics and Religion in the Islamic West during the Twelfth–Thirteenth Centuries*. London: Routledge.

Fierro, Maribel. 2019. 'Again on Forced Conversion in the Almohad Period.' In Mercedes Garcia-Arenal and Yonatan Glazer-Eytan (eds), *Forced Conversion in Christianity, Judaism and Islam*, 111–32. Leiden: Brill.

Fierro, Maribel. 2020. 'Ibn Tufayl's *Hayy bin Yaqzan*: An Almohad Reading', *Islam and Christian-Muslim Relations*. See https://doi.org/10.1080/09596410.2020.1846448.

Fischel, Walter J. 1961. 'Ibn Khaldun's Use of Historical Sources', *Studia Islamica* 14: 109–19.

Fletcher, Madeleine. 1991. 'The Almohad Tawhid: Theology Which Relies on Logic', *Numen* 38(1): 110–27.

Fletcher, Madeleine. 1997a. 'Ibn Tumart's Teachers: The Relationship with al-Ghazali', *Al-Qantara* 18(2): 305–30.

Fletcher, Madeleine. 1997b. 'Al-Andalus and North Africa in the Almohad Ideology.' In Salma Khadra Jayyusi (ed.), *The Legacy of Muslim Spain*, 235–58. Leiden: Brill.

Forst, R. 2015. 'Noumenal Power', *Journal of Political Philosophy* 23(2): 111–27.

Foss, Clive 2010. 'Muʻawiya's State.' In John Haldon (ed.), *Money, Power and Politics in Early Islamic Syria: A Review of Current Debates*, 75–96. London: Ashgate.

Frank, Richard M. 1974. 'Notes and Remarks on the Tabaʻi in the Teaching of al-Maturidi.' In P. Salmon (ed.), *Melanges d'islamologie a la memoire d'Armand*, 137–49. Leiden: Brill.

Fricaud, Emile. 1997. 'Les Talaba dans la Société Almohade (le Temps d'Averroes)', *Al-Qantara* 18(2): 331–87.

Fromherz, Allen. 2009. 'North Africa and the Twelfth-century Renaissance: Christian Europe and the Almohad Islamic Empire', *Islam and Christian–Muslim Relations* 20(1): 43–59.

Fromherz, Allen. 2010a. *The Almohads: The Rise of an Islamic Empire*. London: I. B. Tauris.

Fromherz, Allen. 2010b. *Ibn Khaldun, Life and Times*. Edinburgh: Edinburgh University Press.

Fromherz, Allen. 2016. *The Near West: Medieval North Africa, Latin Europe and the Mediterranean in the Second Axial Age*. Edinburgh: Edinburgh University Press.

Frye, Richard N. 1983. 'The Political History of Iran Under the Sasanids.' In Ehsan Yarshater (ed.), *The Cambridge History of Iran Vol. 3(1): The Seleucid, Parthian and Sasanian Periods*, 116–80. Cambridge: Cambridge University Press.

Frye, Richard N. 2005. 'Church and State in Iranian History', *Bulletin of the Asia Institute* 19: 27–8.

Frye, Richard N. 2007. 'The Samanids.' In R. N. Frye (ed.), *The Cambridge History of Iran Volume 4: The Period from the Arab Invasion to the Saljuqs*, 136–61. Cambridge: Cambridge University Press.

Garcia-Arenal, Mercedes. 2006. *Messianism and Puritanical Reform: Mahdis of the Muslim West*. Translated by Martin Beagles. Leiden: Brill.

Garcia-Arenal, Mercedes. 2010. 'Conversion to Islam: From the "Age of Conversions" to the Millet System.' In Maribel Fierro (ed.), *The New Cambridge History of Islam Volume 2: The Western Islamic World, Eleventh to Eighteenth Centuries*, 586–606. Cambridge: Cambridge University Press.

García-Sanjuán, Alejandro. 2020. 'Replication and Fragmentation: The Taifa Kingdoms.' In Maribel Fierro (ed.), *The Routledge Handbook of Muslim Iberia*, 64–87. London: Routledge.

García, Sénén. 1990. 'The Masmuda Berbers and Ibn Tumart: an Ethnographic Interpretation of the Rise of the Almohad Movement', *Ufahamu: A Journal of African Studies* 18(1): 3–24.

Gardizi, Abu Said. 2011. *The Ornament of Histories: A History of the Eastern Lands AD 650–1041: The Persian Text of Abu Saʿid ʿAbd al-Hayy Gardizi*. Translated by C. E. Bosworth. London: I. B. Tauris.

Gaube, Heinz. 2012. 'The Syrian Desert Castles: Some Economic and Political Perspectives on their Genesis.' In Fred M. Donner (ed.), *The Articulation of Early Islamic State Structures*, 337–67. London: Routledge.

Gellner, Ernest. 1975. 'Cohesion and Identity: the Maghreb from Ibn Khaldun to Emile Durkheim', *Government and Opposition* 10(2): 203–18.

Gellner, Ernest. 1984. *Muslim Society*. Cambridge: Cambridge University Press.

Gerli, E. Michael. 2013. 'Ibn Tufayl.' In Michael E. Gerli (ed.), *Medieval Iberia: An Encyclopedia*, 421–2. London: Routledge.

Germann, Nadja. 2008. 'Philosophizing without Philosophy? On the Concept of Philosophy in Ibn Tufayl's *Hayy ibn Yaqzan*', *Recherches de théologie et philosophie médiévales* 75(2): 271–301.

Ghobadzadeh, Naser. 2014. *Religious Secularity: Shiite Repudiation of the Islamic State*. Oxford: Oxford University Press.

Ghouirgate, Mehdi. 2015. 'Ibn Tumart.' In Kate Fleet, Gudrun Krämer, Denis Matringe, John Nawas and Devin J. Stewart (eds), *Encyclopedia of Islam, Three*. Available at http://dx.doi.org/10.1163/1573-3912ei3COM32275.

Gibb, H. A. R. 1933. 'The Islamic Background of Ibn Khaldun's Political Theory', *Bulletin of the School of Oriental Studies* 7(1): 23–31.

Gibb, H. A. R. 1955a. 'Constitutional Organization.' In Majid Khadduri and Herbert J. Liebesny (eds), *Law in the Middle East Volume I: Origin and Development of Islamic Law*, 2–27. Washington, DC: The Middle East Institute.

Gibb, H. A. R. 1955b. 'An Interpretation of Islamic History I', *The Muslim World* 45(1): 4–15.

Gibb, H. A. R. 1962. *Studies on the Civilization of Islam.* Princeton, NJ: Princeton University Press.

Gibb, H. A. R. 1969. 'The Caliphate and the Arab States.' In Marshall W. Baldwin (ed.), *A History of the Crusades Volume I: The First Hundred Years*, 81–98. Madison: University of Wisconsin Press.

Gibb, H. A. R. 1982. 'An Interpretation of Islamic History.' In S. Shaw and W. Polk (eds) *Studies of the Civilization of Islam*, 3–33. Princeton, NJ: Princeton University Press.

Gilabert, Pablo. 2018. 'A Broad Definition of Agential Power', *Journal of Political Power* 11(1): 79–92.

Glick, Thomas. F. 2005. *Islamic and Christian Spain in the Early Middle Ages.* Princeton, NJ: Princeton University Press.

Goitein, S. D. 2010. *Studies in Islamic History and Institutions.* Leiden: Brill.

Golden, Peter B. 1992. *An Introduction to the History of the Turkic Peoples: Ethnogenesis and State-Formation in Medieval and Early Modern Eurasia and the Middle East.* Wiesbaden: Otto Harrassowitz.

Goldziher, Ignaz. 1994. *On the History of Grammar Among Arabs: An Essay in Literary History.* Philadelphia: John Benjamins.

Gómez -Rivas, Camilo. 2014. *Law and the Islamization of Morocco under the Almoravids: The Fatwas of Ibn Rushd al-Jadd to the Far Maghrib.* Leiden: Brill.

Gómez-Rivas, Camilo. 2020. 'Berber Rule and Abbasid Legitimacy: The Almoravids (434/1042–530/1147).' In Maribel Fierro (ed.), *The Routledge Handbook of Muslim Iberia*, 89–113. London: Routledge.

González-Ferrín, Emilio. 2015. 'The Disobedient Philosopher: Subtle Humanistic Insurgence in Ibn Tufayl.' In Anne Roberts and Belén Bistué (eds), *Disobedient Practices: Textual Multiplicity in Medieval and Golden Age Spain*, 17–35. Newark: Juan de la Cuesta.

Goodman, Lenn Evan. 1972. 'Ibn Khaldun and Thucydides', *Journal of the American Oriental Society* 92(2): 250–70.

Goodman, Lenn Evan. 1983. 'The Greek Impact on Arabic Literature.' In A. F. L. Beeston, T. M. Johnstone, R. B. Serjeant and G. R. Smith (eds), *Arabic Literature to the End of the Umayyad Period*, 459–82. Cambridge: Cambridge University Press.

Goodman, Lenn Evan. 2019. 'Ibn Khaldun and the Immanence of Judgment', *Philosophy East & West* 69(3): 737–58.

Gordon, Mattew S. 2001. *The Breaking of a Thousand Swords: A History of the Turkish Military of Samarra (A.H. 200–275/815–889 C.E.).* New York: State University of New York.

Griffel, Frank. 2005. 'The Rational Proof for God's Existence and his Unity of Ibn Tumart and his Connection to the Nizamiyya Madrasa in Baghdad.' In Patrice Cressier, Maribel Fierro and Luis Molina (eds), *Los Almohades: problemas y perspectivas Volume 2*, 753–813. Madrid: Consejo Superior de Investigationes Científicas.

Guest, R. 1932. 'A Coin of Abu Muslim', *Journal of the Royal Asiatic Society* 64(3): 555–6.

Guichard, Pierre. 1997. 'The Social History of Muslim Spain.' In Salma Khadra Jayyusi (ed.), *The Legacy of Muslim Spain*, 679–708. Leiden: Brill.

Güner, Ahmet. 2002. 'Maverdi'nin Hilafet Kuramının Tarihsel Arkaplanına Bir Bakış I', *D. E. Ü. İlahiyat Fakültesi Dergisi* 16: 3–36.

Güner, Ahmet. 2003. 'Maverdi'nin Hilafet Kuramının Tarihsel Arkaplanına Bir Bakış II', *D.E.Ü. İlahiyat Fakültesi Dergisi* 17: 227–52.

Gutas, Dimitri. 1994. 'Ibn Tufayl on Ibn Sina's Eastern Philosophy', *Oriens* 34: 222–41.

Gutas, Dimitri. 2000. 'Avicenna's Eastern ("Oriental") Philosophy: Nature, Contents and Transmission', *Arabic Sciences and Philosophy* 10(2): 159–80.

Habib, Mohammad. 1951. *Sultan Mahmud of Ghaznin*. Aligarh: Cosmopolitan.

Haddad, Wadi Zaotan. 1996. '*Ahl al-Dhimma* in an Islamic State: The Teaching of Abu al-Hasan al-Mawardi's *Al-Ahkam al-Sultaniyya*', *Islam and Christian–Muslim Relations* 7(2): 169–80.

Haider, Najam. 2021. 'Zaydism.' In Muhammad Afzal Upal and Carole M. Cusack (eds), *Handbook of Islamic Sects and Movements*, 203–34. London: Brill.

Hakim, Avraham. 2017. 'Context: 'Umar b. al-Khattab.' In Andrew Rippin and Jawid Mojaddedi (eds), *The Wiley Blackwell Companion to the Qur'an*, 218–33. London: John Wiley & Sons.

Hallaq, Wael B. 1984. 'Caliphs, Jurists and the Saljuqs in the Political Thought of Juwayni', *The Muslim World* 74(1): 26–41.

Halm, Heinz. 2001. *The Fatimids and Their Traditions of Learning*. London: I. B. Tauris.

Hamid, Etilgani Abdulqadir. 2001. 'Al-Mawardi's Theory of State: Some Ignored Dimensions', *American Journal of Islam and Society* 18(4): 1–18.

Hamori, Andras. 2013. 'Ibn al-Muqaffa.' In Gerhard Bowing (ed.), *The Princeton Encyclopedia of Islamic Thought*, 232–3. Princeton, NJ: Princeton University Press.

Hanaway, William L. 2012. 'Secretaries, Poets, and the Literary Language.' In Brian Spooner and William L. Hanaway (eds), *Literacy in the Persianate World: Writing and the Social Order*, 95–142. Philadelphia: University of Pennsylvania Press.

Hanne, Eric J. 2004. 'Abbasid Politics and the Classical Theory of Caliphate.' In Beatrice Gruendler and Louise Marlow (eds), *Writers and Rulers: Perspectives on Their Relationship from Abbasid to Safavid Times*, 49–72. Wiesbaden: Reichert Verlag.

Hanne, Eric J. 2004/5. 'Death on the Tigris: A Numismatic Analysis of the Decline of the Great Saljuqs', *American Journal of Numismatics* 16/17: 145–72.

Hanne, Eric J. 2007. *Putting the Caliph in his Place: Power, Authority, and the Late Abbasid Caliphate.* Madison: Fairleigh Dickinson University Press.

Harris, Errol E. 1957. 'Political Power', *Ethics* 68(1): 1–10.

Hassan, Ümit. 1998. *İbn Haldun'un Metodu ve Siyaset Teorisi.* Istanbul: Toplumsal Değişim.

Haug, Robert. 2011. 'Frontiers and the State in Early Islamic History: Jihad Between Caliphs and Volunteers', *History Compass* 9(8): 634–43.

Haug, Robert. 2019. *The Eastern Frontier: Limits of Empire in Late Antique and Early Medieval Central Asia.* London: I. B. Tauris.

Havemann, Axel. 1989. 'The Vizier and the Rais in Saljuq Syria: The Struggle for Urban Self-Representation', *International Journal of Middle East Studies* 21(2): 233–42.

Hawi, Sami S. 1974. *Islamic Naturalism and Mysticism: A Philosophical Study of Ibn Tufayl's* Hayy bin Yaqzan. Leiden: Brill.

Hawi, Sami S. 1975. 'Ibn Tufayl: On the Existence of God and his Attributes', *Journal of the American Oriental Society* 95(1): 58–67.

Hawi, Sami S. 1976. 'Ibn Tufayl's Appraisal of his Predecessors and their Influence on his Thought', *International Journal of Middle East Studies* 7(1): 89–121.

Hawi, Sami S. 1995. 'Aspects of al-Farabi's Thought in the Light of Ibn Tufayl's Criticism', *Islamic Studies* 34(3): 297–303.

Hawting, G. R. 2000. *The First Dynasty of Islam: The Umayyad Caliphate AD 661–750.* London: Routledge.

Hebert, Raymond J. 1991. 'The Coinage of Islamic Spain', *Islamic Studies* 30(1/2): 112–28.

Hernandez, Miguel Cruz. 1992. 'Islamic Though in the Iberian Peninsula.' In Salma Khadra Jayyusi (ed.), *The Legacy of Muslim Spain*, 777–803. Leiden: Brill.

Hillenbrand, Carole. 2007. *Turkish Myth and Muslim Symbol: The Battle of Manzikert.* Edinburgh: Edinburgh University Press.

Hillenbrand, Carole. 2011. 'Aspects of the Court of the Great Seljuqs.' In Christian Lange and Songül Mecit (eds), *The Seljuqs: Politics, Society and Culture*, 22–37. Edinburgh: Edinburgh University Press.

Hillenbrand, Carole. 2020. 'What is Special about Seljuq History?' In Sheila R. Canby, Deniz Beyazit and Martina Rugiadi (eds), *The Seljuqs and their Successors: Art, Culture and History*, 6–16. Edinburgh: Edinburgh University Press.

Hillenbrand, Carole. 2022. *The Medieval Turks: Collected Papers*. Edinburgh: Edinburgh University Press.

Hitchcock, Richard. 2014. *Muslim Spain Reconsidered: From 711 to 1501*. Edinburgh: Edinburgh University Press.

Hitti, Philip K. 1937. *History of Arabs*. London: Macmillan and Co.

Hobbes, Thomas. 1998. *Leviathan*. Oxford: Oxford University Press.

Holzgrefe, J. L. 1989. 'The Origins of Modern International Relations Theory', *Review of International Studies* 15(1): 11–26.

Hopkins, J. F. P. 1954. 'The Almohade Hierarchy', *Bulletin of the School of Oriental and African Studies* 16(1): 93–112.

Hopkins, J. F. P. 1986. 'Ibn Tumart.' In B. Lewis, V. L. Menage, Ch. Pellat and J. Schact (eds), *The Encyclopedia of Islam Volume III*, 958–60. Leiden: Brill.

Hopkins, Nicholas S. 1990. 'Engels and Ibn Khaldun', *Alif: Journal of Comparative Politics* 10: 9–18.

Hourani, George F. 1956. 'The Principal Subject of ibn Tufayl's *Hayy bin Yaqzan*', *Journal of Near Eastern Studies* 15(1): 40–6.

Howes, Rachel T. 2011. 'The Qadi, the Wazir and the Daʿi: Religious and Ethnic Relations in Buyid Shiraz in the Eleventh Century', *Iranian Studies* 44(6): 875–94.

Hoyland, Robert G. 2006. 'New Documentary Texts and the Early Islamic State', *Bulletin of the School of Oriental and African Studies* 69(3): 395–416.

Hoyland, Robert G. 2015. *In God's Path: The Arab Conquests and the Creation of an Islamic Empire*. Oxford: Oxford University Press.

Huff, Dietrich. 2008. 'Formation and Ideology of the Sasanian State in the Context of Archaeological Evidence.' In Vesta Sarkhosh Curtis and Sarah Stewart (eds), *Religion in the late Sasanian Period Volume III*, 31–59. London: I. B. Tauris.

Humphreys, R. Stephen. 1991. *Islamic History: A Framework for Inquiry*. Princeton, NJ: Princeton University Press.

Humphreys, R. Stephen. 2006. *Muʿawiya ibn Abi Sufyan: From Arabia to Empire*. Oxford: Oneworld.

Hurwitz, Nimrod. 2013. 'The Contribution of Earl Islamic Rulers to Adjudication and Legislation: The Case of the Mazalim Tribunals.' In Jeroen Duindam, Jill Harries, Caroline Humfress and Nimrod Hurvitz (eds), *Law and Empire: Ideas, Practices and Actors*, 135–55. Leiden: Brill.

Husaini, S. A. Q. 1976. *Arab Administration*. Delhi: Idarah-i Edebiyat-i Delli.

Huyse, Philip. 2008. 'Late Sasanian Society between Orality and Literacy.' In Vesta Sarkhosh Curtis and Sarah Stewart (eds), *Religion in the late Sasanian Period Volume III*, 148–55. London: I. B. Tauris.

Ibish, Yusuf. 1966. *The Political Doctrine of al-Baqillani*. Beirut: American University of Beirut.

Ibn Abi Zar'. 1972. *Kitab al-Anis al-Mutrib bi Rawd Al-Qurtas Fi Akhbar Muluk Al-Maghrib Wa Tareekh Madinat Fas*. Rabat: Dar al-Mansur.

Ibn al-Athir. 1998a. *Al-Kamil fi'l-ta'rikh Volume 7*. Beirut: Dar al-Kutub al-'ilmiyya.

Ibn al-Athir. 1998b. *Al-Kamil fi'l-ta'rikh Volume 8*. Beirut: Dar al-Kutub al-'ilmiyya.

Ibn al-Athir. 2002. *The Annals of the Seljuqs: Selections from al-Kamil fi'-Ta'rikh of 'Izz al-Din Ibn al-Athir*. Translated by D. S. Richards. London: Routledge.

Ibn al-Athir. 2016a. *The Chronicle of Ibn al-Athir for the Crusading Period from al-Kamil fi'l-tar'ikh Part 1: The Years 491–541/1097–1146 The Coming of the Franks and the Muslim Response*. Translated by D. R. Richards. London: Routledge.

Ibn al-Athir. 2016b. *The Chronicle of Ibn al-Athir for the Crusading Period from al-Kamil fi'l-tar'ikh Part Part 2: The Years 541–589/1146–1193 The Age of Nur al-Din and Saladin*. Translated by D. R. Richards. London: Routledge.

Ibn al-Athir. 2016c. *The Chronicle of Ibn al-Athir for the Crusading Period from al-Kamil fi'l-tar'ikh Part 3: The Years 589–629/1193–1231 The Ayyubids after Saladin and the Mongol Menace*. Translated by D. R. Richards. London: Routledge.

Ibn al-Jawzi, Abu al-Faraj. 1992a. *al-Muntazam fi ta'rikh al-muluk wa-l-umam. Volume 14*. Edited by M. Ata. Beirut: Dar al-Kutub al-'ilmiyya.

Ibn al-Jawzi, Abu al-Faraj. 1992b. *al-Muntazam fi ta'rikh al-muluk wa-l-umam. Volume 15*. Edited by M. Ata. Beirut: Dar al-Kutub al-'ilmiyya.

Ibn al-Muqaffa, Abdullah. 1819. *Kalila and Dimna*. Translated by Wyndham Knatchbull. Oxford: W. Baxter.

Ibn al-Muqaffa', Abdullah. 1989a. *Risala fi al-Sahaba*. In Abdullah ibn al-Muqaffa', *Athar Ibn al-Muqaffa*, 309–24. Beirut: Dar'ul maktab al-'ilmiyya.

Ibn al-Muqaffa', Abdullah. 1989b. *Al-Adab al-Kabir*. In Abdullah ibn al-Muqaffa', *Athar Ibn al-Muqaffa*, 245–79. Beirut: Dar'ul maktab al-'ilmiyya.

Ibn al-Muqaffa', Abdullah. 1989c. *Al-Adab al-Sagir*. In Abdullah ibn al-Muqaffa', *Athar Ibn al-Muqaffa*, 283–307. Beirut: Dar'ul maktab al-'ilmiyya.

Ibn al-Muqaffa', Abdullah. 1989d. *al-Durr al-Yatima*. In Abdullah ibn al-Muqaffa', *Athar Ibn al-Muqaffa*, 327–30. Beirut: Dar'ul maktab al-'ilmiyya.

Ibn al-Qutiya. 2009. *Early Islamic Spain: The History of Ibn al-Qutiya*. Translated and edited by David Jones. London: Routledge.

Ibn Barrajan. 2015. *Idah al-hikma bi-ahkam al-'ibra [A Qur'an Commentary by Ibn Barrajan of Seville (d. 536/1141)]*. Edited by Gerhard Böwering and Yousef Casewit. Leiden: Brill.

Ibn Battuta. 2010. *The Travels of Ibn Battuta A.D. 1325–1354 Volume II*. Edited by H. A. R. Gibb. London: Ashgate.

Ibn Fadlan, Ahmad. 2017. *Mission to the Volga*. Translated by James E. Montgomery. New York: New York University Press.

Ibn Isfandiyar, Muhammad b. al-Hasan b. 1905. *An Abridged Translation of the History of Tabaristan*. Translated and prepared by Edward G. Browne. Leiden: Brill.

Ibn Jubayr. 2020. *The Travels of Ibn Jubayr: A Medieval Journey from Cordoba to Jerusalem*. Translated by R. J. C. Broadhurst. London: I. B. Tauris.

Ibn Khaldun. 1958a. *The Muqaddimah: An Introduction to History Volume I*. Translated by F. Rosenthal. Princeton, NJ: Princeton University Press.

Ibn Khaldun. 1958b. *The Muqaddimah: An Introduction to History Volume II*. Translated by F. Rosenthal. Princeton, NJ: Princeton University Press.

Ibn Khaldun. 1958c. *The Muqaddimah: An Introduction to History Volume III*. Translated by F. Rosenthal. Princeton, NJ: Princeton University Press.

Ibn Khaldun. 1979. *al-Ta'rif bi-Ibn Khaldun wa-rihlatihi gharban wa-sharqan*. Beirut: Dar al-Kitab al-Lubnani li Tiba'ah wa al-Nashr.

Ibn Khaldun. 2017. *Ibn Khaldun on Sufism: Remedy for the Questioner in Search of Answers [Shifa' al-Sa'il li-Tahdhib al-Masa'il]*. Translated by Yumna Ozer. London: The Islamic Text Society.

Ibn Khallikan, Ahmad bin Muhammad bin Ibrahim bin Abu Bakr. 1843a. *Biographical Dictionary Volume I*. Translated by Mack Guckin De Slane. London: Oriental Translation Fund.

Ibn Khallikan, Ahmad bin Muhammad bin Ibrahim bin Abu Bakr. 1843b. *Biographical Dictionary Volume II*. Translated by Mack Guckin De Slane. London: Oriental Translation Fund.

Ibn Khallikan, Ahmad bin Muhammad bin Ibrahim bin Abu Bakr. 1868. *Biographical Dictionary Volume III*. Translated by Mack Guckin De Slane. London: Oriental Translation Fund.

Ibn Khayyat, Khalifa. 2015. *Khalifa ibn Khayyat's History on the Umayyad Dynasty (66–750)*. Translated by Carl Wurtzel. Liverpool: Liverpool University Press.

Ibn Miskawaihi. 1921. *The Concluding Portion of the Experiences of the Nations Volume II: Reigns of Muttaqi, Mustakfi, Muti' and Tai'*. Translated by D. S. Margoliouth. London: Basic Blackwell.

Ibn Qutaybah, Abu Muhammad Abdallah b. Muslim. 1900. *'Uyun al-Akhbar I*. Edited by Carl Brockelman. Berlin: Emil Feber.

Ibn Rushd. 1974. *Averroes on Plato's Republic*. Translated by Ralph Lerner. Ithaca: Cornell University Press.

Ibn Rushd. 1987. *The Incoherence of the Incoherence [Tahafut al-Tahafut]*. Translated by Simon Van Den Bergh. Cambridge: E. J. W. Gibb Memorial Trust.

Ibn Rushd. 2000. *The Distinguished Jurist's Primer [Bidayat al Mujtahid wa Nihayat al-Muqtasid Volume I]*. Translated by Imran A. Khan Nyazee. Reading: Garnet.

Ibn Rushd. 2011. *The Book of the Decisive Treatise Determining the Connection Between the Law and Wisdom & Epistle Dedicatory [Kitab Fasl al-Makal, Risala al-Ihda]*. Translated by Charles E. Butterworth. Provo, UT: Birmingham Young University Press.

Ibn Tufayl, Abu Bakr Muhammad. 1964. *Hayy b. Yaqzan [Falsafah Ibn Tufayl wa risalatahu Hayy bin Yaqzan]*. Edited by Abd al-halim Mahmud. Cairo: Maktabat al-anglu-al-misriyya.

Ibn Tumart, Muhammad. 2007. *A'azzu Ma Yuṭlab*. Edited by Ammar Talibi. Algiers: Wazarat al-Saqafa.

Ibrahim, al-Qasim bin. 1927. *Kitab al-Rad 'ala al-zindiq*. Prepared by Michelangelo Guidi. Rome: R. Accademia Nazionale Dei Lincei.

Ibrahim, Tawfiq, and Ruth Pliego. 2020. 'The Coins of al-Andalus: Ideological Evolution and Historical Context.' In Maribel Fierro (ed.), *The Routledge Handbook of Muslim Iberia*, 171–86. London: Routledge.

Idris, H. R. 1986. 'Hafsids.' In B. Lewis, V. L. Menage, Ch. Pellat and J. Schact (eds), *The Encyclopedia of Islam Volume III*, 66–9. Leiden: Brill.

Idris, Murad. 2011. 'Ibn Tufayl's Critique of Politics', *Journal of Islamic Philosophy* 7: 67–102.

Idris, Roger. 2017. 'Reflection on Malikism under the Umayyads of Spain.' In Maribel Fierro and Julio Samsó (eds), *The Formation of al-Andalus Part 2: Language, Religion, Culture and the Sciences*, 85–101. London: Routledge.

Ighbariah, Ahmad. 2020. 'Ibn al-Muqaffa's Isagoge: An Edition of the Arabic Text with an English Translation', *Journal of Abbasid Studies* 7(1): 57–97.

Ilahiane, Hsain. 2006. *Historical Dictionary of the Berbers (Imazighen)*. Oxford: The Scarecrow.

Ilisch, Lutz. 2010. ''Abd al-Malik's Monetary Reform in Copper and the Failure of Centralization.' In John Haldon (ed.), *Money, Power and Politics in Early Islamic Syria: A Review of Current Debates*, 125–46. London: Ashgate.

Inostranzev, M. 1918. *Iranian Influence on Moslem Literature Part I*. Translated by G. K. Nariman. Bombay: D. B. Taraporevala Sons & Co.

Irwin, Robert. 1997. 'Toynbee and Ibn Khaldun', *Middle Eastern Studies* 33(3): 461–79.

Irwin, Robert. 2018. *Ibn Khaldun: An Intellectual Biography*. Princeton, NJ: Princeton University Press.

Islahi, Abdul Azim. 2014. *History of Islamic Economic Thought: Contributions of Muslim Scholars to Economic Thought and Analysis*. Cheltenham: Edward Elgar.

Issawi, Charles. 1950. *An Arab Philosophy of History: Selections from the Prolegomena of Ibn Khaldun of Tunis (1332–1406)*. London: John Murray.

Jiwa, Shainool. 1992. 'Fatimid–Buyid Diplomacy During the Reign of al-ʿAziz Billah (365/975–386/996)', *Journal of Islamic Studies* 3(1): 57–71.

Jones, Linda G. 2008. 'The Christian Companion: A Rhetorical Trope in the Narration of Intra-Muslim Conflict During the Almohad Epoch', *Anuario De Estudios Medievales* 38(2): 793–829.

Jones, Linda G. 2013. 'The Preaching of the Almohads: Loyalty and Resistance across the Strait of Gibraltar', *Medieval Encounters* 19: 71–101.

Judd, Steven C. 2010. 'Medieval Explanations for the Fall of the Umayyads.' In Antoine Borrut and Paul M. Cobb (eds), *Umayyad Legacies Medieval Memories from Syria to Spain*, 89–104. Leiden: Brill.

Judd, Steven C. 2014. *Religious Scholars and the Umayyads: Piety-minded Supporters of the Marwanid Caliphate*. London: Routledge.

Kabir, Mafizullah. 1964. *The Buwayhid Dynasty of Baghdad (334|946–447|1055)*. Calcutta: Iran Society.

Kafesoğlu, İbrahim. 1972. *Selçuklu Tarihi*. Ankara: Devlet Kitapları.

Kafesoğlu, İbrahim. 2021. *Selçuklular ve Selçuklu Tarihi Üzerine Araştırmalar*. Istanbul: Ötüken.

Kai Kaus Ibn Iskender. 1951. *A Mirror for Princes: The Qabus Nama*. Translated by Reuben Levy. New York: E. P. Dutton & Co.

Kallek, Cengiz. 1997a. 'Ebu Yusuf'un İktisadi Görüşleri', *İslam Araştırmaları* 1(1): 1–18.

Kallek, Cengiz. 1997b. 'Haraç.' *İslam Ansiklopedisi Volume 16*, 71–88. Ankara: TDV.

Kallek, Cengiz. 2003. 'Maverdi.' *İslam Ansiklopedisi Volume 28*, 180–6. Ankara: TDV.

Kallek, Cengiz. 2004. 'Maverdi'nin ahlaki, içtimai, siyasi ve iktisadi görüşleri', *Divan* 17(2): 219–65.

Kassis, Hanna E. 1983. 'Qadi Iyad's Rebellion against the Almohads in Sabtah (A.H. 542–543/A.D. 1147–1148): New Numismatic Evidence', *Journal of the American Oriental Society* 103(3): 504–14.

Kayapinar, M. Akif. 2008. 'Ibn Khaldun's Concept of "Asabiyya": An Alternative Tool for Understanding Long-Term Politics?', *Asian Journal of Social Science* 36(3/4): 375–407.

Kelsen, Hans. 2006. *The General Theory of Law and State*. London: Transaction.

Kennedy, E. S. 2007. 'The Exact Sciences.' In R. N. Frye (ed.), *The Cambridge History of Iran Volume 4: The Period from the Arab Invasion to the Saljuqs*, 378–95. Cambridge: Cambridge University Press.

Kennedy, Hugh. 1981a. *The Early Abbasid Caliphate: A Political History.* London: Croom Helm.

Kennedy, Hugh. 1981b. 'Central Government and Provincial Elites in the Early 'Abbasid Caliphate', *Bulletin of the School of Oriental and African Studies* 44(1): 26–38.

Kennedy, Hugh. 2004. 'Muslim Spain and Portugal: Al-Andalus and its Neighbors.' In David Luscombe and Jonathan Riley-Smith (eds)' *The Cambridge New Medieval History: Volume 4, c.1024–c.1198, Part 2*, 599–857. Cambridge: Cambridge University Press.

Kennedy, Hugh. 2011. 'The Late Abbasid Pattern.' In Chase F. Robinson (ed.), *The New Cambridge History of Islam Volume 1: The Formation of the Islamic World Sixth to Eleven Centuries*, 360–94. Cambridge: Cambridge University Press.

Kennedy, Hugh. 2013. 'The Reign of al-Muqtadir (295–320/908–32): A History.' In Maaike van Berkel, Nadia Maria El Cheikh, Hugh Kennedy and Letizia Osti (eds), *Crisis and Continuity at the Abbasid Court: Formal and Informal Politics in the Caliphate of al-Muqtadir (295–320/908–32)*, 13–48. Leiden: Brill.

Kennedy, Hugh. 2014. *Muslim Spain and Portugal: A Political History of al-Andalus.* London: Routledge.

Kennedy, Hugh. 2016. *The Prophet and the Age of the Caliphates: The Islamic Near East from the Sixth to the Eleventh Century.* London: Routledge.

Kerr, Malcolm H. 1966. *Islamic Reform: The Political and Legal Theories of Muhammad Abduh and Rashid Rida.* Berkeley: University of Los Angeles.

Khan, Muhammad Yakub. 2001. 'A Political Study of Al-Mawardi with Special Reference to the Concept of Legitimacy.' PhD thesis, University of Leeds.

Khan, Qamaruddin. 1983. *Al-Mawardi's Theory of State.* Lahore: Islamic Book Foundation.

Koch, Bettina. 2014. 'Religious Dissent in Premodern Islam: Political Usage of Heresy and Apostasy in Nizam al-Mulk and Ibn Taymiyya.' In Karen Bollermann, Thomas M. Izbicki, and Cary J. Nederman (eds), *Religion, Power, and Resistance from the Eleventh to the Sixteenth Centuries Playing the Heresy Card*, 215–35. New York: Palgrave.

Korkut, Şenol. 2008. 'Ibn Khaldun's Critique of the Theory of al-Siyasah al Madaniyyah', *Asian Journal of Social Sciences* 36(3/4): 547–70.

Kosei, Morimoto. 2002. 'What Ibn Khaldun Saw: The Judiciary of Mamluk Egypt', *Mamluk Studies Review* 6: 109–31.

Köymen, Mehmet Altay. 1966. 'Alp Arslan Zamanı Selçuklu Saray Teşkilatı ve Hayatı', *Tarih Araştırmaları* 4(6): 1–99.
Köymen, Mehmet Altay. 1970. *Alp Arslan Zamanı Selçuklu Askeri Teşkilatı*. Ankara: Ankara Üniversitesi Basımevi.
Köymen, Mehmet Altay. 1975. 'Alp Arslan Zamanı Selçuklu Kültür Müesseseleri I', *Selçuklu Araştırmaları* 4: 75–124.
Köymen, Mehmet Altay. 1976. *Tuğrul Bey ve Zamanı*. Istanbul: MEB.
Kriegel, Blandine. 1995. *The State and the Rule of Law*. Princeton, NJ: Princeton University Press.
Kristo-Nagy, Istvan T. 2009. 'Reason, Religion and Power in Ibn al-Muqaffa', *Acta Orientalia Academiae Scientiarum Hungaricae* 62(3): 285–301.
Kristo-Nagy, Istvan T. 2019. 'Marriage after Rape: The Ambiguous Relationship between Arab Lords and Iranian Intellectuals as Reflected in Ibn al-Muqaffa's Oeuvre.' In Margaret Larkin and Jocelyn Sharlet (eds), *Tradition and Reception in Arabic Literature: Essays Dedicated to Andras Hamori*, 161–88. Wiesbaden: Harasowitz Verlag.
Kruk, Remke. 1991. 'Neoplatonism and After: From Ibn Tufayl to Ibn an-Nafs.' In Arjo Vanderjagt and Detlev Pätzold (eds), *The Neoplatonic Tradition: Jewish, Christian and Islamic Themes*, 57–74. Cologne: Dinter.
Kruk, Remke. 1996. 'Ibn Tufayl: A Medieval Scholar's View of Nature.' In Lawrence I. Conrad (ed.), *The World of Ibn Tufayl: Interdisciplinary Perspectives on Hayy Ibn Yaqzan*, 69–80. Leiden: Brill.
Kukkonen, Taneli. 2009. 'Ibn Tufayl and the Wisdom of the East: On Apprehending the Divine.' In Panayiota Vassilopoulou and Stephen Clark (eds), *Late Antique Epistemology*, 87–102. London: Palgrave Macmillan.
Kukkonen, Taneli. 2011. 'Heart, Spirit, Form, Substance: Ibn Tufayl's Psychology.' In P. Adamson (ed.), *In the Age of Averroes: Arabic Philosophy in the Sixth/Twelfth Century*, 195–214. London: Warburg Institute.
Kuru, Ahmet T. 2020. 'Islam, Catholicism, and Religion-State Separation: An Essential or Historical Difference?', *International Journal of Religion* 1(1): 91–104.
Lacoste, Yves. 1984. *Ibn Khaldun: The Birth of History and the Past of the Third World*. Translated by David Macey. London: Verso.
Lambton, Ann K. S. 1956. '*Quis custodiet custodes*: Some Reflections on the Persian Theory of Government: I', *Studia Islamica* 5: 125–48.
Lambton, Ann K. S. 1968. 'The Internal Structure of the Saljuq Empire.' In J. A. Boyle (ed.), *The Cambridge History of Iran Volume 5: The Saljuq and Mongol Period*, 203–82. Cambridge: Cambridge University Press.

Lambton, Ann K. S. 1984. 'The Dilemma of Government in Islamic Persia: The "Siyasat-Nama" of Nizam al-Mulk', *Iran* 22: 55–66.

Lambton, Ann K. S. 1988. 'Changing Concepts of Justice and Injustice from the 5th/11th Century to the 8th/14th Century in Persia: The Saljuq Empire and the Ilkhanate', *Studia Islamica* 68: 27–60.

Lambton, Ann K. S. 1991a. *State and Government in Medieval Islam*. London: Routledge.

Lambton, Ann K. S. 1991b. 'Dihkan.' In B. Lewis, Ch. Pellat and J. Schact (eds), *The Encyclopedia of Islam Volume II*, 253–4. Leiden: Brill.

Lana, Robert E. 1987. 'Ibn Khaldun and Vico: The Universality of Social History', *The Journal of Mind and Behavior* 8(1): 153–65.

Lane-Poole, Stanley. 1873. 'On the Coins of Muwahhids in the British Museum', *The Numismatic Chronicle and Journal of the Numismatic Society* 13: 147–70.

Lange, Dierk. 1996. 'The Almoravid Expansion and the Downfall of Ghana', *Der Islam* 73: 313–51.

Lapidus, I. M. 1975. 'The Separation of State and Religion in the Development of early Islamic Society', *International Journal of Middle East Studies* 6: 363–85.

Lapidus, Ira M. 2002. *A History of Islamic Societies*. Cambridge: Cambridge University Press.

Laroui, Abdallah. 1977. *The History of Maghrib: An Interpretative Essay*. Princeton, NJ: Princeton University Press.

Lassner, Jacob. 1965. 'Some Speculative Thoughts on the Search for an Abbasid Capital', *The Muslim World* 55(2): 135–41.

Lassner, Jacob. 1980. *The Shaping of the 'Abbasid Rule*. Princeton, NJ: Princeton University Press.

Lassner, Jacob. 1984. 'Abu Muslim al-Khurasani: The Emergence of a Secret Agent from Kurasan, Iraq, or was it Isfahan?', *Journal of the American Oriental Society* 104(1): 165–75.

Latham, J. Derek. 1990. 'Ibn al-Muqaffa and Early Arabic Prose.' In Julia Ashtiany, T. M. Johnstone, J. D. Latham, R. B. Serjeant and G. Rex Smith (eds), *The Cambridge History of Arabic Literature: Abbasid Belle-Lettres*, 48–77. Cambridge: Cambridge University Press.

Lauri, Marco. 2013. 'Utopias in the Islamic Middle Ages: Ibn Tufayl and Ibn al-Nafis', *Utopian Studies* 24(1): 23–40.

Lázaro, Fabio López. 2013. 'The Rise and Global Significance of the First "West": The Medieval Islamic Maghrib', *Journal of World History* 24(2): 259–307.

Le Martire, Corrado. 2022. 'What is the Arab for Zoon Politikon? Ethics and Politics in Ibn Tufayl (d. 581/1185)', *Doctor Virtualis* 17: 79–105.

Le Tourneau, Roger. 1969. *Almohad Movement in North Africa in the 12th and 13th Centuries*. Princeton, NJ: Princeton University Press.

Le Tourneau, Roger. 2008. 'North Africa to the Sixteenth Century.' In P. M. Holt, Ann K. S. Lambton and Bernard Lewis (eds), *The Cambridge History of Islam Volume 2A: The Indian Sub-Continent, South-East Asia, Africa and the Muslim West*, 211–37. Cambridge: Cambridge University Press.

Leaman, Oliver. 1987. 'Continuity in Islamic Political Philosophy: The Role of Myth', *Bulletin* 14(2): 147–55.

Lelli, Giovanna. 2021. *Knowledge and Beauty in Classical Islam: An Aesthetic Reading of the* Muqaddima *by Ibn Khaldun*. London: Routledge.

Lev, Yaacov. 2009. 'From Revolutionary Violence to State Violence: the Fatimids (297–567/909–1171).' In Christian Lange and Maribel Fierro (eds), *Public Violence in Islamic Societies: Power, Discipline, and the Construction of the Public Sphere, 7th–19th Centuries CE*, 67–86. Edinburgh: Edinburgh University Press.

Levanoni, Amalia. 2010. 'The Mamluks in Egypt and Syria: The Turkish Mamluk Sultanate (648–784/1250–1382) and the Circassian Mamluk Sultanate (784–923/1382–1517).' In Maribel Fierro (ed.), *The New Cambridge History of Islam Volume 2: The Western Islamic World, Eleventh to Eighteenth Centuries*, 237–84. Cambridge: Cambridge University Press.

Levi-Provençal, E. 1986. "Abd al-Mu'min.' In B. Lewis, Ch. Pellat and J. Schact (eds), *The Encyclopedia of Islam Volume I*, 78–80. Leiden: Brill.

Levy, Reuben. 1929. *A Baghdad Chronicle*. Cambridge: Cambridge University Press.

Lewis, Archibald R. 1969. 'The Midi, Buwayhid Iraq, and Japan: Some Aspects of Comparative Feudalisms, A.D. 946–1055', *Comparative Studies in Society and History* 11(1): 47–53.

Lewis, Bernard. 1969. 'The Ismailites and the Assassins.' In Marshall W. Baldwin (ed.), *A History of the Crusades Volume I: The First Hundred Years*, 99–134. Madison: University of Wisconsin Press.

Liebesny, Herbert J. 1975. *The Law of the Near and Middle East: Readings, Cases, and Materials*. Albany: State University of New York Press.

Loewe, Herbert M. J. 1923. 'The Seljuqs.' In J. R. Tanner, C. W. Previte-Orton, and Z. N. Brooke (eds), *The Cambridge Medieval History Volume IV: The Eastern Roman Empire (717–1453)*, 299–317. Cambridge: Cambridge University Press.

Lowick, N. M. 1970. 'Seljuq Coins', *The Numismatic Chronicle* 10: 241–51.

Lowry, Joseph E. 2008. 'The First Islamic Legal Theory: Ibn al-Muqaffa on Interpretation, Authority, and the Structure of the Law', *Journal of the American Oriental Society* 128(1): 25–40.

Luce, Mark David. 2009. 'Frontier as Process: Umayyad Khurasan.' PhD thesis, University of Chicago.
Lukonin, V. G. 1983. 'Political, Social and Administrative Institutions: Taxes and Trade.' In Ehsan Yarshater (ed.), *The Cambridge History of Iran Volume 3(2): The Seleucid, Parthian and Sasanian Periods*, 681–740. Cambridge: Cambridge University Press.
Machan, Tim William. 1991. 'Introduction: Late Middle English Texts and the Higher and Lower Criticism.' In Tim William Machan (ed.), *Medieval Literature: Texts and Interpretation*, 3–16. New York: Medieval & Renaissance Texts & Studies.
Machiavelli, Niccolò. 1998. *The Prince.* Translated by H. C. Mansfield. Chicago: University of Chicago Press.
MacIntyre, Alasdair. 1983. 'The Indispensability of Political Theory.' In David Miller and Larry Siedentop (eds), *The Nature of Political Theory*, 17–34. Oxford: Clarendon.
Maddy-Weitzman, Bruce. 2011. *The Berber Identity Movement and the Challenge to North African States.* Austin: University of Texas Press.
Madelung, W. 1985. *Religious Schools and Sects in Medieval Islam.* London: Variorum.
Madelung, W. 2007. 'The Minor Dynasties of Northern Iran.' In R. N. Frye (ed.), *The Cambridge History of Iran Volume 4: The Period from the Arab Invasion to the Saljuqs*, 198–249. Cambridge: Cambridge University Press.
Maghen, Ze'ev. 2007. 'See No Evil: Morality and Methodology in Ibn Al-Qattan al-Fasi's Ahkam al-Nazar bi- Hassat al-Basar', *Islamic Law and Society* 14(3): 342–90.
Mahdi, Muhsin. 1957. *Ibn Khaldun's Philosophy of History: A Study in the Philosophic Foundation of the Science of Culture.* London: George Allen and Unwin.
Mahdi, Muhsin. 1987. 'Alfarabi.' In Leo Strauss and Joseph Cropsey (eds), *History of Political Philosophy*, 206–27. Chicago: University of Chicago Press.
Mahdi, Muhsin. 1990. 'Philosophical Literature.' In M. J. L. Young, J. D. Latham and R. B. Serjeant (eds), *Religion, Learning and Science in the 'Abbasid Period*, 76–105. Cambridge: Cambridge University Press.
Maimonides, Moses. 2002. *The Guide for the Perplexed.* Translated by M. Friedlander. Skokie, IL: Varda.
Makdisi, George. 1961. 'Muslim Institutions for Learning in Eleventh-Century Baghdad', *Bulletin of the School of Oriental and African Studies* 24(1): 1–56.
Makdisi, George. 1970a. 'The Marriage of Tughril Beg', *International Journal of Middle East Studies* 1(3): 259–75.
Makdisi, George. 1970b. 'Madrasa and University in the Middle Ages', *Studia Islamica* 32: 255–64.

Makdisi, George. 1973. 'The Sunni Revival.' In D. H. Richards (ed.), *Islamic Civilization, 950–1150*, 155–68. Oxford: Bruno Cassirer.

Makdisi, George. 1981. *The Rise of Colleges: Institutions of Learning in Islam and the West*. Edinburgh: Edinburgh University Press.

Makdisi, George. 1990. *History and Politics in Eleventh-Century Baghdad*. Aldershot: Variorum.

Makki, Mahmoud. 1992. 'The Political History of al-Andalus.' In Salma Khadra Jayyusi (ed.), *The Legacy of Muslim Spain*, 3–87. Leiden: Brill.

Malik bin Enes. 1982. *Al-Muwatta of Imam Malik ibn Anas*. Madina: Diwan.

Malti-Douglas, Fedwa. 1991. *Women's Body, Women's Word: Gender and Discourse in Arabo-Islamic Writing*. Princeton, NJ: Princeton University Press.

March, Andrew F. 2019. *The Caliphate of Man: Popular Sovereignty in Modern Islamic Thought*. Cambridge, MA: Harvard University Press.

Marchart, Oliver. 2007. *Post-Foundational Political Thought: Political Difference in Nancy, Lefort, Badiou and Laclau*. Edinburgh: Edinburgh University Press.

Marcinkowski, M. Ismail. 2001. 'Rapprochement and Fealty during the Buyids and Early Saljuqs: The Life and Times of Muhammad ibn al-Hasan al-Ṭusi', *Islamic Studies* 40(2): 273–96.

Marin-Guzman, Roberto. 1994. 'The 'Abbasid Revolution in Central Asia and Khurasan: An Analytical Study of the Role of Taxation, Conversion, and Religious Groups in its Genesis', *Islamic Studies* 33(2/3): 227–52.

Marlow, Louise. 1997. *Hierarchy and Egalitarianism in Islamic Thought*. New York: Cambridge University Press.

Marlow, Louise. 2016. *Counsel for Kings: Wisdom and Politics in Tenth-Century Iran Volume I: The Nasihat al-muluk of Pseudo-Mawardi: Contexts and Themes*. Edinburgh: Edinburgh University Press.

Marmura, Michael E. 1979. 'The Philosopher and Society: Some Medieval Arabic Discussions', *Arab Studies Quarterly* 1(4): 309–23.

Maroth, Miklos. 2018. 'Legitimate and Illegitimate Violence in Arabic Political Philosophy: Al-Farabi, Ibn Rush and Ibn Khaldun.' In Robert Gleave and Istvan T. Kristo-Nagy (eds), *Violence in Islamic Thought from the Mongols to European Imperialism*, 149–64. Edinburgh: Edinburgh University Press.

Marsham, Andrew. 2009. *Rituals of Islamic Monarchy: Accession and Succession in the First Muslim Empire*. Edinburgh: Edinburgh University Press.

Marsham A., and C. F. Robinson. 2007. 'The Safe-Conduct for the Abbasid 'Abd Allah b. 'Ali (d. 764)', *Bulletin of the School of Oriental and African Studies* 70(2): 247–81.

Masud, Muhammad Khalid. 2002. 'The Scope of Pluralism in Islamic Moral Traditions.' In Sohail H. Hashmi (ed.), *Islamic Political Ethics: Civil Society, Pluralism, and Conflict*, 135–47. Princeton, NJ: Princeton University Press.

Masudi. 1989. *The Meadows of Gold: The Abbasids*. Translated and edited by Paul Lunde and Caroline Stone. London: Routledge.

McDermott, Daniel. 2008. 'Analytical Political Philosophy.' In David Leopold and Marc Stears (eds), *Political Theory: Methods and Approaches*, 11–28. Oxford: Oxford University Press.

Mediano, Fernando R. 2010. 'The Post Almohad Dynasties in al Andalus and the Maghrib (Seventh–Ninth/Thirteenth–Fifteenth Centuries).' In Maribel Fierro (ed.), *The New Cambridge History of Islam Volume 2: The Western Islamic World, Eleventh to Eighteenth Centuries*, 106–43. Cambridge: Cambridge University Press.

Meisami, Julie Scott. 2007. *Persian Historiography: To the End of the Twelfth Century*. Edinburgh: Edinburgh University Press.

Melchert, Christopher. 2015. 'The Spread of Hanafism to Khurasan and Transoxiana.' In A. C. S Peacock and D. G. Tor (eds), *Medieval Central Asia: Iranian Tradition and Islamic Civilization*, 13–30. London: I. B. Tauris.

Merçil, Erdoğan. 1989. *Gazneliler Devleti Tarihi*. Ankara: Türk Tarih Kurumu.

Messier, Ronald. 1974. 'The Almoravids: West African Gold and the Gold Currency of the Mediterranean Basin', *Journal of the Economic and Social History of the Orient* 17(1): 31–47.

Messier, Ronald. 2001. 'Re-thinking the Almoravids, Re-thinking Ibn Khaldun', *The Journal of North African Studies* 6(1): 59–80.

Messier, Ronald. 2010. *The Almoravids and the Meanings of Jihad*. Oxford: Praeger.

Miguel, José, and Puerta Vílchez. 2012. *Aesthetics in Arabic Thought from Pre-Islamic Arabia through al-Andalus*. Translated by Consuelo López-Morillas. Leiden: Brill.

Mikhail, Hanna. 1985. *Politics and Revelation: Mawardi and After*. Edinburgh: Edinburgh University Press.

Miles, George C. 1938. *The Numismatic History of Rayy*. New York: The American Numismatic Society.

Miles, George C. 2007. 'The Numismatics.' In R. N. Frye (ed.), *The Cambridge History of Iran Volume 4: The Period from the Arab Invasion to the Saljuqs*, 364–77. Cambridge: Cambridge University Press.

Miller, Ted H. 2001. 'Oakeshott's Hobbes and the Fear of Political Rationalism', *Political Theory* 29(6): 806–32.

Minorsky, V [originally by an unknown author]. 1982. *Hudud al-'Alam. The Regions of the World. A Persian Geography: 372 A.H.–972 A.D.* Translated by V. Minorsky. Cambridge: Cambridge University Press.

Miranda, Ambrosio Huici. 2004. *Al-Tarikh Al Siyasi lil Imbraturiya Al Muwahhidiya.* Translated by Abd al-Wahid Akmir. Rabat: Al Zaman.

Mojuetan, B. A. 1981. 'Ibn Khaldun and his Cycle of Fatalism: A Critique', *Studia Islamica* 53: 93–108.

Moosa, Ebrahim. 2018. 'Recovering the Ethical: Practices, Politics, Tradition.' In Amyn B. Sajoo (ed.), *The Shari'a: History, Ethics and Law*, 39–58. London: I. B. Tauris.

Morgan, David. 2016. 'Persian Empire, Early Medieval (Saffarid to Buyid).' In John M. MacKenzie (ed.), *The Encyclopedia of Empire*, 1–6. London: John Wiley & Sons.

Morgenthau, Hans J. 1948. *Politics Among Nations: The Struggle for Power and Peace.* New York: Alfred A. Knopf.

Morony, Michael G. 1984. *Iraq After the Muslim Conquest.* Princeton, NJ: Princeton University Press.

Morrow, John Andrew. 2021. *Shi'ism in the Maghrib and al-Andalus, Volume One: History.* Newcastle: Cambridge Scholars.

Mottahedeh, Roy P. 1980. *Loyalty and Leadership in an Early Islamic Society.* Princeton, NJ: Princeton University Press.

Mottahedeh, Roy. 2007. 'The 'Abbasid Caliphate in Iran.' In R. N. Frye (ed.), *The Cambridge History of Iran Volume 4: The Period from the Arab Invasion to the Saljuqs*, 57–89. Cambridge: Cambridge University Press.

Mouline, Nabil. 2014. *The Clerics of Islam: Religious Authority and Political Power in Saudi Arabia.* New Haven: Yale University Press.

Mufti, Malik. 2009. 'Jihad as Statecraft: Ibn Khaldun on the Conduct of War and Empire', *History of Political Thought* 30(3): 385–410.

Mufti, Malik. 2019. 'Is Ibn Khaldun "Obsessed" with the Supernatural?', *Journal of the American Oriental Society* 139(3): 681–5.

Muhammad, Mi'raj. 1980. 'Ibn Khaldun and Vico: A Comparative Study', *Islamic Studies* 19(3): 195–211.

Muir, William. 1891. *The Caliphate: Its Rise, Decline, and Fall.* London: The Religious Tract Society.

Murphy, James Bernard. 2011. 'Perspectives on Power', *Journal of Political Power* 4(1): 87–103.

Musa, 'Azz al Din 'Amr. 1991. *Al-Muwahhidun fi al Gharb al-Islami: Tanzimatuhum wa Nuzumuhum.* Beirut: Dar al-gharb al-islami.

Nadvi, Syed Habibul Haq. 1971. 'Al Iqta or Theory of Land Ownership in Islam', *Islamic Studies* 10(4): 257–66.

Najjar, Fauzi M. 1961. 'Farabi's Political Philosophy and Shiism', *Studia Islamica* 14: 57–72.

Nasr, S. H. 2007a. 'Life Sciences, Alchemy and Medicine.' In R. N. Frye (ed.), *The Cambridge History of Iran Volume 4: The Period from the Arab Invasion to the Saljuqs*, 396–418. Cambridge: Cambridge University Press.

Nasr, S. H. 2007b. 'Philosophy and Cosmology.' In R. N. Frye (ed.), *The Cambridge History of Iran Volume 4: The Period from the Arab Invasion to the Saljuqs*, 419–41. Cambridge: Cambridge University Press.

Nassar, Nassif. 1964. 'Le Maitre d'Ibn Khaldun: Al-Abili', *Studia Islamica* 20: 103–14.

Nazim, Muhammad. 1931. *The Life and Times of Sultan Mahmud of Ghazna*. Cambridge: Cambridge University Press.

Negmatov, N. N. 1998. 'The Samanid State.' In M. S. Asimove and C. E. Bosworth (eds), *History of Civilizations of Central Asia Volume IV: The Age of Achievement: A.D. 750 to the End of the Fifteenth Century*, 83–101. Paris: UNESCO.

Nicolle, David. 2013. *Manzikert 1071: The Breaking of Byzantium*. Oxford: Osprey.

Nishapuri, Zahir al-Din [pseudonym]. 2001. *The History of the Seljuqs: An Ilkhanid Adaption of the Saljuq-nama of Zahir al-Din Nishapuri*. Translated by K. A. Luther. Richmond: Personal Edition.

Nizam al-Mulk. 2002. *The Book of Government or Rules for Kings: The Siyar al-Muluk or Siyasat-nama of Nizam al-Mulk*. Translated by Huber Darke. London: Routledge.

O'Callaghan, Joseph F. 2011. *The Gibraltar Crusade: Castile and the Battle for the Strait*. Philadelphia: University of Pennsylvania Press.

O'Kane, Bernard. 2017. 'Architecture and Court Cultures of the Fourteenth Century.' In Finbarr Barry Flood and Gülru Necipoğlu (eds), *A Companion to Islamic Art and Architecture*, 585–615. London: John Wiley & Sons.

O'Leary, De Lacy. 1923. *Arabic Thought and its Place in History*. New York: E. P. Dutton & Co.

Oakeshott, Michael. 1962. *Rationalism in Politics and Other Essays*. London: Methuen & Co. Ltd.

Ogunnaike, Oludamini. 2017. 'Profile: Ibn Khaldun, The Father of the Social Sciences.' In Dorothy L. Hodgson and Judith A. Byfield (eds), *Global Africa: Into the Twenty-First Century*, 10–16. Oakland: University of California Press.

Ohlander, Erik. 2009. 'Enacting Justice, Ensuring Salvation: The Trope of the "Just Ruler" in Some Medieval Islamic Mirrors for Princes', *The Muslim World* 99(2): 237–52.

Oliva, María Dolores García. 2017. 'The Treaties Between the Kings of León and the Almohads within the Leonese Expansion Strategy, 1157–1230', *Journal of Medieval Military History* 15: 150–85.

Olson, Caitlyn. 2020. 'Creed, Belief, and the Common Folk: Disputes in the Early Modern Maghrib (9th/15'h–11th/17th C.).' PhD dissertation, Harvard University.

Omar, Ayesha. 2019. 'Ibn Rushd's *The Decisive Treatise*: A Text for Political Reform', *The Medieval History Journal* 22(1): 131–55.

Omar, Farouk. 1967. 'The 'Abbasid Caliphate 132/750–170/786.' PhD dissertation, University of London.

Öztürk, Mustafa. 2018. *Siyaset İtikad, Din*. Ankara: Ankara Okulu.

Papaconstantinou, Arietta. 2010. 'Administering the Early Islamic Empire: Insights from the Papyri.' In John Haldon (ed.), *Money, Power and Politics in Early Islamic Syria: A Review of Current Debates*, 57–74. London: Ashgate.

Parens, Joshua. 2016. *Leo Strauss and the Recovery of Medieval Political Philosophy*. Rochester, NY: University of Rochester Press.

Parsons, Talcott. 1963. 'On the Concept of Political Power', *Proceedings of the American Philosophical Society* 107(3): 232–62.

Paul, Jürgen. 1994. *The State and the Military: The Samanid Case*. Bloomington: Indiana University Press.

Paul, Jürgen. 2011. 'Arslan Arghun – Nomadic Revival?' In Christian Lange and Songül Mecit (eds), *The Seljuqs: Politics, Society and Culture*, 99–116. Edinburgh: Edinburgh University Press.

Paul, Jürgen. 2013. 'Where did the Dihqans go?' *Eurasian Studies* 11: 1–34.

Paul, Jürgen. 2015. 'Dihqan.' In Kate Fleet, Gudrun Krämer, Denis Matringe, John Nawas and Everett Rowson (eds), *Encyclopedia of Islam, Three*. Available at http://dx.doi.org/10.1163/1573-3912ei3COM26024.

Paul, Jürgen. 2018a. 'Hasanwayh b. al-Husayn al-Kurdi (r. ca. 350–369/ca. 961–979): From Freehold Castles to Vassality?' In D. G. Tor (ed.), *The 'Abbasid and Carolingian Empires: Comparative Studies in Civilizational Formation*, 52–72. Leiden: Brill.

Paul, Jürgen. 2018b. 'Alptegin in the Siyasat-nama', *Afghanistan* 1(1): 122–40.

Peacock, Andrew. 2005. 'Nomadic Society and the Seljuq Campaigns in Caucasia', *Research Papers from the Caucasian Centre for Iranian Studies* 9(2): 205–30.

Peacock, A. C. S. 2007. *Medieval Islamic Historiography and Political Legitimacy: Bal'ami's Tarikhnama*. London: Routledge.

Peacock, A. C. S. 2010. *Early Seljuq History: A New Interpretation*. London: Routledge.

Peacock, A. C. S. 2011. 'Seljuq Legitimacy in Islamic History.' In Christian Lange and Songül Mecit (eds), *The Seljuqs: Politics, Society and Culture*, 79–95. Edinburgh: Edinburgh University Press.

Peacock, Andrew C. S. 2015. *The Great Seljuq Empire*. Edinburgh: Edinburgh University Press.

Peacock, Andrew. 2016. 'The Great Age of the Seljuqs.' In Sheila R. Canby, Deniz Beyazit, Martina Rugiadi and A. C. S. Peacock(eds), *Court and Cosmos: The Great Age of the Seljuqs*, 2–33. New York: The Metropolitan Museum of Art.

Pennell, C. R. 2003. *Morocco: From Empire to Independence*. Oxford: Oneworld.

Perikhanian, A. 1983. 'Iranian Society and Law.' In Ehsan Yarshater (ed.), *The Cambridge History of Iran Volume 3(2): The Seleucid, Parthian and Sasanian Periods*, 627–80. Cambridge: Cambridge University Press.

Piacentini, Valeria Fiorani. 2005. 'Sohar and the Daylami Interlude (356–443/967–1051)', *Proceedings of the Seminar for Arabian Studies* 35: 195–206.

Pierson, Paul. 2004. *Politics in Time: History, Institutions and Social Analysis*. Princeton, NJ: Princeton University Press.

Pišev, Marko, 2019. 'Anthropological Aspects of Ibn Khaldun's Muqaddimah: A Critical Examination.' In *Encyclopédie internationale des histoires de l'anthropologie* 1–23. Paris: Bérose.

Pourshariati, Pervaneh. 2008. *Decline and the Fall of the Sasanian Empire: The Sasanian–Parthian Confederacy and the Arab Conquest of Iran*. London: I. B. Tauris.

Procope, John. 1988. 'Greek and Roman Political Theory.' In J. H. Burns (ed.), *The Cambridge History of Medieval Political Thought c. 350–c. 1450*, 21–36. Cambridge: Cambridge University Press.

Qadir, M. Abdul. 1941. 'The Social and Political Ideas of Ibn Khaldun', *The Indian Journal of Political Science* 3(2): 117–26.

Qina, Umar bin. 2000. *Al-ru'yat al-Fikriyya fī al-hakim wa al-ra'iyya*. Amman: Dar Usama lil-nashr wa al-tawzi'.

Ra'ees, Wahabuddin. 2004. 'Asabiyyah, Religion and Regime Types: Rereading Ibn Khaldun', *Intellectual Discourse* 12(2): 159–80.

Radtke, Bernd. 1996. 'How Can Man Reach to the Mystical Union? Ibn Tufayl and the Divine Spark.' In Lawrence I. Conrad (ed.), *The World of Ibn Tufayl: Interdisciplinary Perspectives on Hayy Ibn Yaqzan*, 165–94. Leiden: Brill.

Regnier, Daniel. 2018. 'Utopia's Moorish Inspiration: Thomas Moore's Reading of Ibn Tufayl', *Renaissance and Reformation* 41(3): 17–45.

Reichenbach, Hans. 1968. *The Rise of Scientific Philosophy*. Los Angeles: University of California Press.

Renterghem, Vanessa Van. 2011. 'Controlling and Developing Baghdad: Caliphs, Sultans and the Balance of Power in the Abbasid Capital (Mid 5th/11th to Late 6th/12th Centuries.' In Christian Lange and Songül Mecit (eds), *The Seljuqs: Politics, Society and Culture*, 117–28. Edinburgh: Edinburgh University Press.

Rezania, Kianoosh. 2017. 'The Denkard Against its Islamic Discourse', *Der Islam* 94(2): 336–62.

Rice, Tamara Talbot. 1961. *The Seljuqs in Asia Minor.* London: Thames and Hudson.

Richter-Bernburg, Lutz. 1996. 'Medicina Ancilla Philosophiae: Ibn Tufayl's Hayy bin Yaqzan.' In Lawrence I. Conrad (ed.), *The World of Ibn Tufayl: Interdisciplinary Perspectives on Hayy Ibn Yaqzan*, 90–113. Leiden: Brill.

Ricoeur, Paul. 1976. *The Interpretation Theory: Discourse and the Surplus of Meaning.* Fort Worth: Texas Christian University Press.

Rizvi, S. Rizwan Ali. 1978. *Nizam al-Mulk Tusi: His Contribution to Statecraft, Political Theory and the Art of Government.* Lahore: Sh. Muhammad Ashraf.

Rizvi, S. Rizwan Ali. 1980. 'Political and Administrative Measures of Nizam al-Mulk Tusi', *Islamic Studies* 19(2): 111–19.

Rizvi, S. Rizwan Ali. 1981. 'The *Siyasat Namah* (The Book of Government) of Nizam al-Mulk Tusi', *Islamic Studies* 20(2): 129–36.

Robinson, Chase F. 2000. *Empires and Elites After the Muslim Conquest: The Transformation of Northern Mesopotamia.* Cambridge: Cambridge University Press.

Robinson, Chase F. 2010. 'The Violence of the Abbasid Revolution.' In Yasir Suleiman (ed.), *Living Islamic History: Studies in Honour of Professor Carole Hillenbrand*, 226–52. Edinburgh: Edinburgh University Press.

Rodd, Francis. 1925. 'Kahena, Queen of the Berbers: A Sketch of the Arab Invasion of Ifrikiyya in the First Century of the Hijra', *Bulletin of the School of Oriental Studies* 3(4): 729–46.

Rosemann, Philip W. 2013. 'Averroes.' In Michael E. Gerli (ed.), *Medieval Iberia: An Encyclopedia*, 131–3. London: Routledge.

Rosen, Lawrence. 2005. 'Theorizing from Within: Ibn Khaldun and his Political Culture', *Contemporary Sociology* 34(6): 596–9.

Rosenthal, E. I. J. 1953. 'The Place of Politics in the Philosophy of Ibn Rushd', *Bulletin of the School of Oriental and African Studies* 15(2): 246–78.

Rosenthal, E. I. J. 1962. *Political Thought in Medieval Islam: An Introductory Outline.* Cambridge: Cambridge University Press.

Rosenthal, Frank. 1958a. 'Ibn Khaldun's Life.' In Ibn Khaldun, *The Muqaddimah: An Introduction to History Volume I*, xxix–lxvii. Translated by F. Rosenthal. London: Routledge & Kegan Paul.

Rosenthal, Frank. 1958b. 'The Muqaddimah.' In Ibn Khaldun, *The Muqaddimah: An Introduction to History Volume I*, lxviii–lxxxviii. Translated by F. Rosenthal. London: Routledge & Kegan Paul.

Rosenthal, Franz. 1983. 'Ibn Khaldun in his Time (May 27, 1332–March 17, 1406)', *Journal of Asian and African Studies* 18(3/4): 166–78.

Rudhrawari, Abu Shujaʿ, and Hilal b. Muhassin. 1921. *Continuation of The Experiences of the Nations Volume VI: Reigns of Taʾi and Qadir*. Translated by D. S. Margoliouth. London: Basic Blackwell.

Rudolph, Ross. 1986. 'Conflict, Egoism and Power in Hobbes', *History of Political Thought* 7(1): 73–88.

Safi, Omid. 2006. *The Politics of Knowledge in Premodern Islam: Negotiating Ideology and Religious Inquiry*. Chapel Hill: University of North Carolina Press.

Saflo, Mohammad Moslem Adel. 2000. *Al-Juwayni's Thought and Methodology: With a Translation and Commentary on* Lumaʿ al-Adillah. Berlin: Klaus Schwarz Verlag.

Safran, Janina M. 2014. 'The Politics of Book Burning in al-Andalus', *Journal of Medieval Iberian Studies* 6(2): 148–68.

Saliba, George. 1998. 'Persian Scientists in the Islamic World: Astronomy from Maragha to Samarqand.' In Richard D. Hovannisian and Georges Sabagh (eds), *The Persian Presence in the Islamic World*, 126–46. Cambridge: Cambridge University Press.

Sanaullah, Mawlawi Fadil. 1938. *The Decline of Saljuqid Empire*. Calcutta: University of Calcutta Press.

Sánchez, Ignacio. 2010. 'Ethnic Disaffection and Dynastic Legitimacy in the Early Almohad Period: Ibn Tumart's *Translatio Studii et Imperii*', *Journal of Medieval Iberian Studies* 2(2): 175–93.

Sato, Kentaro. 2021. 'Isnad of Ibn Khaldun: Maghribi Tradition of Knowledge in Mamluk Cairo.' In Maribel Fierro and Mayte Penelas (eds), *The Maghrib in Mashriq: Knowledge, Travel and Identity*, 399–410. Berlin: De Gruyter.

Savage, E. 1992. 'Berbers and Blacks: Ibadi Slave Traffic in Eighth-Century North Africa', *The Journal of African History* 33(3): 351–68.

Schacht, Joseph. 1955. 'The Schools of Law and Later Developments of Jurisprudence.' In Majid Khadduri and Herbert J. Liebesny (eds), *Law in the Middle East Volume 1: Origin and Development of Islamic Law*, 57–84. Washington, DC: The Middle East Institute.

Schacht, Joseph. 1967. *The Origins of Muhammadan Jurisprudence*. Oxford: Oxford University Press.

Schmitz, Thomas A. 2007. *Modern Literary Theory and Ancient Texts: An Introduction*. Malden, MA: Blackwell.

Searle, John R. 1979. *Expression and Meaning: Studies in the Theory of Speech Acts*. Cambridge: Cambridge University Press.

Serjeant, R. B. 1983. 'Early Arabic Prose.' In A. F. L. Beeston, T. M. Johnstone, R. B. Serjeant and G. R. Smith (eds), *Arabic Literature to the End of the Umayyad Period*, 114–51. Cambridge: Cambridge University Press.

Serrano, Delfina. 2014. 'Judicial Pluralism under the Berber Empires (Last Quarter of the 11th Century C.E.–First Half of the 13th Century C.E.)', *Bulletin d'études orientales* 63: 243–74.

Sevim, A. 1998. 'The Origins of the Seljuqs and the Establishment of Seljuq Power in the Islamic Lands up to 1055.' In M. S. Asimove and C. E. Bosworth (eds), *History of Civilizations of Central Asia Volume IV: The Age of Achievement* A.D. *750 to the End of the Fifteenth Century*, 151–61. Paris: UNESCO.

Sevim, Ali, and Erdoğan Merçil. 1995. *Selçuklu Devletler Tarihi: Siyaset, Teşkilat ve Kültür.* Ankara: Türk Tarih Kurumu.

Shaban, M. A. 1970. *The Abbasid Revolution.* Cambridge: Cambridge University Press.

Shaban, M. A. 1971. *Islamic History: A New Interpretation I* A.D. *600–750 (A.H. 132).* Cambridge: Cambridge University Press.

Shaban, M. A. 1976. *Islamic History: A New Interpretation 2* A.D. *750–1055 (A.H. 132–448).* Cambridge: Cambridge University Press.

Shahin, Emad El-Din. 2015. 'Government.' In Gerhard Bowering (ed.), *Islamic Political Thought: An Introduction*, 68–85. Princeton, NJ: Princeton University Press.

Shaked, Shaul. 1995. *From Zoroastrian Iran to Islam.* Aldershot: Variorum.

Shaked, Shaul. 2008. 'Religion in the Late Sasanian Period: Eran, Aneran, and other Religious Designations.' In Vesta Sarkhosh Curtis and Sarah Stewart (eds), *Religion in the late Sasanian Period Volume III*, 104–17. London: I. B. Tauris.

Sharon, Moshe. 1990. *Revolt: The Social and Military Aspects of the Abbasid Revolution.* Jerusalem: Max Schloessinger Memorial Foundation.

Sharon, Moshe. 2012a. 'The Development of the Debate around the Legitimacy of Authority in Early Islam.' In Fred M. Donner (ed.), *The Articulation of Early Islamic State Structures*, 15–36. London: Routledge.

Sharon, Moshe. 2012b. 'An Arabic Inscription from the Time of the Caliph Abd al-Malik.' In Fred M. Donner (ed.), *The Articulation of Early Islamic State Structures*, 291–7. London: Routledge.

Shatzmiller, Maya. 2009. 'Marinid Fez – Global Order and a Quest for Empire.' In *The City of Fez in World History: an Interdisciplinary Conference, 9–11 October, 2008*, 7–32. Ifrane: Al-Akhawayn University Press.

Sherwani, Haroon Khan. 1942. *Studies in the History of Early Muslim Political Thought and Administration.* Lahore: S. Muhammad Ashraf.

Shorten, Andrew. 2016. *Contemporary Political Theory.* London: Palgrave.

Shoval, Ilan. 2016. *King John's Delegation to the Almohad Court (1212): Medieval Religious Interactions and Modern Historiography.* Turnhout: Brepols.

Siddiqi, Amir Hasan. 1942. *Caliphate and Kingship in Medieval Persia*. Lahore: S. Muhammad Ashraf.

Siddiqui, Sohaira Z. M. 2019. *Law and Politics under the Abbasids: An Intellectual Portrait of al-Juwayni*. Cambridge: Cambridge University Press.

Simidchieva, Marta. 2004. 'Kingship and Legitimacy as Reflected in Nizam al-Mulk's *Siyasatnama*, Fifth/Eleventh Century.' In Beatrice Gruendler and Louise Marlow (eds), *Writers and Rulers: Perspectives on Their Relationship from Abbasid to Safavid Times*, 97–132. Wiesbaden: Reichert Verlag.

Simon, Robert. 1999. *Ibn Khaldun: History as Science and the Patrimonial Empire*. Budapest: Akademiai Kiado.

Sivers, P. Von. 1980. 'Back to Nature: The Agrarian Foundations of Society According to Ibn Khaldun', *Arabica* 27(1): 68–91.

Somma, Bethany. 2022. 'Ibn Tufayl's Use and Misuse of his Predecessors.' In Andreas Lammer and Mareike Jas (eds), *Received Opinions: Doxography in Antiquity and the Islamic World*, 333–54. Leiden: Brill.

Sourdel, Dominique. 1954. 'La biographie d'Ibn al-Muqaffaʿ d'après les sources anciennes', *Arabica* 1(3): 307–23.

Southern, R. W. 1990. *Western Society and the Church in the Middle Ages*. London: Penguin.

Spengler, Joseph J. 1964. 'Economic Thought of Islam: Ibn Khaldun', *Comparative Studies in Society and History* 6(3): 268–306.

Spiegel, Gabrielle M. 1990. 'History, Historicism, and the Social Logic of the Text in the Middle Ages', *Speculum* 65(1): 59–68.

Starr, S. Frederick. 2013. *Lost Enlightenment: Central Asia's Golden Age from the Arab Conquest to Tamerlane*. Princeton, NJ: Princeton University Press.

Stern, S. M. 1964. 'New Information About the Authors of the Epistles of the Sincere Brethren', *Islamic Studies* 3(4): 405–28.

Strange, L. Guy. 1900. *Baghdad During the Abbasid Caliphate*. Oxford: Clarendon.

Strauss, Leo. 1957. 'What is Political Philosophy?' *The Journal of Politics* 19(3): 343–68.

Strauss, Leo. 1959. *What is Political Philosophy? And Other Studies*. Chicago: University of Chicago Press.

Strauss, Leo. 1990. 'Some Remarks on the Political Science of Maimonides and Farabi', *Interpretation* 18(1): 3–30.

Strauss, Leo, and Joseph Cropsey. 1987. 'Introduction.' In Leo Strauss and Joseph Cropsey (eds), *History of Political Philosophy*, 1–6. Chicago: University of Chicago Press.

Stroumsa, Sarah. 2009. *Maimonides in his World: Portrait of a Mediterranean Thinker*. Princeton, NJ: Princeton University Press.

Stroumsa, Sarah. 2019. *Andalus and Sefarad: On Philosophy and its History in Islamic Spain*. Princeton, NJ: Princeton University Press.

Stroumsa, Sarah. 2021. 'The Making of *Hayy*', *Oriens* 49: 1–34.

Sümer, Faruk. 1972. *Oğuzlar (Türkmenler): Tarihleri-Boy Teşkilatı-Destanları*. Ankara: Ankara University.

Tabataba'i, Muhammad Husayn. 1975. *Shi'ite Islam*. Translated by S. Hossein Nasr. New York: State University of New York Press.

Tafazzoli, Ahmad. 2000. *Sasanian Society: I. Warriors II. Scribes Dehqans*. New York: Bibliotecha Persia.

Taneri, Aydın. 1970. *Büyük Selçuklu İmparatorluğu'nda Vezirlik*. Ankara: Ankara University.

Tansar. 1968. *The Letter of Tansar*. Translated by M. Boyce. Rome: Instituto Italiona Per Il Medio Ed Estremo Oriento.

Taylor, Charles. 2007. *A Secular Age*. Cambridge: Belknap.

Taylor, Richard C. 2009. 'Ibn Rushd/Averroes and "Islamic" Rationalism', *Medieval Encounters* 15: 225–35.

Tetley, G. E. 2009. *The Ghaznawids and Seljuq Turks: Poetry as a Source of Iranian History*. London: Routledge.

Thiele, Jan. 2020. 'Ash'arism in the Hafsid Era.' In Ayman Shihadeh and Jan Thiele (eds), *Philosophical Theology in Islam: Later Ash'arism East and West*, 298–336. Leiden: Brill.

Thiele, John. 2022. 'Debates on Divine Attributes in Almohad Times, or Locating the Limits of Human Reason.' In Charles Burnett and Pedro Mantas-España (eds), *Mark of Toledo: Intellectual Context and Debates between Christians and Muslims in Early Thirteenth Century Iberia*, 213–38. Cordoba: UCO.

Tholib, Udjang. 2002. 'The Reign of the Caliph Al-Qadir Billah.' PhD dissertation, McGill University.

Tibawi, A. L. 1962. 'Origin and Character of "al-Madrasah"', *Bulletin of the School of Oriental and African Studies* 25(1/3): 225–38.

Tignor, Robert L. 2011. *Egypt: A Short History*. Princeton, NJ: Princeton University Press.

Titaw, Hamid. 2010. *Al-Harb wa al-mujtami'a bi-l-maghrib khilal al-'asr al-merini 1465–1212/869–609*. Casablanca: Muassasa al-Malik 'Abd al-'aziz.

Togan, A. Zeki Velidi. 1985. *Tarihte Usul*. Istanbul: Enderun.

Tor, D. G. 2002. 'A Numismatic History of the First Saffarid Dynasty (AH 247–300/ AD 861–911)', *The Numismatic Chronicle* 162: 293–314.

Tor, D. G. 2005. 'Privatized Jihad and Public Order in the Pre-Seljuq Period: The Rome of the Mutatawwila',' *Iranian Studies* 38: 555–73.

Tor, D. G. 2008. 'The Mamluks in the Military of the Pre-Seljuq Persianate Dynasties', *Iran* 46: 213–25.

Tor, D. G. 2009. 'The Islamization of Central Asia in the Samanid Era and the Reshaping of the Muslim World', *Bulletin of the School of Oriental and African Studies* 72(1): 279–99.

Tor, D. G. 2011a. 'The Islamisation of Iranian Kingly Ideals in the Persianate Fürstenspiegel', *Iran* 49: 115–22.

Tor, D. G. 2011b. 'Sovereign and Pious: The Religious Life of the Great Seljuq Sultans.' In Christian Lange and Songül Mecit (eds), *The Seljuqs: Politics, Society and Culture*, 39–62. Edinburgh: Edinburgh University Press.

Tor, D. G. 2015. 'The Importance of Khurasan and Transoxiana in the Persianate Dynastic Period (850–1220).' In A. C. S. Peacock and D. G. Tor (eds), *Medieval Central Asia: Iranian Tradition and Islamic Civilization*, 1–12. London: I. B. Tauris.

Tor, D. G. 2018. 'The Abbasid and Carolingian Dynasties in Comparative Perspective.' In D. G. Tor (ed.), *The 'Abbasid and Carolingian Empires: Comparative Studies in Civilizational Formation*, 3–12. Leiden: Brill.

Tor, D. G. 2020. 'The Religious History of the Great Seljuq Period.' In Sheila R. Canby, Deniz Beyazit and Martina Rugiadi (eds), *The Seljuqs and their Successors: Art, Culture and History*, 52–71. Edinburgh: Edinburgh University Press.

Toynbee, Arnold J. 1955. *A Study of History Volume III*. Oxford: Oxford University Press.

Treadwell, W. L. 1991. 'The Political History of the Samanid State.' PhD dissertation, Oxford University.

Treadwell, W. L. 2005. 'The Account of the Samanid Dynasty in Ibn Ẓafir al-Azdi's *Akhbar al-duwal al-munqaṭiʿa*', *Iran* 43: 135–71.

Tumanian, T. G. 2020. 'On the Theoretical Legacy of Abu 'l-Hasan al-Mawardi', *Philosophy and Conflict Studies* 36(3): 572–81.

Turan, Osman. 2008. *Selçuklular Tarihi ve Türk-İslam Medeniyeti*. Istanbul: Ötüken.

Urvoy, Dominique. 1974. 'La Pensée d'Ibn Tumart', *Bulletin d'études orientales* 27: 19–44.

Urvoy, Dominique. 1996. 'The Rationality of Everyday Life: An Andalusian Tradition? (Apropos of Hayy's First Experiences).' In Lawrence I. Conrad (ed.), *The World of Ibn Tufayl: Interdisciplinary Perspectives on Hayy Ibn Yaqzan*, 38–51. Leiden: Brill.

Urvoy, Dominique. 1997. 'The *'Ulama'* of al-Andalus.' In Salma Khadra Jayyusi (ed.), *The Legacy of Muslim Spain*, 849–77. Leiden: Brill.

Usta, Aydın. 2013. 'Ünlü Selçuklu Kumandanı: Sadüddevle Gevherayin.'. In Emine Uyumaz, Muharrem Kesik, Aydın Usta and Cihan Piyadeoğlu (eds), *Erdoğan Merçil'e Armağan*, 96–111. Istanbul: Bilge.

Van Ess, Joseph. 2006. *The Flowering of Muslim Theology.* Translated by Jane Marie Todd. Cambridge, MA: Harvard University Press.

Van Ess, Joseph. 2017. *Theology and Society in the Second and Third Centuries of the Hijra: A History of Religious Thought in Early Islam Volume 2.* Translated by Gwendolin Goldbloom. Leiden: Brill.

Vance, Rupert B. 1944. 'Toward Social Dynamics', *American Sociological Review* 10(2): 123–31.

Venetis, Evangelos. 2006. 'The Iskandarnama: An Analysis of Anonymous Medieval Persian Romance.' PhD dissertation, University of Edinburgh.

Viguera-Molins, Maria Jesus. 2010. 'Al Andalus and the Maghrib (from the Fifth/Eleventh Century to the Fall of the Almoravids).' In Maribel Fierro (ed.), *The New Cambridge History of Islam Volume 2: The Western Islamic World Eleventh to Eighteenth Centuries*, 21–47. Cambridge: Cambridge University Press.

Wacks, David A. 2003. 'The Performativity of Ibn al-Muqaffa's *Kalila wa-Dimna* and *al-Maqamat al-Luzumiyya* of al-Saraqusti', *Journal of Arabic Literature* 34(1–2): 178–89.

Waines, David. 1977. 'The Third Century Internal Crisis of the Abbasids', *Journal of the Economic and Social History of the Orient* 20(3): 282–306.

Walker, Paul E. 1993. 'The Ismaili Da'wa in the Reign of the Fatimid Caliph Al-Hakim', *Journal of the American Research Center in Egypt* 30: 161–82.

Walmsley, Alan. 2010. 'Coinage and the Economy of Syria–Palestine in the Seventh and Eighth Centuries CE.' In John Haldon (ed.), *Money, Power and Politics in Early Islamic Syria: A Review of Current Debates*, 21–44. London: Ashgate.

Walzer, Richard. 1962. *Greek into Arabic: Essays on Islamic Philosophy.* Cambridge, MA: Harvard University Press.

Walzer, Richard. 1963. 'Aspects of Islamic Political Thought: Al-Farabi and Ibn Xaldun', *Oriens* 16: 40–60.

Wansbrough, John. 1978. *The Sectarian Milieu: Content and Composition of Islamic Salvation History.* Oxford: Oxford University Press.

Watt, W. Montgomery. 1964. 'The Decline of the Almohads: Reflections on the Viability of Religious Movements', *History of Religions* 4(1): 23–9.

Watt, W. Montgomery. 1985. *Islamic Philosophy and Theology: An Extended Survey.* Edinburgh: Edinburgh University Press.

Watt, W. Montgomery, and Pierre Cachia. 1996. *A History of Islamic Spain.* Edinburgh: Edinburgh University Press.

Weiss, Dieter. 1995. 'Ibn Khaldun on Economic Transformation', *International Journal of Middle East Studies* 27(1): 29–37.

Wellhausen, J. 1927. *The Arab Kingdom and its Fall.* Translated by Margaret Graham Weir. Calcutta: University of Calcutta Press.

Whitcomb, Donald. 2009. 'From Pastoral Peasantry to Tribal Urbanites: Arab Tribes and the Foundation of the Islamic State in Syria.' In Jeffrey Szuchman (ed.), *Nomads, Tribes, and the State in the Ancient Near East: Cross-Disciplinary Perspectives*, 241–60. Chicago: University of Chicago Press.

Widigdo, M. Syifa Amin. 2021. 'Imam al-Haramayn al-Juwayni's Mobility and the Saljuq's Project of Sunni Political Unity.' In Mohamad al-Merheb and Mehdi Berriah (eds), *Professional Mobility in Islamic Societies (700–1750): New Concepts and Approaches*, 159–81. Leiden: Brill.

Wiesehöfer, Josef. 2001. *Ancient Persia: From 550 BC to 659 AD.* Translated by Azizeh Azodi. London: I. B. Tauris.

Wintgens, Luc J. 2002. 'Rationality in Legislation-Legal Theory as Legisprudence: An Introduction.' In Luc J Wintgens (ed.), *Legisprudence: A New Theoretical Approach to Legislation*, 1–9. Oxford: Hart.

Wolfson, Harry A. 1959. 'Ibn Khaldun on Attributes and Predestination', *Speculum* 34(4): 585–97.

Wolfson, Harry A. 1960. 'An Unknown Splinter Group of Nestorians', *Revue d'Etudes Augustiniennes et Patristiques* 6(3): 249–53.

Yarshater, Ehsan. 1983. 'Mazdakism.' In Ehsan Yarshater (ed.), *The Cambridge History of Iran Volume 3(2): The Seleucid, Parthian and Sasanian Periods*, 991–1024. Cambridge: Cambridge University Press.

Yarshater, Ehsan. 1998. 'The Persian Presence in the Islamic World.' In Richard D. Hovannisian and Georges Sabagh (eds), *The Persian Presence in the Islamic World*, 4–125. Cambridge: Cambridge University Press.

Yavari, Neguin. 2008a. 'Nizam al-Mulk.' In Andrew Rippin (ed.), *The Islamic World*, 351–8. London: Routledge.

Yavari, Neguin. 2008b. 'Mirrors for Princes or Hall of Mirrors? Nizam al-Mulk's *Siyar al-muluk* Reconsidered', *Al-Masaq: Journal of the Medieval Mediterranean* 20(1): 47–69.

Yavari, Neguin. 2019. 'The Political Regard in Medieval Islamic Thought', *Historical Social Research* 44(3): 52–73.

Yousefi, Najm al-Din. 2009. 'Knowledge and Social Order in Early Islamic Mesopotamia (60–193 AH/680–809 CE).' PhD dissertation, Virginia Polytechnic Institute and State University.

Yousefi, Najm al-Din. 2017. 'Islam without Fuqaha: Ibn al-Muqaffa and his Perso-Islamic Solution to the Caliphate's Crisis of Legitimacy (70–142 AH/690–760 CE)', *Iranian Studies* 50(1): 1–36.

Yousefi, Najm al-Din. 2019. 'Confusion and Consent: Land Tax (Kharaj) and the Construction of Judicial Authority in the Early Islamic Empire (ca. 12–183 A.H./634–800 C.E.)', *Sociology of Islam* 7: 93–131.

Yücesoy, Hayrettin. 2006. 'Political Theory.' In Josef W. Meri (ed.), *Medieval Islamic Civilization: An Encyclopedia, Volume 2*, 623–8. London: Routledge.

Zakeri, Mohsen. 1995. *Sasanid Soldiers in Early Muslim Society: The Origins of 'Ayyaran and Futuwwa*. Wiesbaden: Harrassowitz.

Zaman, M. Raquibuz. 2002. 'Islamic Perspectives on Territorial Boundaries and Autonomy.' In Sohail H. Hashmi (ed.), *Islamic Political Ethics: Civil Society, Pluralism, and Conflict*, 79–101. Princeton, NJ: Princeton University Press.

Zaman, Muhammad Qasim. 1987. 'The Abbasid Revolution: A Study of the Nature and Role of Religious Dynamics', *Journal of Asian History* 21(2): 119–49.

Zaman, Muhammad Qasim. 1990. 'Some Considerations on References to the Qur'an During the 'Abbasid Movement', *Islamic Studies* 29(1): 29–41.

Zaman, Muhammad Qasim. 1997a. 'The Caliphs, the Ulama, and the Law: Defining the Role and Function of the Caliph in the Early Abbasid Period', *Islamic Law and Society* 4(1): 1–36.

Zaman, Muhammad Qasim. 1997b. *Religion and Politics Under the Early 'Abbasids*. Leiden: Brill.

Zarrinkub, 'Abd al-Husain. 2007. 'The Arab Conquest of Iran and its Aftermath.' In R. N. Frye (ed.), *The Cambridge History of Iran Volume 4: The Period from the Arab Invasion to the Saljuqs*, 1–56. Cambridge: Cambridge University Press.

Ziya, Hilmi, and Ziyaeddin Fahri. 1940. *İbni Haldun*. Istanbul: Kainat.

Zubaida, Sami. 2003. *Law and Power in the Islamic World*. London: I. B. Tauris.

Zychowicz-Coghill, Edward. 2022. 'Ideals of the City in the Early Islamic Foundation Stories of Kufa and Baghdad.' In Sofia Greaves and Andrew Wallace-Hadrill (eds), *Rome and the Colonial City: Rethinking the Grid*, 123–50. Oxford: Oxbow Books.

Zysow, Aron. 2013. 'Zaydis.' In Gerhard Bowing (ed.), *The Princeton Encyclopedia of Islamic Thought*, 605–6. Princeton, NJ: Princeton University Press.

INDEX

Abbasids, 30
   Abbasid Revolution, 7, 32–6
   Abbasid–Buwayhid cohabitation, 87–91
   Abbasid–Saljuqid cohabitation, 127–31
   birth of, 30–2
   da'wa, 32
Abd al-Hamid, the scribe, 27
Abd al-Malik, 30, 35, 55–9
Abd al-Mu'min, Almohad caliph, 173, 176, 178–9, 182, 186, 191–2, 195–9
Abdullah bin Ali, 35–6
Abdullah bin Yasin, 183
Abu Bakr, 1–2, 39, 59
Abu Kalijar, 81, 94, 111
Abu Muslim, 34, 45–6, 48
Abu Sufyan, 1, 39
Adud al-Dawla, 96, 101–2, 105, 111, 153
Al-Abili, Ibrahim, 227–8
Al-Andalus, 172, 178, 184, 192, 194, 228
Al-Ash'ari, 2-4, 154, 180
Al-Aziz Billah, Fatimids caliph, 91, 110
Al-Baqillani, 96, 101, 110–12, 115, 119, 242, 254
Al-Biruni, 103

Al-Farabi, 6–7
   Ibn Khaldun's critique of, 243
   Ibn Tufayl's critique of, 207–8
Al-Ghazali, Abu Hamid, 17, 20, 160, 168, 173, 188–90, 195, 202, 205, 208–9, 248, 249, 254
Al-Hakim, the Fatimid caliph, 91, 106, 110
Al-Hanafiyya, Muhammad bin, 30
Al-Isfarayini, Abu Hamid, 93, 107, 111
Al-Jahiz, 19, 115
Al-Juwayni, 20, 135, 160, 166, 181, 208, 214
Al-Kunduri, 146, 155, 158, 166, 169
Al-Mansur, Caliph, 30, 36, 40–1, 45
Al-Muqtadi, Caliph, 78, 129–30, 162
Al-Mawardi, 75–122
   his life, 93–4
   on appointing the leaders, 115–18
   on caliphate, 97, 100–4
   on legitimacy, 118–21
   on political rationalism, 96–100
   on religion, 97–8
   on the birth of state in Islam, 99–100
   on the election of the caliph, 109–15
   on the separation of politics and religion, 98

Al-Qadir, Caliph, 84, 86, 91, 93, 103–8, 111–16, 134
Al-Qaim, Caliph, 112, 114, 116, 120, 126–9
Al-Saffah, Caliph, 35–7, 40
Al-Shafi'i, 13
Al-Tai, Caliph, 84, 101, 105, 112–6
Alid groups, 25, 30–2, 34, 37, 42, 88, 111, 185–6
Almohads, 171–9
   Almohad eclecticism, 190
   Almohad elitism, 189–90, 199–200, 205, 207, 209, 216
   Almohad Revolution, 172–6
   Almohad state, 176–9
   Almohad *tawhid*, 180–5, 189, 195–6, 199, 206–7, 214–18, 245
   talaba, 185, 196, 197–200, 202
Almoravids, 171–6, 178, 179, 183–4, 188, 202, 218, 226
Alp Arslan, 128–9, 132, 141–2, 145, 147, 156–8, 169
Anatolia, 31, 86, 141, 145
anthropomorphism, 180–1, 189, 201, 206, 213, 216, 246
Ardashir I, 28, 70–1, 73, 136
Aristotle, 25, 62, 200, 207–8, 212
army, 31, 35, 40, 45–60, 77, 144–7, 163, 192, 224, 234
Arslan Israel, 125
asabiyya, 232–34
assassination, 33, 133

Baghdad, 42–4
   foundation of, 44
   under Buwayhid rule, 87–91, 102
   under Saljuqid rule, 127–34
Baha al-Dawla, 106, 113, 116
Bahram Chubin, 85
balance of power, 2, 81–3, 104
balancing, 82, 84

Basasiri, 111, 120, 127–8, 165
Basra, 25
Battle of Zab, 35
bedouin, 225, 232–3, 235–6, 239, 249
Berber, 18, 32, 171–9, 183, 186–8, 204, 217
Berber revolt, 171
Bougie, 228–9
Buwayhids, 78, 88–91
Byzantine, 71, 84, 128, 142–5, 150, 157

caliphal recognition, 80–1, 86, 101, 128
caliphate, 1, 4, 16, 32, 89, 91–2, 97, 100–4, 119, 123
captivity, 105, 119
causality, (or causal laws), 14, 27, 51, 154, 202, 246–52, 259, 262
centralisation, 69–70
Chagri, 125, 127, 140–1, 143, 155
coinage, 47, 59–60, 80, 82, 92, 102, 106, 116
collective sovereignty, 127, 145–6, 155–6
corruption, 33, 138, 165, 202, 231, 236

Dailami, 89, 90, 110, 127, 149, 234
Damascus, 34–5, 39–40, 91, 167, 173, 231
Dandanakan, 126, 147
dawla, 57, 92, 100, 104, 123
Denkard, 73
dihqan, 25, 33, 69
diplomacy, 134, 143
diwan, 57–9
drinking parties, 134, 157–9

Egypt, 46, 67, 91, 231
electors, 109, 111–14, 116–17, 119
elitism, 189–90, 199–200, 205, 207, 209, 216; *see also* Almohad elitism
empiricism (empirical), 9–12, 17, 20, 27, 62–4, 94, 96, 115, 121, 212, 232, 244–6, 252–5

Fatima, 30, 92, 186
Fatimids, 75, 91–3, 106–7, 110–11, 120, 127–8, 156, 186; *see also* Ismaili
Fez, 175, 178, 224–5, 227–8, 230, 255
formal approach, 10–11, 17

genealogy, 30–1, 85, 92, 107, 109–11, 185–6, 195, 232
general laws, 29, 56, 136, 241, 253, 257
geography, 24, 28, 88, 249; *see also* geopolitics
geopolitics, 36–7
Ghaznawids, 82–3, 85, 87, 104–6, 132, 142
ghulam, 144–5, 147–9, 159, 162
Granada, 18, 191, 204, 220, 225, 228

hajib, 229
Hanafism, 166–7, 169, 183
Hanbalism, 107–9, 167–8, 180
Hargha, 173
heir, 116–18
Hejaz, 31, 44, 82, 91, 1110, 166
heretic, 29, 32, 49, 78, 108, 114, 119, 132, 154, 160, 168, 246, 256
historicism, 10, 12
history, 4, 10, 21, 23, 100
Hobbes, Thomas, 14, 65

Ibn al-Miskawayh, 70, 153
Ibn al-Muqaffa, 1–74
  life of, 25–6, 30
  on analogy, 62–3
  on army and politics, 45–52
  on Iraq, 42–5
  on judiciary, 52–3
  on legitimacy, 64
  on loyalty, 48–9
  on political rationalism, 63–6
  on power, 120–1
  on proto-legislation, 54
  on religion, 64–6
  on state, 52–6
  on Syria, 37–42
  on taxation, 61–3
Ibn Bajja, 207, 210, 217
Ibn Barrajan, 188, 260
Ibn Fadlan, 124, 139, 164
Ibn Khaldun, 18, 20–1, 57–8, 68, 111, 220–2, 225
  his life, 226–31
  on causality, 246–52
  on empirical sciences, 252–5
  on political philosophy, 246
  on religion, 255–6
  on state, 235–40
  on Sufism, 253–4
  political rationalism in, 240–2
Ibn Rushd, 17, 191, 200–2, 227, 247–50
Ibn Sina, 17, 20, 72, 181, 190, 207–10, 214–15, 227, 255
Ibn Tufayl, 18, 20–1, 171
  his life, 190–1, 196–203
  his political thought, 203–11
Ibn Tumart, 172–6, 179–90, 194–202
Idrisids, 185
Ifriqiyya, 182, 186, 194, 220, 222
Imam Ibrahim, the Abbasid, 34–5
Imam Muhammad, the Abbasid, 31–2
India, 19, 87, 105
investiture, 80–1, 84, 87, 105, 117, 126, 179
iqta, 152–4
Iran, 25, 31, 72, 78, 90, 106, 126, 141, 143, 152
Iranian influence, 67–73
Iraq, 26, 37, 42–4, 57, 77–8, 88, 92, 111, 130, 166
Isfahan, 82, 142, 147, 162
Islamic law, 15, 54, 61, 65, 69, 259

Islamic political philosophy, 5–7
Islamic political theory, 7–18
　autonomous variables, 8, 15
Islamic political thought, 3
Ismaili, 75, 91–3, 110–11, 163, 167

Jalal al-Dawla, 82, 94, 103, 111, 116, 119, 144
jihad, 13, 86–7, 124, 187, 192, 202
jizya, 67–8

Kaysaniyya, 31
Khalid bin Walid, 39
kharaj, 67–8
Kharijites, 31–2, 171
khatun, 165
Khazraj, 2
Khusraw I (Anushirwan), 53, 67–9, 71
khutba, 80, 84, 89, 92, 94, 106, 116, 120, 127–8, 130, 196, 199
kingship, 16, 138
Khurasan, 33, 39, 44, 83, 86, 125
　in Abbasid Revolution, 33–4, 37, 41, 45, 46, 52
　see also Khurasanis
Khurasanis, 43, 45, 47–9
Kufa, 25, 30, 34, 37, 43–4, 52

local state, 20, 75–6, 78, 81
law, 4, 15, 53–6, 61–3, 95, 137, 183, 237–8
legitimacy, 9, 22, 27, 32, 42, 60, 63–4, 76, 81, 83–7, 100, 105, 118–21, 128–9, 134, 139, 176, 184–5, 192–6, 204, 217–19

Machiavelli, Niccolò, 14, 120
Madrasa, 160, 162, 166–9, 244
Maghrib, 24, 171–3, 179, 180, 185, 194–5, 220–4, 234, 245
Mahdi (or Mahdism), 173, 181, 185–8, 194–6, 217

Mahmud Gawan, 19
Maimonides, 199–200
Makramids, 82
Malik Shah, 128–30, 132–3, 144, 146, 148, 152, 157, 159, 161–4
Malikism, 174, 183–5, 188, 194
Manzikert War, 128, 133, 192
Marinids, 220–6, 228, 230
Marrakesh, 175, 178, 191, 197, 223–4
Marwan II, 27, 35, 40–1
Masmuda, 174–6
Mawali, 31–3, 188
mazalim, 60, 98–100, 136, 239
millennial groups, 34, 48
mirrors, 134
Morocco, 91, 173, 178, 220
Mu'awiya, 30, 39, 59, 239–41
Muhammad bin al-Hanafiyya, 30–1
Mukhtar, 31
Muslim East, 20, 171–3, 189
Muslim West, 20, 171–2, 186, 220
Mu'tazila, 17, 19, 21, 93, 108, 180–1, 190, 247
mysticism, 18, 188, 203, 205, 207–10, 213–15, 218, 253, 261

naqib, 32, 46
Nasr bin Sayyar, 33–4, 40, 52
Nesa victory, 125
Nishapur, 28, 93, 125–6, 142–3
Nizam al-Mulk, 123–70
　life of, 132–3
　on *ghulam*, 147–8
　on *iqta*, 152–3
　on legitimacy, 139
　on nomadic culture, 139–46, 150–2
　on Persian impact, 154–6
　on religion, 165–9
　on state, 134–9
　on the origins of state in Islam, 135–7
　on women, 161–5

Nizamiyya College, 135, 167–9
norms, 2, 5, 7–11, 13–14, 18, 63, 94, 108, 113, 115, 121, 218, 220, 241
North Africa, 18, 91, 172, 186–8

Oakeshott, Michael, 17–18
oath, 85, 94, 195, 240
Oghuz, 124
Oman, 82, 88, 92
overlapping approach, 3, 13, 17–18, 258

Pahlavi, 25, 28, 72–3
patronage, 52, 85, 140, 165, 200
Persio-Islamic, 125, 134, 139–46, 153
Plato, 5, 202, 242
plundering, 125, 140–2, 144–5, 149
political authority, 24, 47, 51, 53–4, 56, 60–1, 63, 80, 89, 98, 100, 104
political power, 13–15
political rationalism, 16–18
prose, 28, 221
provincial order, 75–85
provincial state, 82; *see also* local states
public interest, 97, 121, 241–3

Qabusnama, 27, 160
Qadi Iyad, 184, 260
Qadiri creed, 107–8
Qahtabah ibn Shabib, 35, 46
Qarakhanids, 80, 124–5, 129
Qarmati, 92, 108
Qur'an, 2, 49, 68, 107, 181, 187–8, 252, 256
Quraysh, 2, 110

rationalism, 17
Rawandiyah, 48
reason (*or* reasoning), 4, 17, 64–6, 95–7, 112, 115, 135–6, 180, 184, 203, 207, 212–13, 244–7

reflectivism, 12–13; *see also* historicism
religious powers, 95, 97, 101–4, 108, 114, 121
religious view of politics, 3–5

sacral (or divine) kingship, 73, 154-6
Saffarids, 80–4, 87
salary, 51, 137, 257
Saljuqs, 94, 120, 123, 124–7, 128–31, 134, 139–43, 146–52, 155–6
Samanids, 72, 78, 82–5, 87, 90, 92, 124–5, 143, 261
Samarra, 77
Sanhaja, 174–5, 178, 183, 186, 193
Saqifah, 1–2
Sasanid, 26, 68, 132
Sawad, 57, 68, 142
scribes, 27–8
Sebuktigin, 113
Seville, 178, 226
Shafi, 13, 108, 129, 132, 160, 165–9
Shi'a, 30–3, 42, 44, 75, 87–93, 107, 185
shihna, 130, 163
Sijilmasa, 174, 224
siyasah, 98, 243
social organisation, 235–6, 238
solidarity, 4, 8, 233
Spain, 172, 174, 195, 220, 222, 225–30, 234, 245, 250–1
state in Islamic history, 56–60
state–society relations, 22, 139
steppe tradition, 155
sub-provincial state, 82–3
Sufyani revolts, 40
Sulayman bin Jarir, 112
Sunna, 49, 62
Sunni restoration, 104–8
Sus valley, 120, 173–4
Syria, 34, 36–42

Tahirids, 78, 80, 82–5
ta'ifa kings, 172, 178, 184, 198234, 250
Taj al-Mulk, 161–4, 169
Tamyiz, 175
Tansar, 70–3
tawhid, 180–5; *see also* Almohad *tawhid*
taxation, 9, 33, 51–2, 57, 61, 67, 69, 102, 127, 133, 175, 221
temporal power, 20, 75–6, 78, 89, 97, 100, 102, 104–5, 108, 110, 114–15, 119, 121, 128, 260
Terken Khatun, 161–2, 164
theological-philosophical rationalism, 17
titles, 80–2, 140, 150, 170, 234
Tlemcen, 175–6, 196, 226, 229–30
Tugrul, 18, 94, 120, 125–8, 130, 141–5, 155
Turkmens, 140–2, 144–8, 150, 153
Tutush, 141

Umar, caliph, 25, 27, 39, 55, 57–9, 68
Umayyads, 31–3, 35, 39
umran, 235, 237, 239–40, 243, 249, 256
Uqaylids, 91, 120, 128, 135
Uqba bin Nafi, 187
usurpation, 120–1, 135
Utopia, 5, 207, 218

violence, 13, 35–6, 137, 183, 198
vizirate, 102

wine (and political rationalism), 156–60; *see also* drinking parties

Zayd bin Ali, 88-9
Zaydis, 88–9
Zayyanids, 196, 220–1, 225–6, 228
Zenata, 173, 178, 234
zindiq, 29
Zoroastrianism, 25, 29, 68–9, 72